Dancing with the Revolution

ENVISIONING CUBA

Louis A. Pérez Jr., *editor*

Envisioning Cuba publishes outstanding, innovative works in Cuban studies, drawn from diverse subjects and disciplines in the humanities and social sciences, from the colonial period through the post–Cold War era. Featuring innovative scholarship engaged with theoretical approaches and interpretive frameworks informed by social, cultural, and intellectual perspectives, the series highlights the exploration of historical and cultural circumstances and conditions related to the development of Cuban self-definition and national identity.

ELIZABETH B. SCHWALL

Dancing with the Revolution
Power, Politics, and Privilege in Cuba

The University of North Carolina Press *Chapel Hill*

This book was published with the assistance of the Authors Fund of the University of North Carolina Press.

© 2021 The University of North Carolina Press
All rights reserved
Set in Arno Pro by Westchester Publishing Services
Manufactured in the United States of America

The University of North Carolina Press has been a member of the Green Press Initiative since 2003.

Library of Congress Cataloging-in-Publication Data
Names: Schwall, Elizabeth B., author.
Title: Dancing with the revolution : power, politics, and privilege
    in Cuba / Elizabeth B. Schwall.
Other titles: Envisioning Cuba.
Description: Chapel Hill : The University of North Carolina Press, [2021] |
    Series: Envisioning Cuba | Includes bibliographical references and index.
Identifiers: LCCN 2020044098 | ISBN 9781469662961 (cloth) |
    ISBN 9781469662978 (paperback) | ISBN 9781469662985 (ebook)
Subjects: LCSH: Dance—Political aspects—Cuba. | Dance—Cuba—
    History—20th century. | Cuba—Politics and government—1959–1990. |
    Cuba—Politics and government—1933–1959.
Classification: LCC GV1632.C9 S38 2021 | DDC 792.8/097291—dc23
LC record available at https://lccn.loc.gov/2020044098

Cover illustration: Dancers of the Teatro Nacional de Cuba, including Luz María Collazo on the far left. Courtesy of Danza Contemporánea de Cuba.

For my family with love
For my teachers with gratitude
For Cuban dance makers with admiration

Contents

Figures

Acknowledgments

Perhaps unsurprising for a book about dance, this project began with movement. In my formative decades, Kathy Chamberlain, Suzette Mariaux, and Shannon Werthmann instilled a studious devotion to dance. As an undergraduate, Ze'eva Cohen, Rebecca Lazier, and Tina Fehlandt inspired a playfully curious regard for a form that I thought I knew so well. Too many dancers and dance teachers to name have continued to nurture my passion for movement, intentionally or inadvertently inspiring me to continue working on this book despite any faltering along the way.

As I experimented with making dance a historical research project, pivotal mentors encouraged my interests. T. K. Hunter advised the first kernel of this book as a junior paper and nominated it for distinction, giving me the greatest possible gift: confidence. Her untimely death means that I cannot personally thank her for giving my intellectual interests a fighting chance. She gave me so much, even though as a non-tenure-track faculty member, she remained chronically undersupported by the academic institutions that employed her. Jeremy Adelman introduced me to Latin American History and advised an embryonic version of this work as a senior thesis. He has remained a gracious interlocutor whenever I have circled back for advice. In graduate school and beyond, I have benefited from the heartening guidance readily offered by Pablo Piccato, Lynn Garafola, Nara Milanich, and Caterina Pizzigoni. They have read countless drafts and provided crucial feedback, first on my dissertation and then on this manuscript. Their intellectual fingerprints are all over any of the persuasive parts of this book. To these brilliant and giving educators at Princeton and Columbia, I owe many thanks and strive to pay forward their lessons of history and collegiality.

Cuban colleagues and institutions made this project possible. Centro Juan Marinello and the tireless Henry Heredia somehow always managed to secure research visas and letters of introduction despite endless bureaucratic hurdles. Pavel García Llagostera, the assiduous archivist of Danza Contemporánea de Cuba, gave me unconditional access to a meticulous and thorough collection of press and programs. Martha Nolazco Torres in the Sala de Arte at the Biblioteca Nacional José Martí diligently pulled all the dusty files she could find from a back room during a scorching, sleepy August research

trip. Caridad Díaz Cardoso at the Centro de Documentación y Archivo Teatral, Teatro Nacional de Cuba, was a model of professionalism, arriving early
each morning and readily chatting over lunch about Cuban archives. Giselle
Odette and Rainer Schultz facilitated my access to the Archivo General del
Ministerio de Cultura, and once there, Maritza Sota and her team of archivists helped me tremendously. Marlene Villalón Pérez warmly welcomed me
at the Museo Nacional de la Danza, arranged an interview with the director
Pedro Simón, and shared her home, family, and cooking on more than one
occasion. Cuban ballet scholar Ahmed Piñeiro took time out of his busy
schedule to share invaluable resources. Gabriela Burdsall and her father,
Kahlil Piñeiro, met with me to discuss the amazing life of the late Lorna
Burdsall. In Camagüey, Heidy Cepero Recorder provided direction and
friendship. Fernando Sáez connected me to important institutions and interlocutors in Santiago de Cuba. Luz María Collazo and Isidro Rolando generously shared memories and personal archives that shaped this book in many
ways. Archivists at the Archivo Nacional de Cuba, Archivo Histórico Provincial de Santiago de Cuba, and Ballet de Camagüey also facilitated my efforts
to find dance histories stored in their institutions.

Much-needed moments of friendship and dance intervened in my archival
hustle in Cuba thanks to the Núñez Castillo family and Tomás Guilarte. I first
owe thanks to Eddy Veitia for introducing me to both. I stayed for months at
a time in the home of Belkis, Jorge, Jorgito, Javier, and Joel Núñez Castillo.
Belkis not only fed me the most delicious food on the island but also signifi-
cantly aided my research. She and Fara Teresa Rodríguez, both former personal secretaries to Alicia Alonso, arranged numerous interviews with major
ballet figures. Meanwhile, after the archives closed, I had the great fortune to
take dance classes from the peerless Tomás Guilarte. In transit before and
after, he shared his knowledge of modern dance and facilitated (with Rosario
Cárdenas) an interview with Ramiro Guerra. Tomás, his lovely wife, Marnia,
and their children, Carolina and Carlos Andrés, had me over regularly on
Sundays for food and conversation. I would have been lost without their
kindness.

Conducting research and processing my findings outside of Cuba equally
depended on the support of many. Alma Concepción, Muriel Manings, Célida Parera Villalón, Sonia Calero, Susan Homar, Sonia Daubón, Carlota Carrera, Osmay Molina, Víctor Gilí, Bettina Ojeda, Petra Bravo, and Yvonne
Daniel aided my research in Princeton, Miami, New York, San Juan, and San
Francisco. When I was at Columbia, first as a student and then as a needy
alumna, Yesenia Barragan, Sarah Beckhart Coppinger, Amy Chazkel, Joanna

Dee Das, Andre Deckrow, Alan Dye, Julia del Palacio, Fabiola Enríquez Flores, Eric Frith, Marianne González Le Saux, Romeo Guzmán, Sara Hidalgo Garza, Mariana Katz, Paul Katz, Ana Isabel Keilson, Daniel Kressel, Ariel Lambe, Caitlin Liss, Daniel Morales, Rachel Newman, Ivón Padilla-Rodríguez, Victoria Phillips, Laura Quinton, Alfonso Salgado, Paul Scolieri, and Seth Williams provided advice and feedback. Yesenia, Joanna, Ana, Ariel, Rachel, and Alfonso deserve special mention for providing ready comment, and in some cases, housing during research trips over the years. From other institutions, I thank fellow scholars of Cuba for their camaraderie and help: Alexis Baldacci, Devyn Spence Benson, Maya Berry, Melissa Blanco Borelli, Anita Casavantes Bradford, Michael Bustamante, Michelle Chase, Jorge Duany, Raul Fernandez, Daniel Fernández Guevara, Cary García Yero, Eric Gettig, Lillian Guerra, Anasa Hicks, Jesse Horst, Jennifer Lambe, Raquel Otheguy, Daniel Rodríguez, Rainer Schultz, Franny Sullivan, Lester Tomé, Kelly Urban, and Grete Viddal.

Money and institutional support kept this project going. I benefited from grants and resources provided by Columbia University's Institute of Latin American Studies and Graduate School of Arts and Sciences, the Goizueta Foundation Graduate Fellowship Program at the University of Miami's Cuban Heritage Collection, the Doris K. Quinn Foundation Dissertation Write-up Fellowship, the Center for Iberian and Latin American Studies at the University of California, San Diego, and the multicampus consortium UC-Cuba.

After I graduated, a Mellon Dance Studies in/and the Humanities Postdoctoral Fellowship at Northwestern University provided the resources for me to keep researching and the time for me to keep writing. I have Susan Manning to thank for the incredible opportunity, as well as for her warm mentorship. To colleagues at my institutional home at Northwestern, the Kaplan Institute for the Humanities—Tom Burke, Jill Mannor, Megan Skord, Wendy Wall, Jessica Winegar, Danny Snelson, Sarah Dimick, Kaneesha Persard, and especially my patient, funny, and brilliant office mate Hi'ilei Hobart—thanks for filling each day with friendship and inspiration. I am also indebted to others in Evanston and Chicago, including Eleanor Ellis, Emily Maguire, Lauren Stokes, Helen Tilley, Sherwin Bryant, Tessie Liu, Paul Gillingham, Paul Ramírez, Lina Britto, Abram Lewis, Douglas Ishii, Harris Feinsod, Nell Haynes, Lizzie Leopold, Rachel Russell, Keith Rathbone, Ashley Johnson Bravery, Alexandra Lindgren-Gibson, Ramón Rivera-Servera, Jorge Coronado, the University of Chicago Latin American History Workshop, Jenai Cutcher, and the Chicago Dance History Project.

As I continued hopping around, landing next in the Bay Area with short stints in New York, I was fortunate to find nurturing communities and colleagues. At Stanford, Janice Ross and the Mellon Dance Studies in/and the Humanities provided another opportunity to teach and much-needed extra salary that went toward research expenses. At the University of California, Berkeley, I benefited from feedback on my sixth chapter and regular camaraderie offered by the Berkeley Latin American History Working Group: Maria Barreiros Almeida, Margaret Chowning, Evan Fernández, Rebecca Herman, Clare Ibarra, Kyle Jackson, Craig Johnson, Gisselle Pérez-León, Miles Culpepper, and Elena Schneider. Marian Schlotterbeck, José Juan Pérez Meléndez, Julio Aguilar, Lucía Luna-Victoria Indacochea, and everyone involved in the University of California, Davis Latin American History Workshop commented on my fifth chapter, giving me much-needed direction. Over two sessions, the Latin American History Workshop at Columbia University provided help on my introduction, chapter 4, and epilogue. A generous fellowship at the Center for Ballet and the Arts (CBA) at New York University supported my work in many ways. CBA connected me to María Cristina Anzola, who provided an invaluable perspective on Cubans visiting Venezuela in the 1970s. The CBA fellowship also allowed me to conduct extensive oral history interviews with Caridad Martínez, who gave over fifteen hours of her time and remained incredibly open about her past, effectively reshaping the seventh chapter of this book in the process. To Caridad, I am deeply indebted and grateful.

While I struggled to rewrite and improve the material, editors and readers provided calm and clarity. Louis Pérez and Elaine Maisner regularly met with me at conferences to hear about my progress, urge me on, and explain next steps. Two anonymous reviewers of my manuscript offered well-taken provocations and welcome words of encouragement. I am also very grateful to scholars who read revised chapters despite busy schedules: Susan Leigh Foster, Hannah Kosstrin, Jennifer Lambe, Michael Bustamante, Devyn Spence Benson, Alejandro de la Fuente, Anasa Hicks, Ariel Lambe, Joanna Dee Das, Anthea Kraut, Susan Manning, Michelle Chase, Alfonso Salgado, Pablo Piccato, and Heather Rastovac Akbarzadeh. Maya Berry also provided regular insights and invited me to present at the University of North Carolina, Chapel Hill, where workshop attendees importantly shaped my revisions. Nara Milanich directed me to Pat Payne, who expertly and artistically improved a crucial image. As I prepared to resubmit, Elena Schneider and Margaret Chowning read the entire manuscript, soaring above and beyond for an itinerant colleague. Elena also connected me with Alexis Esquivel, who generously shared his beautiful art for the epilogue. On top of this considerable aid, Elena continues to field last-minute queries, offering a model of integrity, kindness, and brilliance to which I can only aspire.

My most precious collaborators are the hardest to adequately thank. My parents, Marcia and Fred Schwall, have fielded countless worried calls, read through boring pieces of writing, helped with travel logistics, and provided endless love and encouragement every step of the way. My hilarious and effortlessly good-natured brother, Brian Schwall, has cheered me up and on through the years. My husband, Danillo Graziosi, has patiently and willingly weighed in on so many issues surrounding this book as it coopted countless discussions during walks and meals. I can never fully articulate my appreciation for his unwavering support and companionship. All I can do is record my gratitude for everything he has done and continues to do. As our most beautiful collaboration to date danced in my belly and now rests in my arms, I embrace, in warm thanks, the life we spin together.

I often lost sleep worrying that I would forget to thank someone. My profoundest apologies if I did. The many who have helped to shepherd this project to completion brought out the best in the material. As for the mistakes inevitably herein, I take full responsibility.

Dancing with the Revolution

Introduction

Here the only thing everyone is going to have to dance with,
whether they want to or not, is with the Revolution.
—Fidel Castro, 1959

In photographs from the early 1970s, Cuban modern dancers appear ready for battle. In one image, four men clutch rifles, a woman raises a flag, several stare down an imagined enemy, and two women defiantly thrust their hands into the air (see figure I.1). Luz María Collazo, the woman on the far left with her open hand raised and leg extended in a firm but buoyant stance, did not remember the photo shoot. Isidro Rolando, her longtime colleague and friend who appears in other images in the series, recalled it fondly. As a gentle breeze and loud street noises spilled through an open window in Rolando's living room, he reminded Collazo and explained to me that the photographs had inspired posters that appeared on each block of the main drive, Paseo, which leads toward the Plaza of the Revolution in Havana. Dancers improvised to embody official annual themes from the previous decade and a half: the Year of Agrarian Reform, Year of the Literacy Campaign, and others. Although the abstracted figures on the final posters did not look like dancers, they had "poetry" and "certain movement," which indicated their source.[1]

Their moving militancy glossed a more complicated backstory. A few years earlier, the government had censored the modern dancers, causing a company crisis and a "very painful moment of much confusion," according to Collazo.[2] However, modern dancers persisted, staging new works and advocating behind the scenes. Shortly thereafter, they appeared on posters to model revolutionary accomplishments. Their aggressive stances, then, above all reflected their resolve, honed after years of cultivating and navigating their relationship with the state. They fought to secure a place along Paseo, and by extension, in Cuban cultural and political life. Because of their work, dance became an important cultural expression of the Revolution, and dancers, compelling avatars of full-bodied investment in political projects.

The history of dancers like Rolando and Collazo provides important insight into Cuban politics writ large. In 1959, Fidel Castro and his 26th of July Movement led a broad coalition to declare a revolutionary "triumph" against the ousted leader, Fulgencio Batista. Dancers, like other Cuban citizens, built

FIGURE I.1 In the studios of the Teatro Nacional de Cuba, modern dancers improvise moves inspired by annual political themes in the early 1970s. Luz María Collazo stands on the far left. Photographer unknown. Source: Archivo de Danza Contemporánea de Cuba. Courtesy of Danza Contemporánea de Cuba.

on precedents to forge tactical relationships with the new regime, and revolutionary ideals motivated their subsequent actions. For dancers, political prompts led to particularly vivid outcomes: they defensively lunged and raised their fists in the photograph, for instance. Their bodies in motion evidence how politics in Cuba were not just spoken but also performed. Dancers in fact had particular capacity to express adhesion to the revolutionary project, as well as critiques thanks to the nonverbal nature of their art. Moreover, dancers like Collazo publicly conveyed revolutionary support as illustrated in the photo shoot, despite recent backstage drama and any disaffection it may have caused. Ultimately, even as the Revolution inspired dancers, final aesthetic outcomes remained the product of their individual imaginations and physicalities. Thus, dance foregrounds the requisite performances of public support, the shrouded tensions, and the spaces for agency involved in literally and metaphorically dancing with the Revolution as an idea and a concrete ruling structure. Just as dancers became emblems of Cuban citizens in the posters, I see their stories as emblematic of broader political histories on the island. Consequently, examining how dancers partnered with the state reveals the ideological forces, physical movements, bold performances, and poised resilience inherent to navigating politics in revolutionary Cuba for dancing and nondancing citizens alike.

To explore these political histories, I examine concert dance developments from 1930 to 1990. This means focusing on staged choreography rather than revelry or ritual dances that often occurred outside of nationalized institutions. During the crucial period of the 1930s through the 1950s, Cuban dancers and audiences established the social and cultural importance of concert dance. After 1959, dance makers—an expansive term that refers to performers, teachers, choreographers, company directors, and students—built on precedents to create revolutionary dance institutions and productions. Mixing the old with the new, dance makers instructed, entertained, employed, and politically provoked Cubans in a revolutionary context. As a result of their efforts, by the 1980s Cuba had become an internationally renowned dance center.

Scholars have often attributed concert dance achievements in Cuba to official cultural policies, but dance makers were not passive beneficiaries (or victims, depending on the political perspective).[3] They in fact spearheaded hallmark dance developments. The active stances that Rolando, Collazo, and their colleagues took to embody revolutionary politics for the photo shoot encapsulated their energetic role in securing resources to build audiences and establish their art as intrinsic to revolutionary culture. Their efforts paid off. Castro saw companies off at the airport, attended their performances with visiting dignitaries in tow, and referenced their distinctions in major speeches. However, their status was never a foregone conclusion. Dance makers had to contend with authoritarianism and fight to assert power as they brought a cultural industry into being in collaboration with officials who ranged from obliging to hostile to apathetic to everything in between.

Along with examining dance makers' hard-won power, this history breaks new ground by foregrounding the kinesthetic rather than the visual, discursive, or aural dimensions of Cuban politics.[4] This focus reveals that bodily movement became an important medium for political expression in Cuba. Performers at times exuded a militant political message, as in the photo shoot. In other instances, dancers questioned the status quo in ways impossible elsewhere. The state came to control the press and censor art, but movement arguably offered greater opportunity for ambivalent messaging given its nonverbal physicality, ephemerality, and general lack of fixity in contrast to literature, film, visual art, theater, and music.[5] This allowed dance makers to challenge racial prejudices by staging the music and dances of Afro-Cuban rituals as the state policed such practices, thereby indirectly questioning punitive policies. Homosexual dancers and choreographers retained a public platform through dance in the late 1960s and early 1970s, despite social prejudice and the threat of persecution by a homophobic state. A younger generation of dancers in the 1980s criticized decades of censorship and self-censorship. Dancers also performed apolitical works like the nineteenth-century French ballet *Giselle* or abstract dances about the beauty of African sculpture. Political and apolitical choreography won the hearts and minds of audiences around the world, cultivating revolutionary solidarity and international profiles in the process. Whether political leaders harnessing militant gestures for posters or dance makers choreographically defying social norms, Cubans recognized and capitalized on the political force of dancing bodies.

In addition to performative politics, the history of concert dance exposes privileges based on race and class in revolutionary Cuba despite official rhetoric of socialist equality. Juxtaposing developments in ballet, modern dance (renamed "national dance" in the 1970s and "contemporary dance" in the 1980s), and so-called folkloric dance reveals that racialized and classist hierarchies indelibly structured the field before and after the 1959 Revolution. Ballet in twentieth-century Cuba denoted whiteness and had elite connotations due to its European origins and early history on the island, which involved mostly white, middle- and upper-class students, professionals, and patrons. Starting in the 1950s, white and African-descended Cuban modern dancers adapted techniques from the United States and Europe by integrating elements from Afro-Cuban culture and positing blackness as a marker of Cubanness in national modern dance aesthetics.[6] Folkloric dance in Cuba refers to theatrical versions of ritual and popular dances, such as those performed in the religious practices of *Regla de Ocha* known as Santería, *Reglas de Congo* known as Palo Monte, the male initiation society Abakuá, as well as social and popular dances like rumba. "Folkloric" can have pejorative connotations, but Cuban folkloric dance makers embraced the term and created revolutionary productions.[7] The lines between ballet, modern dance, and folkloric dance in Cuba remained fluid as dancers and choreographers trained and worked across the forms. Nevertheless, examining the carefully constructed genres together reveals that the historically white, elite ballet enjoyed a privileged position in Cuba, especially when compared with modern and folkloric dance, which both drew upon Afro-Cuban popular culture. Consequently, modern and folkloric dance became notable, though often underappreciated, realms for racial justice activism, wherein African-descended dance makers and their white allies challenged intersecting racial and class prejudice by celebrating black culture on stage and advocating for their art behind the scenes. As a result, concert dance highlights social inertias and justice struggles in revolutionary Cuba.

In other words, this book makes three principal contributions by providing novel insights into power, politics, and privilege in Cuba. First, Cuban dance makers fought for and secured degrees of power as they made the island into a world-renowned dance center. Second, concert dance became an important means for political expression in the limited revolutionary public sphere. Third, ballet, modern, and folkloric dancers enjoyed disparate levels of privilege before and after 1959, and as a result, many dance makers remained on the front lines of challenging persistent racial and class inequalities. This history reframes understandings of the Revolution as charismatic leaders like Fidel Castro, so often central to scholarship on Cuba, fade to the background and as artful dancers frustrate absolute state control.[8] By focusing on concert dance, I argue that Cuban citizens did not march in lockstep behind the Revolution, but literally and metaphorically danced with it. This means that while entwined with the state, dance makers dynamically engaged with revolutionary governance, maneuvering every step of the way.

In dancing with the Revolution, artists did not simply resist or comply with a monolithic state, an abiding narrative that originated with Fidel Castro himself. In 1961, Castro famously told artists and intellectuals that only art "within the Revolution" had a right to exist.[9] With this statement, he reaffirmed a broader Manichean worldview in which artists acted for or against the Revolution. Yet, as many observers then and since have noted, Fidel never clarified what fell within revolutionary parameters. Dancers (like artists of other media) took advantage of the wiggle room and interacted with a multifaceted state in far more complex and contradictory ways. Newly available materials from the Cuban Ministry of Culture archives and oral history interviews evidence the constant negotiations, frequent disagreements, and routine consensus between company directors and administrators on the one hand and cultural bureaucrats on the other. Sources also reveal that key clashes and coalitions happened within companies, between rank-and-file dancers and company leaders. For instance, lower-class, African-descended folkloric dancers had to face racist and classist aggressions from middle-class white choreographers and company administrators, as well as cultural bureaucrats. As for fraught coalitions, homosexual dancers received crucial protection from, along with preemptive internal policing by, company leaders who aimed to shelter them from a punitive homophobic state. All of this transpired within nationalized dance institutions, making the dichotomy between cultural producers and the state a false one. As historian Michael Bustamante points out, "in a socialist country . . . at a certain point, the state becomes you and me."[10] Indeed, ambiguities and vacillations riddled the relationship between dancers, company directors, bureaucrats, and political leaders, all arguably representatives of the state.

Dancing with the Revolution involved more challenges for cultural producers than often recognized.[11] African-descended dance makers in particular waged an uphill battle for their art due to racism and classism. Indeed, the preeminence of ballet in republican and revolutionary Cuba reveals the persistent privileging of whiteness and elite taste, despite official claims of radical social change.[12] As historian Devyn Spence Benson concluded in her study of post-1959 antiracist campaigns, policies resulted in an "unfinished revolution" as racism and antiracism continued to coexist.[13] Even though racial and class prejudices were impossible to fully shake, some dance makers valiantly tried. Black intellectual Rogelio Martínez Furé promoted the politics of racial justice by cofounding the first professional folkloric dance company, advising productions, and protesting bureaucratic mistreatment, all to expand appreciation for Afro-Cuban cultural producers and popular culture. In subtler but no less significant ways, black modern dancers like Collazo and Rolando trained and rehearsed year after year to garner local and international accolades. Through these actions, dance makers fomented important changes to their profession and revolutionary culture broadly speaking, despite persistent prejudices.[14] As modern dancers aggressively posed for the posters above Paseo, they evidenced their familiarity with battle, whether fighting against national enemies or stifling attitudes.

Dancing with the Revolution fleshes out these ideas in seven chapters that move forward chronologically and thematically. The first two chapters focus on how ballet became a valued national art and how Cubans explored race and nation through dance in the 1930s through the 1950s. The rest of the book traces how dancers innovated after the 1959 Cuban Revolution. Chapter 3 examines the racial and class prejudices that guided revolutionary dance institutionalization in the 1960s, as well as how African-descended dance makers challenged these structural inequalities. Chapter 4 analyzes how dancers, choreographers, and company directors across the genres navigated homophobia and choreographed critiques of gender and sexual norms in the late 1960s and early 1970s. Chapter 5 investigates how the dance establishment made dancing and watching dance part of mass education campaigns in the 1960s and 1970s, and chapter 6, how concert dance became a lucrative export and part of internationalist politics in the 1970s and 1980s. Chapter 7 studies ruptures in Cuba as the first revolutionary generation came of age, and as post-1959 concert dance institutions began to show their age in the 1980s. Although the epilogue reiterates major conclusions and how historic developments shape the present, the core analysis focuses on 1930 to 1990. The narrative ends before the 1990s and early 2000s, when a political and economic crisis, catalyzed by the fall of the Soviet Union, shook Cuban society and culture. According to dancers, the decades before the crisis amounted to a bygone golden age of Cuban concert dance. Their stories provide historical insights into the shimmering achievements, devastating disappointments, and mundane muddling through of a particular era and help to explain historical precedents for post-1990 cultural productions examined by other scholars.[15]

For historians of Cuba, a focus on concert dance not only provides insights into power, politics, and privilege but also challenges accepted chronologies of Cuban political developments. Cubans came to value ballet and explored race and nation choreographically before Fidel Castro and the Revolution promoted expansive cultural developments and championed antiracism. After 1959, revolutionary dance institutionalization consolidated by the mid-1960s, earlier than other realms of the economy and politics. Additionally, the late 1960s and early 1970s—often sweepingly characterized as a bitter, gray period of heightened repression and didactic expression—also witnessed exciting developments as nonprofessional dance expanded within Cuba and as professionals cultivated international profiles even while dealing with homophobia and censorship at home. Finally, scholars have thus far presumed that the fall of the Soviet Union in the early 1990s brought sudden openings to culture and society in Cuba. Cuban dancers in fact pushed for such reforms in the late 1970s and 1980s. Concert dance developments across six decades feature changes over time at unexpected tempos and catalyzed by different historical figures than often presumed, namely, dancing Cubans, not political elites or cultural bureaucrats.

For historians of Latin America, Cuban dance developments contribute to social histories in the region during the Cold War. Dance makers hustled to meet material needs—as ballet students securing scholarships in the 1940s, as displaced concert dancers working in cabarets in the 1950s, as folkloric dancers fighting for increased salaries in the 1960s, as ballet dancers lobbying for more food rations in the 1970s, or as young choreographers searching for rehearsal space in the 1980s. Examining their everyday lives as much as possible contributes to ongoing discussions of how people lived in a charged political atmosphere during the Cold War in Latin America. For the past decade, historians have looked beyond clashing superpowers to understand how diverse social actors shaped contemporary political projects and ideological struggles during the Latin American Cold War.[16] Recently, historians of Cuba have joined the conversation to refocus attention to the Revolution "from within."[17] Contributing to these efforts, this book zeroes in on individual dance makers and the ground they covered to understand the social history of revolutionary cultural producers. When considering the photo shoot, for instance, I not only examine the aesthetic outcome but also wonder about the process. Was improvising the tableau difficult? On the contrary, Rolando explained, they "all were militants. . . . It was part of quotidian life."[18] Such comments reveal how life outside of studios and theaters, which included guard duty, military drills, food scarcity, and sacrifices, informed performance work. Routine practices and spectacular events overlapped, and accounting for both provides fuller understandings of politics during the Cold War.

For historians in general, I make a case for attending to dance, a rich, important, and often-overlooked realm of human experience.[19] Dance, necessarily racialized and gendered depending on who is moving, articulates power relations while also providing opportunities to subvert them. Appreciating the analytic value of dance need not translate to studies focused on performance like this one. Instead, I suggest that greater attention to dance while analyzing other realms of human experience provides deeper understanding of what it meant to move through the world. After all, performance by definition disappears upon its realization, as does history. The challenges and opportunities of studying dance historically invite reflection on how to examine the consequential and ordinary movements that people made and what human actions reveal about their context.

For dance scholars, my call for humanistic attention to moving bodies adheres to the central precepts of the diverse field of dance studies. Without question, I stand on the shoulders of scholars who have written histories of dance across time and space.[20] However, my particular approach differs from books for cultural, literary, performance, theatrical, and dance scholars, which use historical context to understand dance. Here, I use concert dance to understand historical change in Cuba. This flipped equation means tracing how larger structures and processes played out in the field of concert dance. Rather than focusing on repertory, this study analyzes structural inequalities, institutional building, mass education campaigns, internationalism, and generational shifts across sixty years of concert dance development. Looking as much behind the scenes as on stage, I examine Cuban dance makers as activists who haggled with governments and as artists who impressed audiences, all to secure a place on national and international stages.[21]

My work would have been impossible without existing scholarship on Cuban dance. In Cuba, scholars have published invaluable chronologies, interviews, retrospectives, and theoretical studies on dance. Notably, many of these authors were historical subjects in their own right. For instance, modern dance scholar Fidel Pajares Santiesteban participated in the photo shoot with Collazo and Rolando soon after joining the modern dance company in the early 1970s (figure I.2). He and others in Cuba have written to preserve and promote the histories that they participated in making. Their works of historical advocacy emphasize boundless achievement and revolutionary synergy.[22] As an outsider who has analyzed bureaucratic documents not yet considered by these and other scholars, I account for the very real challenges that Cuban dancers faced even in revolutionary times. I also diverge from existing work written on and off the island in looking across genres to understand how these distinctions (fraught with racialized and classed connotations) developed in the first place and how concert dance, broadly speaking, operated in Cuban politics and society.[23]

Finally, for readers of any background interested in Cuban dance generally, I write for you as well. Most people with even passing knowledge of Cuba and Cuban dance have likely heard of the late ballerina Alicia Alonso, who became a world-renowned performer and visible revolutionary supporter. She figures importantly in this history, and I met the nonagenarian in 2015. The interview was brief, around thirty minutes, and despite her age and visual, hearing, cognitive, and mobility limitations, she spoke in true dancer fashion by using her body. Her long fingernails tapped, and her fists hit the desk to emphasize certain points; her head moved constantly up and down, side to side. At one point, she confirmed a central premise of this book. Not answering my original question, she delighted me in asserting, "Well, in the beginning, [it] was ourselves and a few persons who helped us. . . . And then after we *proved* that we could be ballet dancers and have a great company . . . the state, the government, start[ed] to subsidize and pay for everything. . . . Since then, they have been helping us . . . all the governments."[24] I follow her lead and show how dancers fought to prove their worth to "all the governments" before and after 1959. However, I also look beyond Alicia's towering persona to detail the experiences of lesser-known artists like Rolando and Collazo, who choreographed and performed revolutions in the era of Alicia Alonso.

FIGURE I.2 Another image from the early 1970s photo shoot features Isidro Rolando (*center*) and Fidel Pajares Santiesteban (*far left, second row*). Photographer unknown. Source: Personal archive of Isidro Rolando. Courtesy of Isidro Rolando.

Before diving into their histories, I pause to note that during the six decades covered, racial terminology shifted and took on different connotations. Cubans employ a range of adjectives to indicate racial and ethnic background, such as *mulato* (mixed race), *mestizo* (mixed race), *negro* (black), *blanco* (white), and *gente de color* (people of color), among others. In cases where individuals used a specific word or phrase to refer to race, I do as well. For Cubans with African ancestors, I use "African descended," "people of color," "black," and "Afro-Cuban" interchangeably when terminology and how individuals identify remain unclear.[25] When discussing cultural practices, such as religious beliefs, music, and dances produced by or closely identified with Cubans of African descent, I use the terms "black" and "Afro-Cuban." These choices fail to represent the variety of experiences that individuals have with racial formation, politics, and identity as well as the diversity of Cubans engaged with cultural practices glossed as "Afro-Cuban." These terms mostly show the limits of language to reflect the histories of Cuban people, who interacted with unsteady racial categories and produced diverse cultural expressions.

To close, I return to the epigraph by Fidel Castro, where he mandated that Cubans "dance . . . with the Revolution." On March 22, 1959, Castro denounced racism, which elicited backlash particularly from white Cubans, who feared integration in public and private life.[26] Castro addressed critics on the television news program *Ante la prensa* the next day by clarifying that he would not force interracial intimacies on desegregated dance floors, but that he did demand unity behind the young political project. To reiterate this point, he asserted, "Here the only thing everyone is going to have to dance with, whether they want to or not, is with the Revolution [*Aquí con la única que van a tener que bailar, aunque no quieran, es con la Revolución.*]."[27] Although Castro spoke metaphorically, concert dancers literally enacted this mandate by partnering with the state. However, they did not passively follow the state's lead as Castro may have hoped. Upon taking the state's extended hand, they deftly moved in and out of sync with official dictates. Indeed, dancing with the Revolution meant drawing on tools honed in earlier decades. It also resulted in varied, sometimes contradictory choreography. At times dancers embodied revolutionary fervor for commemorative posters. At others they celebrated Santería religiosity or reinterpreted a French ballet. The photo shoot of dancing militants that Rolando warmly remembered is part of this story, but it is only the beginning.

CHAPTER ONE

Valuing Ballet in the Cuban Republic

Look, I do more with my feet than you and all those men with your titles.
—Alicia Alonso, 1956

On January 8, 1949, thirty-five thousand Cubans packed into the Stadium Universitario in Havana for a free performance by Ballet Alicia Alonso, Cuba's first professional ballet company.[1] This was nearly three times the capacity of the twelve-thousand-seat stadium, and ten thousand people had been turned away. Company cofounder Fernando Alonso bragged, "The audience was standing in the field, on the steps, on the chairs, on the roof, etc. It was in short the most impressive sight that Cuba has ever seen."[2] From 1949 through 1955, Cuban ballet dancers reached mass audiences in Havana, Santiago de Cuba, Camagüey, Pinar del Río, and even Miami.[3] In Santiago de Cuba, one such performance changed a life. Jorge Lefebre, a *mulato* art student from a poor family, watched Ballet Alicia Alonso at the Antonio Maceo Stadium. The performance catalyzed a series of encounters and opportunities that launched his international ballet career.[4] As these large performances and Lefebre's personal trajectory show, ballet had achieved a relatively expansive and esteemed place in Cuban society, becoming entertainment, passion, and even vocation for many by the 1950s.

This chapter charts how and why Cubans came to value ballet from the 1930s through the 1950s. As for how, it started with civic associations and talented dancers like Lefebre promoting ballet as discussed in the first two sections. Appreciation eventually percolated up to the Cuban state as examined in the last section. This order of interest, from citizens to the government, evidences how ballet was the product of performer and audience activism and implicated in civil society from the moment of its inception in Cuba. As for why, ballet was an expression of whiteness and elite sensibilities. The form had roots in bourgeois culture and sociability in Cuba, which was sustained by an extensive associational culture and increasingly powerful white women of Cuban high society.[5] Bolstered by these connotations, structures, and advocates, ballet secured a privileged position in Cuban national culture by the late 1950s. From such heights, ballet would thrive in subsequent decades, as later chapters will detail.

With these assertions, I offer a revisionist interpretation of Cuban ballet history in line with recent scholarship on Cuba's republican period. Traditional narratives about ballet emphasize victimization by neglectful (at best) and tyrannical (at worst) governments before 1959, which contrasted sharply with enlightened, supportive revolutionary leaders.[6] While perhaps well founded, such characterizations fail to recognize the considerable leverage that ballet dancers and supporters possessed by the late 1950s. In fact, this period encompassed key ballet developments as dancers and supporters honed artistic visions, advertised ballet's social significance, and cultivated networks that bolstered its cultural and political capital in Cuba. Examining the period known as the republic "on its own terms," I join recent scholarship on the first half of the twentieth century, especially by historians Irina Pacheco Valera, Jorgelina Guzmán Moré, and Cary García Yero, who have shown that cultural institutions and policies developed over these decades laid the institutional foundations for what followed.[7] Equally, I apply dance scholar Susan Foster's theorization about "valuing dance" and offer a case study for how dancers, students, audiences, and eventually governments in republican Cuba came to esteem ballet as a resource for personal and national development.[8] With a revisionist eye, sold-out performances that enamored ballet converts like Lefebre backed up Alicia's claim in the epigraph that her supple feet, not to mention those of her students and colleagues, did so much.[9] Notably, they brought a dynamic Cuban ballet tradition into being before 1959.

Making a Cuban Ballet "Dynasty"

The official Cuban ballet historian Miguel Cabrera first saw Alicia Alonso on television. Cabrera later recalled the magical moment when "Alicia appeared on the screen as though she were a fairy."[10] Esteem and even love harbored by Cabrera and others contributed importantly to creating what became an Alonso ballet "dynasty," as one article in the main Havana weekly *Bohemia* called it.[11] The distinguished family included the triad of Alicia the ballerina, Fernando (Alicia's husband) the pedagogue, and Alberto (Fernando's brother) the choreographer. Making the Alonso ballet "dynasty" involved talent and hard work, crossing borders, and competitive energies, as well as meaningful partnerships between professionals and adoring audience members like Cabrera.

The dynasty began with well-off families that included a musical matriarch, Laura Rayneri de Alonso. In 1934, she became president of Sociedad Pro-Arte Musical (Pro-Art Musical Society), which had been founded in 1918 by white, bourgeois women, who believed that high culture could "enlighten and educate" Cuban audiences. Although originally focused on music,

starting in the 1930s the women of Pro-Arte supported dance, bringing notable performers of modern dance, Spanish dance, and ballet to Cuba.[12] Additionally, Pro-Arte organized the country's first ballet classes in 1931. Ballet,
declamation, and guitar classes for youth cost a modest additional amount a
month for members (half of a peso in 1946, for instance).[13] Russian émigré
Nicolai Yavorsky, who resided in Havana at the time, taught the first ballet
classes. His students included the sisters Blanca (Cuca) and Alicia Martínez,
who had an army veterinarian father and a mother who was a "well-educated
seamstress with ambition."[14] They lived in a large apartment in the privileged
Vedado neighborhood in Havana and matriculated in Yavorsky's classes in
the summer of 1931. The brothers Fernando and Alberto Alonso were also
among the early students. Living in a house in Vedado, their distinguished
family included a father, who was an accountant for a U.S. trading company,
and a mother, Laura Rayneri de Alonso, who was a pianist, member of Pro-
Arte, and president of the organization from 1934 to 1948. In 1932, Alberto
enrolled in ballet classes, and his older brother Fernando followed three years
later.[15] The Martínez and Alonso families provide insight into the backgrounds of the first generation of Pro-Arte students.

Ballet likely appealed to Havana's prominent families because it reportedly
built character and physical health, thereby fostering a robust nation. Pro-
Arte publications claimed that teachers combatted dilettantism and developed students with "a serious spirit of the artistic profession, . . . a sense of
collective responsibility, and a consciousness of moral commitment."[16] The
high society magazine *Social* emphasized ballet's health benefits in a series on
female fitness. One article featured Yavorsky contending that ballet "is one of
the most complete and ennobling exercises known to educate the body." The
article concluded that the edifying activity resulted in "bodily perfection."[17]
In a student performance program, an essay eulogized ballet for cultivating
"mental concentration, and a force of memory that are not common in other
forms of physical exercise." Such personal benefits in turn improved the national body politic: "The present interest in the study of ballet in our country
is a very encouraging sign for the future, because it contributes to improving
the physical health and artistic education of our youth and of generations to
come."[18] This resonated with an idea long promoted by Pro-Arte that cultural
activity "renders great service to the homeland [*patria*]."[19] Promoters, then,
imbued cultural activities like ballet with great consequence as a means for
personal and national betterment.

Ballet also contributed to national reputations when Cuban dancers earned
accolades abroad. Through their achievements, ballet went from an admira-

ble pastime to a serious profession. From 1935 to 1941, Alberto Alonso danced with the Europe-based Ballets Russes de Monte Carlo directed by Yavorsky's old friend, Colonel de Basil. Then, from 1944 to 1945, he performed in Hollywood and with the company Ballet Theatre (today American Ballet Theatre) of New York. In 1941, Alberto returned to Cuba and became the director of Pro-Arte's ballet school, a position that he held on and off until 1960.[20] Meanwhile, Fernando and Alicia Alonso traveled to New York in 1937, married, and had their daughter Laura. They trained with premier "Old World" teachers residing in New York and performed in Broadway musicals and with ballet companies, including Lincoln Kirstein's Ballet Caravan (a predecessor of the New York City Ballet) and Ballet Theatre.[21]

Alicia Alonso in particular epitomized Cuban balletic potential as she became an internationally renowned ballerina. In her first year with Ballet Theatre, she performed leading roles to critical acclaim. In 1940, dance critic John Martin opined, "She showed herself to be a promising young artist with an easy technique, a fine sense of line and a great deal of youthful charm."[22] At the end of the performance season, Martin flagged her as one of several artists "of less than stellar rank who belong among [the] season's assets."[23] In November 1943, she performed the title role of the ballet *Giselle*. Originally staged in nineteenth-century France, it tells the story of a young peasant girl who falls in love with a prince disguised as a villager. When class differences keep them apart, Giselle dies of a broken heart. Martin found that "Miss Alonso acquitted herself with brilliance," and her technical foundations were "so strong that perfection seem[ed] only a matter of time."[24] Already in 1945, Martin saw improvement, predicting that the "extraordinarily brilliant young ballerina from Cuba will one day be one of the great Giselles."[25] Alicia had mastered a classic in ballet repertories, indicating her arrival in the upper echelons of the art. Her fame reached beyond the ballet world, as she appeared in the magazines *Life*, *Norte*, and *Newsweek* in 1944, and the magazine *Mademoiselle* chose her as one of the ten most outstanding women of 1946.[26]

Alicia's ballet achievements profited Cuba, according to admiring compatriots who decided to organize a tribute for her. Led by arts critic José Manuel Valdés Rodríguez, the Comité Organizador del Homenaje Nacional a Alicia Alonso (Organizing Committee for the National Homage to Alicia Alonso) included Laura Rayneri de Alonso and Paulina Alsina de Grau (the widow of Cuban president Ramón Grau's late brother), among other notables. Given "the exceptional merits of Alicia Alonso, recognized unanimously by world critics," the committee campaigned to honor her with the Carlos Manuel de Céspedes award, the highest distinction for civilians.[27] The effort succeeded, and for the tribute on August 5, 1947, Alicia performed with Pro-Arte students.[28] After a "prolonged and warm ovation" from the audience, Alicia received a diamond-encrusted cross that was purchased with donations from friends and admirers.[29] With the Céspedes award, Alicia received the title *Dama*, and the government released a commemorative postage stamp with her photo.[30] Already in the late 1940s, Alicia was a national idol thanks to her achievements and adoring fans.

Her success also brought financial gains and symbolic trappings of stature. In 1940, as a dancer at Ballet Theatre, Alicia began with a salary of twenty-five dollars per week. By the 1946–47 season, Alicia received two hundred and fifty dollars per performance week, and this rate generally continued, depending on the length and location of performances.[31] To put Alicia's fiscal ascent in perspective, Fernando, who began his professional ballet career at the same time, started at forty-five dollars per week in 1938 with a troupe led by Mikhail Mordkin, and reached ninety-five dollars per performance week in his final year with Ballet Theatre during the 1947–48 season.[32] In addition to money, Alicia secured signifiers of status. In 1945, for instance, a contract stipulated that Alicia must receive "first" or principal role casting and be listed as "ballerina."[33] In the 1950s, when Alicia was a guest artist with the Ballet Russe de Monte Carlo, billing issues dominated correspondence between her agent and company administrators.[34] These flourishes evidenced Alicia's stature and contributed to her fame at home.

Adding heroic dimensions to Alicia's prominence were her vision problems. In 1941, Alicia discovered that the retina in her right eye had detached. After two surgeries in New York, she resumed daily classes only to experience further issues. Back in Cuba, a specialist found that the retinas on both of her eyes had detached. He operated immediately, ordered total bed rest, and predicted the end of her dance career. By most accounts, Alicia lay immobile with her eyes covered for eighteen months, though some have claimed twelve and others, twenty-four.[35] Ballet historian Célida Parera Villalón challenged the mythic proportions of Alicia's story. Parera Villalón, the first cousin to Alberto and Fernando Alonso, worked as a Pro-Arte administrator before leaving Cuba in 1959. She later recalled Alicia on bed rest, "for a period of 4 months, not 1½ year[s] as legend has it."[36] Regardless, there are two undisputed points. First, Alicia eventually recovered and returned to New York to continue her meteoric rise. Second, her determination and accomplishments despite her visual disability defined her public persona.[37] As famed U.S. choreographer Agnes de Mille wrote in 1990, "What makes her unique, what makes her different from all predecessors, all rivals, is one simple fact: Alicia is blind."[38]

The internationally experienced Alicia, Fernando, and Alberto reunited in 1948 to form the first professional ballet company in Cuba. A major catalyst came when Ballet Theatre experienced financial problems, canceled its fall season, and suspended activities until further notice. A panicked Fernando wrote to Ballet Theatre director Lucia Chase, "We received your communication about Ballet Theatre's Fall Season being cancelled. Alicia and I are absolutely dumbfounded. It will be approximately 9 months lay-off by the time we start again! That is terrible! . . . Because of your position in the Ballet World, it should be comparatively easy for you to suggest something for us to do before Ballet Theatre starts operating again."[39] Worry, however, gave way to excitement. With no prospects, Fernando and Alicia returned to Havana with fellow furloughed Ballet Theatre dancers in tow. They joined forces with Alberto to found the Ballet Alicia Alonso. It had a nationalistic, even anti-imperialist resonance by stealing away the best ballet dancers from New York. John Martin noted in 1948, "If the Ballet Theatre should decide not to carry on, this might be the organization to replace it, with its headquarters 'right in the middle of America,' as Fernando Alonso puts it."[40] U.S. hegemony had frustrated Cuban sovereignty since the nation won independence from Spain in 1898, so the fact that fifty years later ballet appeared to have a more promising future in Havana than in New York attached consequential and lasting nationalistic dimensions to the Alonsos' actions.

Although the Alonsos collaborated on the Ballet Alicia Alonso, they also pursued independent dance projects. In 1950, Alberto founded his own company, Ballet Nacional. Also that year, Fernando and Alicia opened their school, Escuela de Ballet Alicia Alonso. Alberto, Pro-Arte's ballet school, and Ballet Nacional remained on one side with Fernando and Alicia, Escuela de Ballet Alicia Alonso, and Ballet Alicia Alonso on the other. Competition along with collaboration characterized the relationship between the Alonso brothers and their respective enterprises.

A rivalry developed between the schools of Pro-Arte and Ballet Alicia Alonso. In 1953, an article in the popular magazine *Gente* claimed that only Ballet Alicia Alonso's school created quality dancers. Pro-Arte administrator Parera Villalón wrote a letter to the editor that challenged this portrayal, and a public back-and-forth continued in subsequent editorials.[41] Meanwhile, performance programs for the Escuela de Ballet Alicia Alonso asserted that it offered "the most complete education that can be obtained in the art of dance," thanks to Fernando's internationally inspired, locally adapted technique and Alicia's illustrious example. Advertisements also emphasized the school's large teaching staff and extensive curriculum, which included ballet, pointe, adagio, variations, folkloric, Spanish, character, and modern dance, as well as classes in music, history of art and dance, costume design, applied anatomy, and makeup.[42] The passionate promotional efforts went beyond institutional (or sibling) competition. The schools vied for students and their tuition.

Young dancers ultimately benefited from the growing institutional landscape. The schools, for instance, provided options for different clientele. According to Laura Alonso, her parents' school "was for professionals," whereas Pro-Arte allowed students to dance for fun, regardless of talent or future plans.[43] Later star ballerinas Josefina Méndez and Loipa Araújo remembered receiving quality training from Pro-Arte, but reaching a limit and advancing their career with Ballet Alicia Alonso's school. According to Méndez, who began studying at Pro-Arte in 1948, Fernando visited Alberto's class in 1955 and selected her, Araújo, and several others to perform with Fernando and Alicia's company.[44] In this case, the brothers worked together to transform talented students into burgeoning professionals. Building a strong Cuban ballet establishment remained the overarching goal for not only the Alonsos' schools but also their professional ballet companies; however, Alberto's Ballet Nacional and Fernando and Alicia's Ballet Alicia Alonso had different philosophies on how to achieve this end.

Alberto and his collaborators believed that advancing national ballet depended on egalitarian artistic collaboration. According to program essays, the Ballet Nacional had an unprecedented structure that favored "the collective above the individual." Choreography featured all dancers equally, an "artistic mode that accords with the ideology of the present time," rather than "anachronistic" formats that highlighted a single dancer. Toward this end, dancers and other personnel participated in monthly executive meetings to avoid "the imposition of the will of a single person, which in many cases can degenerate into a dictatorship that promotes disharmony and demoralization, creating a hostile environment."[45] Although never naming names, the author seemed to allude to Ballet Alicia Alonso, which revolved around Alicia and likely catered to her wishes. Another program described the Ballet Alicia Alonso as a transitional step in the development of Cuban ballet, with Alberto's democratic Ballet Nacional as the apotheosis.[46]

Whereas the Ballet Nacional fostered collaboration among Cuban equals, the Ballet Alicia Alonso embraced foreign influences and artistic hierarchies. A 1951 Ballet Alicia Alonso program claimed that the company did not harbor "extreme nationalisms" and instead saw foreign artists and techniques as fundamental to Cuban dance development. Indeed, the Ballet Alicia Alonso had welcomed foreign influences since 1948 when the company premiered with New York dancers from Ballet Theatre. International exchanges continued as Alicia regularly performed abroad and brought foreign guest artists and teachers back to Cuba with her. Also diverging from the Ballet Nacional and its interest in equality, "the Ballet Alicia Alonso believe[d] in artistic and human hierarchy," based on the idea that meritocracy advanced ballet in Cuba and the world.[47]

Additionally, Fernando and Alicia on the one hand and Alberto on the other disagreed on the relationship between concert and commercial dance. Out of economic necessity, Fernando and Alicia had performed on Broadway early in their New York careers but ultimately described such genre crossings as problematic. A 1952 Ballet Alicia Alonso program described ballet as "sacerdotal," requiring daily devotion; moreover, "performances before television cameras produce a disastrous result on theater performances and constitute a serious threat to the artistic level of the Company."[48] By contrast, Alberto and his dancers appeared not only on concert dance stages with Ballet Nacional but also on television and in cabarets, since Alberto directed the Conjunto de Bailes del Teatro Radiocentro (Dance Ensemble of Radiocentro Theater) and Ballet de CMQ Televisión (Ballet of CMQ Television) and choreographed for the Montmartre, Sans Souci, and Riviera cabarets from 1951 to 1959. His dancers moved seamlessly between these performance spaces, as illustrated by the career of Alberto's second wife, Elena del Cueto. She began training at Pro-Arte, taught ballet at the school, performed with Ballet Alicia Alonso, and became a founding member of the Ballet Nacional.[49] She also starred in Alberto's television and cabaret spectacles, reportedly "elevating" Cuban dance through her "harmonious lines."[50] A picture of del Cueto in pointe shoes, a tutu, and a tiara, striking a position outside of ballet vocabulary (off-balanced, turned in, with her arms stuck out on either side in a showy gesture), illustrates how the ballet-trained dancer had an onstage persona that defied genre conventions.[51] Alberto later described cross-genre dialogues as generative, allowing him to experiment with mixing popular dance and ballet.[52] By elevating ballet above commercial enterprises, Alicia and Fernando sought to build distinction, while Alberto challenged classed, racialized divides between (white, elite ballet) art and (racially mixed) popular culture.[53]

These tensions had an overall productive effect. The fact that Alberto created the Ballet Nacional only two years after the Ballet Alicia Alonso indicates the robustness of the nascent ballet establishment. Along with professional companies, new civic associations of dancers and patrons formed in the late 1940s and 1950s Havana. Club Ballerina (1945–47) consisted of Pro-Arte ballet administrators and audience members, and Alberto founded an association of artists and fans to support his Ballet Nacional.[54] Alicia and Fernando followed this model and organized the Asociación Alicia Alonso Pro-Ballet (1952–58), Institución de Ballet Alicia Alonso (1952–56), and Patronato Ballet de Cuba (1955–61) to abet their dance initiatives.[55] These institutions reflect a broad appreciation for ballet. As Fernando proudly claimed, "People speak about the ballet in street cars, buses, restaurants, offices, etc."[56] The growing associational and institutional landscape revealed artistic differences, crucial alliances, and the involvement of audience members in ballet initiatives.

Cuban ballet moved in multiple directions, touching receptive audience members like Miguel Cabrera. These projects evidenced familial collaborations and tensions, but overall, consolidated the Alonsos' status as cultural trailblazers. A 1953 article on Laura Alonso, the fifteen-year-old daughter of Alicia and Fernando, niece of Alberto, and granddaughter and namesake of Laura Rayneri de Alonso, reiterated this point. Below rehearsal photographs, the caption described "Laurita," now an aspiring ballerina, receiving feedback from her parents. The generational exchange, the author contended, proved "that the dynasty is established."[57]

Ballet and the People

The Alonso ballet dynasty existed within a much larger ballet community. By the time Jorge Lefebre, for example, came into contact with the Ballet Alicia Alonso during a mass performance in Santiago, he had already studied ballet in his hometown. Decades later, he described, "Ballet then was an elite matter. There were two schools in Santiago . . . and finally, the one . . . that was more progressive admitted me." His interlocutor explained to readers, "Lefebre was poor and also *mulato*."[58] Even though ballet was part of elite, predominantly white, sociability, it also touched the lives of Lefebre and other Cubans beyond exclusive circles. Individuals from different class, racial, and geographic backgrounds experienced ballet as entertainment and pastime. Their diverse experiences indicate how valuing ballet involved different constituents across the country sharing and shaping the contours of the form.

Lefebre's first ballet school in Santiago grew out of local initiatives and connections with Havana. Local elites founded the Sociedad Pro-Arte Musical de Oriente ("Pro-Arte de Oriente" for short) in 1940, which was part of a larger expansion of the society into Manzanillo, Cienfuegos, Holguín, and Camagüey.[59] Pro-Arte de Oriente brought famed foreign dancers to perform in Santiago, including Alicia Markova and Anton Dolin in 1947 and 1950 and

Nora Kovach and Istvan Rabovsky in 1955.[60] A peer arts organization, Sociedad Filarmónica de Santiago de Cuba (Philharmonic Society of Santiago de Cuba), also contributed to balletic activities by inviting Ballet Alicia Alonso to perform in November 1948.[61] However, most importantly, Pro-Arte de Oriente began offering ballet classes with Bulgarian Georges Milenoff, who had ended up in Cuba on tour and had taught at Pro-Arte in Havana.[62] After Milenoff left a "bad impression," Pro-Arte de Oriente invited Yavorsky to replace him in 1946.[63] Yavorsky had taught at Pro-Arte in Havana from 1931 to 1939, until disagreements with the leadership prompted him to leave.[64] He cobbled together work, choreographing for a casino in Havana in 1941, teaching physical education classes in primary schools in 1944, and briefly running his own ballet school in Havana.[65] Eventually, Yavorsky negotiated contracts with Pro-Arte de Oriente to teach three times a week in Santiago as well as regular classes in the nearby towns of Bayamo and Manzanillo.[66] Yavorsky taught only a few months in eastern Cuba before his untimely passing in 1947.

Before his death, Yavorsky, and Milenoff before him, taught Lefebre's future teachers in Santiago, as well as future revolutionary dignitary Vilma Espín Guillois and her sister Nilsa. Vilma studied ballet from 1939 to 1949, and in a studio photograph, she wears a flowing dress, long hair loose, and pointe shoes, appearing to revel in her elegant pastime.[67] Alongside the Espín girls, notable fellow students Vivian Tobío and Clara Ramírez performed works by Milenoff in a 1944 program.[68] After Yavorsky died, Ramírez became the main teacher at Pro-Arte de Oriente, directing Vilma Espín and her peers in a 1949 production that included Tobío.[69] By the time Lefebre sought out ballet classes, Ramírez still taught at the elite Pro-Arte de Oriente, and Tobío, at the local cultural center Casa Heredia. Pro-Arte de Oriente remained exclusive. For example, when the organization's president found out that one student lived in the humble Mexiquito neighborhood of Santiago, she threw him out.[70] Lefebre remembered encountering similar prejudices. Born in the Sueño neighborhood of Santiago, he was the grandson of a white, French émigré and a poor, Cuban *mulata* woman, making him part of the "dispossessed branch of Lefebres."[71] The humble scion began taking ballet classes with Tobío at the Casa Heredia. He also painted and created costumes for a Pro-Arte de Oriente production of *The Sleeping Beauty*. In this capacity, he connected with Ramírez and began training with her. She then invited the talented teen to perform in Holguín, where she also taught.[72] Lefebre's experiences reveal that the Santiago ballet establishment had undeniable elitism but also offered rare chances for a few exceptional, lower-class students to advance in the exclusive art.

The fact that Lefebre followed Ramírez to Holguín also indicates that Santiago was one of several provincial towns with ballet schools, attesting to the form's increasing popularity across the island. Like studios in Santiago, those elsewhere had symbolic or concrete connections to Havana and the Alonsos specifically. In 1948, local enthusiasts in the eastern town of Palma Soriano founded the Escuela de Ballet Alicia Alonso with the "primary purpose to disseminate and enhance the art of classical dance." Nothing in the founding documents suggests a formal connection with Alicia or Havana, but instead, the school appears to have singlehandedly chosen the name to honor the famed ballerina.[73] By contrast, a formal connection between the Alonsos and Camagüey ballet institutions developed thanks to Martha Matamoros Cordero. Born in Havana, Matamoros studied at Pro-Arte and taught at the Escuela de Ballet Alicia Alonso. In 1952 she relocated to Camagüey, where she opened a ballet school, as well as one in the nearby town, Ciego de Ávila. Fernando and Alicia eventually visited, assessed her students, and verified an official affiliation with the Escuela de Ballet Alicia Alonso in 1954. Matamoros entered a relatively robust ballet landscape in Camagüey, which included a school founded by Gilda Zaldívar Freyre, the daughter of a diplomat who had trained abroad, and the Salón de Ballet del Colegio Zayas. One notable student, Vicentina de la Torre, trained with Zaldívar Freyre, the Salón de Ballet del Colegio Zayas, and the Escuela de Ballet Alicia Alonso in Havana. She went on to found her own ballet school in 1957 and a professional company (the Ballet de Camagüey) in 1967.[74] The relatively small ballet world meant that real or imagined connections to the Alonsos were common and often crucial for success, given the grassroots nature of these enterprises.

Ballet students strategically cultivated these connections, as seen in Lefebre's trajectory. After the Ballet Alicia Alonso performance in Santiago, an inspired Lefebre found Alicia and Fernando to discuss the possibility of training in Havana. Fernando took his name and address, and within a few months, a scholarship arrived. At seventeen, Lefebre relocated to Havana, despite familial opposition based on financial concerns. He began training in the capital around 1953.[75] Like other individuals enamored of ballet, Lefebre drove ballet growth by securing resources to further his career.

When Lefebre arrived in Havana, he encountered a diverse ballet instructional landscape that had been developing for two decades alongside the more famous schools of Pro-Arte and Ballet Alicia Alonso. In 1931, Sylvia de los Reyes y Delgado had founded the Sociedad Infantil de Bellas Artes (Children's Society of Fine Arts), where the U.S.-born ballerina and Spanish dancer Sol Fernán Flor (née Ina Cadwell) taught. Sylvia Goudie and Magali

Acosta studied with Flor and went on to found their own studio in Havana in 1949.[76] Another civic association, the Lyceum and Lawn Tennis Club founded in 1928, also offered dance classes. The Russian émigrée Anna Leontieva taught ballet for the Lyceum in the 1940s, as did Alicia Alonso's sister Cuca Martínez in the 1950s.[77] Russian émigrée Nina Verchinina, a former dancer with the Ballets Russes de Monte Carlo and student of German modern dance, also taught in Havana. One notable student, Ramiro Guerra, had started studying ballet with Alberto Alonso at Pro-Arte in 1943 but wanted to explore other movement vocabularies. He later described Verchinina's classes taking place in "a small room of a quite reduced apartment. It did not have a wooden floor, and some barres and a mirror were all the equipment. Only four students fit in each class." Despite material limitations, Verchinina imparted a rigorous and disciplined study of musculature and movement.[78] From the Sociedad Infantil de Bellas Artes to Verchinina's in-home classes, a varied dance instructional landscape (beyond the more famous schools of Pro-Arte and Ballet Alicia Alonso) sprang from individual initiative and allowed numerous young people to access dance training before 1959.

As a result, not all ballet students came from rich families. Guerra, for instance, had the benefit of white privilege but grew up in the working-class Cayo Hueso neighborhood in Havana and could not always pay for classes. "No problem, when you have money, pay me," Verchinina assured him.[79] Lefebre also found ways to train without money, not only at Ballet Alicia Alonso's school but also at the public music academy, Conservatorio Municipal de la Habana (Municipal Conservatory of Havana). In January 1948, the Conservatorio began offering "free dance instruction in all its forms."[80] Parents also chipped in by founding the civic association Patronato Pro-Ballet Municipal in 1949 to "defray the expenses that public theatrical presentations occasion" and to build "social relations in order to achieve for the institution, an environment most favorable to its aggrandizement and success."[81] Meetings, such as one on January 18, 1950, involved mothers who met at the Conservatorio to discuss upcoming events and financial needs.[82] The main teachers at the school were Clara Roche, Josefina Elósegui (a Pro-Arte graduate), and Alberto Alonso (who taught at the school until 1953, along with classes at Pro-Arte).[83] Eduardo Rivero, who had a black Jamaican mother and Cuban father of Chinese and African descent, took classes at the Conservatorio. He recalled, "There were the poor [students], black [students]. . . . In that school I saw for the first time Jorge Lefebre, who later was a great choreographer and friend. . . . He left the Conservatorio, when I started."[84] The Conservatorio depended on public and parental funds, involved students of humble backgrounds like Lefebre and Rivero, and effectively evidenced ballet's popularization in the 1950s.

Even more elite organizations worked to expand the reach of ballet. Starting in the 1930s, Pro-Arte targeted Cubans beyond the bourgeoisie, aligning with a larger tradition of charity among Cuban elites.[85] As president of the organization, Laura Rayneri de Alonso lowered membership fees for the summer months and distributed free tickets to students around Havana.[86] Based on available figures for 1946, membership rates ranged from twenty pesos to join plus three pesos per month for the orchestra seats to only five pesos to join and two pesos per month for seats in the second balcony.[87] One former patron told Cuban historian Irina Pacheco Valera that simple consumer choices provided him access to Pro-Arte, or as he put it, "If I had two pesos a month I did not waste them buying Cristal or Polar beers. I went to the concerts of Pro-Arte."[88] White students of modest but comfortable backgrounds also had access to the ballet school, albeit with some hardship. In 1948, a seven-year-old Loipa Araújo, the daughter of a doctor and a teacher, started classes at the Pro-Arte school, which meant "great economic sacrifices" for her family.[89]

Charitable impulses also extended to the Escuela de Ballet Alicia Alonso, which offered scholarships to talented students like Lefebre. Several future star ballerinas in Cuba, including the white dancers Mirta Plá and Aurora Bosch, had similar opportunities thanks to financial aid. Plá came from a "humble family" in the Cerro neighborhood of Havana and began studying piano and eventually ballet at the Conservatorio. After a year and a half at the conservatory, Plá and thirty other students secured scholarships to train at the Escuela de Ballet Alicia Alonso in 1950. An eight-year-old Bosch won a scholarship the following year. Plá and Bosch credited the Alonsos for using personal savings to ensure students without financial means could train. Bosch also recalled anonymous donors funding her summer classes. "It is something I can never forget," she disclosed.[90] These funds could not cover all expenses, however. At fifteen, Plá started giving private ballet lessons from her home to help her family.[91] Similarly, the white Santiago-born Joaquín Banegas also needed extra income to pursue his dance career. He began classes at the Escuela de Ballet Alicia Alonso in 1953 thanks to a scholarship. Previously, he had trained at Pro-Arte de Oriente in Santiago and the Conservatorio in Havana. Although his scholarship covered the cost of classes, Banegas was eighteen and away from his family, so had to work at the Tropicana Nightclub to make ends meet.[92] From securing scholarships to working side jobs, dancers hustled to take advantage of burgeoning dance opportunities.

Studying ballet meant overcoming not only financial hurdles but also prejudices, especially for men. Lefebre studied ballet in secret and claimed that family members "had their reasons" for opposing his dance aspirations, especially concerns about a stable salary.[93] After seeing a friend ostracized for studying ballet, Ramiro Guerra also hid his dance activities by using the stage name Pedro Suárez.[94] Only after successfully completing his legal studies did he tell his family about his dancing: "My university law degree was in my pocket, never used after convincing my family that to be a dancer was neither dishonorable nor a social deprivation, a concept that was acknowledged in my family, though not completely in the general social consciousness, [and this] caused me some trouble from time to time."[95] Although not explicitly stated, assumptions that ballet was a feminine activity presumably haunted aspiring male dancers like Lefebre and Guerra and resulted in only a handful of male students, as confirmed by photos of 1950s ballet classes.[96]

Along with gendered prejudices, racism plagued the few black and *mulato* ballet students. Images from the period confirm a mostly white demographic, and Lefebre's experience in particular indicates how racism limited his ballet opportunities in republican Cuba. When he arrived in Havana, he later recounted, "The [white] girls of Vedado did not want to dance with a black man." Along with homegrown racism, he faced mistreatment by U.S. dancers in the organization: "There was even a [white] North American dancer that threatened to leave if I continued dancing. The scholarship was suspended."[97] Although Lefebre uses passive construction to avoid assigning blame, the fact that the Alonsos honored the U.S. dancer's racist ultimatum evidences a lack of commitment to inclusion. In 1974, Alicia would assert, "Before the Revolution all the academies were private and you had to pay for everything. . . . And of course you had to be white; they never accepted blacks—there wasn't an academy they could get into."[98] Such narratives erase institutions like the Conservatorio, as well as African-descended dancers from working-class backgrounds who studied ballet like Jorge Lefebre and Eduardo Rivero. This statement also fails to reckon with the Alonsos' role in keeping ballet predominantly white in republican Cuba.

With both expansive and exclusive tendencies, the Alonsos formed a tight-knit community with a select group of students. For instance, the white twins Margarita and Ramona de Sáa were eleven when they started training at the Escuela de Ballet Alicia Alonso and fourteen when they performed with the company during its South American tour. As Margarita later described, "Cuban ballet was like a big family. Fernando and Alicia were like my father and mother."[99] Even outside of the Alonsos' circle, there was a sense of ballet community and mutual support. For instance, the white studio owner Sylvia Goudie warmly recalled special audience members at her school's first performance in 1950: "Mami came to the stage and with great emotion asked me, Sylvia, do you know who is there? I did not dare answer. . . . I knew well that I had invited her, and that I had hoped that she would come. Finally Mami said to me, 'It is Alicia Alonso, who has come with her mom!'" Someone snapped a photo of the distinguished spectators; and, the cherished keepsake appeared in a commemorative book celebrating the Studio Sylvia M. Goudie's tenth anniversary.[100] This sense of kinship reinforced the idea that ballet involved a small circle of generally white ballet practitioners with pedigree.

The financial, moral, and instructional support offered by the Alonsos bolstered the dynasty while extending ballet beyond its purview. The mediated availability of ballet, a challenging art mastered by a few, only increased its value in Cuban cultural canons. As ballerina Josefina Méndez asserted about the first time she saw Alicia perform in 1954, "Through her I valued ballet as a great art and decided to improve myself with the aspiration of someday becoming a true ballerina."[101] With similar ambitions, students like Lefebre, Banegas, Plá, Bosch, and Araújo used talent and opportunity to make ballet their life, despite familial background. Ballet classes at the Casa Heredia in Santiago and Conservatorio in Havana gave lower-class students a necessary start that led to scholarships at more elite institutions. With ballet loved and pursued by citizens of different backgrounds across the island, the state began to take notice. Ballet advocates made sure that this attention translated into material support as detailed in the following section.

Ballet and the State

Thanks to artistic accomplishments and advocacy, several Cuban administrations funded ballet in the late 1940s and 1950s. This was in keeping with article 47 of the Cuban Constitution of 1940, which specified, "Culture, in all its manifestations, constitutes a primordial interest of the State."[102] Dancers did not just welcome but demanded financial support based on the premise that ballet furthered national culture and merited official backing. Analyzing how dancers connected with governments before 1959 challenges misleading narratives about prerevolutionary Cuba, like this one from 1973: "The rulers of the day, oligarchs with enrichment fever, did not contemplate ballet among their plans. The company would have to find its way alone."[103] Far from lonely victims, ballet artists in fact successfully secured subsidies from several Cuban regimes. Moreover, when the cultural bureaucracy decreased funding in

1956, the public overwhelmingly supported ballet dancers in opposition to what they viewed as an authoritarian government under Fulgencio Batista. Bolstered by mass support and a precedent of entitlement, ballet dancers inhabited a position of incredible strength by the late 1950s.

In many respects, the same ideas that civic associations and ballet schools had about spreading art for the public good also extended to the government, as evidenced by the Cultural Mission organized in 1950 by the Ministry of Education. The initiative brought dance, film, books, art and archeological exhibits, music, lectures, and theater to the countryside.[104] The goal was to democratize culture under the guiding philosophy that "culture is the patrimony of the people," according to Minister of Education Aureliano Sánchez Arango.[105] The mission's so-called Culture Train left Havana in March 1950 and returned in July, transporting artists to thirty-nine locales, where they performed for an estimated 146,500 people.[106] As part of this mission, geographer Antonio Núñez Jiménez, president of the Havana Speleological Society and Fernando and Alicia's good friend, explained scientific and archeological exhibits. Alicia's sister Cuca Martínez directed a group of ballet dancers, and Ramiro Guerra choreographed popular and folkloric dances.[107] As one commentator declared, "The forgotten *guajiro* [peasant] lives apart from civilization, orphan to the beautiful things of culture. . . . This Cultural Mission that now begins its crusade of art and education . . . is like a light shining amid thick darkness."[108] Such endeavors were "duties of the Cuban state" that contributed to "a new epoch, the marvelous emergence of a more beautiful, free, and just social life."[109] The campaign illustrated the government and cultural producers' shared belief in the link between art and social progress.

The Ballet Alicia Alonso partnered with the government and multiple organizations in resonant balletic crusades. Under President Carlos Prío Socarrás (1948–52), the Ministry of Education sponsored three ballet performances at "$5,000" each: one for the government and diplomatic corps, another for students, and the final one for "the people." The latter two were free for all audience members.[110] (It is worth pausing to note that here and below, I follow the sources, which use "$" to indicate Cuban pesos. To signal U.S. currency, I write out "dollars.") Polar Brewery bankrolled two showings by the Ballet Alicia Alonso, the first of which was free for the Cuban public at the Stadium Universitario in Havana. Such sponsorship reportedly evidenced Polar's commitment to being "the beer of the people."[111] The University of Havana political organization, the Federación Estudiantil Universitaria (Federation of University Students, FEU), also helped to organize performances and lobbied the government and private industry to increase funding for the company.[112] Along with these entities, company members and supporters founded the Asociación Alicia Alonso Pro-Ballet en Cuba (Association Alicia Alonso Pro-Ballet in Cuba), which fought "to obtain a Law in Congress of the Republic that conceded to the Ballet Alicia Alonso, a permanent annual subsidy," and worked to "involve all cultural institutions of the Republic, as well as businesses, industries, and individuals to cooperate for the success of this effort, both economically and socially." Sparse financial information indicates that the monthly membership fees yielded a modest $2,294.80 to support the company and school in 1955.[113] In addition, Fernando and Alicia invested their own money, thousands of dollars according to a later account, in their dance projects.[114] Cobbling together funds was undoubtedly challenging, but the process evidenced the abundance of supporters eager to help.

A piecemeal funding structure, however, made international tours difficult. During the Ballet Alicia Alonso's first international tour in 1948, for instance, a Venezuelan military coup disrupted their Caracas season, leaving them without payment. Fortunately, the University of Puerto Rico, Río Piedras helped the stranded dancers leave Venezuela to perform for a receptive San Juan audience.[115] During a 1949 tour, the organizing impresario filed for bankruptcy after the Cuban dancers arrived in Mexico City, and local Mexican artists, including the famous actor Cantinflas, raised some, but not enough, money for the touring Cubans. To cover the rest, Alicia took out a loan and left the jeweled cross from her 1947 homage as collateral. As the story goes, Alicia's colleagues protested, and she dramatically responded, "We will rescue it when we achieve economic success, but if it is lost, I feel that [by] gaining prestige through our art for our country, I compensate our people, [and] I give back what they gave to me."[116] In this formulation of reciprocity and exchange, ballet "compensated" Cubans for investing in the form and became a gift to the nation as dancers earned intangible but impactful respect from international audiences.[117] When outstanding debts caught up with the company in Chile, Argentinean leader Juan Perón secured the dancers' transport to Buenos Aires, where they successfully completed their tour.[118] In the aftermath, Fernando wrote to his former boss, Ballet Theatre director Lucia Chase, "After a whole year of having the responsibility of the direction of a company, of having to solve unsolvable problems, of dealing with the financial difficulties of a Ballet Company, and of trying to keep all its artists happy, I would like you to know that now I understand you."[119] These headaches inspired redoubled efforts to secure more state funding.

In fact, Fernando had high hopes that the Cuban government would increase its support of ballet. In 1949 he wrote to his friend, Chicago dance critic Ann Barzel, "The Ministry of Education is going to pay for the production of a new Cuban ballet."[120] In a 1950 letter to Chase, Fernando wrote, "The Government is getting more and more interested in our company. The Secretary of Education is giving us quite a bit of help. On the 31th [*sic*] of this month we are having a special performance at the Presidential Palace. We are sure that by next year we will have a very consistent and healthy subsidy from the Government."[121] In July 1951, Minister of Education Sánchez Arango hailed the Ballet Alicia Alonso and its academy for "intense artistic and cultural labor" and pledged more funding for the next fiscal year.[122]

Because of these established alliances, Fulgencio Batista's March 1952 coup raised new questions about state support. Ballet leaders quickly conveyed confidence that the political change would not affect their work. Fernando sent a telegram to Chase two days after the coup, assuring, "Political situation perfectly normal business as usual confirming performances 19th and 21st."[123] The message referred to a performance that featured eight Ballet Theatre dancers just a few weeks after the coup on March 10, 1952. Fernando's statement "Political situation perfectly normal" is both startling and unsurprising. Startling because the coup had considerable repercussions, sparking mass strikes and detentions and ultimately prompting many Cubans to take up arms.[124] Unsurprising, however, because Fernando likely wanted to quell fears and ensure that the New York dancers would follow through with their plans to perform in Havana. Moreover, the coup did not seem to disrupt or radically alter immediate ballet business. The Ballet Theatre dancers arrived, and the March 19 and 21 performance programs were labeled, "Sponsored by the Ministry of Education of the Republic."[125] The regime change also sparked accelerated efforts to push for greater governmental support for ballet.

The campaign started behind the scenes. On April 7, 1952, the Ballet Alicia Alonso drafted a letter to the new President Batista asking to meet and discuss the company's finances.[126] On May 10, 1952, Fernando wrote to the cultural director of the Ministry of Education to make a case for a subsidy increase. He detailed how the company performed for mass audiences in Cuba and abroad. Appealing to elite sensibilities, he described how ballet "strengthens cultural ties with the numerous countries visited, elevates the artistic prestige of our country, [and] proves . . . that Cuba cultivates other rhythms besides the *guaracha*, rumba, and mambo." He also asserted that the existing subsidy of $43,000 annually was "insufficient," financing salaries but leaving almost nothing for sets, costumes, and other production expenses.[127] Antonio Núñez Jiménez, acting as an administrator for the ballet, asked a Venezuelan impresario to send a letter to President Batista advocating for greater ballet subsidies.[128] In

November 1952, the company drafted a memorandum to Batista's wife, Martha Fernández Miranda de Batista, following a recent meeting. The authors summarized key points covered in their discussion. They claimed to need $300,000 annually but were willing to accept $200,000. They hoped that Sra. Batista would speak with her husband about funding possibilities. Erasing past governmental support, the ballet advocates wrote, "We earnestly urge you to be our sponsor [*madrina*; literally, godmother] in this beautiful artistic endeavor. . . . The ultimate solution to the ballet's problems in Cuba will have enormous historical significance, ascribing to the government of General Batista the coveted accolade of being the first of our republican history to recognize and protect an artistic-cultural expression of such high magnitude as the ballet."[129] Highlighting the value of ballet, advocates argued that a partnership would pay political dividends to a supportive state.

Along with these backstage efforts, the ballet company waged an equally aggressive public campaign. Ballet Alicia Alonso programs from August, September, and November 1952 asserted that the current government subsidy (in place since 1949) of about $43,000 annually, or $3,585.33 monthly, failed to cover production expenditures and resulted in the low wages of $55 to $65 monthly (whereas Ballet Theatre dancers, for instance, received equivalent to $80 weekly).[130] On top of that, Havana at the time was the fourth most expensive city in the world after Caracas, Ankara, and Manila.[131] A 1956 article in the popular Cuban weekly *Carteles* noted that a typical ballet production cost $3,861, which was more than the monthly subsidy, and listed the robust annual performing arts funding provided by governments in England ($300,000), Argentina ($1,000,000), Denmark ($150,000), Finland and France (more than $100,000), and the Soviet Union (complete monetary support for over seventy groups).[132] Uncompetitive salaries threatened to deprive Cuba of top dancers, who had to work in other countries or media, such as television.[133] This led to the conclusion that "the Ballet Alicia Alonso need[ed] urgently an annual subsidy of no less than $200,000." This estimate took into account official funds for the Philharmonic ($150,000) and the Police Band ($100,000), both of which did not need to buy backdrops, shoes, and costumes like the ballet.[134]

These issues found an international platform when Fernando submitted a proposal on the future of ballet in Latin America to the Continental Congress for Culture held in Santiago, Chile, in 1953. Organized by the Chilean poet Pablo Neruda, the event was one of several left-leaning international peace and cultural conferences during the 1950s and 1960s.[135] In his proposal, Fernando envisioned the formation of a new regional institution, "Ballet

Latinoamericano," which would comprise a school and company devoted to ballet, modern dance, and the study of the "folkloric richness of traditional dances of the Americas." All governments of Latin America would subsidize the company, and there would be annual festivals in rotating locations.[136] The plan evidenced the Alonsos' hemispheric mindset and their belief that the region needed ballet. Viewed as an enlightening art, ballet aligned with larger social and political discourses in the 1950s about economic and social reform to address "underdevelopment" and promote modernization.[137] The plan also revealed that ballet leaders realized the need to think creatively and even transnationally about funding the art in the region.

Back in Cuba, promoters highlighted the payoffs of balletic achievement. In grandiose terms, authors insisted that ballet broadly fulfilled the spiritual needs of Cuban audiences "to experience aesthetic emotion before a work of art," since humans, regardless of age or background, could understand the "oldest language" of dance.[138] Ballet also reportedly enlightened Cubans, making balletic diffusion "as important as the campaign against illiteracy and for rural education."[139] Moreover, Cuba benefited from a stronger ballet establishment that allowed talented youth to develop professionally at home rather than needing to go abroad. When Cuban dancers did go abroad, they traveled as representatives of the nation, as most notably demonstrated by the "best ambassador . . . Alicia Alonso, today internationally recognized as a premier figure of world ballet."[140] Such dance ambassadors in turn garnered tangible and intangible returns. One article featured a picture of Alicia's legs and claimed that during a recent trip to Buenos Aires, her limbs had earned the "devout awe and admiration of dance lovers" and four million pesos.[141]

A financial arrangement with the state was complicated by the unstable relationship between the Ballet Alicia Alonso and Batista. In 1953, the company commemorated Cuban patriot José Martí's centennial in keeping with the Batista regime's messaging about a "passive" hero rather than "a Martí of action" like his opponents.[142] However, in 1954 the company participated in a protest against the Second Biennial Hispano-American Art Exhibition, which came from Francoist Spain and was sponsored by the Batista government. Joining other Cuban artists and intellectuals angered by the neocolonial and right-wing implications of the exhibit, the Ballet Alicia Alonso performed under the auspices of the FEU with funding from the Polar Brewery as part of protests associated with a counterexhibit known as the Anti-Biennial.[143] Yet, on February 25, 1955, Ballet Alicia Alonso danced at a special gala in commemoration of Batista's "inauguration" ceremony that day.[144] Moreover, soon after the performance, in the spring of 1955, the Ballet Alicia

Alonso changed its name to Ballet de Cuba, emphasizing its public valences in hopeful anticipation of greater official support. In April 1955, Ballet de Cuba directors, dancers, and supporters founded the association Patronato Ballet de Cuba and named the "President of the Republic and Minister of Education Honorary Members of the Patronato."[145]

The ambivalent relationship between ballet and Batista deteriorated in the wake of changes to the official cultural apparatus. On July 27, 1955, presidential decree 2057 created the Instituto Nacional de Cultura (National Institute of Culture, INC), a "specialized and technical state agency through which the Ministry of Education carries out its cultural activity."[146] Initially, the INC supported the Ballet de Cuba, "because [the company] has contributed to the prestige of our country abroad," as a program essay explained.[147] In December 1955, the Patronato de Ballet de Cuba planned to meet with the INC director Guillermo de Zéndegui to procure "the generous help of the Government of the Republic through the National Institute of Culture."[148] Although it is unclear if this meeting took place, the INC changed government funding, but contrary to ballet leaders' hopes. In June 1956, a revised budget allocated $683,051.80 for cultural activities.[149] However, as Zéndegui wrote to Alicia in August, the INC planned to replace the existing subsidy for the Ballet de Cuba with $500 per month (or $6,000 per year, a fraction of the long-standing subvention of $43,000). Alicia penned an indignant response, rejecting the funding framed as a personal favor that aimed to purchase her complicity. *Nuestro Tiempo*, the official organ for the leftist organization Sociedad Cultural Nuestro Tiempo (Cultural Society of Our Time), published the epistolary exchange.[150] It set off a firestorm of protest as Cubans rallied around Alicia and rejected the INC as an incompetent, encroaching part of an authoritarian regime.

The subsequent ballet polemic revolved around whether the Ballet de Cuba was a public or private institution, and therefore, how much government funding it deserved. According to the INC, the Ballet de Cuba was a private enterprise, and since the government had many cultural initiatives to support, the money earmarked solely for ballet seemed unjustifiably large.[151] Decades later in an interview in Miami, Zéndegui recalled that the company's travel abroad and failure to provide more free performances in Cuba had factored into the decision.[152] Ballet supporters countered with statistics on the company's "popular" performances in Cuba (twenty-three for free and forty-one for minimal ticket prices) and highlighted the service rendered to the nation by impressing international audiences over the course of 301 performances abroad by the fall of 1956. The company and its affiliated school had also trained a new generation of Cuban artists and inspired other studios to offer dance instruc-

tion across the country.[153] Furthermore, the Patronato Ballet de Cuba contended that the company was "as private as the Philharmonic Orchestra of
Havana, which has received in years past more than $100,000 annually from the
State ... [or] Pro-Arte Musical, which receives $40,000 annually."[154] These hy-
brid organizations were community cultural initiatives with a mixed financial
scheme, consisting of private and public patronage. Indeterminate status made
the Ballet de Cuba susceptible to personal and partisan politics.

Alicia's supporters and the INC also debated how funding affected expressive freedom. Alicia, for instance, declared that the "state assistance, which we
believe we deserve, cannot signify a loss of artistic independence that we defend as inherent to the exercise of our art."[155] The INC refuted allegations
that it sought to circumscribe expression: "The National Institute of Culture
rejects the unfair and unfounded accusation that we seek to formalize the
Ballet de Cuba or any other institution to limit in any way its independence,
for it is standard for this agency to practice and respect the freedom of cultural initiatives of a private nature, not having made at any time to Mrs. Alicia
Alonso, or any representative of Ballet de Cuba, any proposal that would restrict their freedom of action."[156] In spite of such claims, this raised the question, as one editorial in *Nuestro Tiempo* put it, "Does economic aid from the
State to any cultural institution presuppose submission to the tutelage of the
National Institute of Culture and the loss of its independence?"[157] What did
artists owe for official funds? The unanswered question continued to hang
over the Cuban political and cultural establishment.

The tussle continued and amplified. Periodicals—*Bohemia* on August 26
and *El Mundo* on September 8, 1956—decried the INC and supported Alicia
and the Ballet de Cuba.[158] *Bohemia* featured a cartoon of Zéndegui in a tutu,
parodying the bureaucrat and encapsulating the poor public opinion of him
due to the ballet fiasco (figure 1.1). Thirty-one cultural organizations signed a
public denunciation of the "economic aggression of the Batista dictatorship
against the Ballet de Cuba."[159] María Luisa Rodríguez Columbié, then president of the Lyceum and Lawn Tennis Club, formed the Comité de Defensa
del Ballet de Cuba (Committee for the Defense of Ballet de Cuba), and explained in a 2006 interview, "When the ballet received the blow [*el golpetazo*]
from Batista, ... [it] hurt all of us."[160] The committee and the FEU organized
a free performance at the Stadium Universitario on September 15, 1956, and
twenty-five thousand people attended while Batista's police menacingly sur-
rounded the venue.[161] The prominent FEU militant Fructoso Rodríguez
came out of hiding to make his last public appearance at the performance
before his death at the hands of Batista's security forces in April 1957.[162] The

FIGURE 1.1 This political cartoon by Antonio, satirizing cultural bureaucrat Guillermo de Zéndegui, illustrates how many took Alicia Alonso's side against Batista and his government in a dispute sparked by ballet budget cuts. Source: *Bohemia,* August 26, 1956, 66. Courtesy of the Cuban Heritage Collection, University of Miami Libraries, Coral Gables, Florida.

"Función de Desagravio a Alicia Alonso" (Performance of Redress to Alicia Alonso) had clear political valences, underscored in published notices about the event. As one unequivocal statement put it, "*Bohemia* warmly supports the act that prestigious cultural institutions organized as tribute to Alicia Alonso and . . . a citizenry that desires independent art, not subject to the official yoke as in totalitarian countries."[163]

After the September 1956 performance, the Ballet de Cuba went on a protest tour around the country, ending in Matanzas on November 15, 1956.[164] The program purported to honor the Ballet de Cuba and Alicia for "the glories that they have conquered for our *Patria*."[165] Although the company did not explicitly denounce Batista or the INC in the printed program, audiences likely understood those underpinning political messages due to the press around the controversy. After the Matanzas performance, the company suspended domestic activities until further notice. Although ballet training and performance continued on the island, the Ballet de Cuba conspicuously halted in protest. Alicia performed with some of her dancers in the United States, traveled with Fernando to the Soviet Union, and fulfilled other contracts abroad as the fight against Batista escalated at home.[166]

Dramatic clashes off the stage framed these balletic protests. Throughout the fall of 1956, the armed wing of the FEU, the Directorio Revolucionario, clashed with Batista supporters. Shortly after the Ballet de Cuba's final performance in Matanzas, Fidel Castro and his 26th of July Movement arrived in eastern Cuba on the *Granma* yacht and escaped to the safety of the Sierra Maestra mountains in December 1956.[167] Although the company had worked with Batista in prior years, alliances with the FEU, protest performances, and a moratorium on balletic activities, just as other antigovernment groups ramped up their resistance activities, attached a lasting air of revolutionary rebelliousness to the ballet establishment.

Since ballet became part of the anti-Batista struggle, the political leanings of the Alonsos have been subject to much debate. Alberto and Fernando later claimed to have joined the Communist Party in the 1940s.[168] Their party membership seems likely, due to their participation in Nuestro Tiempo with Fernando serving as vice president and Alberto as a "*vocal*" for the dance section.[169] According to Fernando, artists and intellectuals had initially worked with Batista based on "the fallacy of 'apolitical' culture"; however, they realized that even minor collaborations with the state "would serve the tyranny."[170] This explanation aimed to justify inconsistencies in the Alonsos' relationship with Batista. Alicia, on the other hand, has been described as apolitical. On October 28, 1958, she reportedly told the Venezuelan newspaper *El Nacional* that Cuban political leaders were indistinguishable: "To me, Machado, Grau, Prío, Batista and Fidel Castro all mean the same thing. I am apolitical and have never voted."[171] Gendered dismissals of Alicia have pointed to such statements as signs of her naiveté, assigning political acumen to a calculating Fernando.[172] In fact, if the 1956 clash reveals anything, it shows how Alicia readily entered the political fray to secure state funds and defend artistic agendas. Indeed, ballet dancers had exhibited their eagerness to ally with amenable governments and had practice in cultivating official and public support. After 1959, ballet leaders, even the supposedly apolitical Alicia, would collaborate with the revolutionary government.

Conclusion

Many histories of Cuban ballet point to 1956 as a melodramatic clash between victimized ballet dancers and the tyrannical Batista regime. Such a characterization fails to recognize the considerable leverage that ballet dancers and supporters had at the time. As the proliferation of ballet schools, companies, and associations indicates, Cubans valued ballet and wanted to strengthen and expand the form. Supporters aired their concerns about funding in playbills and periodicals, and they lobbied the government to provide greater resources, pointing to ballet dancers' contributions to Cuban culture and society. When Batista's INC attempted to decrease funding, Alicia and Fernando responded and in many ways won an important battle. For many, they proved what Alicia reportedly remarked to Zéndegui: "Look, I do more with my feet than you and all those men with your titles."[173] Ironically, Dama Alicia had her own titles, and such distinction bolstered her cause. The 1956 clash indicates how far ballet had come in Cuba. Moreover, the conflict served as a cautionary tale to future political leaders and bureaucrats about the political backlash of rejecting the demands of Alicia and Fernando. The republican period, then, was not a stricken way station, but in fact held key ballet developments with lasting legacies. Going forward, ballet would retain its distinguished place in Cuban cultural canons as an art that enlightened national audiences, impressed international observers, and most importantly, deserved considerable state support.

This chapter has shown that ballet artists wielded impressive power and that racialized and classed values—an investment in whiteness and elite sensibilities by way of ballet—became entrenched in ideas about national culture. A program from the 1956 protest performance tour applauded the Ballet de Cuba and Alicia for "the glories that they have conquered for our *Patria*."[174] What national glories, exactly? Ballet ostensibly proved "that Cuba cultivates other rhythms besides the *guaracha*, rumba, and mambo," according to Fernando Alonso.[175] In other words, ballet and its implicit whiteness stood in valuable contrast to popular dances like rumba, which denoted blackness. Thus, under a patriotic veneer, ballet paradoxically fostered populism and elitism simultaneously. On the one hand, the company performed for sold-out stadiums; (some) schools around the country taught ballet to students from different economic and racial backgrounds; and, ballet leaders proclaimed patriotic, anti-imperialist goals. On the other hand, ballet also remained closely identified with the white Alonso ballet dynasty and its (almost entirely white) scions. Cubans seemed to value ballet most for its vaguely democratizing potential and carefully guarded distinction.

Caught in the crosshairs of balletic openings and racialized closings was Jorge Lefebre. The multitalented *mulato* artist studied with the Alonsos thanks to ballet's spread to Santiago and available scholarships, only to encounter racist barriers in the process. Because of these limits, Lefebre left Cuba in 1956.[176] With his experience in mind, the next chapter turns to the racial dynamics of the dance establishment that he entered and then exited.

CHAPTER TWO

Performing Race and Nation before 1959

I have been studying ballet . . . with Alberto Alonso [and] besides, I can dance rituals like: ñáñigo "diablito," afro, some rumba, etc. But I just can't find here in my country what I really want.

—Irma Obermayer to Katherine Dunham, 1953

In 1953, dancer Irma Obermayer, a "daughter of *mulatos* and granddaughter of Germans," wrote an impassioned letter to African American dancer Katherine Dunham.[1] She had ballet training with Alberto Alonso, performed Afro-Cuban dances in elite cabarets in Havana, and yet, felt dissatisfied with the dance scene in Cuba. Meanwhile, the self-described "young Cuban dancer 20 years old and just crazy about the dance" had heard about Dunham's internationally renowned company, which performed works inspired by African diasporic cultures, featuring mainly dancers of African descent.[2] To Obermayer, Dunham's New York–based company offered professionalization impossible to secure in Cuba. As a *mulata* dancer, Obermayer had access to ballet training (but not a career) and found professional opportunities in elite cabarets where she performed spectacularized Afro-Cuban folkloric dances. Meanwhile, professional modern dance did not yet exist on the island, and early modern dance innovations happened solely on white ballet dancers. Obermayer's experiences and her appeal to Dunham evidence how racialized exclusions shaped emerging concert dance genres in Cuba and how Afro-Cuban dancers fought to advance their careers in the face of such obstacles.

African-descended performers like Obermayer were central to concert dance developments in the 1940s and 1950s. This can be seen in the making of the so-called first truly Cuban ballet, performances of Afro-Cuban "folklore" in international festivals and Havana cabarets, and early Cuban modern dance experiments at home and abroad. Ballet remained exclusively for white dancers, but black dancers inspired vanguard choreography. Excluded from ballet, highly trained black and *mulato* dancers performed stylized folkloric spectacles in elite Cuban cabarets. For dancers like Obermayer, who were dissatisfied with career limitations, Dunham's company beckoned and offered experience that was later applied to professional modern dance pursuits on the island after 1959. By analyzing exclusive ballet, exoticized folkloric spectacles, and elusive modern dance in three respective sections, this chapter traces how racial and class prejudices shaped emergent genre distinctions and professional possibilities before 1959. Across different venues, African-descended performers, albeit partially or fully excluded from certain dance spaces, continued to take center stage whether in actuality or by haunting choreography. Haunting, as dance scholar Melissa Blanco Borelli theorizes, involves instrumental but unacknowledged subaltern dancers inspiring and leaving a lingering trace on performances.[3] Terpsichorean ghosts had great power, which was perhaps best evidenced by the uproar they caused. When white, female bodies performed Afro-Cuban dances, they gestured to the black and *mulato* dancers who engendered choreography and remained an absent presence to the discomfort of prejudiced viewers.

Building on chapter 1, this one reassesses concert dance in the 1940s and 1950s by focusing on performed representations of race and nation. First, it challenges the idea that dance makers of the period ignored black culture. For instance, choreographer Ramiro Guerra wrote in 1959, "The black contribution [*la aportación negra*] to our art has been ignored until recently because of those remnants of slavery that still fill our national life with prejudices."[4] By contrast, I demonstrate how choreographers avidly looked to Afro-Cuban culture before 1959 while continuing to privilege whiteness in performances of Cuban nationhood. This established prejudicial conventions that persisted in subsequent decades. Thus before and after 1959, including "the black contribution" did not undermine, but reinforced antiblack prejudices and idolizations of whiteness.[5] Second, this chapter shows how concert dance and cabaret had much in common (contrary to what revolutionary dance makers would later claim), sharing artists like Obermayer and similarly featuring Afro-Cuban culture enacted by white bodies or filtered through the historically white ballet technique.[6] While white bodies and techniques expressed Cubanness locally, black bodies performed Cuban race and nation in Dunham's company, transnationally reconfiguring these constructs in the process.[7] Analyzing Dunham's relationship with Cuban dancers (rather than musicians) for the first time, this chapter thirdly uncovers how Afro-Cuban performers, especially women like Obermayer, "forged diaspora" by connecting with black artists abroad to advance their careers.[8] This chapter then redresses misconceptions about concert dance in the 1940s and 1950s, while also contributing to scholarship on how cultural productions constituted race (both whiteness and blackness), intersected with national projects, and connected to struggles for racial justice in the Americas.[9]

Chamba and the Making of Cuban Ballet

On May 27, 1947, the ballet *Antes del alba* (Before Dawn) premiered with a showing in the afternoon and evening for members of the cultural association Sociedad Pro-Arte Musical (Pro-Art Musical Society). Alberto Alonso choreographed the ballet, Spanish writer Francisco Martínez Allende wrote the libretto, Cuban visual artist Carlos Enríquez made the set and costume designs, and Cuban composer Hilario González created the score. Alicia, her husband, Fernando, and her brother-in-law Alberto Alonso performed the leading roles with students from the Pro-Arte ballet school in the ensemble. The ballet had three scenes that took place in an impoverished Havana neighborhood during carnival season. It told the story of Chela (performed by Alicia), a widow with tuberculosis, who commits suicide by setting herself on fire.[10] The ballet featured a novel choreographic language that fused carnival dances and rumba with ballet technique. It caused a scandal because it represented social tragedies, the lives of lower-class Cubans, and Afro-Cuban popular dances on an elite stage. The production halted after the first day. Despite this controversy and in part because of it, *Antes del alba* became celebrated in post-1959 histories as the first truly Cuban ballet for its socially conscious, distinctly Cuban plot and mostly Cuban creators. Existing discussions center on the Alonsos' daring as they defied the status quo and inaugurated national ballet aesthetics.[11]

This section reexamines the ballet with a shifted emphasis, focusing instead on the traces of Julián Valdés, known as Chamba, a famed rumba dancer of African descent hired to coach Alicia for the ballet.[12] My analysis elucidates the unacknowledged centrality of Chamba, as well as the popular dances he mastered, to the development of Cuban ballet in the late 1940s. I suggest that Chamba and his dances were foundational to Cuban ballet canons despite ghosting performances and historical records.

Chamba's name does not appear in the 1947 performance program, only in memories collected forty years later. Even then, the single mention of his participation in the choreographic process underscores Alicia's talent. In an article commemorating the fortieth anniversary of *Antes del alba*, composer Hilario González describes the famous *rumbero* [male rumba dancer] Chamba teaching Alicia the "*columbia*," a type of rumba "considered very difficult, [and] only for men." González continues, "Thus, the *rumbero* did a step and Alicia repeated it without hesitation. By the third time already the *mulato* had eyes wide with amazement [*los ojos cuadrados del asombro*]."[13] It is possible that Chamba widened his eyes because of Alicia's ability or awkwardness.

Former Pro-Arte functionary and later exile Célida Parera Villalón suggested the latter, asserting that "the cubanized choreography of [Alicia's] brother-in-law [Alberto] escaped her comprehension and style."[14] González's admiration and Parera Villalón's disaffection shaped their memories of Alicia's dancing. These assessments do not venture into the sweaty, material reality of Alicia's rehearsals with Chamba or the choreographic outcome of their collaboration. We can only wonder about the stumbles and recoveries, intricate footwork, swerving hips, shifts in the head and gaze, dynamic facial expressions, decisive hand gestures, and numerous other performance choices that Chamba and Alicia explored together.

Limited information about Chamba's career nevertheless makes clear his expertise in rumba pedagogy and performance. Chamba was the first to open a "rumba academy" in 1938, and master drummer Armando Peraza played for his shows.[15] Chamba often appeared at the Cabaret El Faraón (The Pharaoh).[16] Earl Leaf, a photographer who visited Cuba in the 1940s, described the club as "noted for its expert music, pretty hostesses and garish, blinding French-Italian Moorish décor. Dance-wise, the Faraon [*sic*] rates second to no other pleasure palace in Cuba's capital."[17] The tawdry "*cabaretucho*, a second-rate cabaret," no longer exists. The structure now functions as a car repair shop, and only Pharaoh profiles engraved on the external wall evidence its grandiose past.[18]

Along with Chamba from El Faraón, Alberto Alonso looked to Cuban carnival for choreographic inspiration. In the opening scene of *Antes del alba*, dancers rehearse in the courtyard of a *solar* (slum) while a sickly Chela watches. A group of characters simply listed as "Women and Men" as well as "Little Girls" perform carnival dances. While program notes provide minimal insights into choreographic content, contemporaneous developments outside of the theater indicate what carnival scenes might have looked like.[19]

Carnival had only recently gained official acceptance in Cuba. The Cuban government (under several presidents) had regulated or tried to ban carnival in the early twentieth century with mixed success. Then, a rapidly growing tourist industry and an era of populist, nationalist politics leading up to and following the 1933 Revolution changed official positions.[20] In 1937, Havana mayor Antonio Beruff Mendieta wrote to the well-known scholar of Afro-Cuban culture Fernando Ortiz for advice on whether the Havana carnival of February should be reinstated. Were the events considered "contrary or beneficial to the culture of our people and to the good opinion of us formed by foreigners when they visit," the mayor wondered.[21] Ortiz responded that the performances aligned Cuba with international indicators of progress since so-called civilized nations preserved folkloric customs as an integrationist strategy. Groups of carnival dancers and musicians called *comparsas* encouraged racial harmony and social collectivity, Ortiz claimed. Moreover, Cuban people had a right to enjoy themselves without worrying about the opinion of ignorant foreigners.[22] Reinstating carnival also dovetailed with the populist politics of 1937. That year, Fulgencio Batista, the power behind several presidents, proposed his "Plan Trienal" (Three-Year Plan), which promoted workers' rights, land distribution, public education, and health care.[23] Carnival celebrations of popular culture and nationalism (albeit by and for white high-society) theoretically resonated with these political trends. As Beruff wrote, "To cultivate [carnival] . . . is to Cubanize ourselves [*cubanizarnos*]."[24] Although white intellectuals and policy makers supported carnival, many black and *mulato* intellectuals and activists worried it inhibited progressive agendas, or as historian Alejandra Bronfman asserts in her analysis of these debates, rites did not translate into rights.[25] Despite some reservations, carnival became part of urban life.

As debates about carnival played out in the black press, dancers took advantage of the policy change. Three women spearheaded a new carnival *comparsa* group, Las Bolleras (named for street vendors who sold corn fritters), initially composed almost entirely of black women.[26] According to Cuban musicologist Helio Orovio, "In 1937, a group of enthusiastic cultivators of folklore had the idea to recreate an important aspect of their city customs. The principal founder, María Carballo, . . . with the collaboration of Nieves Fresneda and Manuela Alonso launched the project."[27] After 1959, Fresneda and Alonso would be foundational figures in professional folkloric dance, and carnival no doubt provided them with opportunities to hone their craft. Already in the late 1930s, Fresneda had developed considerable performance expertise after three decades of engagement and practice. As she later described, "the *comparsa* Las Bolleras exactly copied the customs of those black Lucumís with whom I grew up." As a child, she learned *los pregones* (street-sellers' songs), "marked the steps of the rumba that [she] saw danced every Sunday," and watched *los bembé* (Santería religious rituals filled with music and dance) "that the black [people] dedicated to their *orichas* [*sic*], gods of each nation."[28] These performances had a visceral impact, or as she exclaimed to an interviewer, "That African music . . . *Ay hija*! It was very pretty, one has to understand the language of those drums with the heart" (ellipses in the original).[29] Wholehearted performances made the carnivals of 1937 to 1940 "the best of that era," Fresneda claimed.[30] When Las Bolleras took to the streets, nearly thirty couples made spatial patterns while executing "a slow, repetitive step"; Fresneda walked, sang, and danced with a wooden cart that held a pot cooking *los bollitos* (corn fritters) to be distributed to bystanding audience members. The music combined Santería ritual songs and *los pregones* that Fresneda had heard growing up.[31] Although reinstating carnival in 1937 was an elite project, performers like Fresneda seized the opportunity to feature beloved Afro-Cuban cultural practices in annual *comparsas*.

Despite the artistic innovations of black performers like Fresneda and her collaborators, carnival tended to curate a panorama of popular culture for a white national and international gaze. Havana's carnival in February accentuated class differences as the lower classes danced and sang through the streets in *comparsas* while the upper and middle classes stiffly showed off their wealth in *desfiles* (parades).[32] In a 1949 article on Havana carnival, photographs capture mostly African-descended men and women dancing to drum music as part of *comparsas*. A couple of pages later, images feature white women in fancy gowns and tiaras on elaborate floats or in sharp white uniforms marching in military formations as part of *desfiles* organized by the Havana tourist commission. These photographs, a few pages apart in the popular publication *Carteles*, reinforced the idea that a black Cuba and white Cuba coexisted but remained distinct.[33] Of course, not all carnival celebrations in Cuba were the same. In the eastern city, Santiago de Cuba, for instance, carnival in July reportedly featured more socializing across racial and class lines than in Havana, as a result of "boisterous *comparsas*, where black and white and Chinese, rich and poor dance," as another *Carteles* article described.[34]

Costuming added to the spectacle. For instance, men dressed up as women in both the Havana and Santiago carnivals.[35] Mercer Cook, an African American writer, professor, and diplomat, witnessed racial, class, and gender transgressions in Santiago in 1941: "This year, at least, the typical motif for individual costumes seemed to be female and male impersonation. One 'girl' . . . wore a black satin dress, had painted 'her' face jet black, and wore a Jean Harlow blonde wig."[36] Like the male carnival participant in a dress and blackface, performers in *Antes del alba* crossed social, racial, and gender boundaries. White middle- and upper-class ballet dancers pretended to be lower-class *solar* residents, and the elegant ballerina Alicia danced the typically male, Afro-Cuban *columbia*.

Even though carnival had become a widely accepted event, many affiliates of Pro-Arte disdained carnival dances in *Antes del alba*.[37] Alberto recalled mothers angrily watching their daughters practice. "The atmosphere during rehearsals was terrible," he remembered. The unhappy mothers collectively bemoaned, "Girls from the [Pro-Arte Musical] Society dancing conga on stage, that cannot be!" As a result, the creative team closed rehearsals to prying parental eyes. Dancers also seemed resistant to Alberto's efforts to fuse ballet and popular dance. The choreographer reportedly became "very upset . . . in a rehearsal, saying to two sisters who were there: 'And you [two] who are not moving, well I saw you moving at the end of the year in the Miramar Yatch [*sic*] Club.'"[38] "Moving" likely referred to defying ballet paradigms to articulate body parts and cover space to popular rhythms. This anecdote revealed that wealthy students performed popular dances in social clubs, but resisted them in a high art setting. Like their parents, they policed their bodies to reaffirm ballet boundaries.

Along with incorporating common spectacles like carnival, *Antes del alba* also grappled with the pressing health issues of tuberculosis and suicide. Tuberculosis in Cuba was associated with the poorer masses, especially Cubans of African descent in the 1920s and 1930s, and as a result, became part of Batista's populist politics in the late 1930s and 1940s. Suicide also was a common health problem in Cuba and often appeared in Cuban journalism, film, and theater.[39] Chela's suffering from tuberculosis and suicide by fire added relevant drama to the ballet. After observing a young couple that reminds Chela of happier days with her dead husband, she retires to her room, feverish and troubled by visions, as the sounds of carnival rehearsal buzz in the background. In a delirious climax, Chela emerges from her room engulfed in flames (represented on stage with light reflecting on clothes painted with phosphorescence; see figure 2.1) to dance the final "*columbia* . . . until she collapses, dead."[40] According to historian Louis Pérez, "The performance of suicide by fire was typically undertaken as a dramatic street event."[41] Rather than a private death, suicide by fire was radically public and, therefore, ready-made for the stage.

Chela's final, fiery *columbia*, developed by Chamba, Alberto, and Alicia, fused rumba and ballet. Scholars have shown how rumba in the 1930s and 1940s referred to numerous dance and music styles because performers and audiences in Cuba and abroad applied the term widely.[42] Today, the complex of dances referred to as rumba includes the partner dances *guaguancó* and *yambú*, and the male solo dance *columbia*.[43] Cuban elites overwhelmingly disliked rumba. According to 1940s photographer Earl Leaf, "Not until the *rumba* . . . had crossed the sea and taken the world by storm did the Cuban aristocrats recognize it as anything but a vulgar display of exhibitionism by social outcasts. . . . Haltingly and grudgingly, with ill-concealed condescension, they allowed this low-caste, orgiastic plebe within the portals of their sacrosanct nightclub."[44] In contrast to rumba, "Habaneros have never lost their taste for fine Spanish dancing and there is no floor-show in the Cuban

FIGURE 2.1 Costume design by Carlos Enríquez for Alicia Alonso in *Antes del alba* (1947). In the role of Chela, she danced a final, fiery *columbia* inspired and coached by the *rumbero* Chamba. Source: Museo Nacional de la Danza. Courtesy of the Museo Nacional de la Danza.

capital without its team of Spanish dancers," Leaf described. This was part of a larger trend in Europe and the United States, where Spanish dancing was in vogue.[45] Also, Spanish dance was an exponent of folklore rooted in European whiteness in contrast to rumba, which evidenced Cuba's African patrimony. And yet, Alberto chose to foreground rumba (specifically *columbia*) in *Antes del alba*, despite the preferences of bourgeois Pro-Arte patrons.

Although *columbia* may seem a strange choice, the form had moves that resonated with ballet. Take, for instance, *el tornillo* ("the screw"), a *columbia* variation where "a dancer begins a series of rapid turns on one foot, gradually bends the knees, then rises again, all the while maintaining the spin." Along with this description, musicologist Robin Moore posits that *el tornillo* and ballet shared "European origins."[46] Retrospectives about the late *columbia* dancer Malanga (José Rosario Oviedo), a cane cutter from Matanzas province, also connect *columbia* and ballet. One contemporary said that Malanga "was unique as a rumba dancer; he liked to do it on tiptoe, like ballet dancers. . . . Something very characteristic of him was to dance on top of a dining room table with a glass of water on his head, making all the movements of the dance or picking up a handkerchief off the floor without spilling the water."[47] As this recollection underscores, *columbia rumberos* often used props, including "scarves, canes, knives, plates, cups full of water and candles on their head."[48] The virtuosity, control, and ease needed for *columbia* resembled ballet to many observers. The famous *rumbero* Rene Rivero, who danced with Ramona Ajón (known as Estela), provides another example. Rivero's dancing displayed the same acrobatics of *columbia* dancers, as dance scholar Yesenia Fernández-Selier has contended. He masterfully executed *el tornillo* and danced with a full glass of water on his head, for instance.[49] Perhaps Alberto saw Chamba perform a virtuosic *columbia* like those of Malanga or Rivero and then invited him to teach Alicia his spectacularly seamless choreography.

What sequence did Chamba and Alberto fashion for Alicia? No encountered record answers this question, and the possibilities are endless. Perhaps Alicia enacted rapid footwork and turns reminiscent of *el tornillo*. Dancing in pointe shoes could have reminded audience members of Malanga on tiptoe. Maybe the flames engulfing her referenced the candle that *columbia* dancers sometimes held on their heads as they dipped and swerved. However, for Alicia as Chela, virtuosic movement with fire went from a possible threat to a dramatic plot twist. Regardless, aspects of the inimitable Chamba guided Alicia's steps and energy.

Despite the controversial carnival and rumba sequences, critics generally praised *Antes del alba*. One applauded the choreography for working "to channel and give great artistic range to all the 'folklore' that mixes diverse races and civilizations ... without losing the fragrance of the most ignored and humble." The same commentator cited New York dance critic John Martin, who had once claimed that all noteworthy dance had origins in "the vulgar [*el vulgo*]." The author believed Alberto's choreographic "experiment," imperfect but promising, signaled a bright future for Cuban ballet.[50] Another observer more decisively asserted that the ballet opened the "fertile channels to national art."[51] There were some critiques, particularly of the plot by Spanish author Francisco Martínez Allende, who compromised Cuban authenticity and wrote a "vulgar melodrama from a *solar* [*solariego*]" with Chela suffering from an "outmoded illness."[52] One critic saw Chela's suicide as too reminiscent of garish news stories.[53] However, the critical reception seemed to support further showings, not an untimely end. The Pro-Arte associates must have pushed to halt the innovative ballet. Above all, these tensions reveal different visions of race and *cubanidad* (Cubanness), with the Alonsos and the press recognizing that the "fertile channels of national art" emanated from lower-class, African-descended popular culture, while Pro-Arte affiliates defended a whitened Spanish Cuba. Both sides seemed to agree, however, that *cubanidad* at its best was incarnated by white bodies since Alicia, not Chamba, appeared on stage.

Chamba's dances appeared in *Antes del alba* but disappeared from historical discussions of Cuban ballet. The Alonsos never credited Chamba in the original performance program, erasing his contributions as a choreographer and a teacher. Racial and social disparities between the white Alonsos and the *mulato* Chamba facilitated their appropriation and misrepresentation. Similarly, Afro-Cuban dancers such as Fresneda and fellow members of Las Bolleras, who inspired carnival sequences in the ballet, remained anonymous folkloric raw material for refined ballet products rather than respected artists in their own right. However, erased dancers defied oblivion. They became inscribed in Cuban ballet canons through *Antes del alba*. When the *mulato rumbero* taught the white ballerina *columbia*, Chamba and Alicia played with the boundaries between rumba and ballet, black and white, and male and female. Unequal power dynamics, as well as the transgressions possible through dance, shaped Cuban ballet going forward. Perhaps fitting for a ballet about the hours before dawn, the central contributor, Chamba, and his history remain dimly lit. Chamba only entered ballet stages through the mediation of white collaborators and for white audiences, who rejected but could not eliminate his presence.

Íremes and the Making of Cuban Folkloric Dance

While Chela feverishly dreams in *Antes del alba*, masked dancers known as *íremes* appear. The iconic figures come from the Cuban male initiation society Abakuá, originally established by West African men in nineteenth-century Cuba.[54] About the scene, Alberto explained, "I was greatly influenced by 'abakuá' culture in that moment."[55] As further evidence, the cover of some performance programs for Alberto's Ballet Nacional featured an *íreme* dancing with a ballerina (figure 2.2). Alberto was not alone. This section shows how visions of *íremes* also filled the minds of other Cuban choreographers and audience members, who patronized productions featuring what they viewed as esoteric, exotic, and exciting Afro-Cuban ritual music and dance.[56] On the one hand, *íremes*, often performed by white or light-skinned *mulata* women dancing balletic choreography, encapsulated the careful policing of black culture on elite stages as well as the symbolic violence enacted in the process. That is, these gender-bending performances undermined black masculinity central to Abakuá membership and normalized loosely interpreted Afro-Cuban ritual dances for outsider consumption.[57] On the other hand, the undeniably problematic dances became valued staples even in elite Cuban cabarets by the 1950s, and performers of African descent seized upon the professional opportunities they afforded to advance their careers.

The state and public had long demonized Afro-Cuban ritual associations and continued to do so; however, these vibrant cultures intrigued Cuban ethnographers and writers, along with choreographers.[58] For instance, Fernando Ortiz had taken fellow intellectuals to view private ceremonies and then organized the first public concert of music associated with the Afro-Cuban religion, Santería, in 1937.[59] In the early 1950s, he published books on Afro-Cuban music, dance, and theater, and he collected materials about Abakuá that appeared in some published works.[60] Ortiz's student, musicologist Argeliers León, began publishing research on Cuban folkloric music and working with expert Afro-Cuban musician "informants," who had collaborated with Ortiz, including Jesús Pérez and Trinidad Torregrosa in the 1950s.[61] Another notable researcher and writer of the 1950s was Lydia Cabrera. She published ethnographic studies of Afro-Cuban ritual communities in Havana, particularly Abakuá.[62] Afro-Cuban scholar Rómulo Lachatañeré also published important works on Santería in this period.[63] The scholarship generated by white and black anthropologists targeted mostly, but not exclusively, nonpractitioner (assumedly white) audiences. Similarly, white and African-descended

FIGURE 2.2 The cover of a 1950 performance program for Alberto Alonso's Ballet Nacional features an Abakuá *íreme* dancing with a ballerina. Sketch by René Portocarrero. Source: Alberto Alonso and Sonia Calero Papers. Courtesy of the Cuban Heritage Collection, University of Miami Libraries, Coral Gables, Florida.

performers and choreographers explored compelling Afro-Cuban culture on stage for mostly white Cubans and foreigners.

Riveting ritual became titillating when performed by the Grupo Folklórico Cubano (Cuban Folkloric Group), founded by the Ministry of Education in 1951.[64] Dr. Amparo Carrión, a former professor at the University of Havana, directed the group, and Isabel Menocal served as associate director. The troupe had around twenty female performers, mostly students from the teacher's college, Escuela Normal de Kindergarten, as well as a few students from the University of Havana. In 1954, the group of light-skinned women (based on available photographs) went on an "'official mission' of the Cuban government," to perform in the National Folk Festival in St. Louis, Missouri.[65] The Grupo Folklórico performed Cuban social dances contradanza and rumba, as well as choreographed spectacles based on Cuban "folklore" like *Eribangando*.[66] *Eribangando* presumably takes its name from the *íreme éribángandó*, the individual who "leads the procession in Abakuá ceremonies 'to open the way.'"[67] Although this title suggested familiarity with ritual practices, the performance provided a superficial rendering of Abakuá.

In particular, *Eribangando* involved a "travesty dancer" (a woman representing a man) and violent stereotypes, resulting in a sensationalist representation of Abakuá.[68] Starring Isis Pérez Ruiz and Adria Catalá, the U.S. press described, "Adria symbolized a Calbidos [sic] priest-devil forcing slave Isis to dance to the frantic beat of the drums" (see figure 2.3).[69] This scenario disparaged Abakuá men as dangerous threats to women, while titillating audiences with a same-sex encounter between a "slave" and a "*cabildo*" (term used in this case for an Abakuá *íreme*), both played by white Cuban women. The reason a woman played the Abakuá *íreme* may have been out of necessity, since the male cadets who traveled with the company could not get visas for the St. Louis festival.[70] However, the unnamed choreographer, assumedly Carrión, perhaps wanted a woman to represent the Abakuá figure to counter fears of the group, historically misrepresented in Cuba as "a gang of atavistic mystics and criminals."[71] A white woman presumably provided an unthreatening alternative that may have also excited audiences. As Catalá portrayed the Abakuá male, her tight costuming gave audiences fuller view of the curves in her legs and torso. Indeed, as revealed in press coverage of the event, the unaccompanied "Charming Cuban Belles" delighted U.S. onlookers.[72]

Eribangando also presented a racialized version of Cuba that involved not only blackness but also, crucially, whiteness. One U.S. commentator described the Cuban women's physical appeal in terms of idealized white beauty: "The senioritas . . . include some blue-eyed brownettes and real blondes despite

FIGURE 2.3 Isis Pérez Ruiz (*left*) and Adria Catalá (*right*), members of Grupo Folklórico Cubano, perform *Eribangando* in St. Louis in 1954. Photographer unknown. Source: Adria Catalá Casey Papers. Courtesy of the Cuban Heritage Collection, University of Miami Libraries, Coral Gables, Florida.

pure Spanish ancestry since, it seems, not all Spaniards are dark."[73] Such comments reveal racialized understandings of Spanish-descended peoples in the United States at the time, collapsing Cubans and *cubanidad* into a singular "dark" type. The folkloric dancers' fair features challenged prevailing U.S. assumptions about Cuban "darkness," while the choreography embraced these stereotypes by portraying Abakuá on stage. The group of light-skinned dancers presented Cuba as a white nation *despite* traces of cultural blackness. Along with shaping U.S. understandings of Cuba, *Eribangando* also revealed how the Cuban performers themselves understood race and nation. To represent Cuba, they transformed Abakuá, a symbol of dark Otherness, into an expression of racial and cultural fusion by way of white bodies enacting black choreography. The production, then, capitalized on the fact that in Cuba Abakuá sparked "hysterical fantasies and fears of the 'dark' continent" while also being exalted as "custodians of a treasured 'African' past and a national-distinct creole identity."[74] As the Grupo Folklórico represented Cuba internationally, the white dancers performed race and nation by reconfiguring Abakuá blackness to reinforce Cuban whiteness as the outcome of cultural and racial mixture.

Cabarets also featured Afro-Cuban ritual, as seen in the work of famed choreographer Roderico "Rodney" Neyra; however, unlike the Grupo Folklórico, cabarets featured more African-descended artists, including Rodney, who was *mulato*. Born in Santiago de Cuba, Rodney advanced his career in Havana, performing with musical and theater groups associated with the Teatro Payret, CMQ Radio, and the burlesque Shanghai Theater in Chinatown, where tourists and sailors enjoyed evenings of dance, comic routines, live music, female striptease, and nude performances. During these years, Rodney honed his skills and learned how Havana audiences responded to bawdiness. In the 1940s, Rodney worked at the Teatro Fausto and eventually became a choreographer.[75] He also formed the Mulatas de Fuego, which featured, as the name suggests, women of African descent (including famed Afro-Cuban singer Celia Cruz), who reportedly performed his "popular choreography and plastic sense, to Cuban and Hispano-American and also black music . . . of the United States."[76] Rodney also worked with diverse casts in his eclectic choreography for cabarets.

In 1952, he staged a notable work indicative of his approach to ritual as commercial entertainment. Titled *Sun sun babaé* (or *Zunzún Dan Baé*), the production at the elegant Sans Souci cabaret featured Santería songs and dances.[77] Rodney reportedly practiced Santería and asked religious leaders for permission to stage sacred songs and dances for a paying public. By one account, he took his performers to the outskirts of Havana to witness a *bembé*, a Santería ritual involving music and dance.[78] Inspired by these experiences, the production featured some performers dressed in the clothing of Santería religiosity—white garments and colorful beaded necklaces—and a chorus sang sacred songs. Musicians in the production included the renowned drummers Trinidad Torregrosa, Raúl Díaz, and Francisco Aguabella, as well as singer Merceditas Valdés. *Sun sun babaé* also featured a woman in the audience, who became "possessed," though she was actually a U.S. tap dancer planted as part of the show. The performance shocked some in the audience, but for the most part impressed the public, including African American choreographer Katherine Dunham, who attended in 1953 and contracted Aguabella to play for her company.[79] Administrators of the famed Tropicana Nightclub were equally dazzled and hired Rodney as the main choreographer.[80] In subsequent years at the Tropicana, Rodney staged similar works including *Omelen-ko* (1952) and *Tambó* (1957), which extravagantly interpreted Afro-Cuban rituals with $22,000 budgets and casts swelling to eighty people.[81] Although Rodney's productions spectacularly misrepresented Afro-Cuban ritual with gimmicks like "possessed" tap dancers, they also gave talented Afro-Cuban performers like Aguabella exposure, which led to important professional opportunities.

Along with Santería, Rodney also represented Abakuá rituals in productions like *Karabalí* (1955), where women performed "*ñáñiga* liturgy, with all its characteristics, costumes, colors, music, dances, and ornaments." The show reportedly provided "a grandiose setting for exciting dances, in a dazzling feast of rhythm and color." In a photograph of the spectacle, masked female *íremes* in revealing costumes perform a sexualized rendition of the male Abakuá. The production was a hit, and an announcement for *Karabalí* included the claim that Rodney's work at the Tropicana was "the pride of Cubans, jewel of the Americas."[82]

While drawing upon Afro-Cuban culture, the Tropicana and other elite nightclubs equally promoted whiteness. Darker-skinned men and women were singers and musicians, but lighter-skinned women made up the majority of dancers, as evidenced by 1950s entertainment magazines *Show* and *Gente*. Rodney filled his stages with women whom elite audiences supposedly expected.[83] Further promoting a white image, the famed Tropicana utilized ballet in its advertising and shows. A ballerina statue by sculptor Rita Longa, placed in front of the nightclub on December 31, 1949, became the Tropicana's symbol.[84] Additionally, ballet dancers including Leonela González and Maricusa Cabrera (both had appeared in *Antes del alba*), as well as José Parés and Joaquín Banegas, performed at the Tropicana.[85] Parés and Banegas, formerly with Alicia and Fernando Alonso's Ballet de Cuba, needed work after the company suspended activities at the end of 1956. Both men appeared in Rodney's *Prohibido en España* (Prohibited in Spain), which had balletic choreography with a Spanish flair.[86] These productions confirmed Rodney's eclecticism, as well as widespread beliefs about the superiority of ballet. As one celebratory essay described in a teleological way, Rodney created works "from expressive popular choreography to the most demanding demonstration of so-called classical ballet."[87]

Even though white dancers and ballet remained prominent, African-descended dancers and Afro-Cuban dances also appeared on elite cabaret stages.[88] For instance, Irma Obermayer and her black dance partner Tondelayo performed at the Sans Souci in a production titled *Rapsodia afro-cubana* (Afro-Cuban Rhapsody), where she dressed as an *íreme*. In one publicity photo, Obermayer wears the iconic cone hat and a revealing, glittering costume embellished with feathers; she stands on the tips of her toes in a wide, powerful second position *relève* (figure 2.4). Her high arches and taut legs evidence her ballet training with Alberto Alonso, and her costuming attests to her experience with "dance rituals like: ñáñigo 'diablito,' afro, some rumba, etc."[89] Similar to Alicia Alonso enacting elements of Chamba's rumba, Obermayer reproduced traces of the male Abakuá members that inspired her performance. Like Catalá in St. Louis and the dancers in Rodney's *Karabalí* at the Tropicana, Obermayer's *íreme* catered to public hunger for secret and sacred Afro-Cuban dances made more palatable to elite audiences through choreographic whitening by way of casting white or light-skinned *mulata* dancers or incorporating balletic elements. These productions normalized loosely interpreted, spectacularized Afro-Cuban ritual, offered finite opportunities to talented *mulata* dancers like Obermayer, and became a fraught precedent for staged folkloric dance, which emerged as a professional concert dance genre in the early 1960s.

Even though Obermayer exudes undeniable talent in her *íreme* costume, her gifts remained underutilized in Cuba. As she put it, "I just can't find here in my country what I really want, because they are always teaching the same thing and the schools are so slow . . . and so indifferent to the student that it will take me too long to be what I'd like to be."[90] She never attributes the lack of opportunity to racism, but her general disaffection makes clear that a robust dance scene failed to fully include her. The balleticized Afro-Cuban ritual dances for cabaret stages compelled Obermayer to look outside of Cuba for new choreographic horizons. Similar to numerous Cuban musicians of the era, she crossed national borders to pursue her dance dreams.[91]

FIGURE 2.4 Irma Obermayer dressed as an *íreme* for "Danza ñáñigo de Cuba," ca. 1950s. The date and photographer are unknown, but Obermayer sent the image on June 27, 1953. Source: Katherine Dunham Photograph Collection. Courtesy of the Special Collections Research Center, Southern Illinois University, Carbondale.

Katherine Dunham and the Making of Cuban Modern Dance

In contrast to Obermayer's dissatisfaction with opportunities at home, she thrilled upon hearing about Katherine Dunham's school and professional company based in New York. Tondelayo told Obermayer about Dunham, and she admitted, "I have got madly enchanted. . . . It has been like . . . [finding] what you have been whishing [*sic*] and looking for."[92] Along with Tondelayo's introduction, Obermayer may have crossed paths with former Dunham dancer and teacher Walter Nicks, who performed "a ritualistic ballet dedicated to [the Santería *orisha* (deity)] Changó" at the Sans Souci in 1953.[93] Regardless, Obermayer wrote to Dunham, enclosed photographs that evidenced her training and professional experiences, and asserted that working with Dunham would make her "a really good dancer . . . that's my life's dream."[94] The epistolary plea invites the question, why Dunham? This section suggests that Dunham provided professional opportunities to Afro-Cuban dancers like Obermayer, who were excluded from ballet and unfulfilled by cabaret. Not unlike Chamba for ballet and the *íreme* for folkloric dance, Dunham influenced Cuban modern dance through Obermayer and others before modern dance formally existed on the island. However, racialized exclusions and national ideologies erased Dunham, like other African-descended dancers discussed, from Cuban dance histories.

Dunham had long-standing connections to the Caribbean and in the 1940s accelerated interaction with Cuba specifically. After studying anthropology at the University of Chicago, she conducted ethnographic fieldwork on dance in Jamaica, Martinique, Trinidad, and Haiti from 1935 to 1936 and used performance to explore African diasporic cultures in the Americas. Her choreography and company appeared in films, musicals, and concert dance venues, and she established a school in New York. She worked with Cuban music director and composer Gilberto Valdés, as well as drummers and singers Julio La Rosa, Francisco Aguabella, Julito Collazo, Xiomara Alfaro, and Merceditas Valdés, among others.[95] Dunham's connections with Cuban musicians developed during the height of the "Latin craze" when nearly 90,000 Cubans, including entertainers, migrated to New York and Florida and shaped the cultural landscape in the 1940s and 1950s.[96] Partaking in the groundswell, Dunham planned a "Cuban Evening: The Poems and Songs of Nicolás Guillén" in 1946. The program starred Afro-Cuban poetry declaimer Eusebia Cosme and African American writer Langston Hughes with music by drummers "Candido, Julio, La Rosa and Reyes," and singing and dancing by Dunham company members Eartha Kitt, Lucille Ellis, and Tommy Gómez between poetry recitations.[97]

The evening illuminates what historian Takkara Brunson calls the "transatlantic stage" of the period, where black female performers like Dunham and Cosme appeared and at times connected.[98] Cosme was from Santiago de Cuba, orphaned as a minor, and raised by a distinguished family in Havana. She studied music, piano, elocution, and declamation, and in 1934 had her first major performances for the (white) women's associations Lyceum and Lawn Tennis Club and Pro-Arte Musical, as well as at the Teatro Principal de la Comedia in Havana.[99] Cosme recited vanguard poetry that focused on the black experience like the work of Afro-Cuban poet Nicolás Guillén. His collection *Motivos de son* (1930), for instance, represented the lives of lower-class, black Cubans as well as the popular *son* music through quotidian language and rhythms.[100] The verses that Cosme recited evoked dance, and her performances included gesture and rhythm. As Cosme described in an interview, "A bit of dance, some singing, occasionally black instrumentals, diluted, subordinated to the most noble art of declamation. . . . A reciter, above all, has to recite."[101] According to homages by the Cuban black civic association Adelante in their society publication, Cosme eloquently addressed black experiences: "She is black emotion, voice, and rhythm, harmoniously vibrating in the flesh and grace of a woman."[102] In this era of radio and phonographs, Cosme's rhythmically vibrating flesh, her full-bodied grace, in short, the visual impact of her movement, rather than just the sound of her voice, allowed her to convey "all black emotion," in the words of *Adelante* editors.[103] In the late 1930s and 1940s, Cosme performed in Puerto Rico, Venezuela, and several U.S. venues from Carnegie Hall (1938) to Howard (1939, 1946), Northwestern (1940), and Yale (1948) universities, along with the intimate showing at Dunham's School of Dance and Theatre in New York.[104]

Dunham's transnational, bilingual, and mixed media "Cuban Evening" foregrounded bodily performance and female artists to forge diaspora, that is, to build Afro-diasporic linkages across cultural and national boundaries.[105] Guillén's poetry inspired the event, as Dunham wrote to the poet afterward: "Through Dr. Ben Carruthers I became familiar with your works. They impressed me deeply since I am concerned with bringing Cuban culture and folk-lore to the institution of which I am a founder. So deeply impressed in fact, that I staged a 'Cuban Evening' here in one of my studios. It was a great success."[106] Carruthers, a professor at Howard University who also sometimes taught Spanish at Dunham's school, had helped Hughes translate Guillén's poetry into English. Hughes had traveled to Cuba in 1930 and 1931, befriended Guillén, discovered the power of Afro-Cuban percussionists in Havana dance halls, and went on to promote Afro-Cuban artistic production.[107] Carruthers and Hughes facilitated Dunham's encounter with Afro-Cuban artists, but Dunham organized the evening that spotlighted Cosme, who in turn brought the music and movement in poetic texts to life. As the program notes explained, "Afri-Cuban [*sic*] poetry is meant to be read aloud and that of Guillén is brilliantly recreated by Eusebia Cosme." Further accentuating Cosme's centrality, the program clarified that Langston Hughes "assisted" by reciting English translations of Guillén's poetry.[108] As Cuban poet Nancy Morejón noted decades later, Cosme remained an outlier in the era's predominantly masculine world of letters.[109] Despite encountering racism and obstacles to an acting career, Cosme was in many ways the star of the "Cuban Evening." In a reciprocal gesture of appreciation, Cosme sent Dunham a telegram wishing her luck for a November 1946 performance.[110] Their collaboration shows how black female performers notably forged and publicized transnational diasporic networks in this period.

Dunham's commitment to Cuban culture also manifested in her choreography, according to Cuban observers. For instance, Uldarica Mañas, who worked at the Cuban consulate general in New York, warmly praised Dunham's *Bal negre* ("Negro Ball," 1946), which featured "the typical dances of some countries of the Caribbean region, such as Cuba, Haiti, and Martinique," and music by Cuban composers Gilberto Valdés (Dunham's musical director at the time) and Ernesto Lecuona.[111] Cuban numbers like "Son," "Rhumba," and "Ñáñigo" in *Bal negre* led Mañas to conclude, "Given that the musical and choreographic themes are clearly Afro-Cuban, and that our folkloric culture can be admired . . . Cuba should thank Katherine Dunham, who has presented to the New York public a spectacle that shows all the color and richness of our people and our music."[112] Although the production may have sensationalized elements like the often-misrepresented Abakuá culture in "Ñáñigo," the elite, cosmopolitan Mañas believed that Dunham's *Bal negre* paid tribute to Afro-Cuban popular culture by working closely with Cuban collaborators.

Mañas continued to support Dunham by helping to publicize her work and providing advice on a potential tour to Havana. In April 1947, Mañas visited Dunham's studio with Cuban journalist and Communist activist Mirta Aguirre, who then published an article about Dunham in the Communist daily *Noticias de Hoy*.[113] To explore a possible performance in Cuba, Mañas advised Dunham to reach out to José Manuel Valdés Rodríguez, a well-connected arts critic.[114] Dunham sent a representative to Havana, and her Cuban musical director Gilberto Valdés acted as an interlocutor given his friendships with prospective sponsors.[115] However, the performance never came to pass. As Dunham explained to Mañas, her plan to perform in July and August would not work because "theatre managers agreed . . . it was too hot until September." Given Dunham's commitments in Hollywood, a Havana trip seemed unlikely in the fall.[116] In a letter to Valdés Rodríguez, another possible complicating factor came to the fore: racism. Dunham revealed that her representative in Havana "was unable to get in touch with Pro Arte," a common conduit for foreign performers. Dunham admitted, "I am not too surprised as I imagine that there is a certain amount of resistance to present[ing] a Negro company. I feel however that if we should do it independently or with the cooperation of your friend who manages the American Theatre the venture would be just as successful . . . without undergoing the problems which seem to surround . . . these societies."[117] Although Dunham had advocates like Mañas and Valdés Rodríguez, she never secured an amenable contract in 1947.

Despite an inability to perform in Havana, Dunham fostered her commitment to Cuba through her school. Originally founded in 1944 by Dunham and fellow dancer-anthropologist Franziska Boas (daughter of the famed anthropologist Franz Boas), the school had a comprehensive curriculum. Although the women eventually parted ways, Dunham's school opened in September 1945 and retained their shared anthropological objective of using dance to explore diverse societies.[118] By the 1946–47 academic year, the Katherine Dunham School of the Arts and Research, which included the Dunham School of Dance and Theatre, Department of Cultural Studies, and Institute of Caribbean Research, offered "two, three and five year courses leading to professional, elementary and master graduate certificates, in the fields of Dance, Drama and Cultural Studies." Geared toward aspiring performers, choreographers, teachers, and researchers, the robust program of study included classes in the "Dunham Technique & Primitive Rhythms," ballet, modern dance, "rhythm tap & boogie," "classic Spanish technique," percussion, dance notation, dance history, music appreciation, drama, and cultural studies classes like anthropology, psychology, philosophy, French, Spanish, Russian, and Caribbean Social Dances.[119]

Dunham and her school attracted Cuban students. For instance, in 1948, an aspiring Cuban dancer from Bayamo named Alberto Mola Rodríguez wrote to Dunham after admiring her work on film and reading Aguirre's 1947 article. He had reached out to Aguirre, who had connected him to Mañas, who had given him Dunham's address. "I have been very interested by your art that is considered the best exponent of folklore of our race," he wrote, implying a shared African patrimony. He admitted, "Since I believe that I have some abilities for dance and am wanting to progress . . . to be able to show the world the greatness of Afro-Antillean dances, I know that the only place I can develop . . . is in your academy." Although "answered Dec. 1st" is handwritten at the top of the page, I encountered no copy of the response or further evidence of what became of Mola Rodríguez in Dunham's papers.[120] Regardless, the fact that a dancer in the relatively remote eastern town of Bayamo knew of Dunham suggests that many around the island, especially those interested in Afro-Cuban and Afro-Antillean dance, appreciated her art and singular school.

Given Dunham's curriculum and renown, it is both surprising and revealing that the white Cuban dancer Ramiro Guerra did *not* train with her in New York from late 1946 to 1948. Guerra had joined the Original Ballet Russe during the company's tour to Havana in May 1946. He joined them for performances in Brazil from June through August 1946 and continued to their next destination, New York.[121] Once there, Guerra left the company to study modern dance. His teachers included white, U.S.–born dancers Martha Graham, Doris Humphrey, Charles Weidman, and Franziska Boas and Mexican-American dancer José Limón. Decades later, Guerra recalled going directly to Graham's school, never revealing why. Admittedly, Graham had an international reputation and performed in Cuba in 1941, which might explain his decision. With only ten dollars in his pocket, he explained his financial limitations, and Graham allowed him to take classes for free. He also went to the studio of Doris Humphrey and her husband, Charles Weidman, where he took classes with Limón, who Guerra remembered spoke Spanish to him, "giving me a type of welcome."[122] Limón also taught modern dance at Dunham's school during this period, appearing on schedules for the 1946–47 and 1947–48 academic years.[123] Although in one interview Guerra later claimed that he primarily "studied" with Graham but also "received classes" from Humphrey, Weidman, and Dunham, he did not mention Dunham in extended interviews published by his biographer Fidel Pajares Santiesteban.[124] Whether or not he took classes at Dunham's school, Guerra continued to cite Graham as having the greatest impact on him.[125]

Why did Guerra study with Graham and not Dunham? This seems surprising, since Guerra arrived months after Dunham's "Cuban Evening," and the school had such a widespread reputation that it attracted veterans, professional dancers, and actors like Marlon Brando, James Dean, José Ferrer, and Shelley Winters.[126] One explanation is timing. Guerra arrived in New York before Aguirre's 1947 article on Dunham circulated around Cuba. Also, Dunham herself performed abroad with her company for much of Guerra's time in New York, leaving her school in the hands of others.[127] By contrast, Graham was around and once spoke at length with Guerra about her fond memories of performing in Cuba after the attack on Pearl Harbor. Guerra reflected, "It was half an hour of conversation that I will never forget."[128] With Dunham abroad, she could offer no opportunities to connect directly, something that Guerra clearly sought out and valued.

Along with timing, race likely played a role in these historic connections and circumventions. As dance scholar Susan Manning argues, modern dance remained the purview of white dancers, while black dancers like Dunham were categorized as "Negro dance" in the United States. These "mutually constitutive categories" sprang from "interdependent representations of blackness and whiteness," with modern dance as a realm of whiteness—racially unmarked and open for universal abstraction—while "Negro dance" involved blackness—performances that referenced African heritage.[129] Guerra adhered to this racialized distinction, as indicated in a 1959 article he wrote on modern dance history. In it, he mentions white German dancers Harald Kreutzberg, Kurt Jooss, and Mary Wigman, as well as white U.S. dancers Isadora Duncan, Ruth St. Denis, Ted Shawn, Martha Graham, Doris Humphrey, and Charles Weidman, but not Dunham.[130] Moreover, "Negro dance," the U.S. construct for Dunham's work, perhaps struck Guerra as reflecting North American racial segregation, all blackness and no whiteness, and thus antithetical to Cuba's racially mixed national identity. Modern dance by contrast became Guerra's preferred vehicle for combining whiteness and blackness to result in a Cuban fusion.

After returning to Cuba in 1948, Guerra embraced Graham's "white" modern dance to meld with the blackness of Afro-Cuban culture. He later attributed his choreographic interests to his childhood neighborhood of Cayo Hueso, which he remembered pulsating with Afro-Cuban music and dance.[131] Guerra studied these cultural productions after leaving New York, analyzing "Cuban folklore, not only in theory, reading all the books of Don Fernando Ortiz, but also in practice. In those moments it was not easy, but I made contacts in religious circles and could see a lot of Santería dances, and I had the opportunity to study with some of these people, the movements and roots of Cuban folklore, not only in terms of Santería, but also in terms of the rites of abakuá and others."[132] His studies resonated with Dunham's ethnographic research. For instance, in 1935 while conducting fieldwork in Haiti, she was initiated in Vodou. She also represented Afro-Cuban popular and ritual dances in work like *Bal negre*.

Along with similar artistic interests, Dunham and Guerra may have coincided in Cuba and undoubtedly shared interlocutors. Dunham visited Cuba before 1951, perhaps in 1946. In her June 1946 letter to Guillén, she described planning a trip, and a year later, concluded a letter to Valdés Rodríguez by sending "warmest regards to any of our mutual friends particularly Lydia Cabrera and Mr. Ortiz."[133] Then in late 1951, Dunham wrote to Ortiz directly, desperate for recommendations on "two dependable Cuban drummers" with "good knowledge of rhythms and folklore." She referenced a recent encounter with Ortiz: "It was such a pleasure to see you in Havana and I look forward to our next meeting, I hope in the not too distant future. . . . Please remember me to Lydia Cabrera."[134] As Dunham connected with Ortiz and Cabrera in passing and then from a distance, Guerra studied Ortiz's work and observed local Santería faith practices to develop his first major choreography, *Toque* (Drumming Ritual, 1952).

Toque represented an "Afro-Cuban religious experience," according to program notes, with a cast of ten women and nine men. Guerra worked with Ballet Alicia Alonso company members and students from the affiliated academy, where he had been teaching modern dance since 1951.[135] Set to music by Argeliers León, *Toque* had four scenes: "Invocation," "Ritual," "Dance of the Ancestor," and "Dance of Origin." According to the program, the piece did not try to "realistically copy a rite, but to create [one] in accordance with African religious symbols." In particular, the work considered the fusion of male and female attributes "during the fertilizing action."[136] That is, *Toque* portrayed a fertility ritual.

In seeming anticipation of a public outcry, the performance program included essays defending *Toque*. The Cuban writer and feminist activist Renée Méndez Capote, whose daughter Maricusa Cabrera was in *Toque*, wrote one editorial. She described *Toque* as "a very noble attempt of folklore stylization" that drew inspiration from a "popular motif" and fulfilled an intellectual debt to affirm "Cubanness [*lo cubano*] through the ethnological elements that compose it." She also justified the ballet's sensuality, as it provided a "careful and thorough study of a religious rite. . . . In these cases the dances, prayers, [and] songs have a painful flavor that ennobles it, despite its sensuality." Further defending the work, she cited similarities between *Toque* and renowned (and initially controversial) European repertory such as *L'Après-midi d'un faune* (Afternoon of a Faun), choreographed by Vaslav Nijinsky for the Ballets Russes in 1912. Similar to Nijinsky's interpretation of sensual stories inspired by Greek culture, Guerra staged sexually charged Afro-Cuban practices by "stylizing them, elevating them to the category of a work of art. The realization of *Toque*, in Cuba, is the fulfillment of a duty," Méndez Capote concluded.[137] Her essay highlighted the contradictory impulses behind these nation-making exercises: inclusion, but only through "elevation." Although Méndez Capote never mentioned it in her essay, Dunham had resonant aesthetic goals. As Dunham explained to London audiences in 1948, she took "natural primitive movements" and presented them "as highly developed as Russian ballet."[138]

Along with Méndez Capote's essay, the program included a letter from Fernando Ortiz to Fernando Alonso, written a week before the premiere. Ortiz had observed a rehearsal of *Toque* (upon Alonso's invitation) and hailed its artistic and national merits. Identifying Santería deities with the Greek pantheon, he readied the public by writing, "[In the] black ballet you all will hear the beautiful melodies, rhythms, and steps of Changó (Yoruban Apollo), Yemayá (the Venus of Nigeria), Obatalá (the Mother Goddess), and Babalú Ayé (the spirit [*genio*] of disease) . . . filtered through a harmonic, allegorical and choreographic net made with the textures and embellishments of a modernist aesthetic." According to Ortiz, black culture filtered through a "choreographic net" resulted in "aesthetic transculturation," which expressed "national integrity, translated into a language of universal resonances."[139] Transculturation, a term that Ortiz coined in 1940 to describe the merging of cultures in Cuba, gave legitimacy to the performance.[140] In his letter, Ortiz never connected *Toque* to Dunham's artistic projects. Perhaps he assumed resonances with Greek mythology would most effectively persuade viewers to appreciate *Toque*. Moreover, highlighting the resonances between (white) Greek and (black) Santería pantheons perhaps more fully aligned with Cuban national projects than Dunham's African American approach to diaspora. In spite of Ortiz's praise, however, public outrage closed *Toque* after one performance.[141] Although never compared, Guerra and Dunham had much in common in the 1950s, as they similarly featured Afro-Cuban culture in concert dances and similarly received public critique for eroticism.[142]

While Guerra and Dunham remained on uncoordinated parallel trajectories, Irma Obermayer made contact with Dunham in June 1953. Dunham responded favorably: "Your letter interested me because it seemed to express a serious interest in the kind of company we are. We travel all over the world presenting the folklore of the Caribbean and North and South America with dignity and beauty and I like to have dancers who have feeling for the importance of this."[143] Dunham shared the expenses to bring Obermayer for an audition in Los Angeles, where the company was performing.[144] By November 1953, Obermayer had a scholarship to study at the Dunham School in New York, alongside other Cuban students.[145] Obermayer eventually joined the company in Europe from April to June 1954, but by July she had decided to leave.[146]

Dunham invited her back in the fall of 1955, and Obermayer responded favorably, explaining her foreshortened time with the company in 1954 and her interest in returning:

> I really think you are more than great and [a] genius.
>
> I cud [*sic*] not see that before. I only saw your bad side. I saw you [as] selfish and naughty, but now I understand, and I don't blame you at all.
>
> I can only admire your great value.
>
> I want to ask you for something. I wonder if you will ever accept.
>
> I want to be your pupil. See that I'm not asking you to be your simple chorus girl again but your *pupil*. I want you to help me be a good artist and do something interesting with myself, without needing a partner or depend[ing] on anybody.[147] (Double underlined in source.)

Obermayer's letter alludes to Dunham's reputation as a strict taskmaster.[148] However, Obermayer equally recognized Dunham's genius and saw her as the ideal mentor for a serious African-descended dancer and choreographer, especially a woman ("without needing a partner"), although race and gender never explicitly factored into her appeal. With a new assertiveness, the internationally experienced Obermayer did not want to be a "simple chorus girl," but an independent artist like Dunham.

While it is unclear how Dunham responded, she undoubtedly continued trying to arrange a performance in Havana. In May 1955, Pro-Arte reached out about featuring Dunham in their 1955–56 season, but by the time Dunham responded favorably over a year later, the Pro-Arte season was already set.[149] Dunham also tried to collaborate with Cuban composer Ernesto Lecuona.[150] Lecuona, then rehearsing for a debut at the Tropicana Nightclub, informed Dunham that the cabaret's choreographer, Rodney, wanted to bring her to perform. He also admitted, "Here there is the belief that you do not want to come to perform in Cuba now."[151] Perhaps she wanted to perform in a theater, not a cabaret, and demurred on entertainment venues like the Tropicana. As different institutions and protagonists in Havana tried to organize a show that never came to pass, rumors circulated. And there was some truth to them. In January 1956, Dunham traveled to Havana to assess the situation.[152] She found the touring prospects bleak, "because at the moment there is every evidence of revolution. The country is undoubtedly in a serious economic crisis."[153] Although the economic and political situation made her nervous, Dunham continued to pursue possible bookings.[154]

Dunham also retained connections to the island through Ortiz and Cabrera, who sat on the board of her Institute for Caribbean Research. She remained hopeful for a future encounter: "For many years I have tried to arrange that our show go to Havana and the Cuban people of all kind and classes have been waiting for us. It has never worked out to be possible financially. . . . No impresario in Cuba at the moment has the money to make our guarantee." She then requested a sizable investment from a U.S. patron to fulfill a long-awaited appointment with the Cuban people and to support research: "I would be happy to use the time that we are there to make a brief survey along with my two friends Ortiz and Cabrera in order to report exactly what is still extant in Cuba of the African religious cults."[155] Although this trip never happened, in subsequent decades Dunham remained in close contact with Cabrera especially.[156] In the end, the busy performer seemed wary of Batista's Cuba; meanwhile, other countries in Latin America, Asia, Australia, the Pacific Islands, and Europe beckoned.[157]

One Cuban dancer would join Dunham in Europe: Jorge Lefebre, a *mulato* ballet dancer from Santiago who had danced with Obermayer in Havana. In all likelihood, Obermayer returned to Havana sometime after her October 1955 letter to Dunham, and once there, connected with Lefebre. Obermayer choreographed their routines, and they performed on Havana television programs before securing a contract in Miami in 1956. After their stint ended, Lefebre headed to New York. He wanted to dance in the Broadway musical *West Side Story* but ended up training with Ballet Theatre and at Martha Graham's school. "Soon they sent me to see Dunham," he remembered. Assumedly, "they" included the teachers he was training with at the time. Perhaps racialized presumptions prompted the anonymous recommenders to see the Afro-Cuban Lefebre as a natural fit for Dunham's school and company. He also likely had heard of Dunham from Obermayer. Regardless, Lefebre auditioned, and within a month, he received a phone call from a representative, signed a contract, and headed to Monte Carlo to join Dunham's company on tour. While Lefebre was training and performing in transit, the ballet master and company member Lenwood Morris encouraged Lefebre to not give up on ballet. After performing with Dunham in Europe and the Middle East, Lefebre took Morris's encouragement to heart and left Dunham's company to pursue ballet in Europe. Eventually he connected with choreographer Maurice Béjart and found an artistic home away from home in Brussels.[158]

No professional modern dance company existed in Cuba before 1959, but the people dancing around the genre reveal a great deal about race, nation, and artistic origin narratives. White dancer Ramiro Guerra, the future founder of Cuban modern dance, studied rigorously with Graham, not Dunham,

perhaps because he saw the white Graham as a modern dancer and the African American Dunham as a "Negro dancer." Moreover, Dunham's approach
to blackness may have struck Guerra as distinctly North American and antithetical to Cuban understandings of race and nation, which involved closely
knitting blackness *and* whiteness. Equally possible, Guerra may have resented
Dunham, a U.S. outsider, who developed dances inspired by Cuban popular
culture and gained widespread fame for her work.[159] Nonetheless, his *Toque*
resonated with Dunham's oeuvre by looking to Afro-Cuban culture for inspiration but notably diverged from her work by featuring only white dancers.
African-descended Cuban dancers Irma Obermayer and Jorge Lefebre, who
had ballet training and worked in cabarets and on television, found concert
dance opportunities with Dunham. Dunham visited Cuba several times in
the late 1940s and early 1950s, cultivating lasting connections with Fernando
Ortiz and Lydia Cabrera, but never managed to perform on the island. Elite
societies like Pro-Arte maybe preferred white stars, leaving elite cabarets for
distinguished black performers. These missed connections, whether Guerra
with Dunham, Obermayer and Lefebre with concert dance professions in
Cuba, or Dunham's company with Cuba, evidenced racialized exclusions in
dance experiments that left a lasting legacy. As a concrete connection, Irma
Obermayer joined Cuba's first modern dance company, founded and directed by Guerra in 1959. In an interview, Guerra commented that Obermayer
had "long experience" with professional performance, unlike most other
dancers in his new company. However, once more, he never acknowledged
Dunham.[160]

Conclusion

Performers like Irma Obermayer, Chamba, the *comparsa* dancers of Las
Bolleras, women representing *íremes* in folkloric productions, and Katherine
Dunham have been on the margins or erased from Cuban concert dance histories. Existing narratives focus on white creators like the Alonsos and Guerra,
suggesting that they singlehandedly constructed Cuban concert dance and
made it more inclusive after the Revolution inspired them to do so. This
chapter by contrast has shown how African-descended dancers performed,
taught, choreographed, wrote letters, traveled, and took risks to further their
careers. Their efforts met with exciting opportunities along with frustrating
limitations as choreographers devised, and audiences selectively embraced, a
whitened rendition of blackness to represent Cuba on elite stages. How much
was "too much" blackness depended on opinion and venue, generally accepted

in high-end cabarets targeting white audiences, but not in ballets, for instance, thus reaffirming ballet's rarefied status in turn. These exclusions compelled some dancers to seek out Dunham and forge diaspora through transnational collaborations. The unacknowledged centrality of black and *mulato* dancers, as well as the racialized distinctions between ballet, folkloric, and modern dance that emerged in this formative prerevolutionary period, would have a lasting impact on concert dance developments as the next chapter details.

Following the fates of black and *mulato* performers in the 1940s and 1950s exposes similarities in approaches to race and nation on concert and commercial stages. This challenges narratives of difference propagated by revolutionary concert dancers who later rejected dances of the republican era, especially in cabarets. The dismissal was due largely to politics. More specifically, during his regime, Batista worked to increase tourism, as revealed by handwritten lists of hotel room capacities and reports on the tourist industry in his personal papers.[161] Dance makers in cabarets became associated with the Batista-led tourist industry, landing on the counterrevolutionary side of history. Yet, there were tight connections between concert dance and cabaret, artistically and politically. Ballet and cabaret overlapped as white dancers like Leonela González, Maricusa Cabrera, José Parés, and Joaquín Banegas, among others, appeared in both. Cabaret dancers also participated in anti-Batista protests alongside ballet colleagues. For instance, on September 15, 1956, twenty-five thousand people packed into the Stadium Universitario to support ballet dancers after Batista's officialdom substantially cut their subsidy; and, dancers of the Sans Souci and Tropicana performed works by Alberto Alonso and Rodney alongside ballets performed by Alicia Alonso and the Ballet de Cuba.[162] In addition to these convergences, dancers, choreographers, and audience members moved readily between venues, performing or watching Afro-Cuban-inspired ballets and folkloric spectacles in cabarets. Imagined lines between emergent dance genres remained blurry and were often traversed, as Obermayer's trajectory epitomizes. She trained in ballet, performed folkloric spectacles in cabarets, and joined Dunham's company to explore a modern dance aesthetic based on African diasporic culture. Rescuing these convergences shows how politics and cultural pretensions ultimately policed the boundaries between dance spheres in Cuba and identified concert dance (especially ballet) with whiteness and cabarets (especially spectacularized so-called folkloric dances) with blackness curated for a white gaze.

Just as concert and cabaret innovations overlapped and interacted, much connected dance developments before and after 1959. Choreographers like Alberto Alonso and Ramiro Guerra explored rumba, *comparsa*, Abakuá, and Santería choreographically starting in the 1940s and 1950s, only to continue in subsequent decades. Performers like Obermayer and Fresneda influenced the emerging dance scene by appearing in cabarets or carnival before becoming founding members of revolutionary modern and folkloric dance companies, respectively. Across the decades, black dancers also had to fight against prejudices to forge professional distinction. Dancers, choreographers, bureaucrats, and audiences carried forward established practices of distinguishing dance forms based on class and race. Ambivalent efforts to foster racial equality through choreographic inclusion predated 1959, and exclusionary legacies of the earlier era persisted in revolutionary times. Although commentators later would demonize dance enterprises of the 1940s and 1950s as exclusionary and different from what came later, productions across the political divide had much in common.

The next chapter further illustrates this point by tracing dance institutional building after 1959. The process involved African-descended dancers fighting to build careers in ostensibly inclusive revolutionary organizations. Dancers like Obermayer would not need to appeal to Dunham or travel to New York after 1959, but the path to a meaningful dance career remained arduous. African-descended dancers had to devise tactics for thriving in a revolutionary context deeply influenced by what came before.

CHAPTER THREE

Dance Institutionalization after 1959

Along with the image of the multitudes marching toward the future comes the concept of institutionalization . . . which facilitate[s] the natural selection of those destined to march in the vanguard.

—Ernesto "Che" Guevara, "Socialism and Man in Cuba," 1965

Encircled by mournful onlookers, modern dancer Luz María Collazo cried over the prostrate body of Eduardo Rivero as he writhed in pain (figure 3.1). Five years after Fidel Castro and his 26th of July Movement led a broad coalition to declare a revolutionary "triumph" on January 1, 1959, modern dancers rehearsed a dramatic scene from Ramiro Guerra's *Orfeo antillano* (Antillean Orpheus, 1964), a Cuban take on the Orpheus myth with Santería divinities in lieu of the Greek pantheon.[1] The rehearsal photo captures a moment of high theater, but dancers like Collazo experienced equally dramatic developments behind the scenes. In five short years, she went from a teenager with no artistic training to a soloist with a new modern dance company. A black woman from a humble family, she had no expectations of an artistic future. Yet, after 1959 dance makers built new institutions that desegregated high-art spaces, creating opportunities that talented youth like Collazo seized. Her daily life involved classes, rehearsals, and research. She spoke with former prostitutes and poor women in Havana for her role as a licentious woman in *Orfeo antillano*, for example.[2] The Revolution changed her life, and she also shaped it through dance. As Collazo clung to Rivero and wept, her gestures radiated outward, animating fledgling cultural institutions and public conversations about race.

Her experiences were part of a larger process of dance institutionalization after 1959. Institutionalization meant creating new companies and reconstituting old ones. Opportunities opened for African-descended dancers especially. As examined in the first section, new modern and folkloric dance companies had a majority of black dancers, and even the ballet school admitted an unprecedented number of black and *mulato* students, who later joined and thus integrated the majority white ballet company. Institutionalization also meant incorporating prerevolutionary antiblack racism into revolutionary structures, as discussed in the second section. For instance, this manifested in the fact that black folkloric dancers received lower salaries than their

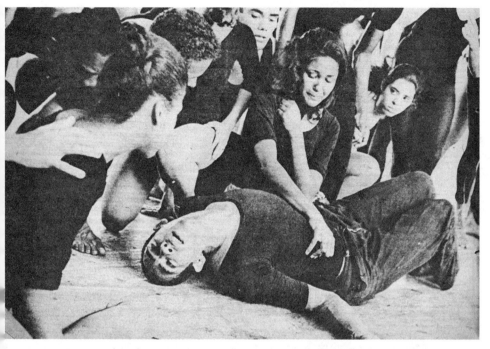

FIGURE 3.1 Modern dancer Luz María Collazo cries over the body of Eduardo Rivero during a rehearsal of the scene "The Death of Orfeo," in Ramiro Guerra's *Orfeo antillano* (1964). Photograph by Rafael Calvo. Source: *Bohemia*, June 26, 1964, 6. Courtesy of the Cuban Heritage Collection, University of Miami Libraries, Coral Gables, Florida.

white counterparts in the ballet company. Equally, white cultural bureaucrats, choreographers, and company administrators bought into prerevolutionary racial stereotypes, characterizing black dancers as lacking discipline and loyalty, linked to poverty, and needing reform or rescue from white revolutionaries. African-descended dancers were not merely victims of structural inequality, however. Black dancers like Collazo took action by performing to distinguish themselves on national and international stages. As modern and folkloric dancers and choreographers displayed the vitality and richness of Afro-Cuban performance on stage, they remade the contours of revolutionary culture. Through their diverse choreographic maneuvers, dance makers from all genres claimed to embody revolutionary ideals, as discussed in the third section. The highly ambivalent process of dance institutionalization, like the larger effort to establish a revolutionary order, involved opportunities, barriers, and undaunted workarounds.

Tracking dance institutionalization answers an often-asked question: how and why did ballet become the most prominent and privileged form after 1959 despite the viable contenders of modern and folkloric dance? Whereas ballet had elite connotations in Cuba, modern and folkloric dance embodied the populist and antiracist objectives of the post-1959 leadership. Observers have attributed ballet's paradoxical predominance to Fidel Castro's benevolence, ballet leaders Alicia and Fernando Alonso's unwavering support for the post-1959 government, and Soviet influence on Cuban society.[3] These explanations fail to account for why other companies, populated by dance makers who vociferously praised the new government, enjoyed less reciprocal support. They also erase dancers' actions by presuming Fidel and his government decided to promote ballet independently or in response to external (Soviet) forces. By contrast, I demonstrate how antiblack racial prejudices within Cuban society and power struggles within the dance community shored up balletic privilege in the 1960s.

This analysis also expands understandings of institutional building and racial dynamics in post-1959 Cuba. As the opening quote by revolutionary icon Ernesto "Che" Guevara illustrates, political leaders considered institutions to be crucial to the Revolution; however, as Che claimed in the same 1965 essay, institutionalization had yet to be achieved.[4] In kind, scholars have characterized the 1960s as a period of organizational chaos and centralized power with Fidel Castro as "the institution."[5] The previously overlooked process of dance institutionalization, however, happened rigorously in the 1960s in contrast to much of the political economy. Moreover, unlike other realms where Fidel starred as *the* institution, dancers took center stage, imagining organizations and bringing them into being. By 1965, they devised a structure that continues to shape the Cuban concert dance landscape today. Notably, these institutions were fundamentally unequal especially for Afro-Cuban dancers. Dance institutionalization vividly confirms what other historians have concluded about the coexistence of racism and antiracism in Cuba.[6] That is, revolutionary institutions gave performers of African descent a place within concert dance, but ingrained prejudices prevented them from gaining equal status to white (especially ballet) dancers. However, concert dance also offered a previously overlooked realm for race activism. African-descended dancers performed political stances that challenged the status quo, making the most of fraught institutions to thrive.

Becoming Dance Professionals

After 1959, dancers of African descent joined white performers on the esteemed stages of Havana. This ended an informal but very real segregation that reserved professional concert dance, previously only ballet, for light-skinned performers. New modern and folkloric dance companies founded in 1959 and

1962, respectively, opened up professional avenues for black and *mulato* dancers. Additionally, a handful of African-descended dancers began ballet training. As performers of different racial and class backgrounds became professionals, they described the development as dreams come true or happy accidents, attributing their achievements to the historic moment. These narratives aligned with hegemonic discourses about the Revolution ostensibly cultivating unprecedented equality, which poor and black Cubans should appreciate.[7] Even though dancers expressed gratitude toward the Revolution, their actions show that they mostly had themselves to thank. Black and *mulato* dancers fought to forge distinction and a new category of revolutionary work. The struggle to wrangle hopes into concrete outcomes within a new political order was not easy or inevitable but nevertheless resulted in moments of pride and joy.

Desegregation in concert dance happened against a backdrop of official antiracist measures. Early in 1959, Castro declared racism to be immoral and incompatible with the Revolution. Historically disenfranchised descendants of enslaved men and women, who had opposed colonialism and servitude for centuries, became symbols of the revolutionary vision. As the black intellectual Walterio Carbonell provocatively asserted in 1961, "Africa has facilitated the triumph of the social transformation of the country. This does not mean that Spain has disappeared. Spain has been Africanized."[8] These openings had limits. In February 1962, Castro declared that the Revolution had eradicated discrimination based on race or sex.[9] Since racism supposedly no longer existed, discussions of the topic became taboo. However, these changes did not deter modern and folkloric dancers from professional performance opportunities or from exploring race on stage.

For childhood friends Eduardo Rivero and Arnaldo Patterson, becoming professional dancers after 1959 realized long-held dreams.[10] Both men of African descent came from families with limited means and had harbored frustrated artistic aspirations until the Revolution. Rivero reportedly came from a "very poor, very humble family" and was one of many Cuban children who "had to abandon their dreams to dedicate themselves to a practical job that resolved household needs."[11] Patterson also described grim prospects subsumed by revolutionary advance: "In 1958 I was an adolescent without a future. I had artistic inclinations; I dreamed, even when I was awake, about being a dancer. My aspirations were realized the same year of the triumph."[12] In 1959, the Teatro Nacional de Cuba (National Theater of Cuba, TNC) became Rivero and Patterson's professional home.

The TNC was the product of preexisting cultural networks and new revolutionary rhetoric. Several members of the prerevolutionary leftist cultural association Sociedad Cultural Nuestro Tiempo, including Isabel Monal, Argeliers León, and Ramiro Guerra, collaborated on an art festival convened by the 26th of July Movement in May 1959.[13] According to the press, "After forging a revolutionary consciousness, the 26th of July [Movement] wants to offer the public a program that rescues its most significant values in the field of art."[14] Leaders appointed Monal to direct the TNC after passing Law 379 in June 1959, which nationalized the theater and charged it with developing "theater, music, ballet, opera, and artistic activities in general."[15] Monal decided to follow the schema of the May 1959 festival with separate departments for each art form and headed by her recent collaborators.[16] The TNC had departments of Music, Dramatic Arts, Modern Dance, Folklore, and Theatrical Extension.[17] Guerra became the director of the Department of Modern Dance and León, the director of the Department of Folklore. From these two departments, modern and folkloric dance companies with a majority of African-descended performers would emerge.

Even before Guerra held auditions for the new Department of Modern Dance, Rivero and Santiago Alfonso, another African-descended dancer, took intentional steps toward eventual dance careers. Rivero started ballet training in 1953 and then sought out Guerra in early 1959 upon hearing that he needed dancers for a television program *Noche cubana*.[18] Rivero auditioned but instead took a job at the cabaret Venecia in Santa Clara. After two months, he received a telegram from Guerra about auditions for a new modern dance company. He immediately left for Havana.[19] Resonantly, Santiago Alfonso began ballet classes in 1955 and performed in cabarets before the Revolution. Although he later asserted that his "technical formation truly began with the Revolution," these early dance experiences undoubtedly built an important foundation.[20]

Alfonso, Rivero, and Patterson, as well as Irma Obermayer, were among the 160 Cubans who responded to an advertisement published on September 11, 1959. It called for people of different backgrounds and physical types to audition for scholarships to take dance theory and technique classes at the TNC Department of Modern Dance with the possibility of becoming a permanent company member after a year.[21] Whereas Rivero, Alfonso, and Obermayer had ballet training and professional performance experience, others had "absolutely no technique." However, Guerra looked for potential and focused on creating a group "formed by the three colors of our nationality. Whites, blacks and *mulatos*," as he later put it.[22] Rivero, Alfonso, Patterson, and Obermayer were among the dancers of African descent who made up two-thirds of the new company. The Department of Modern Dance, later renamed Conjunto Nacional de Danza Moderna (National Ensemble of Modern Dance, "Danza" for short), became the first integrated Cuban concert dance company. Guerra's students celebrate him as the first white company director and choreographer to recruit Afro-Cuban performers.[23]

One black dancer, Isidro Rolando, did not make the cut in September 1959; however, he found other performance outlets before successfully auditioning again in 1961. Rolando worked as an office clerk when he went to the first audition. He had no formal training but always loved to dance and had a natural facility for movement.[24] After his rejection, he successfully auditioned for Alberto Alonso, who needed black dancers for an evening-length work that premiered on April 21, 1960.[25] While working with Alberto, Rolando took classes with modern dancers Guido González de Valle and Manuel Hiram, as well as ballerina Menia Martínez.[26] He also performed on a television program but could not fully support himself by dancing. He worked in a printing office, taking ballet classes during his lunch break and performing after work. "In that era," he explained, "a dancer was looked down upon [*era mal visto un bailarín*] . . . because of the prejudices. And black [dancers], even more so! So [my activities] were practically hidden." Assumedly, Rolando faced presumptions about the financial instability of a dance career and its feminine connotations, not to mention racism. As a result, when he signed a contract to enter Danza in October 1961, Rolando and his colleagues faced an uphill battle to build the reputation of professional dancers.[27]

While male dancers of African descent highlighted ambition frustrated and eventually realized, black and *mulata* women described their arrival to modern dance as accidents of talent meeting revolutionary opportunity. These narratives may reflect gendered expectations that women remain unambitious and out of the spotlight. Take Silvia Bernabeu, who joined the modern dance company in 1960, and later described her involvement in the following terms: "I was a house wife. I did not think seriously about being an artist. Nevertheless, I joined Ramiro's group very young and am almost a founding member. By accident I am a soloist."[28] Whereas Bernabeu stepped into leading roles after a colleague had an accident, another almost founding member, Perla Rodríguez, segued into professional dance as a natural extension of her experiences as a child performer. At three, she began appearing on a children's television show. Meanwhile, her mother was part of a folkloric production that Ramiro Guerra took to the eastern Sierra Maestra Mountains for revolutionary commemorations on July 26, 1960.[29] Perla's dancing mother spoke to Guerra about her talented ten-year-old, who auditioned after the alpine production. Guerra accepted Perla into the company as a student, and for the next decade, she performed youthful roles created for her. Only in 1971 did Perla begin to perform adult roles until her retirement in 1990. "Ramiro Guerra taught me how to be an artist. He never treated me like a child," she asserted. This meant no coddling: "In ten years . . . one time only, he congratulated me. . . . Only one time he said, '*Muchachita*, you danced well,'" she noted matter-of-factly. To Perla, the demanding environment was a gift. Guerra's high expectations shaped her as an artist and a teacher.[30] Downplaying their ambition and exertion, Bernabeu and Rodríguez high-lighted how outside forces like accidents, familial connections, and Guerra's guidance shaped their professional trajectories.

Perla's colleague Luz María Collazo had a history resembling that of her fellow modern dancers. Like Rivero and Patterson, Collazo came from a humble family; like Rolando, she joined the company in October 1961; like Bernabeu, she described her involvement as accidental; like Perla, Guerra played an important role in her career, though with more tension. Although initially interested in acting, she heard about and then auditioned for the TNC Department of Modern Dance. "From that moment dance seduced me," she confided in a 1985 interview. In 2019, she described her early dance experiences as involving "a lot of happiness and enthusiasm," since at eighteen Luz María enjoyed the newfound independence of entering adulthood, having professional direction, and eventually, making money.[31] From 1960 to 1961, Collazo trained in afternoon classes taught by Eduardo Rivero and other company members, who bore pedagogical responsibilities alongside performance careers due to a lack of human resources. She formally joined Danza in 1961 and quickly distinguished herself, becoming a soloist in 1963.[32] She claimed that she lacked ideal physical qualities for dance, "but Ramiro was a magician and he made people dance, and little by little I went deeper into that world, disciplining myself, listening to his dictates." In addition to dancing, Collazo started modeling, becoming the "first black Cuban model," and starred in the Soviet-Cuban filmic collaboration *Soy Cuba* (1964) as María/"Betty." Ramiro was not pleased, since Collazo had to miss classes, rehearsals, and performances for these other pursuits. Nevertheless, dance remained her mainstay through her retirement from the stage in 1995 and beyond as a teacher.[33]

Danza affiliates claimed that the company gave African-descended dancers a lofty artistic career, whereas previously only cabarets and television offered (unsatisfactory) professional outlets. While laying the groundwork for his company, for instance, Guerra published an article that argued, "Black and *mestizo* artists, owners of the powerful expression of their race, escape the grasp of serious art for economic reasons . . . and end up in the vulgarity of commercial art."[34] The trajectories of several dancers including Eduardo Rivero, Santiago Alfonso, and Isidro Rolando do suggest that without Danza, they might have continued performing entirely in cabarets and on television. With Danza, dancers could devote themselves to art not entertainment, or as a 1965 performance program explained, "Human material came . . . from Television and Cabaret, media that before the Revolution did not offer physical or spiritual possibilities to realize a serious or artistic professional perspective. . . . [They now] appear on stage as professionals, a group of dancers . . . creating the foundations of a national dance . . . according to the needs of revolutionary culture."[35] These statements reflect elitist definitions of culture that excluded commercial stages and mass media. Modern dance leaders were not alone in this bias. For example, according to famed writer Guillermo Cabrera Infante, Guerra's choreography had been described as "Rodney converted into art."[36] The reference to Roderico "Rodney" Neyra, the choreographer of the Tropicana Nightclub, dismissed cabaret as trivial and esteemed Guerra's work as serious art.

Despite the self-serving narrative of white company leaders and the Revolution "saving" black dancers from crass commercialism, black dancers rejected the dichotomy by continuing to work and collaborate across imagined lines between highbrow and lowbrow entertainment. Santiago Alfonso, for instance, began working as a teacher and a choreographer at the Tropicana in 1964 while continuing at Danza. He taught modern dance technique to cabaret performers, seeing great value in the training that he received as a company member.[37] While Danza leaders sought to create genre distinctions, dancers moved agilely between institutions and opportunities.

Establishing the status of modern dance reflected not only personal tastes but also desires to reach the echelons of ballet in Cuban imaginaries. Ballet had become a profession in the late 1940s and 1950s and benefited from the international fame of ballerina Alicia Alonso and the advocacy of ballet enthusiasts. After 1959, ballet dancers regrouped and pronounced their alliance with the new government. As the diplomatic relationship soured and then ended with the United States, Cuban ballet had to reorient toward Moscow after two decades of regular exchange with New York.[38] This resulted in physical discomforts, as Alicia's daughter Laura recalled: "We were used to getting toe shoes from the United States and suddenly we started getting them from Russia, and the Russian toe shoe is very thin, or was. . . . So then it would develop bunions and it hurt."[39] Along with throbbing feet, professional ballet dancers faced enormous pedagogical work. They had to train a new generation of dancers to replace foreigners (especially those from the United States), who previously had worked between Havana and New York.[40] Ballerina Aurora Bosch, for instance, remembered teaching ballet classes to young students early in the morning before running to company class and rehearsal.[41] Despite undeniable discomforts and hard work, ballet dancers enjoyed privileges most acutely observed from the outside.

For instance, U.S. expat Lorna Burdsall, a white modern dancer, choreographer, and eventually Danza director, often commented on balletic privilege in correspondence with her family. Burdsall had danced in New York before meeting and falling for Cuban student Manuel Piñeiro, who was studying at Columbia University. She joined him in Cuba in 1955.[42] Piñeiro fought in the Sierra Maestra (earning the moniker "Barba Roja" or Red Beard), and after 1959, he became vice minister of the Interior. Lorna was a founding member of Guerra's new modern dance company at the TNC.[43] In 1963, she described modern dance in Cuba as "growing even if it has to push its roots up through the classical ballet."[44] Then, a decade later, Burdsall summed up: "The ballet is so good here that many people have overlooked the Folklore group and our group.... The ballet gets all the privileges."[45] In other words, modern and folkloric dancers struggled to establish themselves in a nation that so highly valued ballet.

As Burdsall mentions, "the Folklore group," which grew out of the TNC Department of Folklore directed by Argeliers León, faced resonant but distinct challenges in establishing itself. At the TNC Department of Folklore, León worked with expert performers like Nieves Fresneda to theatricalize quotidian faith practices and popular dances. As Fresneda explained in a published interview, "I had known Argeliers León for a long time, when I was in the *comparsa* Las Bolleras, and also for having helped him, like [his teacher] Fernando Ortiz, to demonstrate ... what the dances and customs of the Lucumí were like, because I had seen them when I was little!"[46] Fresneda and others then worked with León to develop the evening programs *Cantos, bailes y leyendas cubanas* (February 1960), *Bembé* (May 1960), *Abakuá* (August 1960), and *Yimbula, fiesta de palmeros* (November 1960). They featured diverse cultural practices like Afro-Cuban Santería, Palo Monte, Abakuá, Cuban popular dances like rumba, and dances from Spain.[47] Fresneda was in her sixties when she took the stage in *Cantos, bailes y leyendas cubanas* and embarked on a new professional performance career. According to a program essay, performers like Fresneda were not "professionals who had acquired these manners of playing, singing and dancing in large periods of study with an academic organization," but "people of the *pueblo*."[48] This picturesque humility, however, belied decades of performance experience and long hours of rehearsal.[49]

Building on this work, Fresneda became a founding member of the Conjunto Folklórico Nacional (National Folkloric Ensemble, CFN) in 1962. In a proposal to cultural bureaucrats, León advocated for a new company made up of "young people . . . from the most humble layers of the population. Not from groups that are already vitiated in dances of cabaret and television."[50] Like Guerra, León objected to commercial venues, which he believed distorted folkloric material for entertainment effect.[51] León garnered support from cultural leaders and recruited his student, Afro-Cuban folkloricist Rogelio Martínez Furé, as well as white Mexican choreographer Rodolfo Reyes, who was in Cuba at the time, to head the new company.[52] In April 1962, Martínez Furé and Reyes held an audition, and over four hundred people showed up. They chose forty-five dancers, drummers, singers, and seven *informantes* (informants). Among the seven *informantes* were Fresneda and Manuela Alonso, founding members of the carnival *comparsa* Las Bolleras, and drummers Trinidad Torregrosa and Jesús Pérez. Also called *bibliotecas vivientes* (living libraries), these *informantes* had expert knowledge in the performance cultures of Santería, Palo Monte, Abakuá, carnival, and Cuban popular dances.[53] The new company members made their living as laundresses, shoemakers, masons, newspaper sellers, bottle collectors, and butchers and had grown up dancing, singing, and playing music in religious and festive contexts. They now applied their knowledge to spectacular renditions of ritual for a theater-going public. Although lacking an official budget, the CFN began rehearsing on May 7, 1962.[54]

The CFN claimed to follow the guiding principle that "there was no white or black folklore, only Cuban folklore, with African roots, in the majority, but also Spanish, Haitian, French, etc."[55] Though promoting an integrationist vision of folklore, the CFN had mostly African-descended performers, giving the company an overwhelming identification with blackness. According to Argentinean company administrator Tamara Satanowsky in August 1962, "The idea was to form a group . . . of black and white personnel, but the . . . budget . . . problem forced the postponement of . . . a school and the teaching of unfamiliar folkloric dances. . . . There was a majority of black personnel as a result."[56] Her statement reveals a desire to dilute blackness in the CFN, which resonates with the whitening impulses that shaped presentations of Afro-Cuban folklore on cabaret stages before 1959.

The "majority of black personnel," in the words of Satanowsky, followed circuitous paths to their performance careers. Drummer and dancer Mario ("Aspirina") Jáuregui Francis had an illustrative nonlinear trajectory. Born in 1932, he had a fourth grade education. "When the Revolution came I was working as a simple worker in road construction," he wrote in a brief autobiographical statement. He had some opportunities as a percussionist, but made a living at the docks when he joined the CFN in 1962. "I worked here a short period because economically I could not solve my situation and that of my family, [and] I returned to the docks," he explained. At some point, he worked at the Tropicana Nightclub before returning to the CFN as a drummer and dancer in 1968.[57] Although the CFN offered an alternative to cabarets, performers like Jáuregui continued to work between these institutions and at times supplemented salaries with nonartistic work to make ends meet. Dance makers from other institutions also became involved with the CFN. Santiago Alfonso, for instance, not only worked at Danza and the Tropicana but also choreographed for the CFN in the 1960s.[58]

The CFN had a majority of black performers because of their undeniable talent and expertise rather than a lack of interest from white dancers. For instance, the Spanish-descended sisters Graciela and Caridad Chao very much wanted to join the company. In the early 1960s, they took classes in modern dance at the TNC with Ramiro Guerra and Eduardo Rivero and in folkloric dance at the newly established Escuela de Instructores de Arte (School of Art Instructors). They wanted to join the CFN, as they explained in a passionate appeal to cultural bureaucrats, but instead received positions as folkloric dance teachers for *aficionados* (nonprofessional dancers). Only in 1965 did the Chao sisters become dancers in the company.[59]

Soon after the Chao sisters, the young black singer Silvina Fabars joined the CFN on February 10, 1966, as part of a younger generation of performers. Born in a small town in eastern Cuba, her father worked in sugar and coffee harvests, and her mother died when she was four. She was twelve when the fight against Batista escalated, and she recalled going with other girls to the mountains to help the rebels by cooking and cleaning clothes. "So, as you see, I also had my small participation in the insurrection," she later boasted.[60] She was fifteen in 1959 and enrolled in a military school in Santiago, where she first began to sing publicly "in cultural activities, with a colleague who played the guitar."[61] She continued developing as an artist while working as a militant in Santiago, building trenches during the missile crisis in 1962 and helping the cleanup effort after Hurricane Flora in 1963. Fabars also participated in festivals and received prizes for her singing. In 1965, she saw a notice about auditions for the CFN and traveled to Havana. Fabars impressed company leaders with her "distinct form" of singing influenced by eastern Cuban musical cultures. After receiving news of her acceptance, she entered the company a week later.[62]

Although performers of African descent like Fabars mostly found opportunities in modern and folkloric dance companies, there were a few black and *mulato* dancers who started ballet training. Pablo Moré and Caridad Martínez were in the first class of students at the Escuela Nacional de Arte (National Art School, ENA) in 1962, and Andrés Williams started training the next year.[63] Ileana Farrés Alonso, a founding member of Guerra's Department of Modern Dance at the TNC, began ballet classes and joined the ensemble of the Ballet Nacional de Cuba (National Ballet of Cuba, BNC) in 1966.[64] However, ballet still remained associated with whiteness. Caridad Martínez encountered these assumptions at her audition to enter the ballet school. As she recounted, "The receptionist who was also a person of color . . . said to my mom, 'Oh, but she passed? . . . Ah, well look . . . be careful because here in the ballet there aren't any black people.' . . . And my mom said . . . 'Well look, if there aren't any, she will be the first!'"[65] Martínez was the only female student of African descent in her class. But things were changing.[66] By the late 1960s, dancers like Moré, Martínez, Williams, and Farrés, who had started their training after 1959, were company members. In 1967, British critic Arnold Haskell noticed the racial mixture that distinguished the BNC from European, North American, and Soviet companies: "A unique detail of the Cuban ballet is the integration of races."[67] However, integration took place slowly, and within Cuba, ballet remained linked to whiteness in contrast to folkloric dance, which became identified with blackness. As one 1970 article claimed, Cuba, the "country of the rumba," identified with "more cultured forms of dance through Alicia."[68] Rumba had connotations of blackness and stood in opposition to the more "cultured" ballet, symbolically identified with Alicia Alonso's white body.

Nevertheless, black performers became concert dance professionals after 1959. An interview with Eduardo Rivero in 1965 illuminated the busy lives of revolutionary artists. Because of his full schedule of classes, rehearsals, and performances, the interviewer had to snag time with Rivero backstage after a show as the echo of applause hung in the air. A still sweating Rivero spoke to the reporter in his dressing room as he removed his makeup and costume, transforming into a "quotidian person." Reflecting on his journey to that moment, Rivero saw sacrifices giving way to joy: "I will always remember my first performance . . . How [could I] forget the moment in which we saw our aspirations, our greatest desires materialize?" (Ellipses in the original.)[69] Rivero's continuous exertion, exemplified even by the rushed interview, had helped to make his dreams come true.

Post-1959 trajectories of dancers like Rivero involved intentional actions meeting revolutionary possibility. This labor of love was filled with liberating movement and expectation. However, soaring hopes often crashed into limits, as illustrated by the fate of Silvina Fabars. Six days after the young singer

joined the CFN, a drummer had a heated exchange with the company director. Angered by the low pay and misrepresentation of cultural practices, he
pulled a gun and began firing. A bullet hit Fabars's neck. She survived, but the
injury irreparably damaged her vocal chords. The tragic incident ended an
exciting beginning.

Harmful Hierarchies

As the violent altercation in the CFN studios made clear, dance institutional
developments ushered in destructive clashes alongside productive collaboration. Rather than a monolithic state pitted against beleaguered artists, a plurality
of people including cultural bureaucrats, company directors and administrators, choreographers, and dancers challenged and undermined each other.[70]
Dance leaders jostled for limited resources and distinction. Some companies
thrived and others withered. Equally, rank-and-file company members like
Fabars got caught in the metaphoric and literal crossfire, suffering from de-
flated salaries, bickering company leaders, racial and class prejudices, and reactionary violence. Power struggles after 1959 resulted in harmful hierarchies
within the field of concert dance. More specifically, white ballet leaders secured a privileged position while modern and especially folkloric dancers
fought for resources and respect.

Fernando and Alicia Alonso attained their privileged status in part thanks
to their relationship with revolutionary notable Antonio Núñez Jiménez, a
geographer and captain in the 26th of July Movement. The Alonsos had been
friends with Núñez Jiménez since the 1940s, and this connection further solidified in 1952 when he married Lupe Velis, a ballerina in their company.[71] In
the early 1950s, correspondence and programs listed Núñez Jiménez as an
administrator in the company and first vice president of a supportive civic
association.[72] Late one night in the spring of 1959, Núñez Jiménez visited Fernando with Fidel Castro in tow. Legend has it that after hours of conversation, Fidel asked Fernando how much money he needed for his company,
Ballet de Cuba. Fernando told him $100,000, and Castro replied, "Take
$200,000 and make it good" (in keeping with the sources, "$" indicates Cuban pesos here and below).[73] This often-repeated story occludes the fact that
Alicia and Fernando had been pushing for $200,000 since the early 1950s.

Then, ballet leaders advocated for and actively shaped a law that would
officialize support for the Ballet de Cuba. In one rejoinder, company representatives wrote, "The Ballet de Cuba and its current directors are not inter-

ested *at all* in having administrative or financial control of the institution, but they do consider essential the freedom of action necessary for artistic production. . . . It would be totally absurd if a functionary of the Dirección de Cultura . . . was the one who determined the hiring of a ballet master, ballerina, or choreographer, without prior discussion with the . . . company directors" (underlined in source).[74] Likely learning from recent trials with Batista, ballet affiliates prioritized artistic autonomy and consistent patronage from the new regime. Law 812 passed on May 20, 1960, and stipulated that the state subsidy for the Ballet de Cuba could never dip below $200,000 annually because "'ballet' constitutes . . . one of the most elevated and beautiful artistic manifestations that already has a tradition in our country."[75]

In addition to securing the Ballet de Cuba's financial future with Law 812, Fernando and Alicia bolstered their company by renaming it. In November 1961, Fernando proposed changing the name to Ballet Nacional de Cuba. This move effectively erased memories of Alberto's Ballet Nacional. As early as 1959, affiliates of Alberto's Ballet Nacional saw Alicia and Fernando encroaching on this name to accentuate their ballet leadership at the expense of others. Dancer and teacher Raúl Díaz Domínguez wrote a letter to the editor, reminding the "public and journalists" that the Ballet Nacional, founded and directed by Alberto, "always functioned . . . without having any union whatsoever with the Ballet Alicia Alonso or the Ballet de Cuba," because of differences in artistic objectives and administration.[76] Fernando, however, argued to cultural bureaucrats that "the Ballet de Cuba is the maximum national expression of the art of classical ballet in our country" and therefore should have "national" in the title.[77] The name change glossed over balletic heterogeneity and integrated different ballet projects into a singular establishment with Alicia and Fernando as the main protagonists.

Choreographers, directors, and dancers from other companies noticed and complained about the centralization of balletic power. In a November 1962 letter, representatives from the Sección de Danza y Ballet (Section of Dance and Ballet) of the recently established Unión de Escritores y Artistas de Cuba (Union of Cuban Writers and Artists) asserted, "At this time we are faced with a split created by the privileges enjoyed by one figure and director of one group, to the detriment of the majority." Although never naming Alicia and Fernando Alonso, the letter went on to charge that the Consejo Nacional de Cultura (National Council of Culture, CNC) seemed to offer "all [its] support to classical ballet," which led to a "sense of competition among the other groups." Dance developments, the authors asserted, should be based on *"the equality of*

*all groups, preventing the hegemony of one over another, and ensuring equal access
for all to material means"* (underlined in source).[78] The authors proposed level-
ing resource allotment and publicity. Their appeal went unheeded. Ballet's exceptionality was accentuated in 1963 when the CNC divided dance affairs into
Ballet (with only Fernando and Alicia's Ballet Nacional de Cuba) and Dance
(with several modern and folkloric dance companies).[79]

These developments had a particularly detrimental impact on smaller experimental companies that defied genre boundaries like Danza Contemporánea (Contemporary Dance [Company]) and the Conjunto Experimental
de Danza de la Habana (Experimental Dance Ensemble of Havana). Danza
Contemporánea, founded and directed by Guido González del Valle, worked
with "different theater groups of the State to solve dance issues."[80] With eclectic training in diverse dance techniques, music, and acting, the company performed modern dances, musicals with the Conjunto Dramático Nacional,
and theatrical productions with the theater companies Teatro Estudio, Grupo
Guernica, and Grupo Milanés.[81] Alberto Alonso's Conjunto Experimental,
meanwhile, created "a national dance synthesis with universal resonance" by
combining ballet, modern dance, and popular dance in ballets, musicals,
modern dances, and pieces about Cuban folklore.[82] Although both companies received some government funding, Danza Contemporánea dissolved in
1965, and the Conjunto Experimental ceased to exist in its original form in
1966. These "failed," largely forgotten dance companies disrupt narratives of
triumphant, linear progression of Cuban concert dance based on companies
like the Ballet Nacional de Cuba, Conjunto Folklórico Nacional, and a renamed Conjunto Nacional de Danza Moderna that still exist today.[83]

Both Danza Contemporánea and the Conjunto Experimental faced logis-
tical challenges. González wrote an emotional letter to bureaucrats in 1964,
recounting how a locked theater and occupied studio meant that one evening
his company had no place to rehearse. He concluded, "Please pardon the perhaps desperate tone of these lines, but believe me they are sincere and I often
feel trapped in a vicious cycle of absurdities and contradictions."[84] Moreover,
the company was allowed only a short season, prompting González to protest
the *"completely ridiculous"* (underlined in source) run of six shows after rehearsing almost a year, calling it "anti-economic, anti-cultural, and completely
mechanical and illogical."[85] Alberto's Conjunto Experimental also had programming problems and short seasons: the company performed just two
months a year rather than the more ideal five.[86]

When Danza Contemporánea and the Conjunto Experimental ceased to
exist, displaced dancers joined larger companies. In late 1964, González met

with Lorna Burdsall about Danza Contemporánea merging with the Conjunto Nacional de Danza Moderna.[87] Although the mechanics of the merger remain unclear, a document from 1965 about Danza Contemporánea stated, "This group was created on March 26, 1963 and already has disappeared."[88] The Conjunto Experimental fused with the Teatro Musical de la Habana (Musical Theater of Havana) in January 1965.[89] Alberto and his dancers worked there for a time before scattering to television (Cristy Domínguez), cabarets (Tomás Morales and Armando Suez), Conjunto Nacional de Danza Moderna (Víctor Cuéllar), and the BNC (Sonia Calero), while Alberto worked as a choreographer and artistic adviser of the BNC and other companies. By the mid-1960s, concert dance institutionalization was complete. The BNC, Danza, and the CFN had consolidated, and smaller experimental groups of the early 1960s were subsumed. While foreclosing opportunities for smaller enterprises, this centralization also meant greater diversification within institutions as individuals brought unique priorities to their new artistic homes.

While ballet enjoyed robust support and experimental companies like Danza Contemporánea and the Conjunto Experimental dissolved, modern and folkloric dancers persisted, but had less from the beginning. Whereas the BNC secured at minimum $200,000 annually in 1960, the budget that year for Guerra's admittedly smaller modern dance enterprise was $48,000, less than a quarter of the ballet's subsidy and modest when compared with the TNC Department of Music budget of $167,000.[90] Although a 1960 budget for León's TNC Department of Folklore has not been found (likely because there was no established subvention), comparing the monthly salaries of performers in the departments of Modern Dance and Folklore shows that the former had considerably more money than the latter. Guerra and León, as directors of both departments, received the same salary of $311.55, suggesting some pay equity within the TNC. However, the twenty-five dancers in the Department of Modern Dance received salaries ranging from $100 to $225 per month while the twenty-nine folkloric artists had salaries of $14 to $34 per month. While modern dancers could support themselves as professional artists, performers in the Department of Folklore had to rely on other jobs.[91] These numbers illustrate stark material differences and a postrevolutionary pecking order, with ballet at the top, followed by modern dance, and then folkloric dance. This reinforced racialized inequalities as mostly white ballet dancers enjoyed the greatest economic security followed by white, black, and *mulato* modern dancers; meanwhile, mostly African-descended folkloric dancers from working-class and impoverished backgrounds experienced the most precarity.

Although modern dance did not have the same level of support as ballet, the company benefited from crucial connections to power via Burdsall, who was married to a revolutionary dignitary and had connections to the United States. "Being a rebel wife, I am exempt from so many things," she wrote in February 1959. "Sometimes I have to fight to pay—money is no payment for what the rebels did for Cuba & everybody knows that."[92] In another letter, she revealed her intimate proximity to power, past and present: "Here I am reclining on the bed of Batista's ex-bedroom across the hall from Raul [Castro] and Vilma [Espín]. . . . I have never seen such luxury."[93] In the 1960s and 1970s, she had access to nice homes, maids, cars, and diplomatic trips all over the world.[94] She also used her connections to support modern dance. For instance, through her husband, Burdsall secured scenic apparatus and air conditioning for the still-unfinished TNC in 1960.[95] Burdsall's revolutionary status seemed to negate any potential disadvantage of her Yankee citizenship, and her connections to the United States continued to pay dividends. Long after the United States and Cuba severed diplomatic relations, her family sent costume fabric and music for modern dance performances when such items became scarce on the island.[96] Although these networks did not eliminate hardships, Burdsall's marital proximity to political leadership, not to mention Guerra's position in dance and leftist circles (evidenced by his connections with the Alonsos and Sociedad Cultural Nuestro Tiempo in the 1950s), likely benefited modern dance to a degree.

Meanwhile, folkloric dancers, first in León's Department of Folklore and then as members of the CFN, had no comparable privileges and faced prejudices due to their age, race, religions, and class. Supporters and collaborators were as discriminatory as detractors. For instance, two bureaucratic proponents of the company, "Gilda [Hernández] and Isabel [Monal,] wanted pretty people . . . younger than forty years [old], but the criteria of being true folkloricists prevailed, even though they were neither young nor pretty," Afro-Cuban co-founder Rogelio Martínez Furé explained during a heated company meeting.[97] Hernández and Monal's reported ideas about beauty had ageist and antiblack valences. Even so, according to white costume designer María Elena Molinet, Hernández and Monal "had faith in the Conjunto, but in other spheres of [the Consejo Nacional de] Cultura, no, instead they thought that [the Conjunto] was a crazy idea. . . . Additionally . . . there was a little fear of both black dance and Santeros and of risking money and having no results, achieving only an exaltation of black rhythms."[98] White choreographer and cofounder Reyes harshly dismissed CFN members as "not very ductile. Their magical-religious mentality makes them distrustful by nature, undisciplined . . . putting their religious interests before their work and the Revolution."[99] León's wife and eventual CFN director María Teresa Linares aired class prejudice when she described members coming "from the most abused social strata" and possessing "bad attitudes."[100] Fear of black religious traditions and racial stereotypes about African-descended peoples as unattractive, lacking discipline, and exhibiting bad behaviors were not new. Racist prerevolutionary stereotypes haunted revolutionary institutions and took on new forms in anxieties over black loyalty to the Revolution.[101]

Adding injury to insult, white company leaders attacked religious beliefs that inspired staged productions. When León proposed a professional folkloric company, he envisioned ideologically malleable young dancers, performing ritual music and dance in an "absolutely materialist plane," displaying their "scientific knowledge" of folklore rather than expressing faith. Toward this end, he recommended regrouping performers according to abilities (rather than shared cultural backgrounds) and applying the "careful work of revolutionary indoctrination."[102] In 1962, Argentinean company administrator Satanowsky asserted, "The goal of the CFN is: Socially, destroy religious myths and bring to the stage for a mass public the dances that are logically reflective of those customs."[103] Even as the CFN offered a space to celebrate Afro-Cuban music and dance, some company affiliates wanted to use the company as a vehicle for eradicating performers' faiths, which they deemed unacceptable.

Salaries reflected and perpetuated inequalities. According to one report, the CFN was the first Cuban performance group composed of working-class "men and women of the *pueblo*," who "continued their habitual labors during the day and at night worked in the Conjunto."[104] They had no choice. While the choreographer Reyes received a comfortable monthly salary of $350, performers earned between $40 and $50 in 1962.[105] By comparison, that same year Alicia Alonso received $1,000 a month and the lowest-ranked BNC members received $300 from an annual budget that had swelled to $963,000.[106] Meanwhile, salaries for Danza ranged from $180 to $350, based on budgets from 1963.[107] Only after the CFN successfully premiered in July 1963 did the financial situation improve. Although precise salaries in late 1963 or 1964 remain unclear, one letter by company costume designers asserted that "increased" salaries and official contracts had helped morale.[108]

Even with better contracts, material discomforts, infighting, and directorial turnover beleaguered the company. As informant Lázaro Ross pointed out in a March 1964 meeting, the CFN rehearsed in a dirty location without running water. Moreover, CFN members often worked eight hours a day, far beyond the four hours stipulated in their contracts, as performer Roberto

Espinosa complained in the same meeting. At another moment, conversation turned to one company member who had nowhere to sleep for undisclosed reasons. A peer suggested that the white company director, Marta Blanco, house the individual. Evidencing class differences between rank-and-file dancers and the director, Blanco demurred apologetically because her recently rehired maid now occupied the previously empty room in her house.[109] Along with these material concerns, infighting among the company leaders had created a toxic environment. Both Blanco and Martínez Furé clashed with choreographer Rodolfo Reyes, and the company's first international tour in 1964 only exacerbated those tensions.[110] Although the 138-day tour was a relative success, it culminated in Blanco leaving (or being removed from) the company. Mexican dancer and choreographer Elena Noriega directed the company briefly in 1965 but quickly left for health reasons.[111] Musicologist María Teresa Linares replaced her.

By the time Linares took the helm in 1965, folkloric dancers' salaries had improved, but historic and ongoing mistreatment culminated in violence. CFN performers earned monthly salaries ranging between $140 and $200.[112] By comparison, in 1964 members of Danza earned either $171 or $238 per month, and in 1965 BNC ensemble dancers earned between $150 and $235, while soloists earned between $285 and $600 and Alicia earned $950 each month.[113] Though pay gaps were smaller, CFN members remained "poorly paid" and worked other jobs to fulfill "their economic needs," Linares noted. This included "modeling for [the Instituto Nacional de Industria Turística, National Institute of Tourism,] INIT into the early hours of the morning," resulting in absences and "a state of physical exhaustion that reduces their productivity."[114] In hopes of improving the situation, Linares assigned CFN members one of three salary categories ("A" with a salary of $250, "B" with $200, and "C" with $180).[115] This rankled some performers, including Miguel Ángel Valdés Bello, who on February 13, 1966, opened fire, seriously injuring Reyes, Linares, and Fabars.[116] While reminiscing in Mexico City, Reyes claimed that Valdés, a member of the initiation society Abakuá, was upset over the publicizing of ritual practices in CFN performances. Indeed, in July 1965 the CFN had just premiered Reyes's *Ciclo Abakuá*, featuring Valdés.[117] The tragic incident underscored two troubling facets of the CFN's history: low salaries and the mistreatment of Afro-Cuban religious faithful and their cultures. This mirrored the revolutionary government's persecution of Abakuá, evidenced by the 458 Abakuá members in Havana prisons alone by 1968.[118]

Fabars got caught in the middle of a longer battle between performers and prejudiced company leaders, bureaucrats, administrators, and choreographers. The story of her recovery reveals how performers collaborated to cope and heal. At twenty-one years old, Fabars was bedridden and unable to talk because of the bullet wound in her neck. She had a risky surgery. Eventually, she returned to the CFN and shifted from singing to dancing. She noted that Santiago Alfonso, Roberto Espinosa, and others "worked with me, whether teaching me or researching my roles or offering me parts in their works." Fabars eventually developed her favorite role, Ochún, through diligence and help from Nieves Fresneda and another founding dancer, Luisa Barroso. As Fabars asserted, "I can say that [Fresneda and Barroso] made me the folkloric dancer that I am today."[119] Ironically, in a national institution where money came from the state, crucial moral support came from fellow dancers, exposing the limits to official sponsorship.

Just as Fabars persisted despite irreparable harm, the CFN forged ahead. Founding musician Fernando Oviedo Alfonso wrote to Fidel Castro about the "anxiety, restlessness, and discontent" of company members in January and February 1966. Castro's companion and assistant Celia Sánchez penned a response that directed Oviedo to contact cultural bureaucrats. In a May 1966 message summarizing this exchange, Oviedo assured cultural bureaucrats that any anxiety and dissatisfaction had already disappeared and that business continued as usual.[120]

Hierarchies developed within socialist Cuba's concert dance establishment. Distinctions had material consequences in the form of salaries, theater space, and publicity. Ballet leaders quickly secured their privilege. Modern dancers enjoyed some connections to political power, which helped to foster their development. African-descended folkloric dancers came from humble backgrounds and staged cultural practices that many white cultural bureaucrats, administrators, and company leaders viewed ambivalently at best and maliciously at worst. Classist and antiblack prejudices intersected to ensure that ballet had the most and folkloric dancers, the least. Even as harmful hierarchies solidified, some dance makers resisted and questioned them. They wrote letters of complaint, joined new companies, spoke up in company meetings, supported recuperating artists, and above all, danced.

Embodying Revolutionary Politics

Even as dance professionals had widely different experiences in the years following 1959, they similarly mobilized to connect their work to revolutionary politics by framing their training and productions as manifestations of loyalty, discipline, and contributions to revolutionary culture. Through these efforts, dancers characterized their art as embodiments of revolutionary politics. Similar discourses, however, resulted in diverse kinesthetic outcomes. These differences accentuate the importance of attending to physical movements, which fleshed out shared revolutionary ideas in unexpected ways. Dancing with the Revolution meant connecting to broader social and ideological projects while staying true to diverse aesthetic objectives.

In a powerful and literal gesture of loyalty, dancers at times took up arms to defend the Revolution from external attack. Andrés Cortina Rueda, a founding member of the CFN, joined the military and defended Cuba during the Bay of Pigs invasion in 1961 and the missile crisis in 1962.[121] In April 1960, the TNC created the first cultural sector militia, and composer Carlos Fariñas led a makeshift troop of actors, modern dancers, folkloric performers, musicians, and administrators in military exercises on site. During the Bay of Pigs invasion, artistic militants were stationed at the theater for seventeen days. After the artistic workday of classes and rehearsals, modern dancers and fellow artists at the TNC received "very old rifles, which [they] ... did not know how to use," and slept intermittently on mats in the theater vestibule.[122] This drama unfolded as modern dancers prepared for their first international tour. The April 1961 Bay of Pigs invasion delayed their departure, but as soon as it was routed, the modern dancers rushed from the TNC to the airport and caught the first flight out of Cuba after the attack. No personal luggage was allowed. "As a result the dancers ... left with their costumes practically on," Guerra later explained.[123] Eduardo Rivero recalled the unforgettable scene of combat and craft as Guerra deplaned in Paris "dressed as a militant with hands full of Santería ritual objects," which were props for the program.[124] As these histories indicate, the daily life of performers in the early 1960s consisted of military service and dramatic departures along with classes and rehearsals.

Ballet dancers, meanwhile, performed aestheticized renderings of revolutionary loyalty in the work *Despertar* (Awakening) about oppressed peoples rising up and overthrowing an authoritarian ruler. The ballet was inspired by the Revolution and dedicated to its fallen heroes.[125] The four-scene ballet resembled a morality play with characters like Oppression, Liberty, Citizen, Executor, Girl, and an ensemble designated as the People. Footage of a 1960 performance in the Soviet Union shows dancers representing the People in ragged clothes, hunched and kneeling on the floor with outstretched hands as though desperate to escape their downtrodden situation. Girl (played by Laura Alonso) breaks away. Two representatives of the oppressive order grab and throw her around until she collapses at the end of a stylized rape scene.[126] In the midst of tragedy, the ballet's heroine, Liberty, inspired resistance. The ballet culminated in a victorious fourth scene, featuring "a dance . . . representing the definitive triumph of the people."[127] *Despertar* performed a blunt balletic loyalty to the Revolution that was not necessarily successful. In a review, Guillermo Cabrera Infante called the ballet "a bad result of the best intentions."[128] Whatever the flatfooted didacticism, *Despertar* successfully projected the linkages between ballet and the Revolution. Evidencing broad public awareness of this alliance, in August 1960 counterrevolutionaries planted a bomb at the company's studios. Fortunately, no one was hurt.[129]

Along with enacting loyalty, dance makers framed their disciplined training as embodying revolutionary commitment. This came through discussions of honing a Cuban modern dance technique in the unfinished TNC studios. As Guerra later remembered, "There was no wooden floor, nor barres, nor doors. The dancers that I chose from the street were . . . wild [*salvajes*]. When I placed them in a diagonal they slipped away."[130] One journalist observed, "Ramiro submitted [dancers] to a rigorous and disciplined work of daily classes that, even in the middle of the labor of rehearsals, did not stop."[131] Whether intended or not, Guerra describing his dancers as "wild" and the journalist highlighting newly instilled discipline implied a racial dimension, as the white Guerra worked with a majority of African-descended dancers. This dovetailed with prejudicial presumptions of the period that black Cubans needed reform, discipline, and guidance from white revolutionaries.[132]

Even as Guerra sought to discipline his dancers, he simultaneously welcomed their influence. In particular, company members of African descent aided the white Guerra in exploring "*lo negro*" or blackness in Cuba, which became a defining characteristic of the emerging technique.[133] Guerra firmly believed that Cuban modern dance depended upon "the direct intervention of individuals of the black and *mestizo* race," who had been denied opportunities "to develop their faculties and augment their spontaneous knowledge of black folklore with a conscious [*conciente*] technique of a universal dance."[134] Although Guerra's evaluation reflects prejudicial subtexts that black dancers' talents were "spontaneous" and valuable mostly (if only) for inspiring modern dances, his dancers undeniably informed technical outcomes. Eduardo Rivero's articulate torso left an imprint, as did Arnaldo Patterson's expressive arms and hands, according to collaborators. Characteristics of present-day Cuban modern dance classes—such as undulating torsos and arms that accompany warm-ups and sequences across the floor—maybe originated with Rivero and Patterson's corporealities. Weaknesses equally had historical weight. Because of "bad" knees (an injury in 1961 followed by chronic pain), Patterson focused on teaching and became a formative *maestro*, who trained generations of Cuban modern dancers.[135] Creating a Cuban modern dance technique was a collective, ongoing process across generations that accommodated the dual forces of disciplinary codification and individualistic interpretation.

Folkloric dancers also emphasized and exhibited their disciplined devotion to art and politics. As black drummer and syndicate leader Jesús Pérez recounted, people from different occupations and backgrounds began "the work of disciplining themselves as artists, for the future great work that awaited us."[136] This "great work" involved not only staging vibrant productions but also winning respect for the cultural practices that they performed. As Afro-Cuban *informante* Lázaro Ross implored fellow dancers in a 1964 company meeting, they must work for the sake of "the religion of almost everyone . . . and for the Revolution, that permits them to manifest all their folkloric and popular dances."[137] Ross's colleagues listened. As a newly appointed CFN director recognized in 1966, "All contributed their artistic skills with the greatest willingness to give their utmost and with the hope that their merits and work will be recognized."[138] Indeed, CFN dancers persisted despite considerable obstacles to achieving distinction. Fabars spoke from experience when she asserted, "Artistic work is [one] of much sacrifice and dedication. The artist must have two essential things: discipline in work and respect. . . . Alicia Alonso is an example in that sense. I admire her a lot, as the world admires her. Other dancers whom I admire and would like to mention are: Nieves Fresneda and Luisa Barroso as well as Perla Rodríguez."[139] Fabars's statement underscores how concert dance, whether ballet, folkloric, or modern dance, demanded discipline and provided an important space for strong women to shine and shape revolutionary culture.

The fact that Fabars found inspiration in Alicia comes as no surprise, since the ballerina became the epitome of feminine discipline and militancy, and these connotations extended to dancers under her leadership—and shadow.[140] An article profiling Josefina Méndez, a ballerina who joined the Ballet de Cuba in 1955, underscored balletic devotion when noting the sweat on her brow and observing, "The life of dancers is rigid and difficult, [and] takes a lot of sacrifice." Sacrifice also meant fidelity to hierarchies, namely, deference to Alicia. In the same profile, Méndez described preparing for the title role of *Giselle*, which she called, "the role of Alicia, who is its ultimate interpreter."[141] While Alicia inspired excellence, she also set an upper limit on the careers of Méndez and other ballerinas of her generation. Any career frustrations that these women faced never appeared in public discussions, but do come up in oral history interviews with family members and colleagues.[142] Disciplined loyalty to the Revolution for ballet dancers also meant closing ranks behind Alicia.

Loyal and disciplined ballet dancers in the 1960s mostly performed traditional works with roots in the elite cultures of Europe and Russia like *Giselle, Swan Lake, Coppélia,* and *Les sylphides.* Of course there were works like Alberto Alonso's *Carmen* (1967), *El güije* (1967), and *La rumba* (1968), which experimented with Cuban folklore and popular dance in ballet, but Alicia loved the classics and had excelled at them since the 1940s. They had pedagogical power, she claimed.[143] Supporters also justified the paradoxical continuation of elite classics in socialist Cuba by underscoring their domestic and international benefits. Essayist Waldo Medina waxed lyrical about workers and peasants patronizing the "great art" of ballet "thanks to the Revolution that renders [it] effective and free."[144] During his famed 1961 "Words to the Intellectuals" speech, Castro noted that the Cuban ballet had received "admiration and recognition in all the countries it visited."[145] Moreover, ballet supposedly took on new forms in a socialist context. One reporter claimed, "In the capitalist world artists have become very egotistical . . . and with our Revolution the artist loses the 'I,' the egoism, to give his [or her] art to the people. Because of this, I can say that the homage is not for Alicia Alonso, the artist, but for the people of Cuba who have made possible the triumph of our ballet."[146] Whether Alicia lost ego is debatable, and if she did not, understandable. While undoubtedly patriotic, Alicia remained a famous ballerina and local hero with long, manicured nails, fashionable clothes, and elegant pearls.[147] Inconsistencies could be reconciled by projecting militancy. A panegyric on ballet claimed that Cubans gave traditional classics "a new life, as if *Giselle,* in effect, were dressed as a militant."[148] Although Cuban Giselles still wore romantic tutus, militant discourse transformed gossamer skirts into another form of fatigues.

Of course, not all ballet artists pledged unswerving deference to Alicia and adhered to a singular vision of revolutionary support. Most notably, Alberto Alonso rebelled by developing experimental companies that defied genre boundaries discussed earlier and through his choreography. In his 1970 *Conjugación* (Conjugation), for instance, Alberto rejected blunt militancy in ballet. He was inspired by the poem *Primera conjugación* (First Conjugation) by Uruguayan writer Amanda Berenguer. Published in the *Casa de las Américas* magazine in 1968, it was dedicated to Che Guevara after his 1967 death. "The true revolutionary is guided by a great feeling of love," Che had famously written; and in kind, the poem lyrically riffed on conjugations of the verb *amar,* to love.[149] Instead of military uniforms and combative gestures, dancers wore

FIGURE 3.2 Dancers perform an abstract ode to Che in Alberto Alonso's
Conjugación (1970). Photographer unknown. Source: Museo Nacional de la
Danza. Courtesy of the Museo Nacional de la Danza.

colorful unitards and embraced lovingly (figure 3.2). Allowing the audience
to grapple with the material in any number of ways, *Conjugación* refused to
didactically celebrate revolutionary icons. Alberto's work exemplifies how the
ballet establishment had greater aesthetic and ideological diversity than existing scholarship tends to recognize.[150]

While ballet projected militancy, even of the ambivalent variety, and distinguished Cuba abroad, modern dancers and their supporters in the press
suggested that their form aligned with the Revolution by promoting integration and equality. According to one journalist, modern dance involved "Cuban dancers 'of all colors,' breaking revolutionary lances against racial
prejudices."[151] Moreover, since modern dancers had racially integrated casts

and less hierarchical ranking compared with ballet, the group was a model of democracy, waging "the most beautiful battle for national art . . . nurturing the revolutionary ideal."[152] Guerra's *Suite Yoruba* (Yoruban Suite, 1960), which opened with a dancer in a cutout of the Virgin Mary stepping through to dance as the Santería *orisha* Yemayá, explored religious syncretism and posited Cuba's national identity as one of racial integration.[153] *Suite Yoruba* ostensibly made Santería cultural practices more "accessible intellectually and emotionally for the spectator with little knowledge of such manifestations."[154] Moreover, modern dance arguably had greater revolutionary relevance than ballet, which seemed inherently distant due to its "courtly antecedents" and codified technique. In other words, as one journalist asked, "How can ballet capture the many battles of the epic Sierra Maestra?" Guido González del Valle editorialized, "Why modern dance? For Revolution."[155] Other reviews conveyed similar opinions as though trying to explain the value of modern dance to readers more familiar with ballet.[156] Tension between modern dance and ballet was so noticeable that U.S. modern dancer Muriel Manings described the "strong rivalry" in her journal while visiting in 1970.[157] To make space for modern dance, supporters argued that the emergent technique better reflected revolutionary ideals than ballet.

Similarly, folkloric dance makers contended that *their* interpretations of popular culture best embodied revolutionary politics. On July 25, 1963, the CFN premiered *Yoruba, Congo, Rumbas y comparsas* at the Mella Theater, and in the program, Martínez Furé described, "The Conjunto Folklórico Nacional emerges to meet a need of our country, which did not possess an institution capable of recovering the dance and musical manifestations of a national character and to integrate them in a definitive form into the new socialist culture. . . . The revalorization and divulgation of this cultural archive is one of the fundamental purposes of the revolutionary process, because only in this way a true culture that reflects the historical reality of our *pueblo* will develop."[158] The first cycle of the program presented the world of the gods with Yoruban music and dance "to create the atmosphere of Santería legends." The second work depicted Cuba's nineteenth-century slave society with a *"tatanganga"* or *"padrino congo,"* that is, a leading practitioner of the Congo-derived Palo Monte appearing with his followers. A danced confrontation (*"el baile de maní"*) gave way to an erotic couple dance (*"el baile de yuka"*) and ended with a friendly, "frenetic *makuta*."[159] The third section showed present-day Cubans dancing rumba and carnival *comparsa*. Martínez Furé's idea to build a new national culture incorporating African-descended knowledge and rituals aligned with other Afro-Cuban intellectuals working in literature, film, and music at the time. Folkloric dance, then, contributed to a broader movement to promote racial justice through the arts.[160]

Like the undeniable elite sensibilities of ballet, folkloric dance had religious underpinnings that seemed to contradict the Marxist secularism of socialism. However, company members continued honoring religiosity. As Martínez Furé wrote, "It is without a doubt that religious elements have played an important role in the creation of many manifestations of our folklore." Program essays explained the pantheons and material culture of worship (e.g., musical instruments, clothing, etc.).[161] CFN productions, from the performance programs to the vibrant music and dance, could be read as testaments to the social role of Afro-Cuban faiths into the present. Moreover, the religious knowledge of CFN members remained crucial for successful productions. The company director explained to a bureaucrat in 1966, "Due to the characteristics of their rites and traditions, only they can carry forward the folklore and the unknown wonders that they hide in their thoughts . . . to the service of Cuban culture."[162] As CFN members drew upon sacred wisdom to build revolutionary culture, they simultaneously nurtured individual faith communities while articulating a devotional nationalism. The seemingly antithetical became mutually reinforcing because for many black Cubans there was no conflict between revolution and religious practices. In fact, there was a convergence, since both systems allowed for opportunities and growth.

Nevertheless, performing and celebrating black culture in the late 1960s remained fraught. The Cuban state increasingly cast religions in general, and Afro-Cuban ones especially, as backward superstitions and obstacles to socialism. This put a new socialist spin on prerevolutionary tendencies to criminalize black culture and religion.[163] The state also called any race-based activism divisive in the late 1960s. When a group of black intellectuals including Martínez Furé tried to submit a position paper on race and culture in Cuba to the 1968 Cultural Congress, cultural bureaucrats dismissed and disciplined them.[164]

Against this backdrop, Guerra created the modern dance *Medea y los negreros* (Medea and the enslavers, 1968), the third work in his mythological trilogy on Santería *orishas* after *Suite Yoruba* and *Orfeo antillano* mentioned above. *Medea y los negreros* transposes the story of Jason and Medea to the Caribbean during the Haitian Revolution. Jason is a European adventurer traveling from Haiti to Cuba with his mistress Medea, an enslaved princess of an African tribe. When Jason abandons Medea for the mixed-race daughter of the landowner Creon, Medea uses Vodou to attack Jason. At the end of the piece Jason, Creon, and two enslaved men whip Medea to death.[165] To develop

Cinco años
en Danza Moderna

FIGURE 3.3 Modern dancer Luz María Collazo models in the all-white clothes of Santería religiosity for a spread simply titled "Five Years in Modern Dance." Photographed by Fernando López. Source: *Revista Cuba*, October 1966, 75. Courtesy of the Cuban Heritage Collection, University of Miami Libraries, Coral Gables, Florida.

the movement vocabulary, Guerra drew inspiration from the two-dimensional imagery of Greek vases, French neoclassical art, and the African-descended dances of Cuba and Haiti. Three women represented different aspects of Medea—Medea the lover, Medea the mother, and Medea the envious—and they reportedly played with equilibrium and disequilibrium as they danced in complicated relation with one another.[166]

Did the piece about racialized violence make a controversial statement about race, religion, and violence, I asked Luz María Collazo, who performed the role of Medea the lover in April 1968.[167] She said no, but brought up a relevant incident that occurred as a model. In 1966, she participated in a photo shoot for *Revista Cuba*, wearing a white hair wrap, dress, tights, and shoes, that is, the all-white clothes that Santería initiates wear (figure 3.3). The spread was simply titled, "Five Years in Modern Dance," and implied that both Collazo and Santería religiosity had informed modern dance developments for the past five years.[168] The images prominently appeared on the front cover and reverse of the back cover, Isidro Rolando gleefully pointed out and exclaimed, "Imagine [*Imagínate tú*]!" By way of explanation, Collazo chimed in, "It was prohibited, the religion." Although perhaps not technically illegal, Afro-Cuban faiths were looked down upon, and functionaries demanded an explanation of the images.[169] Guerra experienced similar interrogation: "When my work about folklore brought me close to the traditional religious cults, to which some of my dancers belonged . . . I was summoned by officials that threw in my face the fact that I was encouraging within the Conjunto religious practices outside the prevailing ideology of that time."[170] Posing in all-white and staging works like *Medea y los negreros*, even when not intentionally transgressive, were bold moves. Collazo, Guerra, and their modern dance colleagues foregrounded black culture and protagonists to invite infinite ruminations on religion and unresolved racial tensions during a period of official silence on the matter.

Dancers connected their work to the Revolution at every turn. They performed revolutionary qualities of loyalty, discipline, and sacrifice and highlighted how their work contributed to the Revolution by garnering international acclaim or fostering antiracist and populist priorities. Although dancers drew on a shared political language, hegemonic theories resulted in diverse choreographic outcomes. Using bodies and movements, dance makers demonstrated the capaciousness of revolution as a concept and a political project.

Conclusion

By the time Collazo appeared in the April 1968 production of *Medea y los negreros*, the dance scene had changed considerably over the previous decade.[171] Before 1959, ballet was the only concert dance form in Cuba, and white ballet dancers portrayed African-descended protagonists on concert stages via suggestive movements or costuming. This changed after 1959 thanks to the desegregation of concert dance, which led to new modern and folkloric companies with a majority of African-descended dancers, as well as more black students training in ballet. Yet, even as the 1959 Revolution opened up professional avenues, prerevolutionary race and class prejudices resulted in different levels of official support that perpetuated inequalities.

In institutionalizing their form, dance makers fought for and secured degrees of power, used their art for political expression, and reaffirmed (in some cases) or challenged (in others) privileges based on race and class. Dancers, choreographers, and company directors spearheaded projects and haggled with each other and bureaucrats. In contrast to other official realms in 1960s

Cuba, Fidel and his bearded comrades existed on the peripheries of dance institutional building, giving dancers degrees of freedom. Consequently, dance makers used their sway to establish dance institutions by the mid-1960s and to convey diverse political stances on hard-won public platforms. Modern dancers performed antiracist integration. Folkloric dancers celebrated Afro-Cuban culture as a revolutionary corrective to decades of injustice. Ballet dancers challenged Cuba's backwater status with internationally lauded interpretations of traditional ballets. Across the genres, performers conveyed revolutionary loyalty and embodied discipline. Although dancers similarly partnered with the Revolution, they experienced vastly different outcomes of their hard work. Aligning with the epigraph by Che, dance institutionalization determined who was "destined to march in the vanguard," rewarding some dance makers and punishing others. This process of "natural selection," to use Che's words, reinforced frameworks in place before 1959 with ballet at the top. However, through backstage advocacy and onstage productions, folkloric dancers especially questioned persistent privileges based on race and class. Moreover, choreographic celebrations of black culture fomented more radical revolutionary cultures despite facing resistance from within and without.

Freedom to move did not mean freedom from pain. Exciting revolutionary opportunities were accompanied by disappointment and hardship. The field of dance encompassed aggressions enacted by cultural bureaucrats, company leaders, and fellow dance makers. It also involved creation and healing. Ultimately, dancers improvised and made hard choices to keep working. This drive came in handy as all dancers, men in particular, contended with homophobia. Dancers had no choice but to address sexual prejudices and promote dance as valid revolutionary work for women *and* men. In the next chapter, these maneuvers take center stage.

CHAPTER FOUR

Choreographing New Men and Women

Nothing prevents a homosexual from professing revolutionary ideology and, consequently, exhibiting a correct political position. In this case, he should not be considered politically negative. And yet we would never come to believe that a homosexual could embody the conditions and requirements of conduct that would enable us to consider him a true Revolutionary.

—Fidel Castro, 1965

To sum up, the fault of many of our artists and intellectuals lies in their original sin: they are not true revolutionaries.

—Ernesto "Che" Guevara, "Socialism and Man in Cuba," 1965

In 1966, ten male dancers with the Ballet Nacional de Cuba (BNC) defected while the company was performing in Paris. They told the international press, "We are not opposed to the revolutionary action of the present regime. But we deplore the arbitrary persecution, . . . which affects anybody showing the least sign of nonconformity either in his way of life, his religious opinions, or simply his clothes. It has become impossible for us to work as artists in such a climate of threats and incertitude."[1] They referred to increased harassment of individuals that the state viewed as nonconformists, including homosexuals.[2] The 1966 defection reveals that dancers were not immune to what they called "arbitrary persecution"; it also evidences their unique power to take action. As cultural envoys, dancers had the opportunity to question policies, whether publicly like the defectors or behind the scenes as dance makers navigated their partnership with a homophobic state.

This chapter examines how dancers, who troubled narrow conceptions of revolutionary gender and sexuality, managed to continue representing Cuba abroad and shaping revolutionary culture at home. Like people in other temporal and geographic contexts, Cuban society and the state regarded dance as an effeminate activity and conflated gender expression with sexual orientation such that male dancers faced widespread presumptions about their homosexuality.[3] Furthermore, as depicted in the epigraphs by political leaders Fidel Castro and Che Guevara, homosexuals and artists both fell in a gray area, considered not enemies but also not full revolutionaries.[4] Homosexual dancers, then, were "not true revolutionaries" twice over for their sexuality and their occupation. This meant that dancers inherently deviated from ideal citizens, which Che theorized in the same essay as "new men and new women," who were hardworking, self-sacrificing, and implicitly heterosexual. However, even as dancers projected images and sometimes harbored desires that diverged from hegemonic norms, dancers stepped into the roles of revolutionary new men and women at home and abroad, as purveyors of revolutionary excellence. Because of these virtues, the homophobic state partnered with dubious dancers. In the process, dance makers suffered a lot but also got away with a lot by touring, choreographing to critique gender norms, and protecting beleaguered male dancers. Their history shows the costs and maneuvers of dancing with a homophobic revolution, as well as dancers' unique power as they leveraged international accomplishments and used their ephemeral form to stage provocations that often dodged censors.

Charting how dance makers navigated revolutionary homophobia provides fresh insights on how repression operated and how citizens responded in Cuba. This chapter shows how discrimination based on race and sexual orientation intersected, as suspected homosexuals of African descent in the folkloric company experienced more extreme repercussions than white ballet dancers, who enjoyed privileges based on race, class, and genre as discussed in chapter 3.[5] Modern dancers also had a vacillating relationship with a suspicious state, but they critiqued gender norms on stage and advocated for official respect behind the scenes. Ballet leaders meanwhile shored up official heteronormative mandates by teaching young boys to perform virile masculinity, while also redefining revolutionary new men to include militants who wore not only olive green fatigues but also tights. Dancers of different sexual orientations, then, did not wholly resist or comply with gender codes, but selectively reconfigured them through movement and discourse. As a result, the history of Cuban dancers differs from familiar narratives of hegemonic homophobia in the Americas during the Cold War because Cuban performing artists remained central to political projects.[6] So unlike other instances where homophobia silenced or sidelined gay citizens, homosexual Cuban dancers, who were not considered "true revolutionaries," continued appearing on highly public platforms at home and sometimes abroad. Without discounting the harm that the state inflicted on artists with diverse sexualities, this chapter foregrounds intentional steps that dance makers took to advance their art in an adverse climate. Toward this end, chronologically ordered actions—a 1970 tour by the folkloric company, then a 1971 modern dance work, and finally a 1973 ballet—provide entry points for each section to analyze how state repression and dancer reactions played out by genre.

My analysis relies on a fraught archive and seeks to honor the radical possibilities of gender and sexual nonconformity while respecting the privacy of the dance makers discussed. The archival materials and press examined come from a homophobic state and its proxies. Reports compile neighborhood gossip and disputed allegations about sexuality. Also limiting, the sources remain overwhelmingly concerned with male homosexuality and only occasionally mention female same-sex desire.[7] Punitive documents reveal how sexuality became an object of obsession for the government, something to document and interrogate. They do not necessarily record the actual desires and behaviors of dance makers. To my knowledge, the men and women discussed in these pages have not spoken openly about their sexual orientations, and I do not claim to know or seek to expose private lives. As a result, allegations should be interpreted as spectacles of official paranoia and prejudice, not revelations. To supplement skewed archival sources, I attend to choreography that held space for more diverse gender and sexual expressions. Dancers used their bodies to suggest alternative modes of being, resonant with the "intimate spaces of autonomy" that anthropologist Jafari Allen richly theorizes in his study of twenty-first-century Cuba.[8] However, unlike Allen's compassionate ethnography of contemporary intimacy, I focus on how dancers performed public roles that did not disclose their unknown, but presumably diverse, desires. That said, if dancers dared intimacies that the revolutionary state defamed, they should be recognized as noteworthy rebels. Some arguably resembled the protagonists in scholar Saidiya Hartman's innovative history of black women's "wayward lives, beautiful experiments," which involved resisting gendered and sexual mandates of the racist, sexist, and violent U.S. state and society in the early twentieth century.[9] In similar and distinct ways, nonconforming Cuban dancers in the 1960s and 1970s may have risked living for social change through quotidian life choices. Although dance makers of different genres endured uneven official reactions to their beautifully wayward actions, they all continued working. Using their status as valued cultural producers, they staged political reflections and provocations about gender and sexuality in revolutionary Cuba.

"As a . . . Revolutionary, I Object": Folkloric Dance on and between Tours

In September 1970, the Conjunto Folklórico Nacional (CFN) set off for the German Democratic Republic, Hungary, Czechoslovakia, Poland, and the Soviet Union, performing fifty-one times over seventy-nine days.[10] This was the company's second international tour and, according to the CFN folklore adviser Juan García, "represented a ratification of the success conquered in France, Belgium, Algiers, and Spain [in 1964] and constituted a great step forward regarding discipline and organization."[11] "Discipline" provides the only vague reference to a key issue in international travel: sexuality. The state wanted to keep homosexual artists from representing Cuba abroad and passed a law in 1971 along those lines.[12] Juxtaposing the experiences of mostly black folkloric dancers to those of mostly white ballet dancers reveals that race and class prejudice intersected with discrimination based on sexual orientation as folkloric dancers experienced greater restrictions on their travel than ballet counterparts. However, performers, regardless of their race or sexual preferences, collectively won rave reviews and the "great sympathy and enthusiasm" of audience members, as the CFN reportedly did in 1970.[13] This section examines how dance makers dealt with intersectional racism and homophobia and continued performing as dynamic new men and women, impressing international audiences even if some private lives deviated from heteronormative expectations.

Sexuality figured into behind-the-scenes discussions as the CFN prepared for its first international tour in 1964. The company had received an invitation to perform at the Théâtre des Nations in Paris, and Cuban cultural bureaucrats planned to send the CFN to Paris, Brussels, Spain, and Algeria.[14] Members of the company, however, believed that the CFN was "not prepared politically or culturally to leave the country."[15] In reality, the company was experiencing internal turmoil. During a series of meetings in March 1964, Mexican choreographer and company cofounder Rodolfo Reyes criticized director Marta Blanco for ineffective leadership; Blanco complained about factionalism and animosity among members; and folkloric adviser Rogelio Martínez Furé faulted conflicts between the directorship, cultural bureaucrats, and Reyes for the poor functioning of the company.[16] Two male members of the company also questioned a choreographer's "intimate friendships" with men. The choreographer responded, "I have made many mistakes and I have criticized myself [*me he autocriticado*] for them. I am homosexual, but I know my obligations as a worker and as a revolutionary. If that causes my expulsion, I accept it." One male member retorted, "All the revolutionary leaders were big womanizers: [nineteenth-century Cuban patriot José] Martí, [Venezuelan Simón] Bolívar and others, they really loved women."[17] Costume designer María Elena Molinet defended the choreographer by saying that no one in the company was "scientifically authorized" to discuss sexuality in relation to character. Company director Marta Blanco also called the charges unfair, "as there are homosexuals that are good revolutionaries and workers."[18] This discussion evidences that homophobia existed within company ranks. Given that two men criticized while two women defended the choreographer, homophobia was perhaps more virulent among men than women. Regardless, the critiques and rejoinders indicate that Cuban citizens in 1964 disagreed on how sexuality impacted revolutionary potential.

Despite backstage tensions, the CFN went on the international tour and earned recognition at home and abroad. Fidel Castro saw the company off at the airport and encouraged the group to bring honor to Cuba: "*¡Pongan bien alto el nombre de Cuba!*" In Algeria, President Ahmed Ben Bella attended two shows and then spent hours at a reception for the CFN at the Cuban Embassy.[19] CFN performers also impressed foreign observers by facing affronts with aplomb. In Spain, some "*gusanos*" (term for counterrevolutionary Cubans, literally meaning worms) yelled insults, threw stink bombs, and released small white rats in the theater to provoke confusion. The show went on. Spanish observers, according to an internal Cuban memo, claimed that the incident "consolidated the name and prestige of Cuba even more." Moreover, the functionary continued, the CFN offered a powerful symbol since the company of mostly black Cubans showed "the World that humble people of our *pueblo* . . . are representing Cuba and that the people previously discriminated against, the people previously without opportunity, now have the same rights in a more just society."[20] This assertion insinuated that the state instrumentalized black, lower-class CFN dancers to project an image of inclusion and justice abroad. It also evidenced how touring dancers embodied the Revolution's diverse new men and women for foreign audiences and Cuban bureaucrats alike.

Although the CFN enjoyed successes during the tour, problems like defections and infighting also arose. Three dancers defected. One internal report called the first defector a "traitor who not only betrayed his comrades, but also his religion, previously persecuted in Cuba and his race discriminated against and without opportunities, renouncing the extraordinary honor to represent Cuba abroad, with that religion and with that black race to which he belongs."[21] This statement implied the paternalistic trope of (expected) black gratefulness for ostensible white "generosity" that dates back to the time of slavery.[22] It exposed the emptiness of Castro's 1962 claim that racial discrimination no longer existed in Cuba and displayed persisting prejudices against Afro-Cuban religions that inspired folkloric productions. Along with defections and the racially charged denunciations that they elicited, the company leadership wavered. Due to irreconcilable differences, Blanco returned to Cuba mid-tour, and Rogelio Martínez Furé provisionally took charge.[23]

Then, there was a scandal involving Martínez Furé on a beach in Spain. The Spanish police found Martínez Furé and a Chilean friend "one on top of the other" and charged them with sodomy. However, they were released quickly from police custody due to a lack of evidence and Cuban intervention. An official that accompanied the CFN reported, "The next day we appeared in court . . . only paying the fees and expenses that had been caused by the matter and everything was fortunately resolved."[24] Martínez Furé vehemently denied the charges and explained to cultural bureaucrats that he had jumped into the water to help his Chilean friend, who had started to struggle while swimming. The moment Martínez Furé got him safely to the beach, the Spanish police approached and asked for their documents. Upon his return to Cuba, Martínez Furé received a message that he had lost his job and salary due to "immoral acts." He wrote an appeal to bureaucrats that insisted, "The notification and its conclusions are very unjust and as a man, Cuban, and revolutionary, I object."[25] This incident and outcome dramatize how male dance makers like Martínez Furé lived with extreme precarity under the thumb of homophobic police states that managed the globe from fascist Spain to Communist Cuba (not to mention the capitalist United States and beyond) in the 1960s. The incident also underscores how the Cuban government policed dance makers' private lives and then disciplined them accordingly.

The encounter on a Spanish beach in 1964 stopped Martínez Furé from leaving Cuba for almost two decades and resulted in an array of humiliations at home in the intervening years. For instance, he had a fuzzy relationship with the CFN until 1974. A 1965 performance program credits him with authoring libretti but does not include him in the list of company administrators.[26] Documents from 1967 and a 1968 program list Martínez Furé as the folkloric adviser of the company.[27] Then, available CFN performance programs from 1970, 1971, and 1972 do not have his name anywhere.[28] The erasure might be due not only to the 1964 incident but also to his involvement with a group of black intellectuals, who received different degrees of sanction after advocating in 1968 for an open discussion of the taboo topics of race and racism.[29] And yet, regardless of his formal relationship with the CFN, Martínez Furé continued to work in cultural production, publishing articles and translations in periodicals and advising drama companies in Havana.[30] Martínez Furé then reappears in CFN materials with a vengeance in 1974 and following years. Programs feature (or once more credit) his writing about folklore and involvement in creating dance works, especially as a librettist.[31] In preparation for a trip to socialist countries in November 1976, an administrator asked officials to consider "the case of Rogelio Martínez Furé, historian of the Conjunto . . . given that we have observed in him magnificent conduct in his work."[32] Despite this advocacy, Martínez Furé did not travel internationally until 1982. After this resumption, he left almost annually, participating in international conferences and festivals through the 1980s and 1990s.[33] The disputed incident on a Spanish beach resulted in the harsh sanction of Martínez Furé and likely factored into the state not sending the CFN abroad again until 1970.

Nevertheless, the fact that Martínez Furé continued to work in the late 1960s and early 1970s indicates that he successfully disputed allegations about his sexuality or that he had enough political and cultural capital to insulate himself from harsher punishment. For instance, no evidence suggests that he was sent to forced labor camps euphemistically called Unidades Militares de Ayuda a la Producción (Military Units to Assist Production), which the government established to "reeducate" so-called anti-socials including homosexuals from 1965 to 1968.[34] Although the government halted the camps in 1968, police continued to target individuals showing signs of nonconformity, whether behaviors like same-sex desire or physical traits like hairstyles and clothing part of global youth culture (i.e., miniskirts and short hair on girls and tight pants and long hair on boys) that supposedly showed a predilection for decadent, capitalist culture and blurred traditional gender norms. Then, during the Primer Congreso Nacional de Educación y Cultura (First National Congress of Education and Culture) in late April 1971, a commission mandated that homosexuals could not teach youth or represent Cuba abroad.[35] During this repressive period, the disgraced Martínez Furé managed to continue working, though intermittently, which attested to his relative power as a valued cultural producer.

Like Martínez Furé, the CFN still performed and even questioned sexual norms and racial ideologies onstage, while remaining Cuba-bound between 1964 and 1970. In the late 1960s, the CFN appeared in the all-black theatrical production *María Antonia*, which explored gender, sexuality, race, and class in Cuba. By Eugenio Hernández Espinosa, the play tells the story of María Antonia, a woman of African descent who loves a boxer named Julián and enchants a chemistry student named Carlos. It ends tragically with María Antonia poisoning Julián and Carlos stabbing María Antonia to death. Director Roberto Blanco described the work as depicting the "*supermacho*" and "*superhembra*" (extreme masculinity and femininity) to destroy and transcend them.[36] In 1967, Grupo Taller Dramático in collaboration with the CFN premiered *María Antonia* and drew a record twenty thousand people to eighteen performances in October.[37] However, the Afrocentric play polarized the public into defenders and detractors of its daring exploration of racism, the culture of black slums, everyday violence, female sexuality, and Cuban machismo. At the height of its success, the government suspended the work.[38] Nevertheless, the CFN appeared in seventeen performances of *María Antonia* with the Grupo Ocuje in late 1969.[39]

Dance imbued María Antonia with strength and dignity, challenging stereotypes about her gender and sexuality. A later version of *María Antonia* by Cuban filmmaker Sergio Giral provides insights into the CFN's unrecorded dances in the late 1960s. Several scenes involve ceremonies, including a powerful one at the end. In a crowded room, men and women dance together, surrounding María Antonia as she fervently moves to the music with her eyes closed. The religious event differs considerably from the adversarial interactions María Antonia has with people throughout the play. Angered wives confront her for seducing their husbands, and lovers violently use her body for their pleasure. Contrarily, as the religious community dances around her with precision and strength, the promiscuous María Antonia reaches unprecedented levels of dignity.[40] Martínez Furé aptly asserted that the "songs and dances in the midst of *María Antonia* are supreme acts of life."[41] He likely identified with the idea of creative expression as vital, given his continued art making despite official mistreatment.

To fully understand how folkloric dancers fared, it is helpful to compare their experiences with those of mostly white ballet dancers. In contrast to Martínez Furé and the folkloric dancers, who went years without touring after 1964, the BNC performed abroad almost every year despite the fact that the government suspected several ballet dancers of homosexuality. Just two years after ten male ballet dancers defected in Paris as discussed in the opening, the BNC appeared in the cultural programming before the 1968 Mexican Olympics. In a letter marked confidential, the Consejo Nacional de Cultura (National Council of Culture, CNC) director Eduardo Muzio bemoaned the timing of the trip. Cuba was in the midst of a "full revolutionary offensive . . . with the transformation of many customs of our society that are not the best for the formation of a new man." However, canceling the trip would have threatened relations with Mexico "and would have been exploited by our enemies, so we decided to administer the second alternative of eliminating the cited cases and running the risk with the cases that we sent." Bureaucrats had to contend with the international fame of dancers, whose absence could attract critical attention from outside observers. Given that calculation, Muzio worked with the Ministry of the Interior to determine which dancers seemed unlikely to cause problems in Mexico like the "treachery of the 10 that abandoned the group in Paris."[42] Dancers were divided by rank, gender, evaluation of either "positive" or "negative," and labeled as homosexual. To illustrate, three of the thirteen male dancers in the corps de ballet listed as "positive" had "homosexual" in parentheses next to their name, whereas all ten corps de ballet men listed as "negative" had "homosexual" parenthetically next to their name.[43] Ultimately, nine company members, including soloists and technical staff, were not allowed to travel. Eight dancers, a few of whom supposedly had "problems of homosexuality," went to Mexico because they had previous experience traveling abroad without incident.[44] Shortly after ten male ballet dancers caused an international scandal in Paris, most of the BNC traveled to Mexico, in striking contrast to the CFN, which remained in Cuba for six years after Martínez Furé's quiet, disputed incident on a beach.

Ballet dancers also continued to travel despite continued defections, interactions with exiles, and sexual exploits. In 1971, two "homosexual dancers" defected in Spain and Canada. On the same tour, ballerina Alicia Alonso's Miami-based sister sought her out in Montreal, which "created a serious political problem" because Alicia had instructed dancers to stay away from Cuban exiles while on tour.[45] Reports on a 1972 tour read like a paranoid gossip column, enumerating activities deemed questionable, such as dancers spending evenings with foreigners, buying material items with food per diems, and wayward sex—extramarital affairs, two different couples having sex in the same room at the same time, threesome propositions, and suspected sexual activity between two women.[46] Based on the documents analyzed, only two professional ballerinas were suspected of homosexuality, and both married men. The paucity of archival material suggests that the revolutionary state worried more about gay men and that nonconforming ballerinas often passed as straight.[47] Regardless, the careful documentation reveals that although ballet dancers were subject to invasive state surveillance in and beyond Cuba, they ultimately escaped extreme repercussions for condemned behaviors, especially compared with folkloric dancers.

In large part, ballet artists benefited from the status of BNC leaders Alicia and Fernando Alonso, who regularly challenged bureaucratic efforts to restrict any company member's travel. In preparation for the 1968 Mexican engagement, bureaucrats had "to sustain a firm position before the pressure above all from the *compañera* Alicia, who believed that the entire group should have gone to Mexico."[48] In a 1972 directive, the new CNC director Luis Pavón instructed, "Try to convince Alicia and Fernando that they [(five individuals)] should NOT leave [on the upcoming tour]. In case it causes a crisis for one/several/all of the mentioned, give them the OK to go and in-form us. Handle this situation with great tact."[49] Bureaucrats could not enact a fait accompli, but had to contend with the powerful Alonsos. Given the reality of worrisome ballet dancers abroad, bureaucrats circulated rules for travel in 1974. Mandates called for "disciplined and moral conduct according to socialist principles and watching for its fulfillment in the rest of the delegation." This meant not interacting with exiles, reporting any plan of desertion, not going in private cars or "accepting invitations for meals, outings, or parties without authorization," not accepting a contract for personal artistic work, and not speaking with the press without authorization.[50] Since ballet (unlike folkloric) dancers never ceased traveling abroad, cultural bureaucrats had to devise guidelines to try to control them.

Dancers from the folkloric and ballet companies experienced the state's homophobic aggressions. Yet, the privileges of whiteness ensured that even though the BNC had a relatively high number of dancers defect and defy state norms in their private life, the company continued to travel, albeit with regular surveillance and concessions in the form of so-called risky dance makers staying home. The CFN had members that the state presumed to be homosexual, and sexual prejudices joined with racist and classist logics to limit their movements. From 1959 to 1975, the BNC went on twelve performance tours and the CFN, six.[51]

Nevertheless, the CFN continued to work despite restrictions. The company critiqued gender norms and racial prejudice in *María Antonia* and performed applauded repertory abroad in 1970. Actions off the stage also helped to bolster their cause. Upon returning from its 1970 tour, for instance, the CFN briefly rested before working in the 1971 sugar harvest to exceed its output from the previous year.[52] By continuing to contribute to artistic and political agendas, folkloric dancers refused to allow official sanctions to define their role in Cuban culture and society. Like Martínez Furé wrote in 1964, as revolutionaries, they objected. Resonant but distinct repression and resilience also characterized the experience of modern dancers, as examined in the next section.

"Joyful Irreverence": Satirizing Sex in Modern Dances

In 1971, modern dancers prepared for the premiere of Ramiro Guerra's new work, *El decálogo del apocalipsis* (The Ten Commandments of the Apocalypse). The dark satire created a world turned upside down, based on inverted commandments. For example, the eighth scene, "The Canticle of Canticles," upended prohibitions against adultery with the antipodal commandment

"You will fornicate [*fornicarás*]." The exploration of sex included a man performing the role of "chaste José," reciting fragments of biblical verse as a group
of nymphs strip him of clothes. At first, José resists modestly, but eventually,
he comes to enjoy the undressing with "blatant delight."[53] Perhaps the nymphs
skipped and José transitioned from restrictive movements to more expansive
ones as he embraced his newfound sensual freedom. No image clarifies the
choreography of this particular scene. In fact, *Decálogo* never premiered. The
government canceled the production two weeks before opening night in the
first clear instance of censorship in revolutionary concert dance. This section
examines how modern dancers choreographed works like *Decálogo* and took
action offstage to question hegemonic ideas about gender and sexuality. The
government policed and censored modern dancers, but failed to fully erase
their provocations. A disrobed "chaste José" never appeared before a large
public but left an imprint on those who arranged and witnessed his unveiling.

Initially, modern dance accommodated official stances on revolutionary
masculinity, since Cubans reportedly viewed the technique as "less effeminate than ballet, so the boys who wanted to dance would run less of a risk [of
homosexuality]."[54] Perhaps this partially derived from the fact that a man,
Ramiro Guerra, spearheaded the movement in contrast to ballet, which remained firmly identified with ballerina Alicia Alonso. Equally, the content of
early modern dances likely bolstered this assumption. For instance, the company's premiere in 1960 featured Guerra's *Mulato* about racism in colonial
Cuba and *Mambi* about independence fighters. In both, male dancers wore
soldier uniforms or suits, performing familiar male figures from history. Later
that year, the company premiered *Suite Yoruba*, which included the Santería
orisha Changó, described in the press as "a warrior who represents the virility
of man."[55] Roles like soldiers and virile gods aligned male modern dancers
with narrow conceptions of revolutionary masculinity.

However, official concerns about modern dancers' "morality" (often a
stand-in for sexuality) undermined whatever credibility they gained by performing traditional masculinity on stage. This became evident in 1964 when
French choreographer Maurice Béjart, director of the Brussels-based Ballet
du XXe Siècle (Ballet of the Twentieth Century), chose modern dancers in
the Conjunto Nacional de Danza Moderna ("Danza" for short) to collaborate on a work celebrating the brotherhood of nations.[56] Officials collected
information on Danza members to determine whether they should travel
abroad. This resulted in thirty single sheets of paper, each with an artist's
name and short sentences about the individual. Nineteen have no date but
occasionally reference an upcoming trip to Brussels, and the other eleven

have the date September 11, 1964. The reports contain disputable claims about sexuality, as well as basic information about revolutionary affiliations and workplace attitudes.

Not all cases of suspected male homosexuality were treated the same in the 1964 investigation. High-profile company members who exhibited revolutionary fervor, had a good work ethic, and tried to hide their sexual orientation garnered reluctant acceptance from the unnamed authors compared with men who ostensibly flaunted their homosexuality. The report on choreographer Ramiro Guerra, for instance, dispassionately observed that he "supports the Revolution and cooperates with the [Committee for the Defense of the Revolution,] CDR, when it is necessary to do economic work. . . . He is 40 years old and is homosexual. On occasions he has been seen entering his apartment with unknown men."[57] The memo on Afro-Cuban soloist Eduardo Rivero details his family background:

Eduardo Rivero Walker

Resides on 58 Street #2713 between 27 and 29, Marianao, with his siblings who are integrated in the Revolution. One of his sisters is the President of the CDR. . . . Their mother can be found in the United States.

Eduardo is homosexual. He married . . . one month ago, as had been proposed by the director of the Conjunto Lorna Burdsalt [*sic*], who wanted to take him on tour, but feared he would fall back into homosexual acts.

. . . He is a hard worker and disciplined. . . .

¡Venceremos![58]

Among the other twenty-eight individuals analyzed in the same series, nine other men were labeled homosexual. Harsh language denounced one man as a "homosexual, of the type that flaunts it [*homosexual, de lo que alarde*]," by interacting with "effeminate elements" and leading "a life of few morals."[59] A report on another individual excoriated his "horrible moral conduct," evidenced by "frequent scandals" with other gay men.[60] The author severely judged men who exhibited their sexual orientation—through embodiment, whether clothes or mannerisms, and actions like conspicuous trysts—in contrast to men who tried to pass as straight.

In addition to sexuality, reports evaluated personal relationships as a reflection of an individual's character. For instance, a female dancer displayed "incorrect moral conduct," even though she reportedly supported the Revolution, because she had "gone out with different men when she was living with her previous husband."[61] A musician was politically "indifferent," drank too much, and had a son who regularly missed school and had pulled a knife on another boy, leading to the conclusion that the musician had "very low" morality.[62] Therefore, actions that undermined the traditional family—like adultery or having a misbehaving son—joined homosexuality as unacceptable to the state. These judgments were often based on observations made "by the neighborhood [*por su barrio*]," suggesting that officials interviewed neighbors, tapping into a network of "citizen spies," to use historian Lillian Guerra's term.[63] Like folkloric and ballet dancers discussed earlier, modern dancers experienced official monitoring and policing of their private lives. Although the reports did not stop modern dancers from working in Cuba, they did ultimately limit their travel abroad.

After weeks of excited preparation, a few days before the company's departure in late September 1964, the government canceled their trip. In her 2001 memoir, Burdsall, then the director of Danza, described fighting the decision: "I ran around knocking on doors and tried in vain to get in touch with other 'important' people who might be able to turn the tide of events, even my husband [Manuel Piñeiro in the Ministry of the Interior], but alas, time was against us. . . . The tactic of waiting until the last minute to cancel our trip made it impossible."[64] In a letter to her mother, Burdsall surmised, "The trip was too expensive a proposition for 36 dancers, drummers, etc. Since there were major changes in the Culture Council that's why the change of plans— the new director just put into office didn't approve the plan—the worst part was the 'axe fell' just before we got on the plane. If we had known before it wouldn't have been such a blow. Oh well, modern dancers are used to struggles and revolutionaries are used to struggles so being both we'll pull out of it fast."[65] Adding insult to injury, she reported a couple weeks later, the BNC "got to go on their trip to the Soviet Union . . . but they were lucky because they left before the restriction got too tough." This prompted her to lament, "Why does life have to be such a tragedy sometimes[?]"[66] Burdsall later learned that Alicia Alonso danced with Béjart in Brussels instead of Danza.[67] Her letters exude deep disappointment and apparent obliviousness to official concern about modern dancers' "morality."

Despite the 1964 setback, Danza did travel abroad in 1969. They performed in Hungary, Poland, Czechoslovakia, Romania, and the Soviet Union from September through November 1969.[68] On the one hand, the 1969 opportunity seems strange due to the timing and performers involved. As for timing, Cuba was in the midst of a tense moment that included a "revolutionary offensive" followed by a nationwide sugar harvest with the target of ten million tons by 1970. As for performers involved, modern dancers with ambivalent morality (according to the 1964 reports) represented Cuba abroad. On the other hand, given the destination of Socialist Bloc countries in 1969, control by Cuban handlers in partnership with local authorities was likely more complete than in capitalist Brussels, where modern dancers had planned to visit in 1964. Comparing the 1964 prohibition and 1969 allowance suggests that destination rather than "morality" or the political climate at home determined whether dancers were able to travel abroad. Regardless, it is notable that modern dancers like Guerra and Rivero traveled in 1969 despite the fact that the state believed that they were homosexual. Internal reports by Cuban officials who accompanied the modern dancers on their trip, called their behavior "magnificent" and ascertained that "due to their discipline and constant desire to work," the dancers should represent Cuba abroad again in the near future.[69] Critical acclaim and good behavior seemed to partially absolve them of previously perceived sins.

Modern dancers not only traveled abroad in 1969 but also retained a highly public platform to stage critical commentaries about gender in 1970 with Ramiro Guerra's *Impromptu galante* (Impromptu Gallant). The satire explored the biblical story of Adam and Eve with "joyful irreverence," charting how the "sinful duality" played out in "all men and women of the universe," as the sexes compete for dominance.[70] *Impromptu galante* examined "*hembrismo*," defined as coquetry, and "*machismo.*" Costuming and stage design were minimalist: bare-chested men wore leggings, and women wore unitards; they danced on an empty stage with the backdrop and wings raised and only large wooden boxes to manipulate.[71] Guerra also made the entire auditorium the stage by having dancers run through the aisles and swing on rope ladders hanging from the balconies. The fifty-minute production reportedly had the feel of an impromptu party; indeed, dancers improvised to generate ironic material. As Guerra asserted in a 1970 article, "Satire penetrates the choreography, until it is what moves everything." The combative but playful ethos comes through one moment when soloist Ernestina Quintana reclines on the back of Gerardo Lastra as two dancers perch on top of a tall wooden box to watch (see figure 4.1). Quirky give-and-take also permeated the audience's experience. "Spectators have no choice but to participate or run away," the same article contended, and those who stayed shaped the outcome. At the end of the work, one member of the public selected one of three endings— victory for women, victory for men, or a clash between the two.[72] If women won, they formed a huge "vagina" on stage (in later descriptions, Guerra leaves the mechanics of this configuration to the imagination) while the faces

FIGURE 4.1 Modern dancer Ernestina Quintana playfully perches on fellow company member Gerardo Lastra's back during a scene in Ramiro Guerra's *Impromptu galante* (1970). Photographer unknown. Source: Guerra, *Coordenadas danzarias*.

of Greta Garbo, Marlene Dietrich, Marilyn Monroe, and other sex symbols appeared on a screen behind them. If men won, they formed a "tower" (phallus) as the faces of "Rodolfo Valentino, Tyrone Power, Robert Taylor, Humphrey Bogart, and other gallants and movie stars" flashed in the background. If the discordant ending was chosen, men and women fought loudly before images of an atomic bomb explosion.[73] The possible endings refused heterosexual consummation, instead depicting harmonious homosocial groups or destructive gender conflict.

The unconventional composition and ending arguably make *Impromptu galante* a "queer dance," to use the term coined and richly explored in the volume edited by dance scholar Clare Croft. According to Croft, queer dance consists of diverse, contradictory impulses that disrupt social norms: "Queer is a wide-ranging set of notions and practices that collide: a state of conflicting, generative modes of existence. . . . By embracing a messy, heterogeneous, even possibly contradictory queer, dance forges community, not in spite of, but through and with challenges and contradictions."[74] I interpret Guerra's *Impromptu galante* as a queer dance, applying a label that did not exist in 1970 and that he might have continued rejecting.[75] Although Guerra never declared a transgressive intent, nor did reviews indicate that the audience picked up on such meanings, the dance invites an alternative reading. For instance, Guerra projected iconic actors believed to have had same-sex relationships as well as heterosexual ones, like Greta Garbo, Marlene Dietrich, and Rodolfo Valentino.[76] Even more boldly, the piece posited that same-sex relationships offered a peaceful alternative to explosive heterosexual confrontation. As dancers ran through the auditorium or invited audience participation, they defied theatrical (perhaps as a signifier of social) norms that confine performers to the proscenium stage (and heteronormative gender roles). This cultivated unexpected community with onlookers "through and with challenges and contradictions," as Croft outlines. The queer valences of *Impromptu galante* suggest the possibility that the stage offered a space for questioning heteronormativity and celebrating nonconformity in Cuba during a repressive period.[77]

Continuing this inquiry, Guerra's next work, *El decálogo del apocalipsis*, was a "satirical mystery" that questioned biblical teachings and precepts about sex. The work had ten scenes with four of them dealing most conspicuously with sexuality. One inspired by the parable of the prodigal son had a huge male/female doll that represented a parental figure. Dancers who personified children attacked the dad/mom doll with props shaped like genitals. In a scene alluding to the Tower of Babel, dancers climbed a large metal structure and yelled out sexually charged obscenities in different languages. A vignette based on the parable of ten virgins featured women in extravagant clothes, who were guided by the Whore of Babylon and encountered the seven-headed beast in Revelation. In a scene inspired by the Canticle of Canticles, dancers in flesh-colored costumes with flowers painted over their genitals staged four episodes: first, a black man and a white woman danced erotically in a "prelude and peep show"; second, nymphs stripped "chaste José" as discussed above; third, dancers manipulated objects in a "phallic configuration"; and fourth, dancers in duets, trios, and quartets eventually formed a mass of "confused bodies" that alluded to an orgiastic encounter.[78] In later discussions of the work, Guerra never clarifies the movements further, so we can only imagine the interracial duet, disrobing, dancing with phalluses, and mass of bodies touching suggestively.

Along with provocative narrative elements, the two-hour production featured unconventional use of space, sound, and audience engagement. Parts of the piece took place in the gardens, stairs, and vestibules around the Teatro Nacional de Cuba (TNC). Performers also sang and spoke as they relocated, and audience members followed them around. For the erotic Canticle of Canticles, the audience watched voyeuristically while standing on stairs leading down to the lobby of the Sala Covarrubias, located several meters below ground level, where the dancers performed the scene. This made the public an active part of the exploration of sex, violence, and social turmoil. Residents in the neighborhood near the TNC, known as La Timba, provided an attentive audience during the year and a half it took to rehearse the piece.[79]

I interpret *Decálogo*, like *Impromptu galante*, as a queer dance. According to Croft, "Queer performance becomes a kind of pedagogy, teaching someone what it might look like or feel like to refuse norms, particularly those related to gender and sexuality."[80] *Decálogo* taught this lesson by representing the psychedelic sixties' rejection of moral codes. According to Guerra, the work offered "reflection, not moralizing or didactic, but documentary and observant while critical in its ironic mockery." Additionally, it reflected on how in parts of the world, "marginal groups like hippies and gays established genres and systems of living ... that until then were not considered possible in any society."[81] The Canticle of Canticles focused on the sexual permissibility of the era. "Chaste José" went from covering up and reciting biblical verse to uncovering and reveling in new freedom; in other words, he came out of a metaphoric closet. Although Guerra never explicitly stated this, the choreographer did reveal that the scene "implied flashes of a '*gay* aesthetic'" (italicized English term in the original), perhaps the hiding of one's true self and then reveling in dropped façades.[82] Other parts of the production also encouraged audience members to reflect on sexuality. For instance, dancers enacted architectural choreography by using their bodies to create a tower (phallus) reminiscent of the soaring José Martí memorial in the nearby Plaza of the Revolution.[83] The juxtaposition perhaps mocked the defensive hypermasculinity of the Revolution. Regardless, the provocative scenes constructed no overt narrative, leaving viewers to piece together (queer) lessons from the open but charged material.

The inexplicit, suggestive choreography also made the work seem dangerous to the regime. Two weeks before the premiere on April 15, 1971, the government canceled the widely advertised *Decálogo*. Ironically, the open rehearsal format allowed the production to enjoy a limited audience before the state had a chance to intervene. Scandalized audience members also may have informed bureaucrats of its content. According to Burdsall in her 2001 memoir, "During the course of rehearsals, word spread that there were pornographic elements and phallic symbols flying. . . . All of this was just too much for some of the pseudo-puritanical 'cultured' bureaucrats."[84] The cancellation happened in the immediate lead up to the Primer Congreso Nacional de Educación y Cultura in late April 1971. During the congress, Comisión 6 Medios Masivos de la Comunicación (Commission 6 Mass Media of Communication) covered "pornography in Cuban art" and mentioned Guerra's *Decálogo*.[85] This dispute compelled Guerra to leave the company permanently. For the next seven years, he choreographed nothing. Accounts remain vague about whether this was mandated, a personal choice, or some combination of the two. During a 2014 interview, he preemptively stated that he would not discuss *Decálogo* with me. The silence speaks volumes. The topic remained a sensitive one and potentially problematic to discuss with an outsider, especially from the imperialistic United States.[86] Following the fiasco, Guerra devoted himself to researching and writing about dance. As Burdsall explained in a 1972 letter to her mother, "Ramiro is no longer with us—he decided to dedicate himself to translating dance books."[87] Although separated from what had been his life's work, Guerra considered himself lucky. He continued to receive his salary during the dark moment.[88]

After Guerra left, Danza persisted but faced an uncertain future due to official sanction and proposals made by ballet leaders. In late 1972, Burdsall confided in her mother:

> The ballet is desperate for modern works & wants us to fuse with them. This would be the *end* of mod[ern] dance in Cuba since Fernando & Alicia never respected mod[ern] dance. They only want some black dancers & some mod[ern] works to build up their company. I just spent a week writing a paper on modern dance, its ideology, concepts, and 12 years of mod[ern] dance in Cuba; it will go to everybody important & let's see what the outcome is. . . . Mod[ern] dance . . . gets invitations to Canada, Italy, Switzerland, Belgium but we never get to go! Ballet gets sent instead.[89] (Underlined in source.)

To Burdsall, the Alonsos' proposal and the fact that modern dancers rarely traveled pointed to a larger underappreciation of the genre. It also reflected a decade of tension as the integrated modern dance company struggled to gain the same kind of state support that the mostly white ballet company enjoyed. Burdsall sent her "paper on modern dance" to CNC director Luis Pavón and requested a meeting to discuss its contents.[90]

In the document, Burdsall protested years of mistreatment by the CNC and demanded resolution to these failings. When the CNC took charge in 1962, modern dancers "had the first impressions of a lack of support." Even students noticed lukewarm official backing. According to Burdsall, "The fact that the Conjunto de Danza Moderna had little support and prestige has made the work of the teachers at the Escuela Nacional de Danza Moderna very difficult," because students "lacked motivation and reason for choosing this art as a career."[91] Evidencing this disaffection, matriculation rates dropped from thirty-seven new students in 1966–67 to twenty-nine in 1969–70, twenty-four in 1970–71, and eleven in 1971–72 before rebounding for the next decade and a half.[92] Burdsall also objected to the labeling of *Decálogo* as pornography during the 1971 congress:

> The act of criticizing the work before the participants of the Commission VI, and arriving at a generalized opinion about the Conjunto without deeply analyzing the labors and works that had been realized since the beginning or having someone of modern dance present to defend the national line of the said group, was in our opinion a great mistake and an injustice. The result was the implementation of an extremist policy, eliminating from the repertory all the works of the choreographer of the work in question. In the recent months, the company has changed director five times and only one of them formed a council [of artistic advisers]—the others simply imposed artistic criteria without adequate knowledge of modern dance and did not ask those of us who had some experience, [for] our cooperation.

This instability affected the "discipline and morale of the members," and Burdsall went on to suggest how the CNC could improve the situation.[93] Her position as the wife of the powerful Manuel Piñeiro likely gave her the political capital to so boldly rebuke the CNC.

Prominent cultural bureaucrat Armando Quesada penned a reaction to Burdsall's report. His words provide insight into how officialdom viewed and dealt with valuable homosexual dance makers. Skirting accountability, Quesada called Burdsall's memo a "biased analysis" that blamed the CNC rather than internal problems and "unresolved contradictions without solution between the Ballet Nacional and the Conjunto de Danza Moderna, while its main ideologues survive." He believed nonetheless that modern dance and ballet "should be fully developed, without trying to eliminate one for the other." About Danza and its future, he wrote, "Currently, the Conjunto de Danza Moderna is at its best moment after the departure of Ramiro Guerra. Furthermore I ask permission to incorporate Ramiro Guerra as choreographer of the Conjunto[;] authorizing him would end the contradictions and complaints of Lorna, because in the end it is what she wants. Doing that we will be able to stabilize and neutralize. After all there are other homosexuals that work with less talent and even more problems than Ramiro Guerra."[94] In this revealing final statement, Quesada demonstrated the cultural bureaucracy's approach to talented "homosexuals"—they were allowed to work when causing few "problems" and politically beneficial (neutralizing Burdsall's complaints).

Although the CNC never reinstated Guerra in Danza, perhaps because he refused the offer, conditions improved for the company soon after Burdsall's report, as illustrated in letters to her family. In February 1973, she had accepted the position of artistic director: "As they have been asking me since last year but since there was a general director who would have been above me that I didn't like, I didn't accept. Now we have a new general director whom I like & so I accepted."[95] In March 1973, Danza performed for a Peruvian delegation, and Fidel Castro was at their performance for the first time in the company's history. He congratulated the dancers after the performance, which left everybody in the company "floating on air."[96] In October of that year, she happily reported, "The Conjunto is on the up & up & we have all kinds of ambitious plans this year."[97] In January 1974, Burdsall wrote, "We have had good audiences, lots of publicity, etc. The result of all this is that modern dance is finally come into the Love! The film institute will film *two* of our dances in March in color. This will be hard work but worth the effort. Especially if we could win some money to spend on leotards and tights which are always badly needed" (underlined in source).[98] And then in April, she asserted, "Modern dance has finally been 'discovered' and we are at last coming into the fore. . . . In October we celebrate our fifteen[th] anniversary and will perform 15 of our best works. There is also talk of tours to Europe, etc. but that I refuse to believe until it happens. Although this time things are different and I doubt if something like the Brussels trip will repeat itself."[99] As Burdsall hesitantly presumed, circumstances had changed since 1964. The company's recuperation in 1973 and 1974 evidences the power of Burdsall's backstage advocacy and nuances understandings of the early 1970s, known as the *quinquenio gris* (gray five years), a dark period of repression and limited creation in Cuba. Although modern dancers experienced harsh aggression on the part of a homophobic state, they also continued creating and found unprecedented support in the span of a few years.[100] In 1973 or 1974, at the time of this ascent, modern dancers also posed for photographs that inspired commemorative posters (discussed in the introduction to this book), signaling their recently consolidated revolutionary prestige.

Modern dance developments from the failed 1964 tour through the failed 1971 premiere and its aftermath show how the state undeniably harmed modern dance without halting the movement completely. Although the government believed leading modern dancers like the white Ramiro Guerra and African-descended Eduardo Rivero were homosexuals, Danza toured abroad in 1969 and staged bold critiques of gender and sexual norms in *Impromptu galante* (1970). Modern dancers eventually crashed into restrictions when censors canceled the premiere of *Decálogo* in 1971. Guerra later contended that this resulted in "almost twenty years of cultural delay in this art."[101] Indeed, Guerra's exit from the company was so disorienting that dancer Luz María Collazo considered leaving. However, she ultimately stayed. As she later explained, although "Ramiro already was not there, he had formed me, so I should defend what he had created, should defend my truth."[102] Taking ownership over the previous decade, dancers kept performing to honor Guerra's legacy. As modern dancers posed for commemorative posters in the early 1970s, their defiant postures encapsulated their determination to defend modern dance and their "truth," to use Collazo's term. Appearing on Cuban and international stages allowed them to keep alive and build upon innovations like the outing of "chaste José" in Guerra's disrupted *Décalogo*. The state temporarily circumscribed who witnessed Danza's queer dances without eliminating the impact of their choreographic legacies.

"Virile" Men and "Utterly Feminine" Women: Creating a Cuban School of Ballet

In 1973, ballet dancer Orlando Salgado sat propped up by one arm with his back erect and legs slightly bent in front of him on a darkened stage. The single spotlight accentuated muscular contours in his arms, chest, back, and legs, all on full display in his minimal costume of slight red briefs. The svelte figure opened the ballet *Canto vital* (Vital Song, 1973), which, "from the choreographic point of view . . . [explored] the expressive possibilities of masculine dance."[103] The ballet starred four young Cuban male dancers: Salgado, Jorge Esquivel, Andrés Williams, and Lázaro Carreño. They were products of the so-called Cuban school of ballet, that is, the unique approach to ballet that developed on the island in which men and women performed gender difference and heterosexuality. Developing these polarities was a defensive tactic. It helped convince homophobic officials and audiences that male ballet dancers were athletic, muscular men who upheld revolutionary gender norms. However, as this section concludes, heteronormative dictates ultimately failed to control how audiences read the new men and women formed by the Cuban school of ballet.

Cuban ballet leaders worked to mold a new generation of dancers in a revamped system of revolutionary academies, starting with the Academia Municipal de Ballet de la Habana (Municipal Academy of Ballet in Havana). Law

742, passed on March 13, 1961, nationalized the school in keeping with the government's "primordial interest" in culture and vocational training, as well as the "interest and aptitudes of the people of Cuba to dance in all its manifestations."[104] In July 1961, over nine hundred children auditioned for two hundred and fifty scholarships, which covered transportation, meals, shoes, dance clothing, academic courses, and dance training.[105] In return, "dance artists and citizens . . . can put their professional capacities to the service of the Country. Consequently, the teaching will mobilize around this dual focus . . . the aesthetic education of children and the integration of their civic consciousness," a foundational school document explained. This included, it continued, "the happy sacrifice of personal egos when collective work requires it."[106] The first year was a conditional one, asserted article 7 of the school's bylaws. To continue, students had to possess physical ability, discipline, and "other essential characteristics indispensable to the profession."[107] As Cuban children of different racial and class backgrounds started free ballet training, they entered the state's fold as beholden young artists and were inculcated with revolutionary values, including heteronormativity.

Recruiting boys to join this effort was an uphill battle. Dance leaders had to overcome familial resistance based on "erroneous prejudices of some families," stemming from homophobia and assumptions about the effeminacy of ballet.[108] The Academia Municipal de Ballet planned to produce "a lot of publicity [*propaganda*] and a curriculum that, in terms of men, presents dance as what it is and should be, besides an art, a way to achieve the totality of masculine physicality, the development of strength as well as grace and elegance, and a supreme aesthetic expression of *virility*" (underlined in source).[109] To ensure that boys developed a virile movement quality, the school's bylaws stipulated that male students take technique classes "separated from the girls so that they do not imitate their gestures."[110] The school also had boys take classes in "gymnastics and sports, which provides a virile stamp . . . converting them into responsible men of their artistic profession."[111] The obsession with virility suggests a fear that homosexuals would penetrate the ballet establishment. Young boys were trained to combat this threat to balletic ranks.

To bolster the cause, ballet leaders resorted to drastic recruitment methods. Ballerina Aurora Bosch joked about "kidnapping" the brothers of female auditionees by promising gymnastics, fencing, and weightlifting classes, rather than dance.[112] The Cuban ballet also overcame familial resistance by recruiting boys from orphanages. For centuries in different parts of the world, governments had enlisted orphan boys in state projects as soldiers, sailors, or colonial settlers. Russia began channeling orphans into dance

when the Moscow Orphanage began offering ballet classes in 1773, and outstanding students joined the Bolshoi Ballet in 1794.[113] In the 1960s, Cubans
auditioned male orphans, never citing any precedent or contemporary as inspiration. Ballet teachers had the boys do exercises from gymnastics, fencing,
and boxing to determine their physical capabilities.[114] A 1961 memo on the
Havana orphanage Hogar Granma listed sixteen ballet scholarship recipients,
including Jorge Esquivel Estrada, who would later premiere in *Canto vital* and
become the first Cuban-trained male partner to Alicia Alonso.[115]

Selected boys joined an extended ballet family. Housed in the nice Havana neighborhood of Miramar, the scholarship students were taken to
movies, concerts, and dance performances to further their "cultural formation." Dance training helped with discipline, according to teacher Joaquín
Banegas, who described making an unruly orphan his assistant, "to illustrate
the positions of the arms. The boy, with rare talent, captured and assimilated
the most difficult combinations and each day his uncommon poise and elegance became more notable. . . . The restless character was none other than
Jorge Esquivel, today the most outstanding male figure of Cuban ballet."[116] In
this anecdote, ballet redirected children like Esquivel toward an auspicious path
of productivity, purpose, and ability to contribute to revolutionary society.

Along with instilling discipline, the ballet establishment adopted young
boys to monitor their gender and sexual development. Cuban architect Ricardo Porro claimed decades later that ballet teachers "began recruiting students among the *guajiros* [peasants] in the countryside, or in orphanages . . .
to ensure that they were uncontaminated by the virus of homosexuality."[117]
This adhered to Cuban medical theory at the time, which held that environment, family, and upbringing shaped sexuality.[118] Moreover, this reflected
post-1959 idolization of *guajiros* as "authentic Cubans," who most reliably
supported Fidel and his revolutionary movement during the guerrilla war.[119]
Recruiting *guajiros*, arguably the truest revolutionaries, to dance perhaps
aimed to undercut the "original sin" (to use Che's phrase in the epigraph) associated with artists. Regardless, ballet leaders intervened at an early age and
formed children according to the values and priorities of the field. The inter-
ventionist state and ballet family (sometimes metaphoric and sometimes real
like the Alonso clan) carefully policed gender and sexuality within balletic
ranks to corroborate heteronormative standards of Cuban society.

Ballet boys had redemptive potential, according to observers. One article
enthused, "The Socialist Revolution has challenged myths and many prejudices that existed previously in Cuba. One of them made families stop their
sons from starting to study dance at a young age. Today, all children with

FIGURE 4.2 Boys in ballet class exude discipline and general dance (and battle) readiness. Photograph by Osvaldo Salas. Source: *Mujeres* 4, no. 8 (August 1964), 79. Courtesy of the Cuban Heritage Collection, University of Miami Libraries, Coral Gables, Florida.

vocation and aptitude study ballet."[120] Another journalist suggested that talented male students would undermine old prejudices by learning "the essential qualities to contribute to the technical, spiritual, and moral development of the new society." In the accompanying photo, boys exude discipline. Uniform in clothing and pose, muscles flexed, and organized in straight lines, they appear ready to charge (see figure 4.2).[121] Dance teachers ostensibly revolutionized instruction to cultivate masculinity within ballet, thereby solving long-standing prejudices. Such efforts, however, reaffirmed rather than eradicated narrow mandates about gender and sexuality.

Although never stated, the ballet establishment seemed to be creating a new generation of virile ballet boys who would avoid the state policing experienced by professional male dancers in the mid-1960s. Police arrested ballet dancer Julio Medina, for instance, with the intention of incarcerating him. His friend informed Alicia, and she "came in person as soon as she could and that is what saved [him]."[122] She also intervened discreetly, making phone calls to defend other dancers.[123] The precarious situation compelled ten male ballet dancers, including Medina, to defect in Paris in 1966. Those who remained had something of a safe haven in the ballet. As one disgruntled ballerina conceded in 1969, "Homosexuals . . . take refuge in the ballet because they have always been well received by Alicia and Fernando who have been their protectors (above all the former) and all of them including those that stayed in Paris say so."[124] Alfredo Guevara, director of the Instituto Cubano del Arte e Industria Cinematográficos (Cuban Institute of Cinematographic Art and Industry), confirmed that the police "could not touch anyone," that is, homosexual artists, in the ballet company because Alicia had the power to protect her own.[125] Along with intervening to mitigate state policing, Alicia and her colleagues worked to create future heteronormative male dancers who ideally would not have these problems by being widely regarded as ideal new men.

Despite this campaign, parents remained wary of ballet for their sons, especially in the provinces. Ballet schools in the eastern cities of Santiago and Holguín only had a few male students, one *Bohemia* article noted, but teachers remained hopeful that this problem would go away with the "education of our audience [and] the liquidation of remnants of the past."[126] While parents avoided enrolling sons in ballet, Cuban mothers reportedly adored "the ethereal figure of the ballerina," and "almost all young girls dream of being a ballerina."[127] Mothers dreaming of ballerina daughters, young girls aspiring to dance, and boys remaining outside of oneiric frameworks were not unique to Cuba.[128] Nevertheless, Cuban dance leaders characterized the gender gap as an indicator of backwardness. As Fernando said in an interview with a visiting U.S. journalist, "In some of the more undeveloped regions there is still objection to dance as a profession for boys. But it can be overcome." Fernando went on to claim that the island boasted between three and four thousand ballet students, a third of whom were boys.[129] Despite his hopeful projection to a foreign observer, six years later a ballet teacher in Santa Clara bemoaned, "Many boys demonstrate aptitude, but encounter disapproval from their parents. We talk to them, but unfortunately, old beliefs about dancers still exist that inhibit our work."[130] Widespread presumptions that ballet was a feminine activity, tendencies to conflate gender nonconformity and sexual orientation, and homophobia persisted.

Fears about the link between ballet and homosexuality also bedeviled the Escuela Nacional de Arte (National Art School, ENA), where students from the municipal ballet academy went for upper-level instruction. Built on the grounds of a former country club in the luxurious Cubanacán neighborhood of Havana, ENA symbolized how the new government prioritized art, rather than elite capitalists.[131] Despite these utopian intentions, a former ENA student, ballerina Caridad Martínez, recalled her friends' heart-wrenching expulsion for suspected homosexuality.[132] Mandatory *autocrítica* (self-criticism) sessions publicly denounced students for homosexual tendencies along with other purported sins. Mexican-born dancer Alma Guillermoprieto and U.S.-born Muriel Manings were guest teachers at ENA in 1970, and both describe attending an *autocrítica* session. According to Guillermoprieto, a male modern dance student wanted to take ballet classes to improve his technique, which led to the accusation that such a request evidenced homosexuality.[133] In her journal, Manings recorded that students were "accused of 'liberal tendencies' in relation to their criticism of curriculum, . . . their companions outside, homosexual attitudes or religious attitudes. Each student's marks were recited & criticism of work in all areas discussed by both admin[istrators], faculty & students. Some of the reactions were very emotional (when areas of a personal nature [were] discussed)."[134] Like professional dancers, students endured wide-ranging surveillance and critique as authorities publicly humiliated them for behaviors like their desire to cross-train in ballet, friendships, religions, and academic performance. However, unlike professional counterparts, ENA students were kids. Their justifiably emotional reactions evidenced the adolescent trauma part of dancing with the Revolution.

Ballet, then, had to be a robust physical activity to prove its revolutionary capacity, a mandate that some believed was still unfulfilled. Carlos Rafael Rodríguez, a longtime Cuban Communist and political leader, gave a speech at ENA and suggested that masculine dancers had yet to become widely accepted: "We believe that masculinity is compatible with the profession of the dancer and vice versa; and we believe that here in this school is the source . . . of dancers of the future, of dancers free of those manifestations, free of those vices. . . . I want to say that in the future all youth will be revolutionary, energetic, cutters of cane, and dancers."[135] His statement about "dancers of the future" free of homosexual "vices" sounds like a threat. Male dancers could and must be revolutionary (i.e., exhibit traditional masculinity and heterosexuality), but had yet to arrive fully at such ideals.

Overcoming considerable obstacles, the ballet establishment produced the first generation of professional male ballet dancers trained in revolutionary institutions. Dancers like Esquivel, Salgado, Carreño, and Williams graduated from ENA and joined the BNC in the late 1960s. In 1973, Azari Plisetski, a Soviet choreographer and Alicia's dance partner since 1963, decided to choreograph a work that celebrated this new generation of male talent. The outcome was *Canto vital*, which premiered in Havana on March 1, 1973.[136]

The fifteen-minute piece to music by Gustav Mahler featured four men in briefs of different solid colors performing choreography that put the power and bravado of Cuban male dancers on full display. The protagonist in red

FIGURE 4.3 Azari Plisetski's *Canto vital* (1973) celebrated the new generation of hypermasculine male dancers of the Cuban school of ballet. The original cast members pictured are (*standing from left to right*) Lázaro Carreño, Orlando Salgado, and Andrés Williams with Jorge Esquivel on the ground in front. Photographer unknown. Source: Museo Nacional de la Danza. Courtesy of the Museo Nacional de la Danza.

represented Man, and the other three male figures personified elements of nature: beasts of the earth, birds of the sky, and fish of the sea.[137] The man in red begins seated in a spotlight on a darkened stage. Flexing his muscles and stretching, he moves to the side and watches as the other three men enter in turn. The choreography is athletic with explosive jumps, runs, dives to the floor, powerful kicks, and lifts. The music and choreography remain light and vigorous. Each man has a solo, showing off his vital strengths. To a lilting section of music, urgent and pensive, the man in red dances and then has duets with each figure, in which they mimic each other's movements in accord and competition. The flurry of action culminates with the protagonist on the floor and his peer in blue standing on his chest, holding with angular, wing-like arms to the shoulders of the men in green and yellow on either side of him. They disassemble, the man in red rises, and the other three men make a platform with their bodies for him to climb. After the triumphant ascension, the four men dance together and end in a tableau that suggests harmony between man and nature (or harmony between men), as captured in figure 4.3.[138]

The feminine counterpart to *Canto vital* was Cuban choreographer Alberto Méndez's *Tarde en la siesta* (Afternoon Siesta), which also premiered on March 1, 1973. Like *Canto vital*, the work featured four dancers of the same sex, but in this case they were all women—Mirta Plá, Marta García, María Elena Llorente, and Ofelia González. Set in 1900 Havana, a "gray" era for women, four sisters with the revealing names of Consuelo (Solace), Soledad (Loneliness), Dulce (Sweetness), and Esperanza (Hope) "debate in their idle and conformist environment."[139] They each wear long, white dresses designed to reflect their different ages and personalities. The soft white costumes and delicate choreography to piano music by Cuban composer Ernesto Lecuona help convey the atmosphere of a sleepy afternoon. The women often spend breathless moments suspended on the tips of their toes with their legs extended, whether behind, in front, or to the side, as though reaching beyond what their patriarchal world allowed. Esperanza deferentially waltzes side to side in her solo, while Dulce exudes a subtle sensuality upon taking center stage in a deep lunge with her head thrown back. Gestures accentuate emotions: Soledad's hand over her pining heart, Consuelo's protective hold on young Esperanza's shoulders, or sweet embraces between sisters.[140] In sharp contrast to the muscular *Canto vital*, *Tarde en la siesta* creates a world of affect, characteristic of traditional feminine qualities. Juxtaposed on the same program, the works epitomized the gender dipoles created by the Cuban school of ballet, which New York dance critic Walter Terry described thusly: "Cuban men are *macho*, that is, they wear their virility like a cloak of honor. . . . The distaff side of the Ballet Nacional is utterly feminine."[141] The ballerinas of *Tarde en la siesta* performed the "utterly feminine" ideal of a bygone era that informed the gender roles of revolutionary new men and women formed by the Cuban school of ballet.

Even though *Canto vital* celebrated powerful male dancers, the work also featured homoerotic choreography as sweating, scantily clad men touched and interacted on stage. It is unlikely that Plisetski intended, or that most contemporary observers perceived, queer valences. The athletic choreography and story about man prevailing over nature did, after all, celebrate traditional notions of male strength and dominance. Moreover, the longevity of the work suggests that contemporary observers did not see homoeroticism. *Canto vital* became a regular part of the repertory and a tribute to the Cuban male ballet dancer, known for his hypermasculine style. However, reading *Canto vital* as a queer dance that contradictorily forged community brings out elements in the choreography, archive, and context of closeted homosexual dancers and audience members that were arguably there but never acknowledged.[142]

It is possible that sexual subtexts appeared only to those looking for them. Dance scholar Jennifer Campbell has shown, for instance, how Depression-era New York ballets included elements of gay subculture, homoerotic costuming, and manly, though campy, same-sex partnering that some audience members may have recognized as referencing homosexual behavior.[143] A letter written by Fernando Alonso on May 15, 1973, a few months after the premiere of *Canto vital*, corroborates this possibility. He complained about a small public at recent performances, and more emphatically and rudely, "*always a fixed group of ~~people~~ fags* [*maricones* (written in pencil above the crossed out word)] *that never leaves*" (underlined in source).[144] Scholars have noted the popularity of ballet among homosexual male audiences in Europe and the United States, and it appears the same may have been true of post-1959 Cuba.[145] Whether or not intended, the hypermasculine new men in *Canto vital* seemed to foster queer pleasure among a group of devoted, presumably gay, audience members.

Even though ballet leaders adhered to revolutionary gender and sexual norms, audience members could use performances to embrace feelings and identities decried by officialdom. The Cuban school of ballet produced men who wore "their virility like a cloak of honor," as Terry put it.[146] They trained in the shadow of state policing and performed virile new men regardless of their sexual orientations. The muscular *Canto vital* was at once homage to traditional masculinity and arguably a vector for homosexual desire. This paradoxical coexistence shows the transgressive potential of dance in revolutionary Cuba. Choreography developed in a homophobic context gave some citizens a chance to enjoy unadorned male bodies in motion.

Conclusion

Although the revolutionary state's homophobia has long been recognized, focusing on concert dance provides new insights on how repression worked. Discrimination based on sexual orientation intersected with racial prejudice, as an allegedly gay, black folkloric dance maker and his colleagues experienced more sanction than predominantly white ballet dancers. Moreover, homosexual repression went beyond state agents, as company members monitored the sexual behaviors of colleagues and subordinates. For instance, male folkloric dancers criticized a homosexual choreographer in 1964; modern dance leader Lorna Burdsall encouraged Eduardo Rivero to marry to counteract homosexual tendencies; and Alicia and Fernando Alonso developed a new and supposedly improved generation of virile male ballet dancers.

Simultaneously, dance leaders resisted state aggressions against their own, whether Alicia fighting to include homosexual dancers on tour or Burdsall taking CNC director Pavón to task for censoring Guerra's *Decálogo*. Bureaucrats vacillated, at times cracking down by canceling the 1964 modern dance tour to Brussels, and at others, relenting by allowing some "negative" ballet dancers to perform in Mexico in 1968. As bureaucratic correspondence about dancers reveals, dealing with homosexual artists meant weighing political risks and benefits. If barring high-profile ballet dancers from Mexico could attract negative attention, bureaucrats allowed them to perform before the Olympics. If Guerra's *Decálogo* struck someone as pornography before an important international cultural conference, officials shut it down. Taken collectively, negotiations between bureaucrats and dance makers around issues of gender and sexuality provide a much more complex picture of the homophobic Cuban state in the late 1960s and the repressive *quinquenio gris* of the early 1970s. The government could not summarily incarcerate or silence homosexual dance makers because they were too valuable to promoting revolutionary culture.

Along with how repression worked, this chapter shows how dancers responded, and in doing so, displayed their capacity to challenge narrow conceptions of new men and women. Rogelio Martínez Furé objected to sanctions against him, "as a . . . revolutionary" in a strongly worded 1964 letter. Burdsall affirmed modern dancers' status as revolutionaries in shaking off the 1964 derailed tour and in demanding better treatment after the 1971 censorship. Homophobic leaders even seemed to recognize dancers' revolutionary significance, given that the government did not send suspected homosexual dance makers to rural labor camps while carting off countless citizens from 1965 to 1968. Even though dubious dance makers experienced humiliations like restrictions to their travel, sidelining within the companies that they founded, and in at least one case, censorship, they continued working at home and sometimes abroad, enjoying some insulation from the worst possible fates due to their political and cultural capital. Thus, even though Castro and Che left out homosexuals and artists from the category of "true revolutionary," they hardly had the final say. Through choreography and advocacy, dance makers reframed the construct to include dancers with diverse desires. Regardless of private lives, the projected message was the same: dancers were revolutionaries tried and true.

Dance makers' unique power within Cuba was on full display in choreography that questioned gender norms and held space for sexual nonconformity. From the tragedy of *María Antonia* to the satire of *Impromtu galante*, performers explored the often-destructive consequences of traditional masculinity and femininity. Additionally, dance makers intentionally or unintentionally created work that reflected on homosexuality or appealed to gay viewers. In *Decálogo*, Guerra later explained that "chaste José" represented a "*gay* aesthetic," as the figure came out of his clothing (a figurative closet) to embrace his sexuality. In *Canto vital*, homosexual ballet fans watched stunning male dancers touch in a paean to male fraternity. The state recognized the transgressive power of *María Antonia* and *Decálogo* and suspended the productions, while *Impromptu galante* and *Canto vital* dodged censorship despite queer valences. Both censorship and permission exhibited the power of dance to express politics. Its nonverbal ephemerality at times provoked state repression, and at others, thwarted efforts to contain it.

Even though professional dancers and the government tussled over gender and sexuality, they found common ground when it came to building a mass public of dance artists and connoisseurs. Starting in the 1960s and accelerating in the 1970s, the government wanted to develop an enlightened citizenry that embodied socialist equality by having the time and means to create art, a pastime previously reserved for the privileged few. Dance leaders equally wanted to firmly integrate concert dance into the daily lives of Cubans to secure a place for their art in revolutionary culture. A large, diverse public also promised to attenuate the presence of homosexual male audience members. For instance, in the same 1973 report about gay fans cited earlier, Fernando advocated for "the mass diffusion of the art that we represent."[147] He hoped to make citizens of different backgrounds and behaviors into ballet enthusiasts. The campaign to make ballet, and concert dance more broadly, into a mass entertainment derived from revolutionary ideals about artistic democracy, as well as revolutionary patriarchy with its affiliated homophobia. To these initiatives, with their soaring aspirations and curious complications, the next chapter turns.

CHAPTER FIVE

Dancing Public

We in the field of culture have to widely promote the participation of
the masses ... [so] that cultural creation is the work of the masses and
enjoyment for the masses.

Art is a weapon of the Revolution. ... The condition of the intellectual
does not grant any privilege. Their responsibility is to contribute ...
with the *pueblo* and within the *pueblo*.
—First National Congress of Education and Culture, 1971

After official statements including those in the epigraph, a performance by
young folkloric dancers closed the April 1971 Primer Congreso Nacional de
Educación y Cultura (First National Congress of Education and Culture).
Perhaps the dancers staged the aggressive Palo, playfully flirtatious Yuka, or
lively Makuta from the Congo series that they rehearsed for a journalist reporting on the recent showing. Unquestionably, they impressed congress attendees, who buzzed with questions: "Who were those kids that so skillfully
performed the folkloric dance? How is it possible that students ... could offer an artistic program of such varied nuances? Where did they come from,
what was their preparation, and how did they reach that level of achievement?"[1] The dancers were students at the Vento Vocational School, a model
for Cuba's prestigious Lenin School and approximately six hundred other
secondary schools built in the countryside in the 1970s. Vento students received a rigorous technical and scientific education, as well as instruction in
the arts.[2] As Vento *aficionados* (literally translates to "amateurs") took the
stage offered by the state and danced for discerning audiences, they evidenced the existence of a dancing public, meaning a public for concert dance
with members who perform themselves.

Creating a dancing public, wherein concert dance became "the work of
the masses and enjoyment for the masses," involved the dual objectives of
teaching Cubans to dance and to watch dance in the 1960s and the 1970s.[3]
The opening section examines the first objective by focusing on the *aficionados* movement, which began in the 1960s and took off in the 1970s. I use the
original Spanish *aficionados* rather than "amateurs," because the translation
can have belittling connotations and fails to express the talent and passion of

performers like the Vento students who opened this chapter. *Aficionados* trained in and performed especially folkloric dance (from Afro-Cuban and popular culture) but also modern dance (especially conditioning and compositional lessons). Through folkloric and modern dance, everyday Cubans of different racial backgrounds corporeally experienced concert dance as entertainment and political action. Meanwhile, ballet remained the purview of individuals with specific (especially white) bodies, ostensibly predisposed and specially formed from an early age. The ballet establishment had to find different popularization methods and so championed the second objective—to make Cubans into a knowledgeable public. As discussed in the second section, ballet dancers in particular, but also modern dancers, tried to teach Cubans to enjoy their productions in the 1960s. However, these initiatives reinforced the divide between dance experts and learners, so by the 1970s, all professional dancers tried with mixed success "to contribute . . . with the *pueblo* and within the *pueblo*."[4] This meant cultivating an image of equality mandated by the 1971 congress, as discussed in the final section.

Although previously overlooked, teaching Cubans to dance and to watch dance figured importantly into educational and cultural initiatives that became hallmarks of the Cuban Revolution. Rather than evaluating state agendas or famed educational projects like the 1961 Literacy Campaign and the nationalized school system, this chapter focuses on cultural intermediaries who implemented official dance education programs and the dancing public that sprang from these initiatives.[5] This focus shows how in the 1960s dance professionals laid the groundwork for popularization campaigns before the state declared this priority during the 1971 congress. As dance makers cultivated *aficionados* and audiences in the 1960s and took advantage of reinvigorated educational priorities in the 1970s, they exhibited power as deputies in a state-led project to educate the masses. Simultaneously, targeted dancers and audience members gave meaning, from unbridled passion to disruptive boredom, to these democratizing projects. In other words, this chapter contends that even though the state labeled art "a weapon of the Revolution," implying central possession and control, dancers of different levels of professionalism and their publics actually wielded and shaped cultural armaments in the 1960s and 1970s.[6]

Concert dance histories reveal the ambivalent outcomes of democratizing projects, which had the patronizing aims of enlightening and disciplining the masses. In revolutionary Cuba (like in the Soviet Union and the capitalist world), a narrow definition of culture persisted, wherein political leaders, cultural bureaucrats, and artists esteemed the fine arts as a tool for education and uplift.[7] Paradoxically, while the state and professional artists clashed over gender and sexuality during the repressive late 1960s and infamous *quinquenio gris* (gray five years) of the early 1970s, they collaborated on mass dance education thanks to shared cultural pretensions.[8] On top of elitist understandings of culture, democratizing programs only enabled diverse *aficionados* to practice folkloric and modern dance, while predominantly white professional dancers performed ballet. This in turn reinforced racialized professional hierarchies. Equally, not all audiences were eager or quiet, and as a result, professional dancers reprimanded them, reaffirming their status as privileged experts working to mold the masses in partnership with the state.[9] Like other revolutionary projects, creating a dancing public involved fraught ideals, dubious methods, and mixed outcomes as dance leaders partnered with the state in aggressive democratizing programs that popularized art while reasserting hierarchies.

Although this chapter examines Cuba's dancing public, the sources provide a particular, partial view of audiences. Statements about spectators come mostly from dance leaders, cultural bureaucrats, and foreign observers. Extensive but by no means exhaustive or accurate attendance statistics collected by the cultural bureaucracy are more useful as cultural artifacts than as representation of reality, revealing more about officials than audiences.[10] Only a couple of letters from audience members appeared in the archive. Thus, understanding the dancing public was an elusive, frustrated fixation for Cuban dance makers, and so it remains for me as well.

Aficionados: Passions and Professions in the 1960s and 1970s

Although no known visual record of the Vento students' 1971 performance exists, visiting British filmmaker David C. Stone captured rare footage of a rehearsal two years prior. Vento students warm up with sequences from Cuban modern dance and then segue into folkloric practice, advancing through space with *orisha* dances in a school auditorium. Live drummers and singers accompany the students, and all of the performers drip with sweat, appearing to revel in the heated fury of music and dance.[11] The scenes above all show how dance became a dynamic, rigorous part of daily lives. This section examines how professional folkloric and modern dancers, teachers, and choreographers worked with *aficionados* to develop ostensibly auxiliary passions. In the process, the line between dance as passion and profession was regularly traversed in the racially diverse field of folkloric dance especially, but also modern dance, while being reaffirmed in the predominantly white ballet.

Although *aficionado* dance became a major state priority and more organized in the 1970s, it developed alongside professional dance institutions starting in the early 1960s. The Teatro Nacional de Cuba (TNC) initiated a Department of Theatrical Extension in July 1960 to support *aficionados*, and Marta Blanco, the future director of the Conjunto Folklórico Nacional (CFN), took charge of the initiative. In 1961, Theatrical Extension affiliates collaborated with the TNC Departments of Modern Dance and Folklore to organize an eleven-day Primer Festival Obrero-Campesino (First Worker-Rural Peoples Festival) in Havana, which featured more than forty performances by theater, music, and dance *aficionados* from all over the country.[12] Young professional dancers choreographed for *aficionados*, including African-descended modern dancers Irma Obermayer, Eduardo Rivero, and Arnaldo Patterson, as well as the future CFN cofounder, white choreographer Rodolfo Reyes. Although the performance programs offer no descriptions of choreographic content, titles provide some indication of what happened on stage. For instance, Obermayer's *Fiesta campesina* (Rural Party) and Rivero's *La bayamesa* (Cuba's national anthem) indicate the popular and patriotic aesthetics that professionals choreographed for *aficionados* in early 1961.[13]

In April 1961, following the successful festival, the Escuela de Instructores de Arte (School of Art Instructors) began to train people to teach *aficionados*. During a televised roundtable about the school, Fidel Castro described art instructors as coming from the same democratizing energies that created the 1960 Agrarian Reform, the 1961 Literacy Campaign, and broader social welfare initiatives. The revolutionary government provided families with "free housing, electric light, water, medical services, medicines, the *Círculo Social* [Social Center], and also . . . instructors of theater, music, [and] dance." Instructors were to cultivate new habits, tastes, and pastimes in *aficionados*, and to look for "all those children who have this [artistic] vocation . . . to come to the National Academy of Art," Fidel elaborated.[14] In this formulation, artistic democracy and meritocracy worked together, as instructors worked with diverse students and channeled the most talented youth into more rigorous programs.

Given the significance of *aficionado* instructors for recruitment, professionals helped to train them. Operating out of the TNC and then the Hotel Copacabana, dance instructors-in-training had classes in dance technique, literature, social sciences, natural sciences, math, and political ideology.[15] Alberto Alonso was the first director of the school, and professional dancers in his company Conjunto Experimental de Danza taught folkloric and popular dances as well as basic modern dance technique. Eventual affiliates of professional companies and the professional school, Escuela Nacional de Arte (ENA), also taught instructors, including U.S. expats Lorna Burdsall and Elfride ("Elfrida") Mahler and Mexican modern dancers Rodolfo Reyes and Waldeen de Valencia. Notable graduates of the instructors' school, Teresa González and Graciela Chao, worked in rural communities, and eventually became teachers at ENA and professionals at the CFN.[16] The Escuela de Instructores de Arte, then, allowed dance professionals to engage with young talent and experiment with dance pedagogy. It also gave students, who later became art instructors, professional performers, and teachers, access to quality dance education.

Art instructors and *aficionados* became emblematic of revolutionary enlightenment and democratization. An article rhapsodized about art instructors: "Cuban youth occupy a place in the forefront of the struggle for building a new social system without exploiters or exploited. . . . Nothing is more beautiful than the sight of these young men and women who are trained as art instructors, children of our workers and peasants, humble sons of the people."[17] Another article on folkloric *aficionados* from eastern Cuba proclaimed, "For the first time in Cuba the working-class can develop its artistic vocation."[18] These groups from across the country performed in the recurring national festival, Festival Nacional de Aficionados, which took place in 1963 and 1964, twice in 1965, and in 1966, 1967, and 1970.[19] During the 1964 festival, *aficionados* reportedly partook in "healthy entertainment" that allowed them to "join our professional artists . . . in their daily fight for better art."[20] These events and related activities expanded dance audiences as well. For instance, by 1964, an estimated twenty-two thousand farmers had seen performances by new instructors and *aficionados*.[21] These early efforts laid the groundwork for developments after the 1971 congress championed education for, and art by, the masses.

In the 1970s, dance became part of a well-rounded education for all citizens.[22] Bureaucrats devised a plan in 1971, which incorporated dance in childhood education. As they saw it, "Throughout history man has demonstrated that Dance and Play are fundamental parts in life development, that they are integral aspects to culture and education; therefore, it is extremely important for society in general and educators in particular, to understand the importance of movement in a human being . . . [as] a fundamental medium of communication and creative expression." Given these truths, educators should incorporate movement as early as possible "to really create a new man for a better world."[23] According to another document, students should start with "Cuban folklore (popular dances)," including the zapateo, *son*, and cha-chachá, then take classes in "Latin American folklore" like "trote" from northern

Chile, "bomba" from Mexico, and "cumbia" from Colombia, before covering "international folklore," meaning Russian, Czechoslovakian, German, and Scandinavian dances. Each class unit had specific instructions: students should listen to the music of the cha-cha-chá, walking to the beat, and marking the rhythm with claps "1-2-3; 1-2," for instance.[24] Along with official lesson plans, published guidebooks directed dance instruction. One reference book on Afro-Cuban dances—like Palo, Abakuá, rumba, and the carnival dances *comparsa* and conga—included dance histories and instructions on how to enact complex physical movements.[25] With these curricula and publications, diverse folkloric dances, whether Russian, Mexican, or Afro-Cuban, became the mainstay of dance as part of physical education for Cuban students across the island.

Jorge Fraga's 1973 documentary *La nueva escuela* (The New School) about schools in the countryside illuminates how students brought these verbal instructions to life. In one scene, mostly lighter-skinned students wear school uniforms and perform the partner dance *son*, popular since the 1920s with "elements from Spanish and African (Bantú) music, blended in a particularly Cuban style."[26] Appearing on an open-air stage for their peers, some dancers have serious, concentrated faces while others smile. Several students who come into the frame slyly watch their peers out of the corners of their eyes to follow what comes next as they shuffle step in embraced pairs, making spatial patterns on the stage. In another scene, students mostly of African descent perform Palo dances. To the pulsating accompaniment of drums, girls wear simple white dresses and headscarves while boys dance bare-chested, wearing white-and-red-striped trousers. Boys and girls have two white lines etched on their cheeks. They repeat a buoyant running step with weight on one foot and kicking the other behind as their arms pump up and front or down and back with each jump-run through space. The music changes, and the dancers put their fists on their waists and shimmy their shoulders as they perform footwork front and back, side to side, meeting one partner and then finding the next, resulting in a wavelike effect as the dancers move in different directions.[27] The demographics of the two folkloric performances suggest race-based casting with lighter-skinned students performing *son*, a popular dance associated with cultural and racial fusion, while African-descended students performed ritual Palo dances more closely identified with blackness.

It is no surprise that young *aficionados* performed *son* and Palo, since folkloric dance aligned with shifting domestic and foreign policy priorities in the 1970s.[28] Cuba more readily embraced Soviet political and economic models following a failed ten-million-ton sugar harvest in 1970, and in kind, the cultural bureaucracy supported *aficionado* folkloric dance, which mirrored the long tradition of amateur folk troupes in Soviet Bloc countries.[29] Moreover, Afro-Cuban folkloric performance also dovetailed with 1970s foreign policy interests in Africa, where the Cuban state supported postcolonial struggles especially in Angola.[30] As Burdsall observed in a letter about a 1972 trip to Africa that her husband, Manuel Piñeiro, and Fidel made, "Fidel is on a folklore kick these days and they saw many groups dance and sing and play native instruments."[31] From an ideological standpoint, folkloric dances were believed "to strengthen the national consciousness of the people, helping them identify with their own historical-cultural reality."[32] From a practical standpoint, folkloric dance was more accessible to bodies of different ages and backgrounds.

Modern dance also figured into *aficionado* programs, since it provided basic conditioning and instilled political values with "*danzas revolucionarias*," revolutionary dances choreographed collectively based on "the life and work of the people."[33] Burdsall had a leading role in *aficionado* curricula in the 1970s, which also helps explain why modern dance became part of official programs.[34] To teach students how to choreograph, a guidebook recommended exercises to "develop creativity" by experimenting with rhythms, spatial design, symmetry and asymmetry, and dynamics like "to hit, float, shake, press, twist, flow, whip, [and] touch." For thematic content, the same manual encouraged students to choose a historic event or issue "from contemporary life focused on the needs and aspirations of the Cuban people in its Socialist Revolution and . . . people of other countries in their fight against imperialism, for peace and in the construction of socialism."[35] These lesson plans ironically promoted individual creativity and hegemonic official agendas simultaneously.

Meanwhile, ballet leaders supported some *aficionado* initiatives but highlighted their limitations. In June 1972, a group of 112 *aficionados* formed the Grupo Experimental de Ballet Universitario (Experimental Group of University Ballet). At an event celebrating its commencement, Alicia and Fernando Alonso and ballerina Loipa Araújo spoke about the "importance of creating a group of ballet *aficionados* at the University of Havana."[36] Ismael Albelo, a former member of Ballet Universitario, recalled working with Ballet Nacional de Cuba (BNC) teachers and choreographers in the company's studios, and official reports filed by the BNC confirm this collaboration.[37] However, ballet leaders also reiterated professional distinction. In a memorandum, Fernando Alonso stated, "*We are not against mass instruction of Ballet,* on the contrary, but it is imperative that someone who is going to be dedicated to this art begins training from eight years old as correctly as possible to not develop defects and bad habits [that are] very difficult to correct.... In none of the other arts *is the problem of developing the body as an instrument ... as important*" (underlined in source).[38] He distinguished between *aficionados* who began ballet later in life and students who trained from a young age in a professional school. Although some *aficionados* had the opportunity to enjoy ballet as a physical activity, the line between professional and nonprofessional ballet dancers remained firmly in place.

Meanwhile, professional modern and folkloric dancers commonly advised, taught, and choreographed for multiple *aficionado* groups, evidencing regular, dynamic collaboration across professional lines. In 1973, the Conjunto Nacional de Danza Moderna ("Danza" for short) advised six modern dance *aficionado* groups.[39] In 1978, Danza (by then, renamed Danza Nacional de Cuba) worked with an *aficionado* group of soldiers in the Fuerzas Armadas Revolucionarias (Revolutionary Armed Forces).[40] CFN members also taught and choreographed for *aficionados* and served on juries for *aficionado* festivals.[41] The Cuban press highlighted the significance of professional guidance, which maintained "constant quality" to ensure "the artistic level required."[42] Although collaborations across levels of professionalism reinforced the status of modern and folkloric dance experts who oversaw *aficionado* productions, these distinctions were not fixed.

For instance, *aficionados* sometimes transitioned from nonprofessional to professional. Modern dancer Eddy Veitia started performing in 1965 with a medical syndicate *aficionado* group advised by Rodolfo Reyes, and in 1966 he joined Danza. Folkloric dancer and choreographer Roberto Espinosa also started as an *aficionado* before joining the CFN.[43] In Santiago de Cuba, Milagros Ramírez González started her career in 1974 at the Escuela de Instructores de Arte, Caney de las Mercedes, then taught at schools, and took "improvement" courses offered by professional companies. In 1982 she became a dancer, teacher, and eventually director of a professional folkloric company in Santiago, the Conjunto Folklórico de Oriente (Folkloric Ensemble of Oriente). The company in its entirety, as well as other Santiago folkloric groups, transitioned from *aficionado* to professional in the 1960s and 1970s.[44] The Havana-based folkloric company Patakín also started as *aficionado* before becoming professional. Available records on Patakín's history demonstrate the porous, surmountable lines between different dance instructional institutions and between *aficionados* and professionals.

The company sprang from devoted students, who took advantage of varied dance educational resources at their disposal. On March 8, 1968, thirty-five *aficionados* formed a new group named "La Kalunga."[45] To develop their skills, they took classes in acting, dance technique, pantomime, and diction, as well as supplementary courses in art and theater history, musical appreciation, folkloric theory and practice, and language at the local school for art instructors. According to later artistic director Bebo Ruiz, "Because of the impossibility of obtaining the necessary budget to constitute itself as a professional group, all the members entered the Columna Juvenil del Mar [marine youth column], where besides performing labor specific to the organization . . . the members performed labors as art instructors in the detachments of the Column."[46] In the meantime, the company won awards at *aficionado* festivals and eventually had the chance to perform on the same program as professional groups. Then, Patakín became a professional company in 1973.[47] In April of that year they performed outside of Havana and Matanzas at cultural centers, theaters, schools and a sugar mill and for U.S. volunteers part of the solidarity group, the Venceremos Brigade.[48] In 1977, Patakín had its first season at the Mella Theater in Havana, and in 1978, the company had its tenth anniversary show *Patakín dice Patakín*, which included Congo, Yoruba, Abakuá, and rumba dances.[49] Although documents and journalistic discussions of Patakín wane after 1978, the company provides insight into the interconnected worlds of *aficionados*, art instructors, and professional schools and companies. Enterprising dancers took advantage of free courses to improve their technique and performed in festivals that proliferated in the 1970s. This allowed them to hone their talents and professionalize. Their actions evidence how members of a dancing public gave content and meaning to *aficionado* programs imagined and implemented from above.

Like the dancers of Patakín, Teresa, the main character of the fictional film *Retrato de Teresa* (Portrait of Teresa, 1979), took her performance work very seriously. Directed by Pastor Vega, *Retrato de Teresa* dramatizes gender inequality in revolutionary Cuba despite the 1975 Family Code, which mandated that men and women share domestic burdens. It was an important cultural event, "a controversy, a continuing public debate," seen by approximately 250,000 people in the first two weeks.[50] It tells the story of Teresa, a mother of three who works at a textile factory and volunteers with her union's *aficionado* folkloric dance company (portrayed by the real *aficionado* folkloric group Conjunto Folklórico Universitario Baile de "La Chancleta," and featuring choreography by the CFN's Juan Jesús García). Teresa's husband jealously resents her after-hours commitments to the *aficionados*. Success at work and motherhood are not enough, she tearfully explains to her furious husband after a late rehearsal. Fulfillment comes from feeling needed and useful, and indeed, she plays a key role in gathering resources and making costumes for the *aficionados*. When she considers quitting because of her marital discord, a colleague encourages her to continue: "To me it appears that with the *aficionados*, you can do a lot more if you want to." She affirms his projection. Upon separating from her husband, she redoubles her participation and helps the group win well-deserved distinctions. As one dancer proudly boasts in a syndicate meeting, "Everybody says we dance like professionals!"[51] Besides staging professional-quality work, Teresa and her colleagues commit fully to this auxiliary passion in ways that go beyond their amateur status.

Aficionado dancers are key to understanding the history of Cuban concert dance and cultural production more broadly in the 1960s and 1970s because professional dancers were imbricated with *aficionados*. Creating a nation of *aficionados* reaffirmed the status of professionals, while also equipping talented citizens to blur these lines. The conflicting impulses to distinguish and democratize coexisted, and this ironic tension accounts for the contradictions inherent to making the fine art of concert dance a mass activity in socialist Cuba. Additionally, a focus on *aficionados* nuances depictions of the late 1960s and early 1970s. While professional artists struggled to survive the repressive period, *aficionados* thrived. With less bureaucratic oversight, *aficionado* folkloric and modern dancers worked with teachers armed only with guidebooks for honing boundless creativity. Ambitious students took advantage of varied institutions and sometimes moved to the status of professional artist. Even when they did not, *aficionados* devoted body, mind, and soul to their dance passions.

Dancers as Teachers: Enlightenment and Control in the 1960s

Along with teaching Cubans to dance, professionals instructed publics on how to *watch* dance, especially in the 1960s. This involved dance professionals working to create interest in and refine consumption of their performances. Their campaigns provide indicators of existing demand and watching practices, as well as the institutional muscle of each genre. That is, as ballet leaders, and to a lesser extent modern dancers, worked to popularize their form, they exhibited anxieties about public interest, reacted to what they viewed as problematic audience behaviors, and indexed their resources to promote dance appreciation on a national level. These dance education programs also had a disciplining intent, designed with paternalistic valences to teach Cubans how to watch dance "properly."

In contrast to ballet and modern dance, folkloric performances throughout the 1960s seemed to attract Cubans without a problem. In one of the first folkloric productions staged by the TNC in 1960, so many people tried to attend that they did not all fit into the auditorium, and the crush of people caused commotion.[52] A large public also patronized CFN performances, as evidenced by the 1964 film *Nosotros, la música*. In scenes of the bustling Mella Theater lobby before a CFN production, people mill around and socialize. Several audience members put their heads under the curtain to talk to dancers warming up on stage as the camera pans across their backsides.[53] The casual, celebratory mood suggests that CFN performances were an enjoyable, regular part of many Cubans' lives. In 1970, visiting U.S. dancer Muriel Manings corroborated this ambiance in her journal, characterizing a recent CFN performance thusly: "Audience response great, truly pack[ed] theater!"[54]

Admittedly, archival traces provide an incomplete picture of folkloric audiences, addressing only Havana publics even though the CFN made regular trips to the provinces. In 1967, for instance, the company gave twelve performances in Pinar del Río, four in Matanzas, seven in Oriente, five in Camagüey, ten in Las Villas, five in Isla de Pinos, two in Varadero, and two in Cienfuegos, along with numerous shows in Havana throughout the year.[55] Performances had audiences ranging from the hundreds to the thousands, such as one performance in Santa Clara where an estimated three thousand people watched the CFN stage Abakuá and Congo dances on December 2, 1967.[56] Nevertheless, available documents provide little evidence that the CFN worried about building audiences in the 1960s when compared with modern and ballet companies in that decade. Perhaps the CFN had no time to worry about spectators as it struggled to survive racial and sexual prejudices.[57]

Modern dancers, by contrast, emphasized the need to acclimate Cubans to the relatively new form. Dancer and choreographer Gerardo Lastra commented, "Since the founding of the company [in 1959], the intention was to create a public and a taste for this genre of dance that did not exist in Cuba before the triumph of the Revolution." To better connect with audiences, Lastra continued, the company "began to work within a folkloric vein, subjects that were very close to popular preferences."[58] Indeed, Ramiro Guerra's early modern dances drew inspiration from Cuban folklore. He also choreographed with a plot for the benefit of unseasoned viewers. In a 1960 interview, Guerra explained, "I am not against abstract dances, on the contrary. But if now I insist on dance with a plot . . . it is because we are creating a public, and for this public it is easier for them to understand modern dance based on a plot. The public reacts better."[59] Although somewhat condescending, this statement evidenced how an imagined unschooled audience exerted influence and shaped choreographic content in professional modern dance.

The 1962 film *Historia de un ballet* (History of a Ballet) demonstrates the folkloric and plot-driven approach of the early years. The documentary "explained" Cuban modern dance by showing Guerra and his collaborators in their creative process for *Suite Yoruba* (Yoruban Suite, 1960). Modern dancers take a ferry to the humble neighborhood of Regla across the bay from Havana, where they observe the music and dances of Santería ceremonies. One scene shows Guerra conferring with costume designer Eduardo Arrocha, who meanwhile sketches a man dancing for the *orisha* Changó. The film eventually moves from the ethnographic encounter to modern dance rehearsal and performance. On stage, modern dancers present stylized versions of the dances observed in Regla with Irma Obermayer as an elegant Ochún and Santiago Alfonso as a fierce Changó, for instance.[60] In subsequent years, Danza screened the documentary during demonstrations to help explicate the origins and objectives of Cuban modern dance.

To further publicize their work, Danza went on national tours to farms, factories, and work centers in the early 1960s.[61] In 1963, Guerra described such performances as instructive for all involved: "Dance that we present to farmers has a lot to do with teaching. We, after presentations, have a half hour of conversation with them. And you should have seen the things they said and what they taught us! There is no doubt that it was, for us, a rich experience. The farmers commented in a direct, precise way, because they saw, in its simplest forms, something of their quotidian endeavors. They located immediately expressions of sadness, love, struggle, [and] action, in an amazing way."[62] Similarly at a work center in 1965, modern dancers performed excerpts, screened *Historia de un ballet*, and took questions from the audience. An article recounted how Lorna Burdsall, then director of the company, "explained the numbers ... and offered general concepts about contemporary dance. The workers asked questions that were amply answered.... The workers applauded a lot and said they would go to the Mella Theater to see ... the new choreography."[63] In 1966, Danza performed for an estimated twenty-seven thousand spectators during a monthlong tour around the country. The spectacular *Suite Yoruba*, along with other unnamed works, reportedly enthralled "audiences distinct from the Havana public. The agricultural worker, farmer, citizen of rural communities, understands all expressions of art.... When the man of the countryside applauds a dance phrase, his perception is not dulled by 'dilettante' prejudices, and communication is better, more pure."[64] These statements show how the state-controlled press, and likely dance makers, fetishized "pure" rural Cubans as indicators of broad artistic sensibilities and modern dance's relevance to the masses.

As Danza worked to increase understanding and interest in modern dance, ballet leaders began resonant initiatives earlier and more aggressively. For instance, the BNC worked to build a ballet public with regular international ballet festivals. After the first festival in 1960, which reportedly turned the island into a world stage, the second festival in 1966 had a more pedagogical aim.[65] As ballerina Alicia Alonso explained, "The people learn in these performances. . . . Their eyes become accustomed to watch, appreciate, discover details, and differentiate the perfect turn from one with small errors. . . . There are *pueblos* that know a lot about 'ballet' because of a tradition that sometimes stretches [back] several centuries. The Cuban people . . . learn and acquire knowledge with incredible rapidness, because they are offered good 'ballet' constantly. It is not the same to read a book one time a week as learning, reading, every day."[66] These festivals, described by one Cuban journalist as "a kind of harvest of art and culture," gave Havana audiences a large dose of ballet.[67]

Yet, rather than a forced educational medicine, ballet became a welcome treat for Cubans, according to foreign observers at the 1967 festival. British critic Arnold Haskell observed (condescendingly, based on a conceit of Cuban provincialism), "One can almost compare it to the delirium of the multitude for soccer or, in our days, for pop singers. The ovations in the spectacles are colossal. . . . The technique and style of the dancers are the object of heated discussions in intermissions with a general knowledge of dance that can do nothing less than surprise." In particular, Cubans avidly debated their favorite ballerina in the first generation trained by Fernando and Alicia— Aurora Bosch, Loipa Araújo, Josefina Méndez, and Mirta Plá—whom Haskell dubbed "the four jewels." Haskell claimed that when a ballet performance aired on television, the sounds of the program and conversations about the dancers filled homes and spilled onto the streets of Havana.[68] Another article on the 1967 festival described a high demand for seats: "Obtaining tickets to see the invited and Cuban dancers in any show of the Festival was difficult. Ballet lovers formed lines for three days—and nights—outside the García Lorca theater." Fortunately, viewers could watch even without a coveted ticket, since "the shows were televised to bring the festival to the entire country."[69]

While impressive in size and fervor, Cuban audiences also struck observers as problematic. In a roundtable on Cuban ballet, Haskell said that audience enthusiasm "tended to get out of control" and suggested that their passion now "should be cultivated [and] educated, to protect the treasure." Bulgarian critic Teodosi Teodosiev chimed in: "The night of May 30 the conduct of the public surprised me. . . . It was the height of an anti-artistic delirium. . . . The love of dance should serve to help and not spoil the art." Fernando Alonso added that "improper demonstrations" interrupted performances and adversely impacted dancers' concentration.[70] While undoubtedly imperious, these judgments nevertheless reveal the great passion that Havana audiences had for ballet. They also indicate that ballet leaders and spectators had different priorities. While leaders wanted to educate, discipline, and control the public, audiences wanted to watch freely and enjoy loudly.

Further evidencing a devoted public, some audience members penned letters of complaint and congratulations. One woman wrote to object to the system of unassigned seats. People lined up two or more hours before performances to secure a good seat, she explained. Since she worked at the national library until 7:30 P.M., she could only arrive minutes before showtime and always struggled to find a decent spot. Pleading for assigned seats, she concluded, "The show is supposed to be for workers. Why obstruct and hinder them?"[71] Along different lines, a fisherman in the port of Havana wrote to congratulate Alicia on the awards that she had received while on tour to Paris in 1966. Several years later, he wrote once more to eulogize the ballerina in careful cursive: "Alicia Alonso is an artist, is beauty, is the world."[72] These letters provide a glimpse into how ballet figured into the lives of Cubans whether as a regular after-work activity or object of breathless veneration.

U.S. journalist Marian Horosko picked up on this clamorous knowledge and fervor while visiting Havana. She noted that the audience "always seemed to be chattering" as ballerina Marta García performed in the nineteenth-century French ballet *La fille mal gardée* (The Wayward Daughter). After enthusiastic applause for García "suspended in the air" in a delicate "piqué passé" balance on one leg, Horosko concluded, "This was no ordinary audience, but one cultivated through the years to respond, appreciate, and obviously, to discriminate." Fernando explained the extraordinary public as a product of accessibility: "The audience seats are always sold out. . . . School children don't pay, and the adult tickets are one or two dollars. Everyone has enough money, the average worker making about $250 per month. The only question is what to buy with it! Performances provide the answer. It's the first time we have been able to afford culture."[73] Fernando's politicized explanation to the foreign observer strategically characterized revolutionary society with idyllic strokes of economic possibility and cultural achievement. Although failing to acknowledge aggressive campaigns to expose Cubans to concert dance, Fernando rightly foregrounded how cheap ticket prices allowed working-class Cubans, like librarians and fishermen, to attend shows regularly and develop strong opinions about ballet.

Despite a devoted Havana following, the BNC wanted to reach citizens unfamiliar with the art. This priority reportedly emerged after a tour to socialist countries from October 1960 to May 1961. While abroad, the BNC performed for mass audiences and wanted to have similar encounters at home. They also planned to share anecdotes about their experiences in socialist countries with the Cuban public.[74] So in the fall of 1961, ballet dancers toured the Cuban provinces Oriente, Camagüey, Las Villas, and Matanzas, performing twenty times for an estimated 58,300 spectators. Along with performances, the ballet company gave talks (*charlas*), where dancers answered questions about socialist allies and ballet in general. Several sessions were recorded and broadcast over local radio stations. The tour allowed ballet dancers to witness firsthand "the extraordinary interest of the *pueblo* in the art of ballet," a report claimed.[75]

Following this initial foray, in 1962 the BNC performed for workers and soldiers. Two thousand construction workers, who had expanded the BNC studios in Vedado and built the ballet school of ENA, watched selections from the comic nineteenth-century French ballet *Coppélia* "with great curiosity . . . and with enthusiastic demonstrations of approval and sympathy," according to Fernando. Dancers then met with their audience "to discuss the show, receive their impressions, and also offer them an explanation of it." Fernando concluded, "It has been a very interesting experience, this exchange and camaraderie between workers and dancers."[76] Weeks later, in early October 1962, the BNC began a national tour and performed in the eastern part of the island during the missile crisis. One itinerary put the company in Guantánamo on November 1, just days after the standoff with the United States ended.[77] Years later, a Cuban journalist described how the ballet dancers performed even though there was no electricity and they had to hum their musical accompaniment. They believed that "soldiers in the tension of war" should enjoy "a deserved rest of instruction and recreation."[78]

In 1964, the company returned to Guantánamo to perform for soldiers in less dire conditions. Once again ballet offered respite from regular schedules and an honorable pastime, according to Cuban observers. The production supposedly contrasted with the entertainment consumed by nearby U.S. soldiers—"Superman and pornographic magazines," an article in *Bohemia* presumed. Before or after the performance, soldiers spoke with ballerina Josefina Méndez, who wore her tutu as she explained pointe shoes (figure 5.1). "A soldier smiles as he caresses the satin of the shoe," the caption narrated.[79]

FIGURE 5.1 From left to right, a soldier strokes a pointe shoe as Alicia Alonso (in fatigues) watches, and ballerina Josefina Méndez (in a tutu) explains something, perhaps the mechanics of dancing on the tips of the toes. This encounter took place during a ballet presentation in Guantánamo. Photograph by Osvaldo Salas. Source: *Bohemia*, August 14, 1964, 64. Courtesy of the Cuban Heritage Collection, University of Miami Libraries, Coral Gables, Florida.

FIGURE 5.2 Alicia Alonso in an aggressive sequence as soldiers watch and register mixed reactions during a 1964 showing of Azari Plisetski's *La avanzada* in Guantánamo.
Source: Museo Nacional de la Danza. Courtesy of the Museo Nacional de la Danza.

He may have enjoyed, self-consciously posed, or smirked at the encounter. The BNC also performed the militaristic *La avanzada* (The Front-Line Charge, 1963), where dancers in fatigues enacted aggressive sequences like the one captured in a photograph of Alicia in a wide transitional lunge, mouth open in mid-shout, and arms thrown back as though ready to charge (figure 5.2). Although Alicia committed fully to combat on stage, the soldiers behind her seem less convinced. They watch slouched in their seats with blank faces. One man smiles in the second row behind his comrade smoking a cigar. His exceptional emotional response could have registered excitement or ridicule for the stylized representation of military action by the elegant ballerina and her poised colleagues.

Such initiatives dovetailed with broader educational and developmental aspirations. As organizers for a 1966 art appreciation course that featured BNC dancers and targeted Cuban workers explained, "Fidel said that we were going to fight a battle against a lack of culture [*incultura*]. This battle began with the Literacy Campaign [of 1961] and the Plan of Art Appreciation is part of that battle."[80] Two years later, the BNC launched its own crusade. From June through December 1968 and then again in June and July 1969, "artistic brigades," under the direction of the Sección Sindical del Ballet Nacional (Syndicate Section of the National Ballet) and in collaboration with the Confederación de Trabajadores Cubanos (Confederation of Cuban Workers), gave eleven demonstrations to factories and schools.[81] The first session took place on June 11, 1968, for nine hundred University of Havana students. Ballet administrator Sara Pascual discussed ballet history and its origins in Cuba followed by a demonstration where teacher Joaquín Banegas explained the moves performed by advanced ENA student Amparo Brito and BNC dancer José Medina.[82] Later sessions followed a similar format and often ended with dancers handing out tickets for upcoming performances, making them "accessible to workers who cannot wait in line."[83] The BNC encouraged attendance by asserting, "The Theater is a means of cultural development."[84] Workers reportedly exhibited "curiosity" about the topics discussed, evidencing how each encounter "closely connect[ed] artists to the workers."[85] Didactic performances ostensibly furthered broader national development by piquing workers' artistic interests and bringing cosmopolitan artists and provincial audiences into close contact.

Although avid audience members at times showered dancers with flowers and interest, not all sessions had such halcyon hues.[86] On September 24, 1969, the BNC performed a mixed program—Alberto Alonso's neoclassical *Espacio y movimiento* (Space and Movement) to music by Igor Stravinsky, the non-narrative European ballet *Les sylphides*, and Alberto's *Carmen* inspired by Georges Bizet's opera—for students from the military institute, Institutos Técnicos Militares. After entering the auditorium "very disciplined," the students began to talk loudly, throw paper, and "produce a very deplorable demonstration of a lack of education and culture," according to an emotional letter written the next day by Fernando Alonso. When the show began, the students shouted suggestive and racially charged epithets, such as "Pinch her [*Pellízcala*]" and "Go, black [man], you are in your groove [*Vaya, negro, estás en tu salsa*]," causing female dancers to flee the stage crying. One affiliate implored the students to quiet down, since "behavior in a theater or a public place is also an indication of the cultural level of the country." The BNC had never encountered such conduct, and making matters worse, the students "demonstrated such a lack of elementary education and [such] cultural backwardness despite being in the hands of our Revolution." This marred the "exemplary conduct of those who wear the honorable olive green uniform.

That's why what happened hurts more," Fernando bemoaned. The incident also made clear "the need to emphasize the correct behavior" for watching ballet. He concluded, "The situation . . . must be tackled with the greatest urgency, in order to eliminate underdevelopment, both of a material and cultural order."[87] After hearing about what happened, Raúl Castro sent flowers with a note of apology to Alicia, who responded that dance leaders, not the students, were to blame, since they had not "offered artistic education to those people."[88] While the Alonsos used veiled terms like "underdevelopment," the students in fact exhibited racism and machismo in a cultural event meant to evidence Cuba's enlightened citizenry.

Along with disregarding bourgeois codes of conduct in the theater, the catcalling, all-male military students accentuated the gendered dynamics of performances.[89] As dance scholar Ann Daly writes, "In modern Western culture, the one who sees and the one who is seen are gendered positions. The possessive gaze is 'male,' while the passive object of the gaze is 'female'—regardless of the dancer's or spectator's sex."[90] In the 1969 performance, male audience members became aggressors, and both female and male dancers, their targets. The incident signaled a "lack of respect [*falta de respecto*]," to use Fernando's words. It effectively emasculated Fernando and his male dancers, who were unable to fulfill a traditional male role of shielding ballerinas from comments, paper projectiles, and public humiliation.[91] Even though the Cuban ballet establishment pushed male dancers to perform virility and heteronormativity, the military students eroded this image in a single performance. Respect for dance professionals, which could be expressed through attentive watching, went beyond ideal performance conditions. It was about authority, control, and reaffirming the masculinity of Fernando and his male dancers.

Throughout the 1960s, ballet and modern dancers worked to create an audience and refine consumption, and in doing so, reinforced a gap between performers and audience members. If audience members appreciated or insightfully commented on choreography, dance makers reacted with surprise, bemusement, and ultimately condescension, revealing their presumptions about a naive and malleable public. As further proof, a three-week modern dance appreciation course that Guerra taught in 1969 was titled, "To conquer a dance public: Film, television, and mass theater."[92] The term "conquer" reflects a muscular approach to dance education carried out by masculine-coded authority figures acting as teachers and enforcers. When audiences showed too much enthusiasm or not enough reverence, dance leaders disparaged them like overactive children and decried their ignorance and backwardness. Dance makers never asked what the audience envisioned as the ideal viewing experience. However, such a query was perhaps unnecessary, since Cuban spectators applauded enthusiastically, talked freely, and effectively choreographed their participation in revolutionary dance experiences.

Dancing by and for the Workers: Equality and Privilege in the 1970s

Aware that dance education initiatives reinforced a gap between performers and audiences, dance makers spearheaded efforts in the 1970s to break down the fourth wall by using mass media, inviting audience members to perform, and working in the fields alongside spectators. In other words, dancers performed equality with audience members during the decade. This also allowed male dancers to reassert their adherence to traditional gender norms by emphasizing that they were workers who performed masculine-coded physical labor. Although these efforts provided a compelling image of politically committed, normative dancers, they also accentuated privileges that dancers (especially in the BNC) had secured thanks to the nature of their artistic labors. This flew in the face of the 1971 congress, which claimed that intellectuals had no privileges, as quoted in the epigraph.[93] Despite these expectations, dancers guarded entitlements that sprang from their status as valuable artistic weapons of the Revolution.

In the 1970s, modern dancers continued to expand audiences and also worked alongside them, building on their 1960s initiatives. Records from 1976, for instance, indicate that Danza regaled an estimated 10,231 people in Isla de Pinos and Havana with Víctor Cuéllar's *Panorama de la música y danza cubana* (Panorama of Cuban Music and Dance), an abstracted history of Cuban social dances like the danzón, cha-cha-chá, rumba, and mambo. Havana performances that year also took place in theaters, Danza's studios for small groups, and in textile, perfume, soap, and ice cream factories.[94] As modern dancer Clara Luz recalled, "We did an annual tour with a duration of a month and a half. We went to the sugar mills, [and] I remember that we participated in the cutting of sugar cane and at night we offered a formidable performance, sharing with the workers."[95] With regular appearances around the country, festive choreography featuring stylized popular dances, and manual labor in sugarcane fields, modern dancers shifted from trying to conquer viewers in the 1960s to striving to commune with them in the 1970s.

The Conjunto Folklórico Nacional also increased, or at least more carefully recorded, popularization efforts by compiling statistics and promoting folkloric appreciation in the 1970s. Available records on the CFN's activities in

March 1974, for instance, indicate that the company appeared at a hospital, broadcast a show on television, and performed rumbas, carnival *comparsa* dances, and *los pregones* (street-sellers' songs) for tobacco workers at a stadium that accommodated five thousand audience members in Pinar del Río. During the rest of 1974, the company also toured Holguín, Victoria de las Tunas (now Las Tunas), Matanzas, Varadero, and Camagüey, performing in schools, a sugar mill, theaters, a park, and an air force base for thousands of agricultural workers, students, and soldiers.[96] Meanwhile, folkloric adviser Rogelio Martínez Furé gave seminars to small groups and on the radio about the CFN, as well as Latin American, Caribbean, and African cultures.[97] He explained, "Our didactic programs have a fundamental objective to awaken the interest of our people in their folkloric traditions," which not only entertained but also enriched understandings "about our history, our struggles for national liberation."[98] In performing widely to teach the public about folkloric music and dance, the CFN aimed to counter the prejudicial devaluing of Afro-Cuban culture.

Additionally, the CFN strove to connect with Cuban audiences as fellow revolutionaries by harvesting sugar. A 1973 memo, for instance, indicated that the CFN worked in the sugar harvest that year.[99] In a published interview, Martínez Furé claimed that company members participated in "sugar harvests, productive work, [and] industrial projects wherever needed. . . . And many times, in the place where they have given their productive efforts during the day, they have offered their art on improvised stages at night. For the members of the Conjunto, there are two things that are one: the Revolution and Folklore."[100] By cutting cane and then performing, productive and artistic labors fused, becoming an indivisible political act. Moreover, this allowed the CFN to adhere to the 1971 congress mandate that artists contribute "with the *pueblo* and within the *pueblo*."[101]

Along with working alongside audience members in the fields, the CFN began informal, participatory performances on Saturdays on the patio of their studios in Vedado. A 1975 memo informed cultural bureaucrats that the new "didactic programming" provided extra rehearsal and further disseminated their work.[102] It aimed to attract "a more heterogeneous public (from school children, to workers, professionals, artists, and foreign visitors)."[103] An open rumba where company members danced with each other and spectators closed each performance, hence the name Sábados de la rumba (Rumba Saturdays), a tradition that continues today. Even before the interactive rumba, religious audience members often swayed and sang as the CFN performed Afro-Cuban ritual dances and songs.[104] The weekly event broke down barriers between private rehearsal and public performance as well as between performers and audience members. This radical sharing continues, meaning that the CFN has danced with countless Cubans over the decades.

The BNC, by contrast, danced with audience members in rare political events, like the culmination of a ballet history course for transportation workers from late 1971 through early 1972.[105] The performance at the Ciudad Deportiva stadium featured ballet professionals including Alicia Alonso and dozens of transportation workers in pieces like *La guagua* (The Bus), the traditional ballet *Pas de quatre*, and the militant ballet *La avanzada*.[106] The Cuban press eulogized, "There they merged into a single mass, dancers and transport workers, the hat of the bus driver and the pointe shoe, giving the almost 12,000 spectators a triumphant display of revolutionary art."[107] The 1972 event received hyperbolic praise compared with the CFN's less-celebrated Rumba Saturdays, which mobilized exponentially more participants over the decades. For observers, professional performers and spectators dancing rumba together weekly seemed to offer less radical border crossing than distinguished ballet dancers and humble bus drivers staging a couple of ballets.

While ballet professionals only occasionally danced with the public, they purported to appear annually in front of dozens to hundreds of thousands of audience members in contrast to the thousands reached by the CFN and Danza. During regular seasons at the García Lorca Theater, the company enjoyed large audiences, an estimated 30,390 people over four months and twenty-four shows in 1973, for example.[108] Beyond regular theater appearances, the BNC occasionally gave special mass performances at the indoor sporting arena Ciudad Deportiva. A reported ten thousand people attended, accommodating more than the García Lorca Theater's "1000 spectators . . . always the same 'group,'" in the words of one cultural bureaucrat.[109] Another report surmised that in 1971 alone, the BNC performed for 278,577 people, including an estimated 36,415 people in the provinces.[110] Even if numbers do not represent reality, they index the BNC's unrivaled resources to reach many Cubans in events that were carefully documented.

Numbers provide little insight into the conditions and emotions involved as dancers appeared before thousands of people around the country; however, audiovisual material and oral histories fill these gaps. In a film clip, ballet dancers Caridad Martínez and Fernando Jhones perform the ballet *Muñecos* (Dolls) on wooden planks in a field. The duet depicts dolls coming to life at night, falling in love, and mourning the sunrise and imminent end of their time together.[111] No audience appears, but the film viewer becomes the proximate eye-level audience member, inhabiting a position of intimacy characteristic of these open-air, rural showings. When I asked Martínez about this performance and others in fields across the island, she described them as exciting and memorable. Cuba developed a large, diverse audience for ballet thanks to regular national tours, she proudly contended. Moreover, she exclaimed, "In the country[side], it was, oh, so much fun!" She recalled dancers putting props on the floor, an audience member reaching for the items, and performers indicating "no" with a smile and slight shake of the head. "They loved it. I loved to perform in the country [side]," she affirmed. Was it ever uncomfortable to dance on makeshift stages? I wondered. "I didn't care! Sometimes [there were] holes, [it was] slippery, but who cares?" she responded.[112] Despite the possibility of dangerous floors, Caridad had fond memories of connecting with new audiences. This passion came through her and Jhones's touching performance of *Muñecos* in an anonymous Cuban field.

Along with regular seasons and national tours, the BNC enjoyed large audiences during international ballet festivals. Festivals were proposed, discussed, and then canceled in 1968, 1970, and 1971 due to financial and political challenges before and after the failed 1970 sugar harvest.[113] However, they did take place in 1974, 1976, 1978, and 1980, and continue to be a biennial event. Although a few programs featured Cuban folkloric and modern dancers, the festival as a whole remained a platform for ballet. Live performances happened outside of Havana for the first time in 1976 (Matanzas and Camagüey) and continued in 1978 (Matanzas and Isla de Juventud) and 1980 (Matanzas, Camagüey, and Isla de Juventud).[114] Although festivals targeted "publics formed by students, workers, soldiers, etc.," this goal was difficult to implement.[115] An individual who identified himself only as "a revolutionary ballet lover [*un revolucionario amante del ballet*]" wrote a letter of complaint about the 1974 festival. In particular, he noted that many of the best seats reserved for invited guests (presumably bureaucratic, political, and cultural leaders) remained empty. At the same time, "almost violent" authorities struggled to keep order outside of theaters as regular citizens fought to secure tickets.[116]

The ballet establishment also reached Cubans through mass media. On October 27, 1969, the radio program *Ballet* aired for the first time on the station CMBF Radio Musical Nacional. Lasting thirty minutes daily and one hour on Sunday, it transmitted information about dance, music, critical reception, interviews, news, and "other themes of interest."[117] Along with *Ballet*, *El mundo de la danza* (The World of Dance) began airing in 1969. Transcripts through 1976 indicate that programs focused geographically on Cuba, Latin America, and socialist countries, and thematically on ballet, though with regular updates on, and sometimes extended discussion of, modern and folkloric dance.[118] Ballet radio shows were popular enough to lead to another one, *Sobre el ballet*

(About Ballet), which started airing in 1974.[119] These initiatives aligned with state visions of mass media as "powerful instruments of ideological conformation, forgers [of] collective consciousness," according to the 1971 Primer Congreso Nacional de Educación y Cultura.[120]

In addition to radio, the ballet establishment launched the magazine *Cuba en el Ballet* in 1970 and a regular television program, *Ballet visión*. Although covering national and international dance developments, the new periodical mainly focused on the island's place in the larger world of ballet, as indicated by the title, "Cuba in Ballet." As stated in the first issue, the magazine aimed to "make known to the world our achievements and our efforts." Making strides in this international projection, by 1972 the magazine had 416 subscription requests from the Soviet Union.[121] By contrast, the television program *Ballet visión* targeted local audiences. It premiered on February 1, 1972, on Tuesday evenings at 10 P.M. and in 1973 moved to 8:30 P.M. It featured clips of ballet performances, interviews with famous dancers, ballet news, and commentaries on "the history and achievements of traditional classical ballet as well as more contemporary repertory."[122] The two programs that aired in January 1975, for instance, featured Cuban dancers (and a guest artist from Italy) in acts one and three of *Swan Lake*.[123] Only the ballet establishment spearheaded such costly mass media programs, indicating its ability to secure finite resources.

The BNC encouraged viewers not only to learn about concert dance through radio and television programs but also to consider ballet a form of physical labor. During a 1974 lecture demonstration for construction and petroleum workers, Alicia reportedly said, "Ballet is work like all art." The dancers then showed typical daily exercises, like those captured in figure 5.3, underscoring the concentration and physical force needed to advance technically. Inputs and outputs resembled the logic of other industries: "Without effort there is no sugar. Dance either," an article about the demonstration noted.[124] In another encounter, a muscular youth joked that it looked easy to dance. Alicia invited him to reproduce a sequence that included lifting a ballerina, which he was unable to do to his surprise and chagrin.[125] The cheeky audience member implicitly questioned male dancers' masculinity, but perhaps reconsidered upon realizing the strength needed to dance and partner.

Whereas the BNC had to devise special initiatives to reach new publics and find common ground with the masses, the smaller ballet company Ballet de Camagüey (founded in 1967) seemed to epitomize the populist ideal of artists and audiences forming a singular community. Company director Joaquín Banegas claimed that Camagüey ballet professionals "dance for the people and, at the same time, live together with these people, in the majority

FIGURE 5.3 During one of the many lecture demonstrations around the country, ballerina Josefina Méndez (in street clothes next to the tree) explains the moves that the dancers execute for audience members, ca. 1970s. Photographer unknown. Source: Museo Nacional de la Danza. Courtesy of the Museo Nacional de la Danza.

agricultural workers. With this public, when we do not dance, we cut cane, plow the land, in short, the things that allow us a total integration with them."[126] Dancers of humble backgrounds moved from farming with their families, "almost without transition, to being enchanted princesses of *Swan Lake* or *Giselle*." Both Ballet de Camagüey dancers and "the people of the land" in their audience helped to "pulverize" the idea that ballet belonged only to a "privileged caste."[127] Toward this end, the group performed almost entirely outside of Havana and worked in the fields. In 1971, for instance, they appeared in Camagüey, Ciego de Ávila, Santa Clara, Santiago de Cuba, Pinar del Río, and Matanzas and cut sugar cane for five days in April.[128] As a result, the company introduced a "virgin public" to ballets like *Elegía a Jesús Menéndez* (Elegy to Jesús Menéndez), inspired by Afro-Cuban writer Nicolás Guillén's poem about the eponymous black labor activist and sugar worker who was murdered in 1948. One audience member was touched by the performance: "I always have seen ballet on television, but to see it [live] . . . is, ufff, something else. And the most beautiful [thing] is that I understood everything in it: the epoch of struggle of Jesús Menéndez against injustice."[129]

Through clarity and content about black, rural heroes, the mostly white Ballet de Camagüey directly connected with the assumedly racially diverse agricultural laborers in their audience.[130]

Although ballet dancers worked in the fields and connected with rustic publics to project equality, they retained a special status, which some members of the BNC used to avoid agricultural labors. During the nationwide push to harvest ten million tons of sugar by 1970, cultural official Eduardo Conde found only thirty-one out of over seventy BNC dancers "performing effective agricultural labor." He had received excuses about injuries, family responsibilities, work, school, and even plastic surgery, which provoked the dry comment "NICE LITTLE OPPORTUNITY" (all capital letters in the original).[131] Twelve days later, Fernando Alonso responded huffily to Conde's "jocular comments," asserting that the ballet dancers had done the requisite amount of work even though agricultural labor hurt their technical level by taking them away from daily classes.[132] The same day, Conde responded apologetically and closed by sending salutations to Alicia.[133] In this exchange, Fernando defended ballet dancers' right to shirk fieldwork to protect their bodies. Avoiding the 1970 sugar harvest was no trifle, since the government had framed the effort in eschatological terms, calling on Cubans to pick up machetes rather than guns to defend the Revolution.[134] Conde's apologetic concurrence with Fernando demonstrated official recognition of ballet's exceptionality. This highlights a tension between dance as revolutionary work and privilege, the productive body and the artistic body.[135] Despite incongruities, dancers found ways to perform both roles with some adaptations.

Ballet leaders continued to control the scope of voluntary labor. Although "all the collective" carried out agricultural work for three days in January 1972, and sixty-four dancers, a month later, they did not cut sugarcane, for instance.[136] As Marian Horosko reported after visiting Cuba, "The ballet, too, had given time to harvesting, although the members were exempt from cutting for fear of damaged muscles. They are champion coffee bean planters, and their many banners and awards attest to their excellence."[137] Moreover, ballet leaders chose the small number of dancers who would fulfill agricultural requirements.[138] By the early 1980s, Alicia claimed that the government would not allow the BNC to work in the fields out of concern for their physical well-being.[139] Internal documents reveal that the government only developed such concern after the BNC's prodding. Through trial and compromise, a system developed whereby a small number of presumably lower-ranked dancers could fulfill physically less demanding, symbolically necessary duties to prove the BNC's political excellence.

Ballet dancers secured not only exemption from certain agricultural work but also privileges in relation to food. When Castro visited the BNC studios in 1961, he decided to create a dining hall for company members. El Carmelo, a nearby restaurant on Calzada Street in front of the BNC studios, stocked the resulting ballet cafeteria. Initially, the BNC had an adequate amount of food thanks to receiving an "athlete's diet [*una dieta de deportista*]," which halted for unclear reasons in 1965.[140] Ballet dancers experienced shortages like the rest of the population, and in 1974, Fernando complained that the promised cheese, beef, ham, pork product [*jamonada*], and liver had not arrived and that they only irregularly received chicken.[141] Bureaucrats discussed increasing the amount of butter, cheese, milk, and yogurt for ballet dancers in 1975. The BNC also requested to have the Instituto de Nutrición e Higiene (Institute of Nutrition and Hygiene) study the dancers' diet to ensure it aligned with their physical expenditure.[142] In 1978, a report emphasized the physical and mental demands of over seven hours of dancing a day, meaning that a lack of food caused injuries and therefore "directly affected production." Given that dance was about "strength and aesthetics," it was equally important to avoid fatty foods, and the report concluded, "Good nutrition is important."[143]

Although the BNC performed equality by sharing art and sacrifices with fellow citizens, the company also actively sought to mitigate the burdens of agricultural labor and food scarcity. No similar documentation has been found about folkloric or modern dancers, which proves nothing conclusively. It could mean that the dancers did not try, tried without success, or successfully avoided labor and appealed for food in records not preserved or found. Regardless, the case of BNC privileges shows that the dancers resembled other political elites in Cuba. In his 1971 memoir about a trip to Cuba, Jamaican playwright Barry Reckord reflected on material distinctions in a classless society by asking a group of children, "Why does Fidel eat more than your father?" This elicited a variety of responses: the "big fat man" had a bigger appetite, he talked a lot so needed more energy, he was prime minister, and he did not eat more than at least one girl's father.[144] Like Fidel, ballet dancers received special treatment. This was no coincidence. They carefully consolidated political capital through public works and highlighted the demands of their craft. Moreover, they devised a new category of revolutionary work, wherein their art promoted social welfare and accommodated narrow conceptions of revolutionary manhood, not unlike a farmer's harvest or soldier's patrol. In the 1970s, dancers appeared on makeshift stages, and in stadiums, studios, and formal theaters for fellow revolutionary workers, turning each performance into a spectacle of at least symbolic parity.

Conclusion

The 1971 performance by Vento students that opened this chapter signaled the beginning of an increased focus on art making and patronage by the masses. Although 1971 was an important turning point, developments in the 1960s evidence a constant desire on the part of dance professionals to extend the reach of their art (and power) beyond a select cosmopolitan public. From collaborating with *aficionados* to embarking on yearly performance tours to rural areas, factories, and schools in the 1960s, professionals laid the groundwork for popularization campaigns of the 1970s. The state declared a renewed emphasis on the masses in 1971 and partnered with willing professional dancers to implement this program just as officials policed, censored, and humiliated suspected homosexual performers and choreographers. Such ironic coincidences illustrate the impossibility of categorizing state-concert dance relationships at any one moment as entirely positive or negative. Tensions existed, but so did collaborations. Notably, the state did not dictate how these collaborations played out. Dance makers transformed lofty statements like those in the epigraph into concrete popularization programs that furthered their own agendas by expanding and enriching concert dance. Moreover, the *aficionados* and audiences targeted by these programs shaped initiatives imagined by the state and designed by dance leaders. Through performances or vocal watching practices, members of the dancing public influenced concert dance trajectories with their talents and passions.

Although a new dancing public undoubtedly emerged by the 1970s, the outcomes remained profoundly ambivalent. Vento *aficionados* performed folkloric dance in 1971, not ballet, since only folkloric dance, and to a lesser extent modern, opened to wider practice. This reaffirmed ballet's rarefied status as an exclusive (and still mostly white) form. Moreover, audiences were broad and diverse, but did not always behave as dance leaders hoped. For instance, Australian writer Germaine Greer traveled to Cuba for a women's congress and recalled, "The first evening the delegates were taken to a ballet. They arrived stomping and chanting, sat chatting eagerly about the day's doings, and when the dancing had started and silence was finally imposed, a good proportion of them went straight to sleep." They slumbered through a piece about a man-eating plant and a communistic tribute to heterosexual relations, but "woke up with a start to watch the eighth wonder of the world, Alicia Alonso, sixty years old and virtually blind, dance a *pas de deux* with Jorge Esquivel to music by Chopin."[145] Attending a ballet performance was so familiar that delegates comfortably socialized, slumbered, and intuited when to wake up for a Cuban idol. According to literary scholar Michael Warner, "It is even possible for us to understand someone sleeping through a ballet performance as a member of that ballet's public, because most contemporary ballet performances are organized as voluntary events, open to anyone willing to attend, or in most cases, to pay to attend. The act of attention involved in showing up is enough to create an addressable public. Some kind of active uptake, however somnolent, is indispensable."[146] Attendance was often required in Cuba, but behavior remained voluntary. Cuban audiences watched as desired, even if chatting and snoring would have disappointed dance and political leaders. Ultimately, full houses with sleeping audience members encapsulated the ambivalence of idealistic efforts to make all citizens into fine art connoisseurs. Everyone showed up and clapped, but only a portion loved the experience. Some sleepy delegates converted ballet from a dramatic weapon of the Revolution, as the 1971 congress exhorted, into an individual sedative.

Despite these mixed outcomes, creating a dancing public not only contributed to broader efforts to educate and unify Cuban citizens but also strengthened concert dance by cultivating practitioners and patrons in all corners of the island. *Aficionados*, professionals, and audiences variously asserted their power in the process by developing a beloved pastime, captivating viewers nationwide, advocating for more food, and boisterously cheering performers. As a result, concert dance contributed importantly to broader revolutionary educational programs and became integrated into everyday repertories of labor and leisure.

However, Cuban dance makers did not limit their aspirations to the national stage. Along with creating a dancing public at home, performers circulated as commodity exports in a global marketplace. As Cubans danced around the world, they reaffirmed their significance to revolutionary politics. Their ubiquity helps explain why concert dancers were so uniquely powerful in Cuba. They became venerated equals on a world stage and significant vectors of revolutionary politics beyond Cuba. Their cultural and political distinction internationally helped them secure privileges back home. Looking both in and beyond Cuba, the next chapter follows these dance internationalists as they moved across stages and borders to great political effect.

CHAPTER SIX

Dance Internationalism

It's not that we represent the Revolution. We *are* the Revolution.
—Alicia Alonso, 1974

Cuba has three chief exports: cigars, sugar, and Alicia Alonso.
—Agnes de Mille, *Portrait Gallery*, 1990

In 1979, modern dancer Víctor Cuéllar spent a month in Mexico City, enacting what I call *dance internationalism*, a political practice of corporeal cooperation across borders. During his time in Mexico, Cuéllar worked with professional and nonprofessional dancers and tied these artistic activities to international revolutionary politics. As a Cuban article explained, Cuéllar gave "a series of talks . . . about the development of dance, folklore and ballet in our country, about the revolutionary action that made possible its great quantitative and qualitative jump, [and] about the creation of schools and dance groups. . . . Then there was a collective blood donation . . . for Nicaragua by the dancers that were in attendance."[1] In this encounter, Cuban and Mexican dancers radically shared their bodies—choreographically and sanguinely—to support revolution in Nicaragua. Through such activities, Cuban dance went from a weapon in national educational projects as discussed in chapter 5 to an international export that netted symbolic and material gains and propagated revolutionary politics.

Through dance internationalism, Cuba exercised what scholars call "soft power," defined as "culture, values, and policies," rather than "hard power" in the form of military or economic coercion.[2] Scholars have examined Cuban soft power (whether or not labeled as such) in the form of medical and educational expertise, music, and the Cuban news service, Prensa Latina. Dance became an important, previously overlooked vector for Cuban soft power, accumulating "symbolic capital (prestige, influence, goodwill)," not to mention hard currency salaries and honoraria.[3]

Examining this understudied realm provides fresh insights on Cuban foreign policy by shifting away from policymakers to focus on the experiences of dance makers who enacted official cultural agreements.[4] Dance internationalism not only aided the state by generating intangible and tangible dividends but also affirmed dancers' own power. As ballet leader Alicia Alonso claimed in the epigraph, dancers went beyond representatives; they *were* the Revolution and seized the authority inherent to such an embodiment to realize their artistic goals.[5]

Along with Alicia Alonso and her fellow ballet dancers, folkloric and modern dancers contributed importantly to Cuban dance internationalism; however, the fact that Alicia became a well-known Cuban export, as New York choreographer Agnes de Mille quipped in the epigraph, is revealing. As Alicia and her ballet dancers traveled regularly, they accumulated symbolic and material gains, which folkloric dancers especially but also modern dancers had relatively fewer opportunities to enjoy. Dancers of different genres enjoyed disparate levels of privilege at home, and these imbalances were reinscribed through activities (or lack thereof) abroad.

Analyzing dance internationalism as a form of soft power provides a fuller picture of Cuba's place in the world in the 1970s and 1980s because dancers had the flexibility to engage with multiple sites and objectives at once. As examined in the first section, folkloric and modern dancers meditated on Cuban links with Africa just as military involvement in anticolonial struggles on the continent accelerated. The second section discusses how ballet dancers impressed observers in the so-called first and second worlds by exhibiting their shared Western traditions and a distinct Cuban aesthetic. The third section examines how Cuban ballet and modern dancers worked in Latin America to bolster regional solidarity. Cuban dancers propagated these various priorities in Africa, the United States, Europe, the Soviet Union, and Latin America simultaneously. Examining the different choreographic projects together shows how Cuba was both combative and conciliatory as dance makers engaged with ideological friends and foes alike. This juxtaposition also reveals how dancers could concurrently represent different aspects of Cuba's racialized identity in the eyes of international viewers: African blackness, European whiteness, racial mixture, and the loaded notions of exoticism and civility. Dance internationalists, then, accommodated diverse Cuban foreign policy initiatives and racialized national identities, and could do what hard power could not: sidestep the U.S. embargo to flood into countries around the world.

Choreographing Connections with Africa

In 1975, folkloricist Rogelio Martínez Furé completed a libretto for *Palenque*, an experimental folkloric production that dramatized the freedom struggles of enslaved Africans in nineteenth-century Cuba.[6] Also that year, a program honoring the 1975 First Congress of the Communist Party of Cuba featured

modern dancers performing Eduardo Rivero's *Súlkary*, a sensual work inspired by African sculpture.[7] To close the 1975 congress, Fidel Castro addressed over a million people in the Plaza of the Revolution, proclaiming,
"We are ... a Latin-African nation. ... African blood flows freely through our
veins. ... We're brothers and sisters of the people of Africa and we're ready to
fight on their behalf! (APPLAUSE)"[8] Military actions followed. From November 1975 to April 1976, Cuba stunned the world by dispatching thirty-six thousand Cuban soldiers to Angola, beginning over a decade of large-scale operations
to support anticolonial struggles on the continent.[9] Cuban folkloric and modern
dancers had long focused on Afro-Cuban culture, and in the 1970s and 1980s,
they imaginatively staged Cuba's identity as a Latin African nation. Their dance
internationalism choreographically explored the legacies of slavery and racial
solidarity in the African diaspora.

Imagination engendered these choreographic endeavors. In the 1970s,
Martínez Furé theorized imaginative approaches to African and African diasporic culture in his book *Diálogos imaginarios* (Imagined Dialogues). As part
of his discussion, Martínez Furé wrote about the history of the Conjunto
Folklórico Nacional (CFN), and indeed, the folkloric company became a
vector for imagined dialogues about Cuba's African patrimony.[10] Equally,
modern dancers like Eduardo Rivero choreographed to explore old, and in-
vent new, linkages with Africa. Analyzing these productions builds on the
work of historian Christabelle Peters, who "foregrounds the role of imagination as an instrument of collective action" in her analysis of 1970s Cuban racial identities and involvement in Angola.[11] Dances manifested imagined
dialogues into corporeal articulations of connection.

The CFN involved mostly black performers who staged Afro-Cuban
music and dance, effectively foregrounding historic and ongoing linkages between Africa and Cuba. Algerian audiences noticed this during the CFN's
first international tour in 1964, which sparked one Algerian critic to claim,
"They are the ancient slaves of Congo or of Nigeria who express their concerns, their love, their joie de vivre in their religious songs."[12] Despite the
troubling choice to call contemporary Cuban citizens "ancient slaves," the
statement evidences how CFN performances conveyed the legacy of slavery.
These implications gained new geopolitical significance in the 1970s with
Cuba's accelerated engagement in African anticolonial struggles.

In this context, the CFN created and performed *Palenque* (1976). It was set
in 1843 and 1844, known as *La Escalera* or "the year of the lash" when authorities executed, imprisoned, or banished thousands of enslaved and free
African-descended Cubans in harsh response to a planned rebellion.[13] While

staging *Palenque*, Cuban troops streamed into Angola. Their mission was code-named Operation Carlota after the enslaved woman who helped to lead the 1843 revolt.

The over-forty-page *Palenque* performance program featured poems, historical studies, essays, and bibliography on the formerly enslaved men and women who established Cuban maroon communities called *palenques*. According to the program, these ancestors fomented a rebellious spirit that twentieth-century freedom fighters inherited. To connect the past to the present, the playbill featured quotes from Castro's 1973 speech about Cuba's debt to "slave fighters," who were "precursors of our revolutionary *patria*," as well as a 1976 speech about European enslavers, who "probably never imagined that one of those peoples receiving the slaves, would send combatants to fight for the liberty of Africa."[14] The production brought these claims to life.

Although no photographs or films of *Palenque* have been found, an extensive libretto by Martínez Furé provides insight into the performance. He imagined the production proceeding as follows. The curtain opens slowly to a stage bathed in blue light to create a "cold atmosphere like the bottom of the sea." Performers portraying enslaved Africans take different positions "like in the engravings of the chambers [*las calas*] of slave ships." Sacred batá drums (used in Santería religious ceremonies) mark the rhythms of the *orisha* Yemayá, and a captive sings about Spanish enslavers and enslaved Africans. After the song, the lighting shifts to soft pink, signaling daylight and landfall in Cuba. The performers transition from slave ship to quarters, eventually cutting sugarcane to a lamenting song and enjoying precious moments of rest. A dramatic romance develops, as the enslaved José Trinidad and María Regla fall in love despite coming from the competing Lucumí and Congo ethnic groups. However, a white foreman also wants María Regla and jealously kills José Trinidad. The murder catalyzes a rebellion. María Regla decapitates the murderer, and her peers set fire to the sugarcane fields. They escape and establish a *palenque*.[15]

The second half of *Palenque* charts the fateful twists and turns experienced by the now free men and women. Energy shifts from heavy and dramatic to "agile, short, [and] dynamic." Scenes like "study, work and rifle" show the community dividing tasks and learning "the discipline of WORK" (capital letters in the original). María Regla gives birth to José Trinidad's son, the first person born free in the *palenque*, and everyone celebrates. However, "agents of the slave repression" find the *palenque* and attack the inhabitants. Here, Martíncz Furé paused the plot to interject, "The choreography should be inspired by . . . photographs of the Yankee massacres in Vietnam, of the Portuguese

colonialists in Mozambique . . . ; in sum of all the graphic materials that denounce the genocidal methods of imperialism and colonialism in every time
and place." He envisioned the nineteenth-century massacre evoking bloody
struggles for sovereignty in the 1970s. Many die in the ensuing battle, but the
first free man born in the *palenque* survives, and "the rebel spirit runs through
the hills like a wind." Dead bodies littering the stage then come to life, showing the immortality of rebelliousness. Revived fighters perform a warrior
dance to the sounds of Castro commemorating the 1843 uprising as the pre-
cursor of present-day militants. This final scene, titled "One, Two, Three
palenques," alludes to Che Guevara's message to the 1966 Tricontinental Conference, wherein he called for one, two, three Vietnams, that is, for world
revolution. The curtain closes slowly on a stage reverberating with rebellious
songs and dances.[16]

Bringing these scenes to life involved over forty performers and choreography by Roberto Espinosa. Espinosa had started with the company in 1962 and
began choreographing in 1967 for *aficionado* groups and, eventually, the CFN.
About his work, he described, "I really like to highlight the dramatic sense of
dance."[17] Scenes of violence and rebellion in *Palenque* offered ample opportunity for drama to a mixed musical accompaniment of Yoruba, Congo, Arará,
and Carabalí music, as well as "experimental music." The eclectic mix made
the work a part of "tradition and the vanguard," according to collaborators.[18]
The combination encapsulated the dual temporality of the piece. The production about Cuba's nineteenth-century slave society gestured to the 1970s by
celebrating socialist values (a veneration of work and discipline in the *palenque*,
for instance) and by alluding to ongoing struggles against imperialism.

A program essay reflected on the work's boundary crossing: "How to clas-
sify the work *Palenque*? Dramatic dance? Danced opera? Musical drama? . . .
It's difficult to pigeonhole it in one category" (ellipses in the original). Instead, the playbill continued, it was "an experiment . . . where the most heterogeneous elements of song, music, anonymous poetic texts, and dance are
integrated."[19] The amalgamation was "a work of disruption [*rompimiento*]"
that was "profoundly political" and showed the "vitality and force" of folkloric arts.[20] The "heterogeneity of languages," including pantomime, dance,
text, and varied music, led one critic to fault the piece for aesthetic incoher-
ence.[21] Nevertheless, the brazen mixture ultimately aimed "to exalt the eternal rebellious spirit of [the Cuban] people, [and] its long tradition of fighting
against oppression and exploiters."[22] What literary scholar Rosemary Geisdorfer Feal has concluded about Martínez Furé's poetry also applies to the
aesthetically layered dance production: "The language and symbols . . . may

seem fully legible, yet there is hidden content discoverable only through a deep tracing of origins which permits imaginative links to be forged."[23] The difficult-to-pigeonhole dance had a veneer of state rhetoric and deeper meanings about race and connection.

Given Martínez Furé's involvement in censored Afro-Cuban study groups in the late 1960s, his work likely suggested racial solidarity that transcended state visions.[24] The "work of disruption" highlighted racial solidarity instead of nationalism to resonate with a very particular target audience. Martínez Furé told black poet Nancy Morejón in a published interview about the work, "Our *pueblo*, to see their history reflected on stage, has reacted with enormous enthusiasm, laughing, crying, or intervening with their applause or commentaries. . . . Maybe some connoisseur feels uncomfortable in front of certain situations and he shifts in his seat, crying out for songs and dances during scenes that reflect the horrors of slavery, or he wants to feel more sheltered. What interests us is that our people, descendants of those same *cimarrones* [maroons] and *mambisas* [nineteenth-century Cuban independence fighters], be satisfied." *Palenque* was created by and for the descendants of nineteenth-century captive Africans and the majority African-descended anticolonial fighters in Cuba. Martínez Furé acknowledged the unmarked, assumedly white connoisseur who perhaps felt "uncomfortable" watching the horrors of slavery, and left him to squirm in his seat. Foregrounding the ugliness of past and present racial violence (Martínez Furé dedicated the production "to the just fight of brother *pueblos* of Namibia, Zimbabwe and Azania [southeastern Africa], that heroically face the fascist South African regimes"), *Palenque* articulated a powerful dance internationalism.[25] The production aimed to unite African-descended performers, audience members, and transatlantic freedom fighters across time and space.

Like Martínez Furé, Afro-Cuban modern dancer Eduardo Rivero imagined dialogues with Africa. To create his first work, a fifteen-minute romantic duet titled *Okantomí* (1970), Rivero conducted extensive research. "That's why I have so many books about Africa," he explained in 2007.[26] He drew inspiration from "the sculptures of Ifé and Benin . . . which [has] the force, vitality and plastic sense of African culture." The result was *Okantomí*, a Yoruban word meaning "all of my heart."[27] The sensual work starred two dancers of African descent and initially shocked audience members. Rivero recounted, "The first time people started to murmur. It was very grotesque, very animalistic movement, a man squatting, almost on four legs, and people did not understand it. As time went on, there was an overwhelming silence, and when the curtain closed, people were amazed."[28] In a 1974 film of *Okantomí*, Ernestina Quintana performs the female lead and shimmers in all gold, from the paint on her face to her flowing cape, which she often removes and manipulates as a prop. After her introductory solo, her partner Pablo Trujillo leaps onto stage wearing minimal gold trunks that provide full view of his muscular body. Then, they dance together. Sexually charged moments, like one in which they embrace with pelvises pressed together, backs arched, and gaze upward, may have sparked audience murmurs in 1970.[29] The "grotesque, very animalistic" choreography laid bare the stereotypes that informed Rivero's Cuban understanding of an erotic, exotic African continent.

Rivero's colleague, black modern dancer Luz María Collazo, performed the female lead of *Okantomí* at the Champs-Elysée Theater during a Danza Nacional de Cuba ("Danza" for short) tour to Paris in 1977. She cherished "favorable reviews in French periodicals . . . which compared [her] to Lois [*sic*] Fuller, the North American dancer who performed many years in that city at the beginning of the century."[30] Perhaps the flowing cape that Collazo wore inspired the comparison to Fuller, a white North American dancer who in the early 1900s dazzled Parisians by swirling large skirts under elaborate light shows and performing the (appropriative) *Serpentine Dance*, inspired by so-called Nautch dancing from India. The 1977 Parisian audience may have connected the black Collazo to the white Fuller because the women signaled fetishized, exotic Others.[31] Such a comparison also confirmed Collazo's success, as she enchanted a knowledgeable audience in the cultural capital of Paris and reminded them of a venerated dance innovator.

In 1977, along with Rivero's *Okantomí*, Danza toured with his famed *Súlkary* (1971), which also drew inspiration from African sculpture. Simple program notes explain the dance depicting "the relation between man as a symbol of virility and power and woman as an exponent of beauty and tenderness."[32] To convey universality, the single couple in *Okantomí* became three male-female pairs in *Súlkary*. "My choreographies are all very sculptural. I feel inclined toward elements of plastic arts," Rivero reflected years later.[33] Indeed, in *Súlkary* six statuesque dancers flow through poses and gestures to soaring vocals of unspecified ritual music. Three women in nude leotards enter the stage with a quiet though ardent energy, followed eventually by three men in minimal briefs who march, stomp, jump, and emphasize the beat with the long staff that they each carry. As the men and women dance together, the phallus-like props accentuate their charged excitement. Collazo performed in the premiere of *Súlkary* in 1971 and hundreds of times over the next almost thirty years, until she was fifty. "That choreography marked my life," she later said; "I identified with it." About Isidro Rolando, her partner in

Súlkary for over two decades, she reflected, "He helped me a lot always. . . . He is my brother."[34] A filmed version of *Súlkary* from 1974 captures the trust between Collazo and Rolando, as they deftly partner and project a shared energy.[35]

Rivero's choreography had an impact on not only performers but also audience members, particularly in Nigeria during the Second World Black and African Festival of Arts and Culture (FESTAC '77). The event included participants from Africa and the African diaspora, and extravagantly celebrated Nigerian nationalism, Pan-African unity, and utopian modernity by staging a rendition of "global Africa."[36] The famed African American modern dance company Alvin Ailey American Dance Theater also performed, as did groups from Angola, Mozambique, and Senegal, among other countries.[37] On January 22, Danza performed Rivero's *Okantomí* and *Súlkary* at the University of Ifé, and on January 25, in a televised production at the National Theater of Lagos for around 2,500 people, including citizens of Mozambique, Angola, and Guinea. In the latter performance, photographers rushed to the edges of the stage, and incessant camera flashes bathed the performers in sharp white light. Dancer Gerardo Lastra claimed, "Almost each moment was fixed visually and also applauded warmly by the public that showed in this way, and with exclamations of surprise or enthusiasm, the impact that the three pairs of [*Súlkary*] interpreters provoked." The final performance in Nigeria on February 3 regaled five thousand in the stadium at Tafawa Balewa Square.[38] As a U.S. critic described the audience's reaction, "The highly polished [Cuban] troupe received a standing ovation and the warmest response given to any country act."[39] According to Rivero, "In Nigeria one could hear people commenting: 'Look, that is how our grandparents, our ancestors danced.' I do not say it to brag [*darme en el pecho*], [but] it was something that really happened, it is a healthy pride, it is an honor."[40] Although no doubt a crowd pleaser, only further research into the Nigerian press could garner a fuller understanding of how audiences viewed the Cuban interpretation of Africa. However, Rivero's comment does reveal how Cuban dance internationalists saw their work as vehicles for forging connections between Cuba and other parts of the world—in this case, Africa. Rivero's memory also underscores how dance internationalism often went from an imaginative exercise to a concrete performative encounter that had an emotional impact on choreographers, dancers, and audience members from both sides of the Black Atlantic.[41]

As Rivero meditated on distant Africa and shared his choreographic ruminations during short performance tours, other Cuban dancers worked for extended periods in different African countries. Teresa González, a folkloric dance teacher at the Escuela Nacional de Arte (ENA) and eventual director of the CFN, taught in Luanda.[42] The married couple Diana Alfonso and Manolo Vázquez, both members of Danza, taught classes and organized performances in Mozambique. "We learned a lot: you could say more than what we taught them," Alfonso later reflected. The trip had added personal significance because Alfonso returned seven months pregnant with their son.[43] Their Danza colleague Eddy Veitia took their place in Mozambique and described his time teaching there as a "very good experience."[44]

Dancers also contributed to relief and connection during the Cuban military campaign, as depicted in the film *Caravana* (1989) about Cubans in Angola. In the fictional dramatization of reality, Cuban modern dancers Vilma Lara and Idalmis Pacheco perform on a makeshift stage for what appears to be an audience of local Angolans and Cuban soldiers. Lilting music begins and the soloist drifts her arms and leg in front of her, before following the energetic trajectory of her extended limbs and taking soft steps forward. A Cuban soldier, appreciating her pining affect, comments to his peer, "It's true that beauty is a necessity for everyone."[45] Cuban dancers offered not only imagined connections and technical expertise to postcolonial comrades but also emotional respite to countrymen fighting far from home. From the *Palenque* rebellions in Havana to the lyrical gestures in Angolan military bases, cultural soft power and military hard power collapsed into each other as Cuban dancers intervened in theaters of war.

Not all dancers had equal opportunity to reach audiences and colleagues internationally. It is important to note that modern dancers, rather than folkloric dancers, regularly worked abroad for extended periods. The CFN did perform internationally with tours to Guyana, France, and Spain in 1975, Romania, England, Yugoslavia, and East Germany in 1976, the Soviet Union, Bulgaria, Hungary, and Colombia in 1977, Mexico in 1978, Canada and the United States in 1980, Nicaragua and Belize in 1981, Ghana, Angola, Mozambique, and Zambia in 1982, Italy, France, Spain, and Venezuela in 1983, the Soviet Union, Czechoslovakia, Bulgaria, Yugoslavia, East Germany, and Peru in 1984, East Germany, Austria, Switzerland, England, Holland, and Czechoslovakia in 1986, and Angola, the Dominican Republic, and Iraq in 1987, for instance.[46] However, CFN members generally did not teach and choreograph for months at a time abroad like modern dancers. This had material consequences, since international contracts meant salaries in hard currency, as well as professional prestige. While folkloric dancers could only imagine connections, ballet dancers even more than modern dancers enjoyed profitable internationalist opportunities as discussed in the next section.

Ballet Exports

Alicia Alonso and fellow members of the Ballet Nacional de Cuba (BNC) carried out what Cuban minister of culture Armando Hart called "systematic internationalist activity," collectively becoming a distinguished "export" of the Cuban Revolution, to use De Mille's formulation in the epigraph.[47] As they circulated, ballet dancers generated considerable hard currency and at times projected whiteness—as scions of and peers to historically white ballet institutions in Europe, the Soviet Union, and the United States—and at others, nonwhiteness—as products of a racially mixed national culture. Equally, as ballet dancers collaborated with colleagues in Communist and capitalist countries, they toggled between embracing and rejecting politics depending on the context. Dancing between whiteness and nonwhiteness, political and apolitical, Cuban ballet exports became an impressive, alluring, and ubiquitous exponent of the Revolution.

Ballet engagements built on networks forged before 1959 when the Alonsos spent months and years in Western Europe, New York, and the Soviet Union. After Castro came to power, Cuban ballet dancers activated and expanded these connections. In 1967, for instance, Alberto Alonso went to the Soviet Union to create his ballet *Carmen*, upon the request of Bolshoi ballerina Maya Plisetskaya.[48] In doing so, he fulfilled the first instance of external demand for Cuban choreographic services. Subsequent requests for *Carmen* took Alberto to Japan, Czechoslovakia, Romania, Bulgaria, and Spain in the 1970s and 1980s.[49]

As Alberto staged *Carmen* around the world, several European companies invited Alicia to mount and star in her versions of traditional ballets. This included *Giselle* (1972), *Pas de quatre* (1973), and *The Sleeping Beauty* (1974) for the Paris Opera.[50] The Vienna State Opera Ballet invited her to stage *Giselle* (1980), and the Czechoslovakian National Theatre, her production of *La fille mal gardée* (The Wayward Daughter, 1981).[51] Her renditions evidenced the malleability of the nineteenth-century copyright-free legacy, as well as Cuban connections to illustrious performers and choreographers of nineteenth- and twentieth-century Europe, the Soviet Union, and New York. *La fille mal gardée*, first performed in 1789, remains one of the oldest works in ballet repertory. *Pas de quatre* and *Giselle* had origins in the 1840s and involved the greatest ballerinas of the nineteenth century. Alicia initially encountered both in New York. In 1941, when Alicia was a member of Ballet Theatre, choreographer Anton Dolin created a ballet evocative of the by-then lost original *Pas de quatre*.[52] Alicia's creative license with *Giselle* began when she first appeared in the title role with Ballet Theatre on November 2, 1943. She eventually went from adapting one character to revising choreography for her Cuban company in subsequent decades. Choreographer Marius Petipa's *The Sleeping Beauty* premiered in Russia in 1890. When Alicia's version premiered in Havana in 1974, she asserted, "For the first time in the history of our continent *The Sleeping Beauty* is mounted without having to depend on imported versions."[53] Locally crafting and then exporting classics not only suggested Cuban parity with distinguished predecessors and contemporaries but also resulted in sizable financial gains. For instance, Alicia received around twenty-five thousand dollars for staging *The Sleeping Beauty* in Paris.[54]

The 1972 restaging of *Giselle* in Paris had particular significance because the ballet had premiered at the world-renowned Paris Opera in 1841. Alicia, accompanied by her husband and fellow company leader Fernando Alonso and BNC ballerina Josefina Méndez, worked with French dancers from January through the beginning of March to stage Alicia's version of *Giselle*. Alicia danced the title role in five performances, and Méndez, in two.[55] The Cuban press claimed that Alicia "received the double honor of being recognized for her art as a performer and as a choreographer of *Giselle* simultaneously, in the place in which this ballet has a lot of meaning and tradition." The same article also heralded the achievements of "the Cuban school" by way of Méndez, "a young figure created under the direction of Alicia and Fernando Alonso."[56] As Alicia emphasized to the Cuban press, "This was the first time that two Latin American ballerinas danced with the company of the Paris Opera in its theater."[57] French critics reportedly hailed an unspecified "Latin spirit" in the production that gave the ballet "a new vitality, a new significance."[58] This supposedly compelled a Paris Opera administrator to tell Alicia, "*Giselle* was a museum piece, something dead. You with your genius, you have revived it. You have restored it to us."[59] Cuban observers proudly highlighted how dancing compatriots impressed experts in a ballet metropole by restoring classics.

The revitalizing power of Cuban ballet may have come from the company's relative racial diversity. In the late 1960s and 1970s, black and *mulato* students like Caridad Martínez, Pablo Moré, and Andrés Williams, who had started training after 1959, joined the company, giving the troupe a multiracial character that foreigners noticed and appreciated. For instance, British critic Arnold Haskell ascertained that in Cuban ballet, "the fusion of white and black dancers brings a fresh element of great importance."[60] Diverse Cuban dancers excelled in canonic ballets like *Swan Lake*, compelling a Spanish critic to write, "Both Amparo Brito (Odette) and the prodigious black Siegfried, Andrés Williams, showed that the Ballet Nacional de Cuba has a deserved place among the small elite of the best trained [*las primerísimas formaciones*] in classical ballet."[61] The lack of racial demarcation for the white ballerina Brito, who performed Odette in *Swan Lake,* in contrast to Williams, "the prodigious black Siegfried," illustrates how the critic (and his imagined public) presumed the whiteness of dancers. In staging these works, Cubans defied the expectations of many European audience members. As one Italian critic admitted, "The Cuban performance, for the first time in Nervi, has constituted in a certain sense a surprise: the public awaited 'Caribbean' choreography, music, and costumes.... On the contrary, the first time has been occupied by a series of classical fragments, clearly inspired by the Italian and Russian school."[62] It is worth noting that these quotes come from selections of favorable foreign reviews republished in the Cuban publication, *Cuba en el Ballet.* In this carefully curated panorama of European reception, Cuban ballet dancers effectively challenged narrow understandings of the island as an exotic Caribbean Other.

In fact, ballet underscored connections between Cuba and Europe. In an interview with a Spanish critic, Alicia claimed, "The Latino is a little undisciplined, but we are not undisciplined[;] on the contrary, all the dancers are formidable and have nothing to envy of the Europeans. Besides, in our blood do not forget that we have great Spanish strength."[63] Alicia reiterated their European heritage in 1980 when she set her *Giselle* in Vienna, which was the birthplace of the famed, nineteenth-century ballerina Fanny Elssler. Alicia took a floral wreath to Elssler's tomb and credited the ballerina as a foundational figure for Cuban ballet, since she had performed in Havana in 1841 and 1842. *Cuba en el Ballet* carefully covered the trip and reprinted a German journalist claiming that the "Cuban heirs of Fanny Elssler" repaid their balletic forebear and the Austrian people with Alicia's *Giselle.*[64] Although Alicia challenged European preeminence, she ultimately capitulated to cultural and racial hierarchies by heralding Spanish patrimony and ties to Viennese luminaries. In these formulations, European-descended (white) ballet was redemptive.

Alongside traditional ballets, Alicia and her collaborators performed works that explored Cuban popular culture in the 1970s. Building on Alberto Alonso's work like *Carmen* (1967) and *El guije* (1967), which drew upon Hispano-Cuban and Afro-Cuban culture, respectively, several younger choreographers similarly created ballets with Cuban themes.[65] In 1970, the Cuban-born, Belgium-based choreographer Jorge Lefebre staged an Afro-Cuban take on the Oedipus myth, *Edipo rey,* set to percussion.[66] Alberto Méndez, a founding member of Ramiro Guerra's modern dance company before moving to ballet in the early 1960s, created *El río y el bosque* (The River and the Woods, 1973) inspired by Santería mythology. He also choreographed *Muñecos* (Dolls,

1978), a duet between a soldier doll and a "black puppet doll," which was performed by the only black female soloist, Caridad Martínez.[67] Contempora-
neously, Iván Tenorio, an actor and former member of the short-lived Danza
Contemporánea, choreographed *Rítmicas* (Rhythms, 1973), a pas de deux
that explored "the connection between *guaguancó* [a type of rumba] and
pointe shoes," as Tenorio put it.[68] Gustavo Herrera, who worked in television, cabaret, Alberto Alonso's Conjunto Experimental de Danza, the Ballet
de Camagüey, and finally the BNC, created *Cecilia Valdés* (1975) based on the
famed nineteenth-century Cuban novel by Cirilo Villaverde about a tragic,
incestuous romance during Cuba's slave society.[69] These choreographers
drew upon their experiences in other venues like television, cabarets, modern
dance, and experimental companies to create ballets with Cuban themes and
aesthetics. White, black, and *mulato* dancers in the BNC performed these
balletic homages to Cuban culture, alongside traditional European ballets.

The mixed repertory traveled to the United States in 1978. The appearance
was a long time in the making, since Alicia and a couple of dancers made several small-scale appearances in the United States in 1975, 1976, and 1977 before
the full company performed for the first time in 1978. In 1975, after a fifteen-
year absence from New York, Alicia surprised audiences by performing at the
American Ballet Theatre gala. This happened as the Nixon and Ford administrations pursued détente and improved relations with Cuba. These negotiations
accelerated under President Jimmy Carter.[70] As dance critic Alan Kriegsman
explained, "A State Department source in Washington . . . confirmed yester-
day that Alonso's present appearance was in line with recent policy 'clarifica-
tions' allowing Cuban citizens to visit the United States for religious, scientific,
or cultural purposes."[71] Then, in 1976 and 1977 Alicia and several Cuban
dancers again performed in the United States, inspiring "a genuine outpour-
ing of enthusiasm" in the auditoriums and anti-Castro pickets outside the
theaters.[72] As Cuba and the United States anticipated opening embassy-like
Interest Sections in September 1977, organizers from both countries planned
to share the financial burden of the entire BNC touring in 1978: "The Cuban
government will pay the company's travel expenses, and the Kennedy Center
and the [New York] Met[ropolitan Opera House] will pay expenses that the
85-member troupe incurs in the United States."[73] During the historic tour of
the entire BNC to the United States in 1978, the varied repertory included the
canonic *Giselle, Coppélia, Pas de quatre,* and sections of *Swan Lake,* as well as
Cuban innovations like *Carmen, Rítmicas, Muñecos,* and *Edipo rey.*[74]

Unbeknownst to organizers, 1978 would be a year of stagnation and reversal in Cuban-U.S. relations; yet, that did not dampen enthusiasm for balletic

exchanges. A May 11 invasion in Shaba, Zaire, by a small group of former Katangan gendarmes set off a public "shouting match" between Carter and Castro. The United States assumed that Cuba had been involved, and Cuba denied any participation. When the BNC arrived in the United States at the end of May 1978, talks about improving relations had stalled. The United States demanded that Cuba end military involvement in Africa, and Castro balked at Carter's efforts to dictate Cuban foreign policy.[75] These tensions did not manifest in the theater, according to one reporter:

> As the curtain rang down on *Giselle,* the audience reacted as if it had just witnessed a touchdown or a home run with the bases loaded. It was a friendlier climate than anyone could have anticipated considering the circumstances of the troupe's appearance. After all, earlier that day . . . President Carter had assailed Cuba's involvement in Africa at a meeting of NATO allies. Majority Leader Robert Byrd had called for a break in diplomatic relations with Cuba. . . . These political perturbations aside, Cuba's U.S. representative, Ramón Sánchez Parodi, responded to the dance troupe's roaring reception by remarking that "Cuba and the United States disagree about many things but there is one thing about which we are in complete agreement—ballet."[76]

Indeed, Carter even posed for a picture with Alicia in Washington.[77] In a strained climate, ballet became a safe common ground.

The BNC in the United States in 1978 and again in 1979 received warm receptions from eager and curious audiences across the country. In 1978, the BNC appeared in Washington and New York, and in 1979, in New York, Washington, Boston, San Antonio, Houston, Los Angeles, and Berkeley.[78] Dance writer Roger Copeland compared the BNC debut in 1978 to "the triumph of the Stuttgart Ballet in 1969."[79] Before the Stuttgart Ballet, touring Soviet dancers had attracted large, admiring crowds of passionate dance connoisseurs and leftists.[80] Dance, like other cultural productions from jazz to abstract expressionism, figured into the larger global struggle over capitalism and communism. Governments framed artistic success as proof of ideological viability. Watching Communist dancers meant weighing in, however indirectly, on the debate.[81]

U.S. dance critics marveled at the BNC's integration while utilizing racialized, gendered stereotypes to describe the company as a whole. In 1978, dance writer Olga Maynard noted, "The skins of [Alicia's] dancers range through the wondrous shadings of the Caribbean miscegenation, from alabaster to ebony, and all the dancers consort as equals in the Cuban school and company."[82] In this assessment, diverse dancers consorting onstage primarily evidenced inter-racial sex ("miscegenation"). Dance scholar Lester Tomé calls black men part-nering white women in Cuban ballets "interracial choreo-erotics," and indeed, commentators underscored sensuality as characteristic of the BNC.[83] For in-stance, a critic said that Méndez's *Muñecos* offered "new variations on the old toys-come-to-life theme, spiced with Latin sexuality."[84] Whereas Méndez may or may not have intended a sexy twist, Lefebre did. His *Edipo rey*, inspired by "the exotic music of [his] country," amounted to a "sensual work dealing with Jocasta's relationship with her son: mother-son, older woman–younger man, older woman–husband."[85] Perhaps Lefebre commented on the Cuban ballet's unusual family dynamics, as the aging Alicia continued performing and part-nering romantically on stage with much younger, former students like Jorge Esquivel. Regardless, sexuality jumped out to U.S. observers with men exhibit-ing "macho bravura" as they danced with "refined, disciplined, sensual" balleri-nas.[86] Eroticism had racialized implications: Cubans, regardless of skin color, struck U.S. critics as exotic, and implicitly, nonwhite.

Reductive stereotypes of "Latin sexuality" aside, Cubans selectively pro-moted this nonwhite identity and contrasted the BNC's integration to segre-gation elsewhere in the ballet world. In the United States, for instance, black ballet dancers were rare with a handful of standout figures like New York City Ballet's Arthur Mitchell, who went on to found the all-black ballet company Dance Theatre of Harlem in 1968.[87] Alicia boasted about the unique diversity of Cuban ballet:

> So the most wonderful thing . . . is that we presented both the classical and the modern and nobody . . . was at all surprised that our dancers went from the whitest blondes to the blackest blacks. Nobody seemed bothered by that, no one felt it took away from our artistic worth or from what we were doing, because it was obvious that we choose our dancers for the way they dance, not because of their colour. . . . I've seen other companies that have tried to include black dancers, and it's as if they were saying: "Look at us; look how integrated we are!" It's pure exhibitionism, without any real reason, like showing off an animal instead of an artist. It has nothing to do with talent. Here in Cuba it's the talent that counts.

Alicia concluded, "We don't even know how many Black [dancers] we have, how many mulattos and how many whites. I know that we have a lot of talent, and it's all colours, but the most important thing is that we've got artists, revo-lutionary artists."[88] This typically Cuban claim of race blindness did not translate to equal opportunity, as the career of Afro-Cuban ballerina Caridad

Martínez shows. Caridad had access to the upper echelons of the BNC but was barred from roles like Giselle because she "did not have the hair" for the mad scene, when the protagonist's (apparently only straight) hair falls in her face.[89] Yet, even though the BNC was undoubtedly plagued by racism, the company still stood out. Alicia suggested, and observers seemed to agree, that the artistic worth of the BNC increased due to the ostensibly organic racial diversity that sprang from long-standing Cuban ideologies about race and nation, Alicia's notions of meritocracy, and newer revolutionary discourses.

Along with racial diversity, politics also attached allure to Cuban ballet exports. After the fall of the right-wing dictatorship in Portugal during the "Carnation Revolution" of April 1974, the BNC performed for an estimated 75,100 people.[90] In one performance at a stadium, exuberant audience members threw carnations on the stage as the Cubans performed the militaristic ballet *La avanzada* before the flags of Portugal and Cuba. "Why did my presence in Portugal produce such a favorable reaction?" Alicia mused in an interview. "I think it responded to the fact that, for many years, I had been invited to dance in Portugal and I never went. So that admiration . . . responded to my revolutionary position against fascism that previously oppressed the country."[91] By contrast, Alicia dodged political posturing when she performed in the United States in June 1980, just as the refugee crisis known as the Mariel boatlift brought thousands of Cubans to Miami. In an interview, Cuban exile and journalist Octavio Roca asked Alicia about tensions between the United States and Cuba. She demurred, "It is very funny[;]when politicians travel and speak with the press, they are never asked to speak about ballet. Why should it be that ballet dancers have to discuss politics? I am not an expert in politics. . . . Just be sure that I am a Cuban, that I do support the revolution. Then, let me dance."[92] Politics framed Cuban dancers and no doubt added to their intrigue, regardless if Alicia asserted antifascism in Portugal or unadorned revolutionary support in the United States. After years of carrying revolutionary baggage around the world, Alicia possessed considerable political acumen, knowing when to accentuate or avoid ideological discussions.

Political leanings also manifested in less splashy, more mundane ways. In the 1970s, Cuba strengthened relations with the Soviet Union and Eastern Bloc countries, especially in 1972 when Cuba joined the socialist economic community under Soviet leadership, the Council of Mutual Economic Assistance.[93] When I asked Caridad Martínez about how this special relationship impacted ballet, she noted matter-of-factly that Cubans performed almost every year in the Soviet Union and that Soviet companies appeared regularly in Cuba.[94] In this instance, ideological alliances resulted in uninhibited connection (instead of grand political theater), which was not insignificant given the metaphoric curtain dividing the world with concrete consequences. Cuban-Soviet ballet exchanges also became opportunities to highlight parity between the two countries despite the island's economic dependence on the Soviet Union.[95] For instance, in 1975 Loipa Araújo performed the lead roles of *Swan Lake* and *Carmen* with the Bolshoi Ballet, becoming the first Cuban ballerina since Alicia in the 1950s to dance with the famed Soviet company. Araújo also repeated the program when the beloved Bolshoi ballerina Maya Plisetskaya fell ill. This was briefly controversial, according to one internal report. "As an interesting anecdote," the Cuban functionary shared, "when the Kremlin protocol leaders learned that a Soviet [ballerina] would not dance, they raised hell [*pusieron el grito en el cielo*] and immediately called the directors of the Ministry of Culture. The answer was convincing and concise, do not worry yourselves as the quality of the [Cuban] soloist is equal to ours." Despite initial concerns, faith in Cuban abilities won out and Araújo delivered. She enjoyed a "fabulous reception" from discerning Moscow audiences.[96]

The whiteness and nonwhiteness, politics and apolitics of the Cuban ballet made for an irresistible export that generated material gains for individuals involved. Information about monetary compensation for dancers is uneven, but anecdotes indicate considerable payoffs. In 1973, soloists Jorge Esquivel and Orlando Salgado purchased motorcycles while in Odessa. Although such actions were officially frowned upon, bureaucrats decided to allow the transactions because of "the personal characteristics of these *compañeros,* serious and responsible workers."[97] In 1982, Alicia used her honorarium to buy equipment while appearing at a retirement event for her former dance partner, Igor Youskevitch, at the University of Texas, Austin. As a university administrator described it, "On Saturday, the day before the performance, [Alicia] came to me with her honorarium check, which was for $6,000 [U.S. dollars], and she said, 'Cash please.' So I called the president of the university, and he called the president of a local bank, and the local banker opened up the vaults and cashed her check. All day Sunday she and her bodyguards shopped, and when they boarded their flight to Cuba on Monday, they were loaded down with VCRs, tape-recording equipment, slide projectors, and every conceivable thing you could imagine for filmmaking. It was for her school and company."[98] Despite hardening policies under U.S. president Ronald Reagan, the ballerina used money from a public university to help support Cuban ballet enterprises. Such gains equally aided the Cuban government, as it received cuts of the windfall, not to mention the intangible benefit of impressed international audiences. The state in turn "rewarded" dancers by sometimes allowing them to use money earned abroad to address personal and professional needs.

This arrangement did not please everybody. When five ballet dancers including Caridad Martínez performed in Italy, they earned over one thousand dollars per night; yet, they received around fifty dollars daily. The tight funds forced them to cook in their hotel rooms, which was a common practice for Cubans appearing in expensive foreign cities. Sizable honoraria went to the government, which had paid for the dancers' education, training, and salaries. "My school was free, that is true," Caridad acknowledged, "but I paid [for] my school several times." She wryly mused, "I don't know how many careers I paid [off] during the years that I was in the National Ballet of Cuba."[99] Traveling regularly to Europe was a privilege within Cuba that nevertheless revealed to Martínez and others the hardships that Cuban ballet dancers faced in contrast to peers in richer countries.

Through ballet, Cuba had a different relationship with the so-called first and second worlds than generally recognized. Whereas Cuba harbored political animosity toward the United States and depended economically on the Soviet Union, in ballet Cubans collaborated as equals with counterparts in more powerful countries with different ideological leanings. Dancers and audiences around the polarized Cold War world seemed to agree that Cuban ballet had much to offer. This evidenced shared cultural traditions and value systems as Cuba, Europe, the Soviet Union, and North America similarly coveted ballet. Moreover, Cuban ballet dancers stood out, performing traditional ballets (associated with whiteness) as well as ones with Cuban themes, often glossed as exotic and nonwhite in foreign imaginaries.[100] Along with sexualized, racialized difference, Alicia and Cuban ballet colleagues had a politicized allure, whether they embraced or purported to transcend mundane politics. Through these different registers, ballet dancers appealed to foreign hearts and minds. Thus, Cuba became not only a David fighting Goliath through military missions and loud denunciations of U.S. imperialism but also a dancing David, sharing choreography with friends and foes alike.[101]

Dance Leadership in Latin America

Along with imaginatively connecting to Africa during military engagements and proving balletic excellence for profit in the first and second worlds, Cuban dancers became valued regional experts just as official policy toward Latin America shifted. Following Che Guevara's death in Bolivia in 1967, Havana decreased support for armed movements and focused on reestablishing diplomatic relations with governments in the region. This defied U.S. efforts to isolate Cuba by promoting inter-American engagement through trade and cultural exchange.[102] As armed guerrilla fighters went home, dancers perpetuated Cuba's physical presence throughout the region, sharing methods of movement that equipped Latin American counterparts to make revolutions in art not war.

Dancers forged Cuban-Chilean connections even when the countries had no formal relations from 1964 to 1970.[103] In the 1960s, Chilean choreographer Patricio Bunster worked in Cuba. Originally trained as an architect, Bunster discovered dance via German choreographer Kurt Jooss and his company, which performed in Santiago. After the outbreak of World War II, some members formed a dance ensemble at the University of Chile, extending their stays indefinitely. With "eclectic technique," the German dancers created dramatic social messages like Jooss's famed antiwar piece, *The Green Table*, and these priorities influenced Bunster's development.[104] In 1959, Bunster created *Calaucán* (Rebellious Bud) about indigenous peoples fighting to preserve their "land, liberty and culture, from the barbaric colonization of the Spanish conquistadors." He also ran in leftist circles, collaborating with his former wife British-Chilean dancer Joan Turner and her second husband, famed Communist folk singer Víctor Jara.[105] In the early 1960s, Bunster traveled to Cuba to set *Calaucán* on the BNC; then in 1967, he attended an international ballet festival in Havana and participated in a roundtable on Cuban ballet.[106] These collaborations dovetailed with Castro's late 1960s endorsement of Chilean presidential candidate Salvador Allende's electoral (not armed) path to socialism.[107]

After winning the election in 1970, Allende reestablished formal relations with Cuba, making dance exchanges especially propitious, as revealed by increased correspondence about Cuban dance makers traveling to Chile.[108] For instance, Bunster wrote directly to Fernando Alonso, "*I need* you to come to our Department of Dance [at the University of Chile] to give some lectures, to meet with our professors in formation, and if it is possible to give some demonstrative classes" (underlined in source). Chilean dancers had previously worked with Soviet teachers, but Bunster wanted to ensure that "*us Chileans encounter our own form of expression*" (underlined in source). The Cuban ballet provided a model for bold independence: "You all have created a Cuban school in which all your experiences have been assimilated and integrated guided by a spirit, a Cuban national idiosyncrasy.... You will help me give them the courage that we have to have in order to advance on our own paths." Bunster hoped Fernando would come immediately in December 1972, or at the latest March 1973, for three or four weeks. He threw in a flourish of political responsibility, "Cuban-Chilean solidarity, *compañero!*"[109] However, the BNC had commitments elsewhere, such as Alicia setting *Giselle* in Paris and Araújo performing in the Soviet Union.[110] The delay went from temporary to indefinite when a right-wing military coup on September 11, 1973, ended Allende and brought the right-wing dictator Augusto Pinochet to power.

Although Chile became an unviable dance partner, Cuban ballet teachers, choreographers, and performers began working regularly in Mexico, Peru, and Ecuador in the 1970s and 1980s. As Mexican president Luis Echeverría (1970–76) pursued closer relations with Cuba, Mexican dance institutions invited Cuban ballet experts to reorganize training programs, set ballets on Mexican professionals, and audition Mexican dance students to train in Cuba.[111] Ballet linkages formed with Peru after Juan Francisco Velasco (1968–75) reestablished relations with Cuba in 1972. In 1978, a Cuban delegation supported the new international dance festival in Trujillo organized by Peruvian dancer Stella Puga, who called the Cuban ballet dancers "our guide."[112] BNC members visited as delegates and performers in subsequent years, and in 1986, the Cuban-Peruvian ballet exchange expanded when the Ballet de Camagüey formalized a collaboration agreement with Puga.[113] Camagüey dancers, along with choreographer Gustavo Herrera, also figured importantly in Cuban collaborations with Ecuador as part of an agreement formalized in September 1979 under the reformist president Jaime Roldós Aguilera (1979–81).[114] In 1984, Herrera and dancers from the Ballet de Camagüey worked with the Ballet Ecuatoriano de Cámara and Instituto Nacional de Danza (National Institute of Dance) in Quito.[115] That year, ballet teacher María Esther García reflected on her internationalist work in Ecuador and elsewhere thusly: "We did not limit ourselves to what the agreements [*convenios*] established. The cooperation went far beyond what was planned. I felt really good the entire time, and I should say that there, they amply respected the technical criteria of the Cuban advisors, greatly valuing the work that we did."[116] Dancers gave content and meaning to international programs, going "far beyond what was planned."

Through internationalist campaigns, the Cuban school of ballet arguably became for Latin American dancers what Che's canonic manual, *Guerrilla Warfare*, was for leftist guerrillas: methodologies that organized movements and had hemispheric projection. Moreover, like Che, Alicia became an icon, who animated movements beyond her physical reach. As Ecuadorian company director Rubén Guarderas effused when awarding her a medal of recognition, "Thank you, master teacher Alicia Alonso, for your artistic light that illuminates and will always illuminate our America. . . . Your spirit and teachings live in every one of America's dancers."[117] Although Alicia became *the* symbol of Cuban ballet, a diverse band of teachers, performers, and choreographers executed the intense work of dance internationalism.

Enchantment with Alicia and all she represented had its limits, but Cuban ballet dancers never failed to impress, as revealed in the case of Venezuela. Venezuelan president Carlos Andrés Pérez (1974–79) reestablished relations with Cuba in 1974, and in February 1975, Venezuelan ballerina Zhandra Rodríguez performed in Cuba, warmly asserting, "All of us are Latin Americans, as though the same blood, the same family."[118] Despite supposed proximity, divides came up when Cuban ballet dancers appeared in Venezuela a couple of months later.[119] María Cristina Anzola, an impresario in Caracas at the time, helped to bring the BNC to Venezuela. During a conversation in her New York home, she reflected, "When the company came to Caracas they had, I think . . . a mission, which was to prove that socialism or communism is the right thing. So they had a little of that aggressive attitude, in general." Moreover, as Anzola recalled,

> They would sit in a long table and debate . . . what the casting was going to be. I was sitting there waiting because . . . with the casting you could promote, and you would sell tickets better. . . . It would take a long time, and Alicia would always say, "Because we are very democratic, . . . everybody gives an opinion." But there was only one ruler there, and it was her! The whole thing was like a comedy because they all knew it—and I knew it— that in the end, she was going to decide who was going to dance what. . . . But you had to go through that . . . democracy show.[120]

Despite delayed casting, the trip was a huge success with full houses of exuberant audiences. Though not a fan of Castro's politics, Anzola admitted, "I never care[d] one bit that Cuban ballet [was] communist or not; they were just beautiful." Cubans also inadvertently aided local ballet projects: "I wanted to show—and in a way, I was looking at my government—[that] the Latino body can do this. They can have a big company doing the classics. . . . If they did it in Cuba, we could do it too." Her plan worked. The state increased support for Venezuelan ballet.[121] Like in Chile, Mexico, Peru, and Ecuador, Cuban ballet dancers proved balletic possibility and supported local ballet enrichment, regardless of ideological leanings.

Along with ballet specialists, Cuban modern dancers became highly sought after in Latin America. The early 1970s held acute frustrations for Danza, including censorship and few opportunities to perform abroad, but the situation improved slowly but surely.[122] This manifested in 1974, when

Danza went to Panama, traveling abroad for the first time that decade. Burd-sall gushed to her mother, "56 members of the group [went] to help inaugurate the reopening of the National Theatre of Panama.... We gave *five* performances in *three* days, in schools, local theatres, etc. We had thousands of people clapping.... It was a *wild* week since besides all the work of performances and traveling we were invited to luncheons, dinners, receptions, parties & we hardly slept. The last day, today, we heard on the radio that diplomatic relations with Cuba have been reestablished" (underlined in source).[123] Modern dancers appeared at an exciting moment of diplomatic transition and their own professional advance. "We're sitting on top of the world after our successful Panamanian trip and I'm sure it won't be long before we get sent on another. We are probably the best and biggest modern dance group in Latin America," she happily bragged in another letter.[124] Regional distinction had repercussions in Cuba, which Burdsall described in the following terms: "Things have changed here. Modern dance is now a big thing & we are finally respected by everyone."[125] Dance internationalism indexed growing profiles both abroad and at home.

Along with establishing professional reputations, modern dancers projected leftist solidarity as right-wing reactionary violence was on the rise in 1970s Latin America. For instance, Danza performed *Uruguay, hoy* (Uruguay, Today, 1973), choreographed by Teresa Trujillo, who fled to Cuba after a right-wing regime came into power in her native Uruguay. The half-hour work featured thirty-one dancers performing movement and spoken text, "inspired by the fight of this *pueblo*, which fascism wants to silence."[126] In 1978, Burdsall choreographed *Ahora* (Now) about the 1973 right-wing coup in Chile. Set to music and spoken text from the writings of Pablo Neruda, Wilhelm Reich, and Fidel Castro, "the list of murdered and missing people was read, [and] these women, in slow motion, rose to their feet to form a tight line of frozen faces. The light also revealed the clasping of each other's hands before each one left the line, one by one, to walk slowly to meet her fate," Burdsall later described. Adding to its internationalist consequence, Burdsall set *Ahora* on Mexican dancers during a 1980 trip.[127]

In addition to performing solidarities with Latin American leftists, Cuban modern dancers began exporting their technique, starting with Guyana. Such connections dovetailed with geopolitical shifts after Cuba reestablished diplomatic and trade relations with the newly independent Jamaica, Barbados, Guyana, and Trinidad and Tobago in 1972. This gave way to important cultural collaborations like the rotating international Caribbean Festival of Arts (CARIFESTA), which took place in Guyana (1972), Jamaica (1976), Cuba

FIGURE 6.1 Dance internationalist Gerardo Lastra with his students at the National School of Dance of Guyana, ca. 1978. Photographer unknown. Source: Archivo de Danza Contemporánea de Cuba. Courtesy of Danza Contemporánea de Cuba.

(1979), and Barbados (1981).[128] In this context, Danza spent a week in Guyana in 1976, performing under the auspices of a Guyana-Cuba cultural cooperation agreement and reportedly impressing audiences with a "high standard of dance, which was particularly Cuban and Latin American."[129] Guyana then asked Cuba to send a choreographer or teacher to help develop modern dance instruction and a new professional company. The Guyanese government would cover all costs of the stay. Cuba only had to pay for airfare.[130]

Cuban modern dancer Gerardo Lastra directed the National School of Dance of Guyana starting in August 1977 (see figure 6.1), succeeding Lavinia Williams, a U.S.-born dancer of West Indian descent who had shaped dance institutions in the Caribbean, especially in Haiti. In addition to the school, Lastra explored the possibility of creating a professional modern dance company.[131] In a statement to the press, Lastra reflected, "Of course the emergence of such a company will take years and, so far, I am to be here for only 12 months. . . . But this plan is so important to the development of your culture that I am happy to be here even for the very beginning."[132] Although he brought Cuban approaches to modern dance—that is, fusing international modern techniques and local folkloric vocabularies—the "internationalist mission" ultimately aimed to equip Guyanese creators for independent art making.[133] Students took classes in Guyanese folkloric dances from African and Indian diasporic cultures, along with modern dance and ballet.[134] Evidencing their diverse training and repertoire, a 1979 program included *Hold On*, choreographed by Lastra and based on a "negro spiritual . . . expressing the theme of courage and togetherness," as well as *Indian Scarf Dance* choreographed by Mathadyal Persaud, which depicted a "folk dance done in the Punjah region of India" to celebrate rice harvests.[135] According to Lastra, his work in Guyana resulted in exciting dance developments, stronger "currents of sympathy, interest, and respect between Guyanese and Cubans," and deepening "friendship between our countries."[136]

To Guyanese observers, Lastra was an especially important dance figure due to his gender. As one Guyanese article noted, "It is hoped for that with a man as Director, more men will be encouraged to enroll in the new school year scheduled to begin next month."[137] Another article described dance for men as a new concept in Guyana. Lastra noted that similar problems had bedeviled Cuba: "At that time, in my country, many men believed that dancing was not masculine enough and that they would be looked upon as sissies if they became dancers." He went on to clarify how Cuba overcame that problem by creating a "masculine" way of dancing: "At home we have many powerfully built young men in our dance school and the choreography . . . they perform almost always tests them to the utmost. We find too that the dance exercises are perfect for developing . . . muscles . . . and so the dance student is always afforded the opportunity to be trim and healthy."[138] To master the Cuban approach, three Guyanese male dancers even began training in Havana in 1977.[139] Dance internationalism in this instance exposed shared gender norms with Guyanese observers welcoming Cuban approaches to cultivating traditional heteronormative masculinity through movement.

Lastra's activities in Guyana were part of a larger phenomenon. In 1980, for instance, Lastra's colleague Eduardo Rivero spent a year in Jamaica. This exchange was long in the making. The National Dance Theatre Company of Jamaica had performed in Cuba in 1974 and visited Danza's studios for a showing that included Rivero's *Súlkary*. Jamaican choreographer and artistic director Rex Nettleford praised the group for cultivating "a dance theater of the Caribbean with its own characteristics." He suggested that the companies share repertory and invited the Cubans to Jamaica.[140] Six years later, Rivero worked in Jamaica for a year.[141] The son of a Jamaican woman and a Cuban man, Rivero felt special connection with the island: "When I went to Jamaica, it was like arriving to my home, to my family. . . . I staged *Súlkary* on the Jamaican company and created a strong connection, and I even danced *Okantomí*."[142] Rivero's time left a lasting impact on Nettleford's Jamaican company. *Súlkary* remained in active repertory, and Rivero's classes, according to Nettleford, "brought to the Company an articulation of technique, vocabulary, and style rooted in Afro-Caribbean forms with which the Company had been working for eighteen years."[143] In Rivero and Cuban modern dance more broadly, Jamaican dancers recognized a kindred project of exploring African legacies in the Caribbean. Influence flowed in both directions. Upon returning to Cuba, Rivero choreographed an eight-minute piece simply titled *Solo* (1980), inspired by his time in Jamaica.[144] The rich experience paved the way for Rivero's later dance internationalism in the Caribbean, including Grenada and Belize.[145]

International exposure led to new opportunities. As Burdsall put it, "After the Conjunto has made its rounds advertising our teaching we keep getting requests from other Latin American countries to come & study."[146] In response, Cuban modern dancers increasingly traveled abroad to advise and teach. Lastra, for instance, was in Nicaragua for a year "to develop . . . internationalist labor within his specialty," joining other dancers, cultural producers, and civilian experts supporting the country after the leftist Sandinista National Liberation Front took power in 1979.[147] Reflecting on these international projects, modern dancer Isidro Rolando proudly asserted, "Cuban dance already is integrated in the process of dance in Latin America, helping and strengthening this practice in those countries that have solicited our services."[148] Cuban modern dance, like ballet, became a regionally renowned technique that forged international friendships and bolstered the status of highly sought-after Cuban experts.

The regional connections and collaborations enacted by ballet and modern dancers culminated in 1983 with the First Latin American Congress of Dance in Rio de Janeiro. Alicia was chosen to preside over dance leaders from Brazil, Colombia, Chile, Mexico, Venezuela, Uruguay, Paraguay, Argentina, and Cuba.[149] The congress reflected a key political shift in the region—countries like Brazil, Argentina, and Uruguay were transitioning from right-wing dictatorship to democracy in the 1980s. At this moment, Cuban ballet dancers pursued exchanges with these formerly estranged nations. In 1984, the BNC danced in Brazil for the first time in twenty-five years.[150] In 1985 and 1986, Lázaro Carreño was a guest artist in Rio and received "spectacular" reception from "both the press and spectators." He told reporters, "It's exciting to see the fondness that they feel for Cuban ballet, for our school."[151] In 1985, 1986, and 1987, Cuban teacher Karemia Morena taught ballet classes, coached dancers, and led discussions about the Cuban school of ballet in Buenos Aires. Echoing Carreño, she claimed, "There is a great respect for our work and a notable preference for the Cuban school."[152] In 1987, the BNC performed in Uruguay for the first time in twenty-eight years, prompting Uruguayans to wait in long lines to buy tickets. Along with other political notables, Uruguayan president Julio María Sanguinetti attended the show. More dance collaborations between the two countries soon followed.[153]

With Cold War tensions dissipating but not over, a second session of the congress on Latin American dance met in Havana in November 1988 during Cuba's biennial international ballet festival. Just before the meeting, a pro–United States Puerto Rican music institute proposed developing a regional dance organization that snubbed Cuba.[154] With this rebuff in mind, representatives from Argentina, Brazil, Colombia, Cuba, the Dominican Republic, Ecuador, Mexico, Nicaragua, Panama, Peru, Puerto Rico, Uruguay, and Venezuela as well as observers from other parts of the world elected Alicia president of a new foundation in charge of regional dance projects.[155] The new Fundación Latinoamericana y Caribeña de la Danza (Latin American and Caribbean Dance Foundation) had goals that resembled those in Fernando Alonso's 1953 call for a Ballet Latinoamericano. The new organization, like the 1953 proposal, aimed to facilitate regional exchange, promote respect for dance professionals, and support the dissemination of ballet and modern dance in member countries.[156] Thus dance internationalism in Latin America meant realizing long-standing artistic goals by establishing Cuban dancers' regional leadership while furthering recent foreign policy objectives of breaking hemispheric isolation. As guerrilla fighters stayed home, dancers and fellow cultural producers took on added significance as vectors of Cuban intervention and influence in Latin America.

Dance internationalists enjoyed privileges in traveling and working abroad on behalf of the Revolution, but always with caveats. In the early 1980s, master ballet teacher Joaquín Banegas taught an unscheduled private class while furthering the Cuban ballet mission in Mexico. He was taken into Cuban custody, removed from Mexico, and incarcerated in Cuba. Everyone in the BNC knew about this scandal but followed unwritten rules to remain publicly silent. Ballerina Caridad Martínez inadvertently transgressed this mandate by mentioning Banegas during a published interview with Cuban writer Leonardo Padura: "In school I had excellent teachers, friends that, in one form or other, occupy an important place in my development; and, among them, above all Fernando Alonso, Mirta Plá and especially Joaquín Banegas, an excellent teacher that made me understand the discipline necessary to become a good ballerina."[157] The seemingly innocuous credit caused commotion behind the scenes. Padura was fired, and Alicia angrily asked Caridad why she had mentioned the persona non grata. Caridad recalled her horror at witnessing the fate of her cherished teacher and the aftermath of acknowledging his contributions to Cuban ballet. What happened next, I asked. Alicia used her cultural and political capital to get Banegas out: "She resolved it," Caridad answered simply.[158] The incident encapsulates the power and precarity of dance internationalists. Although they were venerated as regional experts, individual monetary acquisition was strictly forbidden. Yet, Alicia's distinction, and that of ballet dancers more generally, undoubtedly helped to secure the release of an insubordinate ballet master.

Conclusion

Dance internationalism involved Cuban performers connecting with diverse corners of the globe through choreography and travel. Folkloric and modern dancers imagined dialogues with Africa, and modern dancers performed and taught on the continent. Cuban ballet dancers highlighted historic and ongoing connections to Europe, the Soviet Union, and the United States, impressing audiences with their whiteness and nonwhiteness, that is, their parity with traditional ballet centers and comparative racial diversity. In Latin America, modern and ballet dancers taught, choreographed, and performed, exporting their technical expertise and becoming regional leaders. Dance internationalists intervened in theaters of war, earned hard currency, and poked holes in hemispheric isolation, contributing to diplomacy, the Revolution, and global dance developments. According to the consummate revolutionary export, Alicia Alonso, dancers went beyond representatives: "We *are* the Revolution."[159] That is, when deployed by the state, Alicia and her fellow dancers grabbed the mantle of revolutionary purpose and proclaimed their ability to connect with Nigerians, Italians, Soviets, Venezuelans, Guyanese, Brazilians, and others through their dance innovations.

Dance internationalism generated both symbolic and material gains. Modern dance director Miguel Iglesias affirmed, "When we travel abroad our goals are to show how a country like Cuba can have a high quality artistic movement . . . and also to generate currency to contribute to the economy, in addition to having the personal satisfaction of being recognized as Cuban artists."[160] Dance internationalists generated hard currency for a cash-strapped state, joining an increasing number of Cuban cultural producers (from only eleven in 1977 to over a hundred in 1982) working abroad.[161] Although data on earnings remain spotty and anecdotal, dance makers contributed to a larger windfall earned by numerous Cuban experts overseas, around fifty million in hard currency or approximately 9 percent of commodity exports to capitalist countries in 1977, for instance.[162] Danced soft power generated prestige and profit that bolstered the status of both the Revolution and Cuban dancers on the world stage.

These gains were ultimately uneven and restricted, however. Folkloric dancers did not have many opportunities to teach abroad for extended periods, while modern and especially ballet dancers spent months or even years engaged in internationalist missions. This had concrete implications. Time abroad gave dance makers honoraria, access to consumer goods, and symbolic capital. Even ballet dancers, who had the most opportunities to enjoy the privileges of international work, faced humiliations, as illuminated by Martínez's memories of meals cooked in Italian hotel rooms or Banegas's punishment for a private class in Mexico. Cuban dance internationalists owed the government for their education and careers, but some wondered, to what degree and at what cost?

The system wherein the Cuban government maintained strict control over monetary gains of international projects struck dancers like Martínez as unfair. The quiet dissatisfaction with the status quo changed the dance establishment slowly but surely in the 1980s. In Padura's interview with Martínez, they discussed not only her valued teachers like Banegas but also her generation. Her answers had a despondent tone. The future seemed fine but not exciting, and certainly not revolutionary. As post-1959 dance institutions aged, dancers fought to revise and update their field. This resulted in works that irreverently questioned the system with experimental aesthetics. As a result, the 1980s in many ways came to resemble the heady and daring early 1960s before dance institutions ossified. As a younger generation burst onto the scene and older dancers reflected on bitter memories, they pushed for a more open dance future from within. The next chapter takes up these generational shifts and sighs.

CHAPTER SEVEN

Opening Dance

OPEN, TO OPEN, OPENING	ABIERTA, ABRIR, ABRIENDO
The visible to the invisible	Lo visible a lo invisible
body to voice	el cuerpo a la voz
detritus to epic	el detritus a la epopeya
viscera to form	la víscera a la forma
movement to gesture	el movimiento al gesto
Metaphor to concept	La metáfora al concepto
Dancer to actor	El bailarín al actor
Dance to posture	La danza a la postura
Muscle to metaphor	El músculo a la metáfora
Concept to sensation	El concepto a la sensación
Form to question	La forma a la pregunta
Question	La pregunta

—Danza Abierta (Open Dance), 1988

The impressionistic text above appeared in the 1988 premiere performance program for the new modern dance company Danza Abierta (Open Dance).[1] The words that bookend the poetic passage—open (*abierta*) and question (*la pregunta*)—encapsulated the ethos of dance innovations in the late 1970s through 1990. Dance makers had fought for and secured considerable political and cultural capital in the revolutionary dance institutions that they had built. Moreover, they retained a public platform despite racial and sexual prejudices and extended their artistic reach domestically and abroad through mass education programs and internationalist initiatives. By the late 1970s and 1980s, dance makers used their degrees of power and ephemeral political moves to push for more open structures. Their political choreographies made the years leading up to 1990 a period of radical experimentation and bold reckoning with revolutionary steps and missteps.

Dance developments happened alongside important political and economic changes. In 1976, the government passed a new constitution, established municipal assemblies called Popular Power, and reorganized the cultural bureaucracy. In December, the Ministerio de Cultura (Ministry of Culture) replaced the Consejo Nacional de Cultura (National Council of Culture), and Armando Hart took the helm. Cultural producers reportedly exhaled a collective "sigh of relief" because Hart was more open-minded than his predecessor, Luis Pavón Tamayo.[2] The beginning of the 1980s was an era of "centralized decentralization," but the latter half of the decade saw a reversal in these trends. As the Soviet Union implemented perestroika (reformation) and glasnost (openness), Castro went in a different direction with *rectificación* (rectification) to address economic errors of recent decentralizing reforms, which supposedly had led to increased inequality and inefficiency.[3] Despite these changes, Cuba's economic problems increased in the late 1980s. Meanwhile, dance institutions formed after 1959 began to show their age, and the first generation of Cubans born after the 1959 Revolution came of age. Dancers like those in Danza Abierta used expressive tools like "muscle" and "metaphor" to promote reform despite official efforts to the contrary.

With a dance perspective, this chapter offers a different understanding of the cultural scene in the late 1970s and 1980s and helps explain what came next. Cuban dancers, like their peers in other art forms, created alternative institutional spaces to air disaffection. These creative energies predated but became acutely apparent during the "Special Period in Times of Peace," a label that Castro coined in 1990 for the devastating economic and political crisis caused by the fall of the Soviet Union. Scholars have argued that this crisis caused an explosion of institutional changes and expressive openings (sometimes short lived) in the 1990s.[4] However, such narratives miss an important legacy of negotiation and creative labor in Cuba. Dancers did not suddenly push boundaries due to external geopolitics like the fall of the Soviet Union in the 1990s, but built a transgressive art praxis to respond to internal inertias and individual needs in the late 1970s and 1980s. By tracing these internal dynamics, I build on the work of Cuban historian Jorgelina Guzmán Moré, who has written about developments in the visual arts, literature, and theater from 1988 to 1992: "These years constituted a moment . . . of change and shaking off of the stagnant and infertile that hindered the progressive advance of Cuban society as a whole. They were years of effervescence and restoration of the revolutionary project, at the same time new paradigms were known and assumed."[5] Looking at dance reveals that the "shaking off" in fact started almost a decade earlier and was a legacy of predecessors, who had innovated in productive tension with various Cuban governments since before 1959. In sum, dancers drew upon existing artistic and political tactics to fill the 1980s with exciting experimentation, and these innovations, not external geopolitics, would lay the foundation for continued opening and questioning in the Special Period.

To analyze these dynamics, the chapter first examines restless youth in the ballet establishment, especially those led by Afro-Cuban ballerina Caridad

Martínez. Martínez and dancers of her generation protested against mismanagement under the unwavering leadership of Alicia Alonso. They wrote letters of complaint, formed a new company, and mounted choreography that a savvy dancing public read as cleverly critical. The second section focuses on older dance makers, who experienced personal and professional changes and moved in new directions. This meant relinquishing longtime company affiliations and sometimes relocating to towns outside of the capital, which reconfigured the dance landscape in Cuba. The third section analyzes vanguard modern dancers associated with and contemporaries to Danza Abierta, as well as Ramiro Guerra, who staged a cynical retrospective. Their work shows the dynamism of Cuban concert dance, decades in the making, as well as the struggles that dance makers had faced and continued to face in dancing with the Revolution.

Restless Youth

Modern dancer Rosario Cárdenas noted in 1979, "There is much restlessness [*inquietudes*] among the young members of the company."[6] This sentiment reflected broader currents as armed struggles of the late 1950s and ebullient improvisations of the 1960s became a receding past. The official institutionalization of a singular heroic Revolution in the 1970s established "expectations that all Cubans, and young people in particular, could scarcely hope to meet."[7] Along with the weight of a monumental history, the decade closed with a recession and more than 100,000 Cuban Americans visiting the island in 1979. During these reunions, citizens reconnected with relatives, who had ready access to consumer goods and very different lifestyles abroad.[8] Although it is difficult to gauge how these visits impacted Cubans, soon thereafter, ten thousand Cuban citizens took refuge at the Peruvian Embassy in Havana, and 125,000 left via the Mariel boatlift in 1980, evidencing a broader climate of discontent.[9] Within this atmosphere, young dancers began rejecting the expectation that revolutionary Cubans remain happy and grateful without indulging in existential problems.[10] They had dissatisfactions and desires to convey.

For one, the Ballet Nacional de Cuba (BNC) offered limited opportunities to younger dancers because older ballerinas, including sexagenarian Alicia Alonso, continued dancing. Her daughter Laura Alonso tried to address this issue in 1984, when she spearheaded a collective dubbed the Joven Guardia (Young Guard) for new BNC members. According to an official announcement, Alicia had conceived of the project while Laura directed it.[11] A document about its goals described the Joven Guardia as a "brigade" of the BNC that "groups the young graduates of [the Escuela Nacional de Arte] ENA and other members of the company . . . 18 to 25 years old with the objective that in the term of four years, they receive a type of post-graduate, technical and artistic complementation for their continued development as dancers."[12] Early on, the Joven Guardia appeared in small-scale, youth-oriented venues like the Lenin School and with ballet students in Matanzas.[13] However, by late 1987, Joven Guardia had matured into an international enterprise, boasting foreign dancers in its ranks and embarking on its first international tour to Nicaragua in December.[14] Joven Guardia provided much-needed opportunities and gestured to broader discontent under Alicia's perpetual shadow.

Restlessness and dissatisfaction at the BNC also pushed principal ballerina Caridad Martínez to take action. Born in Havana, Martínez was part of the first class of ballet students at ENA and joined the BNC upon graduating in 1968. She eventually became a soloist, first soloist, and then principal dancer with the company.[15] In an interview, she discussed her early training and career in positive strokes. She always felt welcome and encouraged despite being the only top-ranking female ballet dancer of African descent. However, in 1975, Fernando and Alicia Alonso divorced, unsettling the ballet establishment and adversely affecting Caridad's experience in the company. She noticed racial prejudices in comments and casting decisions, which she attributed to Alicia's second husband, Pedro Simón.[16] At one point, Caridad asked Alicia about her future. After complimenting Caridad on her technique and artistry, Alicia said that she had a nose and hair "problem." The racist comments "shook me tremendously," Caridad recalled, especially after years of kind support.[17] People around the company noticed and tried to help. Laura Alonso invited Caridad to participate in an internationalist ballet exchange in Canada. A BNC stylist offered to "fix" her hair for roles that ostensibly required flowing tresses. Yet, the antagonistic environment took its toll, and Caridad's self-esteem deteriorated.[18] Along with personal attacks, corruption and mismanagement of the company had reached acute levels by the late 1980s, so Martínez decided to write a letter of complaint with dissatisfied colleagues of her generation like ballerinas Amparo Brito, Rosario Suárez, and Mirta García.[19]

Connecting balletic discontent to the times, Caridad explained, "The letter I wrote was a consequence of perestroika." Theoretically, a complaint went through established channels, but as Caridad reflected, she had an irresolvable issue: "The problem [was] that I am not white!" Her letter did not explicitly mention racism, but in general terms, communicated unresolved problems. Despite hopes of pushing for improvements from within, the letter amounted to a "bomb."[20] Alicia accused them of lying and wrote a counter-letter with representatives of the Communist Party and Communist youth organization.[21] By the fall of 1987, Caridad, Rosario, and Mirta had left the BNC and were with-out pay for two months. Fans collected money for the rogue dancers, and when cultural bureaucrats found out, they reinstated the ballerinas' salaries.[22]

Then, Martínez founded the Ballet Teatro de la Habana (Ballet Theater of Havana), which began working in October 1987.[23] The company consisted of actors, ballet dancers, and modern dancers, working with dramaturges, writ-ers, and visual artists. The name of the company reflected the interdisciplin-ary nature of the balletic and theatrical project. Venturing into uncharted territory was exciting but also difficult. As Martínez reflected, "When I start[ed] . . . my own company, it was when I understood my country. Because, when I was . . . in the National Ballet of Cuba in that moment, it's a privilege. You live totally different than the other people. . . . You have some privileges that other people don't have. And so it was [when I left that] I woke up. I saw how hard it was for everybody. I had a lot of support, from all young artists and journalists, and visual artists, a lot of support from them. So I learned a lot."[24] As Martínez notes, ballet dancers enjoyed very real privileges in social-ist Cuba as valued weapons of the Revolution and cosmopolitan internation-alists. Once out of the company, Martínez "woke up" to harsh realities but also witnessed the crucial horizontal collaborations that nurtured careers when vertical state support was lacking.

Although initially on the wrong side of a dispute that involved gatekeeping institutions, the ballet dancers eventually won backing from cultural pro-moter Nisia Agüero, former BNC administrator Angela Grau, musician Ser-gio Vitier, and modern dancer Miguel Iglesias. These figures helped Ballet Teatro secure rehearsal and performance spaces.[25] Eventually, the new group received approval from the Ministry of Culture. Although their 1987 pro-grams did not indicate official sponsorship, 1988 programs had "Ministerio de Cultura" on the cover, a sign that the Ballet Teatro had official acceptance.[26] Martínez also had an informal connection to the state when Mariela Castro Espín, the daughter of revolutionary dignitaries Raúl Castro and Vilma Espín (a former ballet student herself), began taking classes with Ballet Teatro while dating company member Rubén Rodríguez.[27]

Ballet Teatro's trajectory suggests that by the late 1980s cultural leaders and the bureaucracy saw the benefit of revising the dance establishment. Along these lines, the Ministry of Culture reorganized into different national councils advised by artists and focused on funding small projects to counter "the hypertrophy of established groups without mobility or possibilities of change . . . and with the undeniable loss of creativity of much of our best tal-ent," as Vivian Martínez Tabares, the editor of the journal *Tablas*, wrote in

1989.[28] Although the structural and funding changes only went into effect in 1989, Martínez and her group helped to catalyze them by preemptively striking out on their own.

With Ballet Teatro, Martínez experimented with multimedia performance. This was a natural outgrowth of her friendships with visual artists, actors, scientists, writers, and intellectuals. She felt kinship with visual artists experimenting with "arte calle," performative happenings in the street, and this impulse reflected a broader movement. "It was a social response. It was something inevitable. It was a necessity to express oneself in a freer manner and . . . look for a different language," she explained.[29] This ethos of experimentation manifested in Ballet Teatro's program, *Ciclo de experimentación en la imagen escénica: Danza, teatro, plástica, música, cine* (Cycle of Experimentation in the Scenic Image: Dance, Theater, Visual Arts, Music, Film), which premiered at Havana's Mella Theater in 1987. Writer Miguel Sirgado provided "dramatic advising," and visual artist Gustavo Pérez Monzón created the scenery. Choreographers drew inspiration from literature. For instance, program notes for Martínez's *Hallazgos* (Discoveries) included a few lines of poetry by the Brazilian leftist writer Thiago de Mello to set up the choreography to come.[30]

Also part of the premiere program was *Altazor* by Ballet de Camagüey choreographer Lázaro Martínez. Named for and inspired by Chilean poet Vicente Huidobro's magnum opus, it starred Jorge Esquivel and actor Adolfo Llauradó. Esquivel, a celebrated "son of the Revolution," who had been selected from an orphanage and developed into the first homegrown male dancing partner to Alicia in the 1970s and 1980s, had left the BNC to work with other groups in the country.[31] About his decision, he explained in 1987, "I have not left the Ballet Nacional, because it is part of my life and of my spirit. The BNC is of Cuba and of the Revolution, and I am Cuban and revolutionary. . . . I have decided to look for other forms of liberty, of mobility, to encounter the possibility to dance with different groups[;] they could be classical, modern, [or] contemporary, preferably . . . [to] expose me to a new universe of creation and interpretation."[32] *Altazor* reflected this impulse to find new artistic universes, as program notes for the work explained: "An actor, dancer, [and] four musicians join a choreographer to recite a poem (!), composed by poems of a universal Latin American. A ballet? A recital? A concert? We don't know. It is the result of a craving [*ansia*] to do something beautifully daring, young, revolutionary. . . . Music, Theater, Dance, Poetry and Lighting, unite in this experiment that seeks only the pleasure of the work; to think, dream and enjoy with you all and for all."[33] Artists shied away from categorizing their performance, but asserted their desire to create something "daring, young, revolutionary." Their statement resembles those made in the years immediately following 1959, when then-young dancers sought to break from existing modes. By the late 1980s, a new generation of artists harbored their own revolutionary visions.

Also on the premiere 1987 program was a work choreographed by Esquivel. Titled *Muerte junto al lago* (Death by the Lake), one scene featured Esquivel as a prince hunting four ducks, three white and one black. As he and live ducks wandered around the stage, the audience died laughing. Everyone assumed that the work parodied the BNC with the ducks referencing the generation of three white ballerinas Amparo Brito, Rosario Suárez, and Mirta García, and the only black ballerina, Caridad Martínez.[34] Whether intended or not, audiences gleefully searched for and found sly ridicule in works by the rebel ballet dancers.

Caridad Martínez's *Test* (1988) similarly featured interdisciplinary artistic collaborations and led audiences to imagine daring messages. Visual artist Rubén Torres Llorca inspired the work, and choreographic material came from workshops with the late artist-scholar Randy Martin, who taught while conducting fieldwork on the theater scene in Cuba in the late 1980s. Belgian writer Jean Portante, then married to Cuban writer and fellow Ballet Teatro collaborator Marilyn Bobes, wrote the text for *Test*.[35] The production presented open symbols to the audience for each member to interpret and "test" their relative levels of neurosis.[36] A performance program insert asked audience members to select which of the twelve scenes most and least "pleased them." Additionally, the insert instructed the observer, "Do a self-observation: the relation that exists between the twelve scenes is linked to the cause of your neurosis."[37] In one scene, ballerina Mirta García danced to the familiar time announcement and newsfeed of Cuba's number one radio station, Radio Reloj. Cuban audiences perceived a joke about Alicia Alonso: time was running out for her career. Martínez said that she had no such intention. When the work appeared in Mexico, no one saw a commentary on Alicia, but read closer to Caridad's original goal of meditating on repetitive, mundane routine.[38] Overall with *Test*, Caridad hoped to evoke the emotional distress created by living in Cuba at the moment. "It had become something normal to live stressed. It is normal to have no food and . . . to be below the sun without water . . . in a line to buy something. . . . That is not normal! . . . And it affects you," she explained.[39] Sick of daily discomforts, Martínez and her peers expressed their disaffection on stage.

Another scene of *Test* captured another Cuban neurosis, which Caridad described as a tendency to blame problems on an imagined external force. To represent this quirk, two men, one in a dress and one in a suit, danced neutrally (without so-called gay mannerisms, "*amanerado*"). Slowly but surely, their relationship deteriorated because of external stimuli like disruptive sounds. Audience members saw subversive messaging in the scene, ranging from a commentary on state repression of homosexuals to representations of Fidel. As for the latter, the central committee of the Communist Party called Caridad for a meeting the day after the premiere. The man in a dress had a beard, and the functionaries assumed that he represented Fidel. Caridad chuckled when recounting the incident. The interpretation had surprised her. Her choreography inadvertently functioned like a Rorschach test; if people saw Fidel in the dress-wearing man on stage, she observed, they should investigate why they had arrived at that conclusion. Regardless, the functionaries said that the dancer must shave his beard to eliminate any physical connection to the aging *barbudo* (bearded one). The dancer complied, and Caridad then heard from representatives of the Unión de Jóvenes Comunistas (Union of Communist Youth). They anxiously asked, why had the dancer shaved? Caridad recalled them worrying, "They will all think we made you!"[40] The incident revealed how political entities had different priorities, as the Communist Party suspiciously protected Fidel's image while Communist youth wanted to preserve a façade of free expression. This resulted in slipshod censure.

Rumors of the incident spread, and audience members eagerly went to see the infamous scene.[41] "Excited spectators" filled the Mella Theater for performances of *Test*, noted a journalist. This was impressive because "it has not been something common for the dance groups of the vanguardist sector. . . . There were spectators and above all youth, wanting to enter in the problematic labyrinth that the new work presents."[42] Although unmentioned in the press, the beard scandal likely fed widespread curiosity. Even if only functionaries saw Fidel in the man wearing a dress initially, the public no doubt imagined connections between the now cleanly shaven dancer and Castro. This anecdote illuminates how the Cuban public "looked for a political meaning in everything," and how once on stage, choreography "converted into something else," according to Caridad.[43] Just as spectatorship can be shaped by and reflect social identities as dance scholar Susan Manning has argued, viewing practices also provide telling information about the political context.[44] In revolutionary Cuba, where creators used metaphor to dodge censors and where leaders like Alicia and Fidel clung to power, spectators eagerly contrived renegade meanings in dance productions.

It was actually in another piece that Martínez and her dancers abstractly represented Fidel. Titled *Eppure si muove*, Latin for "and yet it moves," the

FIGURE 7.1 Ballet Teatro de la Habana company members strike an irreverent pose for a photo shoot, ca. 1988. Photograph by Juan Enrique González Careaga. Source: Personal archive of Caridad Martínez. Courtesy of Caridad Martínez.

work reflected on power by focusing on religious and political authority. Lasting an hour and twenty minutes, the work invited viewers to discover "our" (Cuban) identity through a nonlinear production.[45] The work had a defiant tone. As captured in figure 7.1, performers wore gender-bending plain dresses and thrust their middle fingers in front of them, embodying an artful rejection of norms. In another scene, performers danced in military jackets and riffed on Fidel's distinct hand movements. "We had so much fun studying the gestures of Fidel," Caridad recalled. "It is a brand! . . . The finger and the left hand . . . it was very pronounced." The idiosyncratic repertoire inspired movements that reflected broadly on authority. The national religious icon, the Virgin of Charity of El Cobre, also made an appearance, as illustrated in figure 7.2. Although officials did not seem to detect Fidel in the work, the unconventional aesthetics led them to request another meeting with Caridad. She had prepared her "responses" with the help of her friends. At one point, officials asked about her motives, "And what is it you want? A house? A car?" They then started asking about her mother, who had

FIGURE 7.2 Ballet Teatro de la Habana company members wear military jackets and dance in front of the Virgin of Charity in Caridad Martínez's *Eppure si muove*, ca. 1989. Note the dancer in the foreground with extended fingers inspired by Fidel Castro's gestural repertoire. Photograph by Juan Enrique González Careaga. Source: Personal archive of Caridad Martínez. Courtesy of Caridad Martínez.

recently died. Why did they do this, I wondered. To make me feel bad and out of control, Caridad confided. And it worked. "I was at the point of collapsing," she shuddered. However, she had the wherewithal to request a studio, and they gave her one.[46] Opening dance meant abstracting political commentary, accommodating bureaucratic paranoia, preparing answers, holding ground, and negotiating with bureaucrats when the opportunity arose.

Moving in New Directions

As the younger generation questioned authority, established dance leaders moved in new directions. In 1978, Ramiro Guerra, for instance, began choreographing again, seven years after the state censored his magnum opus and compelled him to leave the modern dance company that he had founded in 1959. Now as official choreographer and adviser of the Conjunto Folklórico Nacional (CFN), Guerra created seven works from 1979 to 1982, including two inspired by musical and dance cultures of the eastern Cuban cities Santiago and Trinidad.[47] His reentry into official dance institutions indicated that the repressive environment of the early 1970s had relaxed slightly.[48] Equally, his work exemplified increased exchanges, built on precedents, between Havana-based artists and cultural producers outside of the capital. The Santiago native and CFN soloist Silvina Fabars performed in Guerra's *Tríptico oriental* (1979), which featured Haitian-influenced forms *gagá, tumba francesa*, and dances of Santiago carnival.[49] In this particular performance, Fabars represented cross-island cultural collaborations that started in the 1960s and reached new heights in the late 1970s and 1980s. This section examines the trajectories of Guerra's colleagues Fernando Alonso in Camagüey, Lorna Burdsall in Havana, and Eduardo Rivero in Santiago. Their stories illuminate how an older generation also effected institutional change as they responded to private and professional shifts and embarked on new projects in and out of the capital.

After Fernando and Alicia Alonso divorced in 1975, Fernando relocated. His extramarital dalliance and belief that Alicia should cede the stage to younger dancers reportedly compelled Alicia to confront the cultural bureaucracy with an ultimatum: either Fernando leaves or she would.[50] The break was difficult for dancers like Josefina Méndez, Loipa Araújo, Aurora Bosch, Mirta Plá, and Ramona de Sáa, who grew up with Alicia and Fernando as formative, parental figures.[51] Although Fernando supposedly had several options including directing the ballet academy in Havana or teaching in France, "the highest management of the country requested that he assume the general direction of the Ballet de Camagüey."[52] According to Fernando, the challenge had a rejuvenating effect: "Coming to Camagüey has been like being young again. I have returned to relive those experiences that I had with the Ballet Alicia Alonso but now in a new stage: in that of socialism."[53] Despite these halcyon characterizations, the move resembled internal exile, as Fernando went from leading an internationally renowned company in the Cuban capital to a modest troupe in the interior.[54]

Although divorce catalyzed this change, Fernando's arrival came after years of BNC mentorship of the Ballet de Camagüey. Vicentina de la Torre, who founded the company in 1967, had trained with the Alonsos before 1959, and her Camagüey ballet school became part of the national system that the Alonsos organized after 1959. Also, the inaugural 1967 performance was "in collaboration with the Ballet Nacional de Cuba," featuring BNC soloists and choreographers.[55] These connections continued and deepened when BNC affiliates Joaquín Banegas and his wife Sylvia Marichal became directors of the Ballet de Camagüey in 1969.[56]

The BNC then played a key role during a crisis at the Ballet de Camagüey in the early 1970s. Marichal, Banegas, and almost half of the dancers reportedly "deserted" the provincial company to work in Havana.[57] In April 1973, Banegas wrote a simple memo that he needed to reintegrate into "my work center, Ballet Nacional de Cuba or other responsibility as a teacher."[58] The

BNC and Havana bureaucrats brainstormed possible replacements. The soloist Pablo Moré came up, but Fernando suggested his daughter Laura Alonso, who had recently stopped dancing for health reasons. Bureaucrat Armando Quesada grumbled that the BNC likely rejected Moré because they "would not be able to control" him as they had with Banegas and Marichal and could with Laura.[59] A couple weeks later, a memo accepted the BNC proposal to have Laura direct the Ballet de Camagüey.[60] Meanwhile, frustrated Camagüey dancers in limbo wrote a letter of complaint about bureaucratic ineptitude while faced "with the disappearance of a company that . . . we have managed to handle."[61] Camagüey dance maker Jorge Rodríguez Vede served as interim director until February 1975.[62] Fernando, not Laura, replaced him. Although a retrospective claimed that Fernando left the BNC "to save the more modest group from crisis," an array of factors incited the move, including a history of BNC support, a leadership crisis, and a divorce.[63]

After Fernando's arrival, tensions manifested between the Ballet de Camagüey and the BNC. Letters from 1975 and 1976 evidence that Alicia and Fernando competed over recent graduates.[64] At least one contested dancer ended up at the Ballet de Camagüey, indicating that cultural bureaucrats did not always take one side or the other.[65] In response to the mixed outcomes, Alicia wrote a letter describing a "great personnel crisis" in the BNC as older dancers transitioned to teaching and directing rehearsals.[66] In 1983, Fernando acknowledged, "Always there is a big fight between the Ballet de Camagüey and the Ballet Nacional for the [best] graduates. . . . And so begins not the War of the Galaxies, but the War of the Ballets, which is almost worse."[67]

As the former husband and wife competed, another familial metaphor came to identify the two companies—that of siblings. In an interview, Fernando asserted, "The Ballet Nacional is the big brother."[68] The sibling trope supported the idea that the Ballet de Camagüey and the BNC could coexist harmoniously, akin to the Bolshoi and Kirov, the two internationally acclaimed companies of the Soviet Union.[69] Fernando also used the concept to deflect criticism: "To compare the Ballet de Camagüey to the Ballet Nacional is not fair. This company is very young."[70] Despite inexperience, youth was advantageous as well. When asked the Ballet de Camagüey's "best quality," Fernando answered, "Youth . . . the average age is 23 years."[71] This young raw material offered "an open laboratory for more than one dance alchemist."[72] The "big brother" BNC, by contrast, had mature dancers assumedly more set in their ways, including Alicia, who performed into her seventies.

Nevertheless, the Ballet de Camagüey faced inherent challenges. The first was geography, or as Fernando put it, "600 km between the province and the capital that feels like 600 light years."[73] With less access to artistic collabora-tors, dance critics commenting on their work, and the best medical attention, Camagüey dancers felt frustrated and isolated.[74] The second was a subordi-nate status to the BNC. In 1986, the Ministry of Culture labeled the Ballet de Camagüey's technical level "second category," while the BNC was the first. Fernando called the determination unfair and incorrect.[75] Disappointment endured as evidenced by the fact that over thirty years later, Camagüey dancer Guillermo Leyva brought up the lower status in an oral history interview.[76]

Despite these challenges, Fernando helped the company grow. In 1978, the company relocated from the third floor of a school to a stately complex, which had a workshop for scenery and costuming. That same year, the com-pany went on its first international tour to the Soviet Union, Czechoslovakia, and Romania.[77] More international appearances followed, with trips to Co-lombia, Bulgaria, Poland, East Germany, the Soviet Union, Czechoslovakia, Yugoslavia, Mexico, Belgium, Holland, and France in the 1980s.[78] Fernando also organized collaborations with artists like Gustavo Herrera, Iván Tenorio, Alberto Méndez, Soviet dancer Azari Plisetski, the Belgium-based Cuban couple Jorge Lefebre and Menia Martínez, Alberto Alonso, Lorna Burdsall, and Ramiro Guerra.[79] In this exciting environment, four local choreographers—Francisco Lang, Lázaro Martínez, José Antonio Chávez, and Osvaldo Beiro—created a rich, varied repertory starting in 1979.[80] Fernando also inaugurated a local dance festival in 1982, which continued regularly during the off year of the biennial international ballet festival in Havana (i.e., 1983, 1985, 1987, 1989, and beyond).[81] Fernando also pushed for and secured a number of vehicles for the Ballet de Camagüey, including two buses.[82] In his thank you note to Cas-tro, Fernando pledged to "continue working to elevate the ideological level of the pueblo" through ballet.[83] The Ballet de Camagüey also established a pointe shoe–making factory that reportedly saved the company ten thousand dollars in the first year.[84] Savvy in institutional building, Fernando applied his networks and knowledge to securing resources for the Ballet de Camagüey.

As Fernando connected with distinguished collaborators and built infra-structure, other affiliates worked to preserve the company's history. In 1979, the Departamento de Divulgación (Publicity Department) asked dancers to fill out a questionnaire for the company archives. In 1982, company adminis-trator and historian Manuel del Pino collected autobiographical information about dancers' family background, training, teachers, membership in political and mass organizations, the reason for choosing ballet as a profession, future plans, and "for you, what is ballet?"[85] Completed forms reveal that company members came from all over Cuba, as well as Venezuela, Colombia, Peru,

France, Ecuador, and Brazil.[86] Letters soliciting similar information in 1986 were explicit about the historical stakes of "making a general archive, where each member of the Company has a file, with a first part (biographical), and another technical."[87] "Technical" documents included evaluation forms completed by a committee that observed each dancer and provided feedback on areas for improvement like arm positions, stage presence, and weight.[88]

Although most reports have a formulaic similitude, a trace of political tumult disrupts quiet recording on one questionnaire. At the top of the form is the word "*Escoria*" (underlined in source; literally, flint or chips that fall off a surface but used as a defamatory label akin to "scum").[89] The term was applied to Cubans who left, particularly during the 1980 Mariel boatlift, suggesting that the male dancer who filled out the form was one such refugee. The fact that the document was preserved shows how the company worked painstakingly to build a substantive archive that preserved (and attested to) its significance to Cuban culture. The Ballet de Camagüey's history that archivists worked to preserve illustrates how institutional building often involved personal and professional tensions whether divorce, competition, or exile.

Like Fernando, longtime modern dance leader Lorna Burdsall experienced professional changes as a result of a high-profile divorce. In the 1970s, she left her husband, the powerful Cuban politico, Manuel Piñeiro, after sensing that he was having an affair and retaliating with her own. This had professional repercussions. According to Burdsall in her memoir, "opportunists in the company who were waiting to pounce on my job" reported her romantic evenings while on tour in Hungary and Yugoslavia. "The General Director of the *Danza Nacional de Cuba* changed the lock on my office door on my first day back from the company's successful tour to Europe, leaving me a message that I no longer worked there" (italics in the original).[90] While initially upset, Burdsall made the most of the situation. In 1981, she founded Así Somos (The Way We Are), which had an "educational purpose and humoristic character."[91] The group included highly trained young dancers, painters, actors, and musicians eager for guidance on how to develop as artists. The experimental group retained connections to high politics through Mariela Castro Espín, who was a theater student and member of Así Somos.[92] Perhaps such ties to state power were necessary for challenging the status quo.

The same year that Burdsall founded her company, eleven visual artists mounted the experimental exhibition "Volumen I" in Havana, which "began a process of increasingly radical ruptures with Cuban art traditions."[93] Although Así Somos and Volumen I have never been juxtaposed, they had much in common. Volumen I artists began showing their work in private homes and eventually gained the official acceptance needed to exhibit at important art centers in Havana. The visual artists purported to have national- ist intentions, but embraced cosmopolitanism and rejected what they viewed as the artistic isolationism of their predecessors. Moreover, Volumen I became infamous for using humorous, erotic, and irreverent performative elements for critical ends.[94] Similarly, Burdsall's group started out creating in her apartment before appearing in nonconventional and conventional public places like mu- seum galleries, *casas de cultura* (community cultural centers), schools, the- aters, and outside.[95] Así Somos also claimed to focus on "Cubanness," without obvious Cuban trappings, which Burdsall described as "*avant-garde* pieces in- stead of the expected Afrocuban and popular forms" (italics in the original).[96] Así Somos claimed to possess "a great dose of humor, typical of Cuban idio- syncrasy" and to provoke reflections on love and mankind.[97] Burdsall's artistic priorities—humor, irreverence, cosmopolitanism, and experimentation— aligned with those of Volumen I.

Although led by an older modern dancer, Burdsall's collective was commit- ted to the experiments of the young. Así Somos created "image theater using choreographic movement, poetry, music and properties that often [came] from the personal experiences of company members," a pamphlet explained.[98] The company's debut on October 31, 1981, at the Sala de Teatro Estudio (Hu- bert de Blanck), reflected an interest in costumes, props, and theatricality. As Burdsall later described, "As one of the many props, I used an army surplus white silk parachute.... This huge round globe that floated over the dancers, lit from the inside or the outside, made a very effective setting for our numer- ous inventions."[99] Así Somos took these playful productions around Havana and even abroad. In 1985, for instance, the group staged an exposition of "ki- netic sculpture" at a *casa de cultura* in Havana, performed at the publishing house and cultural center Casa de las Américas, and performed at Stanford University.[100] A critic for the *Palo Alto Weekly* described Así Somos reflecting "the exuberance and creativity of the Cuban youth of today."[101]

Meanwhile, Burdsall's longtime colleague, modern dancer Eduardo Rivero, pursued opportunities outside of Havana similar to Fernando and worked with diverse artists like Burdsall. Rivero founded the Compañía Teatro de la Danza del Caribe (Dance Theater Company of the Caribbean) in Santiago de Cuba on September 20, 1988, and like Fernando in Camagüey, furthered dance developments by building on important precedents. In the mid-1960s, the U.S.-born Elfrida Mahler and Chilean Paulina Politoff had spent a year introducing students to modern dance in Santiago. In 1975, Tania Bell Mosqueda, a Santiago dance teacher who had trained in the school for art instructors, formed a group that provided an important foundation for contemporary dance developments in the city.[102] Rivero entered that scene upon request. His Havana colleagues had been teaching in Santiago to support the creation of a new company. Santiago cultural bureaucrats requested that Rivero stay, and "my definitive placement here in this city was decided," he later explained. Although Rivero embraced this new position, "really, it was not that Rivero made the company," his friend and colleague Isidro Rolando shared.[103] Like Fernando, Rivero ended up outside of Havana due to circumstance and responsibility; like Lorna, he developed multimedia and cross-genre dances.

Rivero's company in many ways provided an institutional culmination of his work as a dance internationalist exploring African and African diasporic culture. Rivero described the company aesthetic as based on modern dance technique and "a profound process of investigating the cultural roots of the Caribbean region and especially the eastern zone of the country."[104] The company location, then, was perfect, since Rivero considered, "Santiago de Cuba . . . the center of the Caribbean, in its geographic location and all the mixture of cultures and races."[105] Although Rivero articulated a politically correct commitment to racial and cultural mixture, his focus on Santiago de Cuba signaled his interest in exploring blackness since eastern provinces have tended to be racialized as the "blackest" in Cuban imaginaries.[106]

With these aims, Rivero shared artistic objectives of cultural producers affiliated with Grupo Antillano. Founded in 1978 by sculptor and print maker Rafael Queneditt Morales, Grupo Antillano focused on black culture in Cuba and the island's place in a larger Antillean world, which historian Alejandro de la Fuente has described as "the world of plantations, slaves, and tropical exports. That was fundamentally a black world." CFN cofounder and adviser Rogelio Martínez Furé was also an important member of the collective. From 1978 to 1982, Grupo Antillano had thirty-two exhibitions, including several abroad in Prague, Sofia, Mexico City, and Surinam. In 1983, the collective had its last group exhibition, dedicated to visual artist Wifredo Lam, who was the group's honorary president and had passed away one year prior.[107]

Although Rivero was not a formal member of Grupo Antillano, he and his longtime colleague Luz María Collazo contributed to their projects. A photograph from 1980 shows Rivero, Collazo, Queneditt, and Lam in the midst of a friendly exchange. Laughing heartily, Rivero looks at Lam, and Collazo, at the camera.[108] The encounter happened soon after Rivero premiered two works inspired by Lam: *Ómnira* (1979), which means freedom in Yoruba and was inspired by Lam's *La jungla* (The jungle), and *Dúo a Lam* (1979), which used rhythm and movement to portray the light, color, and exaltation of life in Lam's oeuvre.[109] The eighteen-minute *Dúo a Lam*, starring Rivero with Collazo, so touched Lam that he made an engraving inspired by Collazo's profile. In 1987, Collazo continued these collaborations by working with a former Grupo Antillano affiliate, visual artist Manuel Mendive. That year, Mendive covered her nearly naked body and those of three other dancers in paint for an art happening at the National Museum of Fine Art in Havana. Collazo, adorned with Mendive's painting, embodied the experimental connections forged between dancers and visual artists during the 1980s. Mendive made a script, gave some direction, and "then us dancers coordinated movements to represent the idea of the painter. I liked . . . to move myself with paint on my skin," she reminisced.[110] Subsequently they went on a European tour with Mendive. She recalled that the dancers were hungry for most of the trip (due to the nearly nonexistent costuming) and caused a "scandal" because the paint got everywhere in the hotels. Hunger and messes aside, Collazo enjoyed the "fantastic" experience.[111]

Rivero's Compañía Teatro de la Danza del Caribe continued artistic objectives of the by-then inactive Grupo Antillano by examining black solidarity and Cuba's Antillean culture. For the company's first program, Rivero created *Mandela* to music by Miles Davis and dedicated to the South African activist and leader Nelson Mandela.[112] Then, in October 1989, the company performed Rivero's *Tributo* (Tribute) to the music of Bob Marley and Jimmy Cliff. The piece underscored political messages in the music, which came from the "ghettos of the Third World," to criticize "racial discrimination, the oppressive regime of apartheid, war, injustice, [and] oppression." To the socially conscious sounds of reggae, the work celebrated "love, unity, and liberty of the people" and offered "a tribute to all our [Cuban] heroes and martyrs and all those that have given their lives or part of them for these principles and ideals."[113] Rivero had dancers from his company and the Santiago-based Conjunto Folklórico de Oriente perform together, reiterating the idea of solidarity across geographic borders and genre divides. The public even joined in; as Rivero recalled, "The curtains could not be closed that day. The public got up to dance with the work, which presented [Bob Marley's] musical composition *War* in a final party to a powerful reggae, which sang of liberty and opposing oppression."[114] As performers and publics danced to reggae, they animated Rivero's long-standing commitment to collectively celebrating black culture in Cuba and beyond.

Like younger counterparts, the older generation of dance leaders moved in new directions in the late 1970s and 1980s. Their histories show how private lives shaped public institutional change. Furthermore, these expansions signaled that dance institutions in Havana had matured to such a degree that distinguished leaders turned to tackling new challenges elsewhere on the island. Revolutionary dance makers accepted these calls of duty, despite the personal discomfort so often part of relocation. For instance, Elfrida Mahler, who taught in Santiago in the 1960s, spearheaded a modern dance mission in Guantánamo in the 1980s. In her late sixties when she left the comforts of her longtime home in Havana, Mahler went to live in simple quarters where only a curtain separated her from other teachers housed in a communal room.[115] The dance aspirations and material discomforts that characterized Mahler's stay undoubtedly resonated with what Fernando, Burdsall, and Rivero experienced upon moving east or leaving large companies for small, experimental ones out of circumstance, choice, or a sense of professional and revolutionary responsibility.

Dancing with Fragments

As the dance establishment fractured in the 1980s, younger and older dance makers innovated with the fragments left by disruptive energies. Young modern dancer Marianela Boán questioned the political present, and veteran dance leader Ramiro Guerra reflected on a bittersweet past. Taken together, these modern dancers' work illuminates what the Cuban dance establishment had achieved (generations of innovative artists) and also what it had lost and lacked (complete freedom of expression) as the 1980s drew to a close. Choreographing, performing, and building dance institutions resulted in a dynamic concert dance scene that nevertheless had long faced hardship due to hierarchies and censorship. To open up new possibilities, dancers seemed to say, they needed to reckon with counterproductive forces and imagine new avenues to a better future.

Like Caridad Martínez and her collaborators in Ballet Teatro, modern dancer Marianela Boán sought to disrupt hegemonies with her choreography. This began as a choreographer for Danza Nacional de Cuba, renamed Danza Contemporánea de Cuba in the early 1980s ("Danza" for short). Her first choreography, *Danzaria* (1978), provides an illustrative case in point. Citing creative lineage to "the world of Ramiro Guerra," as well as Mexican choreographer Elena Noriega, French choreographer Maurice Béjart, and Cuban choreographers Eduardo Rivero, Víctor Cuéllar, and Gerardo Lastra, Boán nevertheless created *Danzaria* "to break with the established."[116] The work depicted two teenagers who "discover love through a relationship of play and provocation," according to program notes.[117] The choreography consisted of big jumps and turns executed by dancers dressed in street clothes, resulting in cognitive dissonance between technical virtuosity and quotidian trappings that confused the company directorship. Boán admitted in a published interview, "This was totally intended, rather a bit subversive." Also illustrative was Boán's *Teoría de conjunto* (Group Theory, 1984), which portrayed a restless, imaginative youth called extravagant by his peers. The group rejects the individual, who in turn underestimates the collective. The conflict is resolved when a girl from the group falls in love with the "different" individual, and transforms him. Sets by Volumen I artist Leandro Soto consisted of two boards with the theory of the group. The first read, "'Live with consciousness [*la conciencia*] of the collective.' (A+B+C)=Group A." The second read "B=C and B=A. 'Live with consciousness to create.' Creation=Love. Therefore B=C=A."[118] The piece encouraged viewers to wonder how love, creativity, and individuality fit within commitments to a collective.

After over a decade with Danza, Boán left in 1988 to found Danza Abierta (Open Dance), a company name that made explicit the group's intentions. In the handbill for the company premiere on December 15–18, 1988, a poem-like text appeared on the first page. It touched on themes like opening, visibility, metaphors, questioning, and mixing media (see the epigraph).[119] The company included young dancers from the CFN, Danza, ENA, and Gabri Christa, a dancer from Curaçao, who had started her professional career in the Netherlands. The company also collaborated with actor and director Víctor Varela, who created two out of four works in the first program.[120]

Before the premiere, the new company needed help and permission. Christa noted in an interview that Danza director Miguel Iglesias provided rehearsal space and feedback on works in progress. Christa guessed that he understood the need for more outlets in the flooded dance scene with more dancers than positions in existing, large companies. Smaller companies like Boán's would take the pressure off and employ dancers.[121] Though aided by Iglesias, Boán and her company ultimately needed permission from officialdom. During a rehearsal for opening night, Alicia Alonso appeared at the Mella Theater to appraise the program. As Christa recounted to dance scholar Suki John, "After what happened with Caridad [Martínez and Ballet Teatro], Alonso had decided her permission was needed in order for a piece to go on. She came to our dress rehearsal with her entourage; she was almost blind but people were telling her what was happening onstage. Alicia was the unofficial head of the Ministry of Culture and said, 'not without my permission.' We were very nervous, [because] there was one piece with nudity. We didn't know until an hour before if we could even do the performance."[122] When I shared this anecdote with Martínez, she suggested that Boán must have shown Alicia a "light" version of her often-provocative work.[123] Regardless, Alicia deemed Danza Abierta's performance acceptable despite any edgy content.

Ironically, with this approval, the company premiered Boán's *Sin permiso* (Without Permission), about the permission—requested, granted, or denied—inherent to creating in Cuba. The work had a "fragmentary structure to maintain an active spectator. . . . The leit motiv of the piece is to raise a hand and ask permission to speak."[124] Journalist Raquel Mayedo commented on the powerful mix of "quotidian gestures and postures with an almost photographic realism" like walking, sitting, and running, as well as the "techniques of [U.S. choreographers] José Limón and Trisha Brown, among many others." This created "new paths toward communicating with the people of today." With pedestrian movements, dancers dealt with "themes as tough [*escambroso*] as unnecessary meetings, double standards, aggression, isolation, self-censorship and censorship . . . among many others," Mayedo continued.[125]

One of the seven dancers in *Sin permiso* on December 15, 1988, Tomás Guilarte, described the choreography to me years later. Dancers raised their hands, only to push their arms forcibly down. They covered their mouths, performing a verbal silence.[126] Yet their articulate bodies spoke. A photograph of the piece shows one woman staring at the audience urgently, blankly, as dancers stretch and float their right arms next to her.[127] Alluding to the expressive strictures that Cuban artists faced, Boán later claimed that *Sin permiso* was "very revolutionary," seeking to "break with everything established."[128] Guilarte affirmed, "In its moment, it was a type of revolution. It was a powerful choreography for the period. It was a period of a lot of control. . . . One almost couldn't speak or say things. So she was very much in the vanguard with it."[129] *Sin permiso* viscerally explored the consequence of expressive limitations. The daring choreography prompted one critic to call Boán's Danza Abierta "one of the most interesting [groups] in the so-called New Vanguard."[130]

Boán perhaps impressed observers due to her experimental methods. She determined to "de-codify herself [*descodificarme*]," which meant breaking with previous approaches to dancing.[131] Boán intentionally worked with young dancers, less set in their ways and more open to new forms of expression. "Like a scientist I needed my laboratory and instruments: a small collective of interpreters, some graduated and others still students of the schools of ballet and dance, they are youth that want to break formalisms and they have formed a very powerful vanguard choreographic movement," she asserted.[132] In later interviews, she further explained, "I was rejecting much of the very folkloricist technique. . . . I think that my work is Cuban. One does not need to worry about being Cuban, nor about whether nationality is present in a work, because in fact it is there."[133] As a white choreographer, she perhaps had less interest in exploring and celebrating Afro-Cuban culture, especially since an older generation like Eduardo Rivero had done it and continued doing it so successfully. Distinct from older choreographers, and like her contemporary, Martínez, Boán admitted her interest in commenting on present-day issues, or as she put it, "I am obsessed with saying concrete things, addressing social problems."[134] These clear critiques signaled a generational shift as dancers wielded their status to question contradictions in their day-to-day lives.

Take for instance Boán's *Un elefante se balanceaba sobre la tela de una araña* (An Elephant Balancing on a Spider Web), in which six performers danced on and around a single chair to reflect "on inertia, boredom, routine, [and] conformism," according to one journalist (see figure 7.3). In the work, Boán rejected the convention of covering large spaces in an aesthetically appealing manner and reflected on Cuban intractability. Reminiscent of Guerra's *El decálogo del apocalipsis* (1971), she also employed spoken word and song.[135] Dancers theatrically explored limitations to Cuban freedom, in this case represented by being choreographically tethered to a single chair.

Along with Boán, the "new vanguard" included several other female choreographers. Isabel Bustos Romoleroux, a woman of Ecuadorian descent who was born in Chile, raised in Cuba, and studied at ENA, founded the dance theater company Retazos (Remnants) in 1987. An announcement about a 1987 performance declared that the "young group . . . based its choreographic creations on the preoccupations of people today, their inner world, and their role in society and history." The group consisted of eight dancers and performed works with titles like *Mujer* (Woman), *Agua* (Water), and *Agonía* (Agony).[136] Modern dance choreographer Rosario Cárdenas also started her own group after working with Danza for almost twenty years. After Danza premiered her acclaimed *Dédalo* (Labyrinth, 1989), she decided to form Danza Combinatoria (Combinatorial Dance), a name inspired by combinatorial formula analysis, which uses combination, permutation, and variation. Cárdenas built upon this branch of mathematics to inspire choreography: she exchanged, combined, and varied to arrive at something new.[137]

Although the late 1980s brought exciting changes to concert dance, vanguard artists also were an extension of the past and rooted in the establishment. For instance, Boán had graduated from ENA and was a choreographer with Danza for almost a decade. In 1981, the company devoted a whole evening to her work.[138] As Mayedo summed up, "From the large companies, young

FIGURE 7.3 Dancers of Danza Abierta experiment with movement around a chair perhaps for *Un elefante se balanceaba sobre la tela de una araña* (1988). Photographs by Fernando Lezcano. Source: *Granma*, October 12, 1988, 7.

dancers leave, wanting to say something new or not, but something of their own. . . . They are not performers in outright contradiction with their collectives, but they are the fruit of the . . . companies."[139] This appraisal contended that even while moving away from their origins, rebel dancers evidenced their training and careers in major institutions. The young choreographers seemed to agree by acknowledging their lineage. For instance, in an interview, Cárdenas explained how Rivero and Guerra had shaped her work.[140]

Meanwhile, a key predecessor of these artists explored remnants of a receding past. In 1989, Ramiro Guerra created *De la memoria fragmentada* (Of Fragmented Memory) for Danza. Guerra had not worked with the company he had founded since 1971, but director Miguel Iglesias invited Guerra to choreograph for the company's thirtieth anniversary.[141] This signaled a public reckoning with Guerra's past, and a 1988 article in the official newspaper *Granma* acknowledged the harm inflicted on modern dance by the "overwhelming incomprehension" that fueled official mistreatment of "the mentioned-forgotten-remembered-honored (and even vilified)" Guerra.[142]

De la memoria fragmentada featured sections from Guerra's famous 1960s works *Suite Yoruba* (1960), *Orfeo antillano* (1964), and *Medea y los negreros* (1968), a trilogy that explored Santería and other aspects of Afro-Cuban culture in spectacular form.[143] It also included references to his censored work, *El decálogo del apocalipsis* (1971). Lasting forty minutes, *De la memoria fragmentada* featured thirty-nine dancers, including some, like Eduardo Rivero, who were no longer with Danza but had returned to dance the roles that they had originated. Also part of the production was the documentary *Historia de un ballet* (1962) about the making of *Suite Yoruba*.[144] Guerra aimed to create "not a depiction of the works as they were staged . . . but a new scenic game of mine, a collision of memory, nostalgia." One critic described the work as "more contemporary, avant-garde," with elements of "dance-theater [and] a tone that utilizes pop and expressionism as a figurative language."[145]

Based on a guide written by Guerra, the work had eight scenes. Scene 1 took place in the vestibule of the theater with dancers performing sections from *Medea y los negreros*, *Suite Yoruba*, and *Orfeo antillano* in the middle of audience members before disappearing into the crowds. Scene 2 began before a seated audience with the curtain opening on a stage filled with smoke. A "mysterious and sly" voice said to the audience, "Memory is populated by fragmented ghosts that only can be conjured through the desacralizing exorcism of parody." Then dancers performed slow-motion movements in "complete and total silence" and eventually disappeared into the smoke. Scenes 3 and 4 included projections of *Historia de un ballet* while dancers in wheelchairs wheeled around and others danced Guerra's choreography. After sequences from *Medea y los negreros* in Scene 5, Scene 6 started with the auditorium completely lit and a screaming siren. Two nurses rushed on stage with a woman on a stretcher, followed by a man in a wheelchair. They began "an absurd dialogue about a work that they should have staged but could not: *Decálogo.*" Then a screen lowered and photographs of *El decálogo del apocalipsis* rehearsals were projected. More dancers in wheelchairs entered and yelled threats at the images. Scene 7 featured a carnival scene from *Orfeo antillano* and figures from *Medea y los negreros*. In Scene 8, dancers appeared on stage and climbed on each other, forming a large mass of bodies. Others in wheelchairs circled the center group. Three stilt walkers with suitcases in hand joined the dancers in wheelchairs while the stage filled with smoke. This happened to the accompaniment of Esther Borja singing lines from the song *Ausencia* (Absence) by Jaime Prats about the impossibility of returning home. In a 2014 interview, Luis Roblejo, a dancer who had appeared in the work, asserted that Guerra criticized Cubans who left to escape the difficult conditions on the island. The curtain fell, and then opened on an empty stage, filled with smoke. After the curtain closed and opened again, only wheelchairs and suitcases littered the stage. Then it closed for the last time.[146]

By revisiting old choreography, Guerra recapitulated the history of Cuban modern dance in the first decade after the 1959 Revolution. However, *De la memoria fragmentada* hardly offered a conventional homage to a career and cultural establishment. Instead, using mystery and irony, it encouraged audience members to question the institution celebrating its thirtieth anniversary. Performers in wheelchairs perhaps alluded to the fact that government censorship had crippled Guerra's career and modern dance developments. Moreover, suitcases referenced the many Cubans who had left, undercutting narratives of cultural and political achievement. The final image, populated only by wheelchairs and suitcases, solemnly closed Guerra's first and final return to choreographing for the company that he had founded. Emptiness came out of revisiting his fragmented memories.

Although the piece conveyed haunting loss, the 1980s boasted a vigorous dance establishment albeit beset by generational conflict, limited resources, and censorship. Dancers fought for and benefited from an opening in the establishment that did not necessarily disrupt hierarchies. Notably, Alicia retained important sway over the Ministry of Culture. Even so, provocations happened with the help and support of other power brokers. Institutions eventually incorporated rebels into the system like when Danza Abierta received official support and Guerra choreographed for his estranged company.

Reworking revolutionary dance meant strengthening creative possibilities from the inside out.

Conclusion

In 1989, founding Danza Abierta member Tomás Guilarte graduated from ENA and left Havana for Guantánamo to work with his former teacher Elfrida Mahler. Mahler directed the dance school where Guilarte had trained and eventually led a professional dance initiative in the province. Guilarte was sorry to leave Danza Abierta, but he had no family (and therefore no housing) in Havana. Fortunately, an exciting professional opportunity awaited him. Guilarte joined a new company that Mahler founded on August 2, 1989. It was the first professional modern dance company in the province and grew out of Mahler's work with talented Guantánamo dancers like Guilarte. Originally called the Conjunto de Danza de Guantánamo, the company eventually became Danza Libre (Free Dance), named after the poetry collection *Versos libres* (Free Verses) by nineteenth-century Cuban patriot José Martí.[147] The company premiered January 26, 27, and 28, 1990, at the Cine-Teatro Guaso de Guantánamo, commemorating the anniversary of Martí's birthday with a program of works by Mahler, Guilarte, and choreographers from Guantánamo and Santiago de Cuba.[148]

The greatest challenge was to build an audience for modern dance in Guantánamo. To do so, the new company danced "in the streets, cinemas, theaters, schools, mountains, [and] countryside."[149] These encounters often involved humiliating experiences. As the company performed before movies, people anxious to watch the film and hostile to male dancers jeered the performers, exhibiting the persistence of homophobic prejudices. Equally trying, the company trekked long distances to dance in remote towns. According to Guilarte, many company members grumbled when Mahler organized difficult excursions to make Guantánamo into a dancing public. However, she ultimately won her battle. Danza Libre remains a notable professional company, and Guantánamo, one of the best places in Cuba to perform modern dance in Guilarte's opinion. He cited Mahler's incredible love of dance and the Revolution to explain the personal sacrifices she endured (and asked her dancers to bear). Mahler's former colleague, U.S. dancer Muriel Manings, echoed this assessment, and simply said, "She was gung-ho. The Revolution was hers too."[150]

Similarly, Cuban dancers embraced the Revolution with all its complexities and inconsistencies, and danced to further its promise. Their careers sometimes meant leaving the comfort of established institutions, relocating, and connecting with diverse artists. Moving in different directions, Cuban dance makers invigorated their field. Their work attested to all that had transpired, good and bad, over the previous sixty years. They used their power as venerated artists to question, as Danza Abierta's manifesto in the epigraph emphasized. Moving bodies became the perfect medium for political provocations. A bearded man in a dress, a collective dance party to close a reggae tribute, an ensemble pushing down their raised hands nonverbally spoke to audience members. Whether intended or not, a versed dancing public saw satires of Fidel, African disasporic solidarity, and critiques of censorship and self-censorship. As a result, dancers and their audiences made the late 1970s and 1980s a vibrant period of reckoning with the past and present to imagine a more vibrant future. The dance establishment was bursting at the seams as the 1980s drew to a close. Constituent dancers remained keenly primed to continue making revolutions—circling around enduring though elusive hopes and choreographing steps toward social change.

Epilogue

Where ideology is strong, bodies must adapt and resist. I am fascinated by the ways our bodies are pushed by ideology and push back, by the spaces in between the rules and off the grid, where bodies come together, settle, and sometimes dance. Soft, responsive, rebellious, local, our bodies are the first victims of ideology, but are finally unconquerable and unsubmissive.

—Marianela Boán

In June 2019, an oppressive heat hung over Havana as the capital celebrated sixty years of the 1959 Revolution and five hundred years of existence. On a painfully bright Saturday, dozens of Cubans and a handful of tourists braved the unrelenting sun to see an outdoor folkloric dance show. Those without umbrellas clustered under scraggly trees offering meager patches of shade. At three o'clock, a woman began collecting five Cuban pesos (approximately twenty cents in U.S. currency) from locals and five convertible Cuban pesos (approximately five U.S. dollars) from foreigners for entry into the Conjunto Folklórico Nacional patio area for a regular Rumba Saturdays event. Families, couples, and friends enjoyed music and dance while casually chatting, smoking, drinking, and eating. A couple of days before, U.S. president Donald Trump had announced new policies ending most educational and all people-to-people travel, as well as cruise ships, to Cuba from the United States. The threat of economic loss cast no apparent shadow over the afternoon. The performance infrastructures that dancers and audiences had created over the decades, which allowed for dancing and watching, expression and enjoyment, despite oppressive heat and punitive geopolitics, deserve recognition as a key revolutionary achievement made by and for the people.

Elsewhere in Havana, evidence of dance dotted the cityscape. Cuban-trained ballet dancer Carlos Acosta, who made his career in the United States and Great Britain in the 1990s, had returned in 2012 to open Acosta Danza. Both a company and school, its highly visible studio sits on the main drag, Línea. Some of the best modern and ballet dancers have joined the private-public enterprise thanks to international funding that allows for higher salaries than those offered in nationalized companies. Stopping by the Ballet Nacional de Cuba, I found the main office, where Alicia Alonso had managed her ballet empire for decades, with piles of furniture and papers creating a dusty cave. In a small opening, Alicia's longtime, hardworking assistant Farah Rodríguez sat at her hefty computer monitor. The office was under construction for the new subdirector (and eventually director), ballerina Vingsay Valdés—the first person not in the Alonso family to formally lead the company. Modern and contemporary dance projects like the excellent MalPaso Dance Company, spearheaded by alumni of Danza Contemporánea de Cuba, also enriched the dancescape. During my trip, they rehearsed for an upcoming U.S. tour in their unbearably hot space without air conditioning at the synagogue on 17th Street in Vedado. Meanwhile, the Conjunto Folklórico Nacional studios some blocks away bustled with weekly class offerings and Rumba Saturday performances.

Dance also cropped up in homes. One evening I watched an episode of ballet scholar Ahmed Piñeiro's weekly television program, *Danza eterna* (Eternal Dance), which focused on British ballerina Margot Fonteyn that week. Modern dance choreographer Rosario Cárdenas appeared several times on television, speaking with newscasters about upcoming events to celebrate the thirtieth anniversary of her company, founded in the midst of youthful rebellion and invention of the late 1980s. Santiago Alfonso, who in the 1960s had worked with modern and folkloric dance companies, as well as in cabarets, appeared as a judge on the new competition dance show, *Bailando en Cuba* (Dancing in Cuba). Dance seemed to be everywhere, but admittedly, I was looking.

Ubiquity does not mean prosperity, however, and a quiet anxiousness seemed to hover over each dance (and nondance) enterprise as a result of political and economic shifts. President Raúl Castro had left office to his selected successor, ending fifty-nine years of the Castro brothers in direct power. In April 2018, hours after his appointment, the new president, Miguel Díaz-Canel, signed Decree 349, which rejected "vulgar" content in artwork. Artists roundly protested the measure as harkening back to the restrictive environment of the 1970s.[1] Along with political challenges, economic ones loomed as a result of a conciliatory Obama administration ending and a hostile Trump administration beginning in 2017. In September 2019, Díaz-Canel warned of an expected fuel and energy crisis due to U.S. sanctions. The ongoing embargo also has hampered the island's ability to fight the COVID-19 pandemic.[2] In this particular moment, the immediate future seems bleak.

Crisis and coping were familiar territory, however. Starting in the 1990s, Cuba experienced acute economic and political crisis during the so-called Special Period in Times of Peace, which equally impacted the dance establishment. Exciting dance continued in the 1990s and 2000s, as scholar Suki John discusses in her book on the subject; however, equally common, dancers left regularly.[3] In the decades after my narrative ends in 1990, dire economic crisis among other factors pushed, and eager foreign collaborators pulled, famed Cuban dancers to pursue opportunities elsewhere. Some Cubans ended up performing and teaching in world-class companies and schools after years of internationalist exchanges. Others chose lucrative commercial gigs, like teaching salsa in Tokyo or Chicago. Others have landed in less distinguished or flashy destinations but still provide excellent training to students in cities all over the world, including San Francisco, Belo Horizonte, Liverpool, Monterrey, and Leiria, to name a few. Perhaps the hardships that Cuban concert dance experienced in the 1990s and 2000s, which included economic crisis and regularly losing valuable dancers and teachers, make any unfolding trials seem mundane or a throwback. Perhaps the worst is yet to come. Although some of my friends and interlocutors may be toying with leaving Cuba, they still take class, rehearse, and perform. Teachers teach. Audiences watch. People keep moving.

In the absolutely ambivalent present, dance enterprises during the sixty years examined in this book shimmered. During a telephone interview, Rogelio Martínez Furé proudly reflected on folkloric "conquests" of post-1959 decades, when he and his colleagues convinced the public and government to value theatricalized popular culture. By contrast, he described folkloric developments of the 1990s and early 2000s to anthropologist Adrian Hearn as problematic for commercializing Afro-Cuban culture for tourist dollars.[4] Similarly, ballerina Caridad Martínez, now based in New York, commented, "There are people that say it was a golden age of ballet." The excitement and energy of the 1960s through the 1980s contrasted with the Ballet Nacional de Cuba of recent years, which had talent, but needed revitalization in her view.[5] Isidro Rolando in Havana inadvertently echoed Martínez, reflecting that his career happened during a "prodigious" era when people devoted themselves to fighting for the intertwined projects of Revolution and Cuban modern dance.[6] While nostalgia factored into these assessments, dance undoubtedly underwent profound changes during the decades covered in this book, giving their characterizations weight beyond mature artists romanticizing bygones. Concert dance took off in the 1930s through the 1950s, and after 1959, artistic vision met political ebullience to result in historic dance developments. Dance makers of African descent like Martínez Furé, Martínez, and Rolando leapt at unprecedented opportunities to become venerated professionals. This book has charted the key developments of this golden age, its causes, consequences, and persistent challenges.

Examining this history reveals that dance makers sought and secured degrees of power as they led, and governments followed, in their metaphoric dance over six decades. Ballet dancers pushed for new students, audiences, and eventually state subsidies in the 1930s through the 1950s, accumulating enough support and political capital to defame the Batista regime for budget cuts. During this same period, dancers and choreographers explored race and nation on elite stages by featuring African-descended art and artists while continuing to privilege whiteness in expressions of Cubanness. This established prejudicial conventions and artistic priorities, which persisted in subsequent decades. Dance makers then took advantage of regime change to advance long-standing artistic goals in new or revamped companies. They institutionalized revolutionary dance by the mid-1960s before other realms of political and economic life. Racial and class prejudices continued to be systemic with historically white, elite ballet enjoying the most privilege. Meanwhile, black and *mulato* dancers used their art and newly won professional status to challenge persistent inequalities. Dancers of different racial backgrounds not only built institutions but also continued to choreograph and perform despite official suspicions regarding especially male dancers' sexual orientation. Their actions evidence that the late 1960s and early 1970s were filled not only with devastating repression but also with vibrant innovation. These same beleaguered professionals also managed to integrate dance into mass education programs in the 1960s and 1970s and internationalist campaigns of the 1970s and 1980s. Capitalizing on their significance to revolutionary culture and politics, dance makers fought to revolutionize their field in the late 1970s and 1980s, well before the onset of the Special Period. The impulses that directed developments overwhelmingly originated with dance makers who jostled to overcome official antagonism in various forms and managed to do so at unexpected moments.

Along with directing their relationship with the state, dancers used their ephemeral, nonverbal form to express politics in a revolutionary public sphere. Folkloric and modern dancers advocated for racial justice through productions like *Yoruba, Congo, Rumbas y comparsas* (1963) and *Medea y los negreros* (1968), which celebrated Afro-Cuban culture and performers as central to revolutionary visions. *María Antonia* (1967) and *Impromptu galante* (1970) critiqued gender norms; *El decálogo del apocalipsis* (1971) featured gay aesthetics with the coming out of "chaste José"; and *Canto vital* (1973) staged homoeroticism, all within a highly homophobic context. Folkloric dancers mounted a paean to Africa with *Palenque* (1976), heralding diasporic rather than national communities. *Eppure si muove* (1988) and *Sin permiso* (1988) critiqued suffocating authority. The fact that some works premiered without problem (*Yoruba, Congo, Rumbas y comparsas, Medea y los negreros, Impromptu galante, Canto vital, Palenque*) while others experienced some degree of censure or questioning (*María Antonia, El decálogo del apocalipsis, Eppure si muove, Sin permiso*) only further attests to the transgressive capacity of movement. Each gesture, sequence, spatial pattern, and stance was laden with meaning. This allowed dancers to convey ideas other artists could not in their fixed, verbal media. Choreographic maneuvers at times stumped officials, who worried (sometimes baselessly and sometimes with good reason) about postures conveying oblique dissidence or deviance. Indeed, Cuban concert dance makers over the decades effectively used bodies and nonverbal movements to make political statements about race, gender, and revolution in a limited public sphere.

Glittering achievements came at a price, and this book has emphasized how pain was equally part of Cuban concert dance history. Harm could be inflicted by a state that barred foreign appearances or censored work, as well as by colleagues, who wielded guns, stunted careers, or defected. Such mistreatment was extraordinarily common, compelling Caridad Martínez to softly assert that everyone was hurt over the decades: "*Todo el mundo* [*estuvo*] *lastimado*."[7] Also causing pain were hierarchies based on racism and cultural pretensions. In my interview with Alicia Alonso in 2015, she confided, "I will tell you a secret. I wanted to show that the Cubans could dance *classical* . . . because every time that you spoke about Cubans—oh, rumba, cha-cha-chá . . . no sir. Classical. They would go, *what*? I would say, classical."[8] The statement reflects the uphill battle she waged against stereotypes emanating from global centers that Cubans solely danced suggestive popular dances. Her hard work paid off. When she started, Cuban dance meant rumba and cha-cha-chá. Today, it also means ballet. However, such a project implicitly diminished the value of (mixed race, popular) rumba and cha-cha-chá while holding up (white, elite) ballet.

To be sure, ballet dancers have enjoyed the most privilege. Lorna Burdsall complained about these privileges in the 1960s; balletic food rations evidenced privileges in the 1970s; and Caridad Martínez realized the privileges she lost after leaving Alicia's jurisdiction in the 1980s. This status continues today. As recent proof, U.S. president Barack Obama delivered his March 2016 speech to the Cuban people in the newly renamed Alicia Alonso Grand Theater of Havana. He met Alicia (and no other dance leader) just before his speech, and Alicia sat a few seats from state power in the form of then president Raúl Castro during Obama's historic address.[9]

Ballet's proximity to revolutionary leadership is well known in Cuba, as illustrated by visual artist Alexis Esquivel's painting *Releve-ción* (2000). In the image, Vilma Espín, a longtime militant, political leader, and the wife of Raúl Castro, wears a uniform shirt and beret on top and tutu and pointe shoes on the bottom with a rifle slung across her back. In the spotlight on a darkened stage, she smiles while standing on the tips of her toes (figure E.1). With the neologism *releve-ción*, Esquivel combines the French ballet term *relevé* for her pose and the Spanish *revolución*, encapsulating the close relationship between ballet and revolution in Cuba. When I asked Esquivel about the painting, he grinned and explained that inspiration came from hearing that Espín had trained in ballet. By mixing military and ballerina accouterments—fatigues and pointe shoes—the painting meditates on the curious, almost ironic combination of the historically bourgeois ballet and socialist revolution. Equally, the painting captures major points of this book: that concert dancers and the Revolution partnered in unexpected and consequential ways and that not all partnerships were created equal.

Institutions and public discourse reinforce these inequalities. In 1998, the Museo Nacional de la Danza (National Museum of Dance) became the official research center of the Ballet Nacional de Cuba. Though purportedly devoted to "dance," the center focuses almost exclusively on ballet under the directorship of Alicia Alonso's second husband, Pedro Simón. Also telling, Alicia, and not modern dance leader Ramiro Guerra, who also passed away in 2019, received a presidential homage upon taking a final mortal bow. President Díaz-Canel (@DiazCanelB) tweeted on October 17, 2019, the day she died, "#AliciaAlonso you have gone and left us an enormous emptiness, but also an insurmountable legacy. She situated #Cuba on the altar of the best of world dance. #Gracias [Thanks] Alicia for your immortal work. #Somos-Cuba [We are Cuba]." Documents from the Ministry of Culture archive, which form the core of this study, also evidence these disparities. Ballet has twenty-five boxes devoted to its past; modern dance, twelve; and folkloric dance, eight.[10] Thus, virtual and material traces, as well as the history I tried to tell, reveal the implications of uneven official regard in revolutionary times.

Concert dance history also underscores the physicality of making revolutions. To contribute to political projects, dancers spent countless hours sweating in class and rehearsal. On stages, they flew across the floor. Devoted audience members waited in long lines for coveted tickets, while others fell asleep and awoke to applaud for an aged Alicia. How Cubans engaged with concert dance—whether performing under a hot sun or sitting through a lecture demonstration in a factory—gestures to a larger, underappreciated movement history of Cuban politics. This study focused on concert dancers and their dancing public, but countless Cubans enacted distinct revolutionary choreographies, like cutting sugar cane, waiting in lines, conducting military drills, and dancing for ritual and revelry, which merit further research. My

FIGURE E.1 Alexis Esquivel, *Releve-ción*, 2000, acrylic on canvas, 100 × 75.5 cm, private collection, United States. Esquivel's painting features revolutionary notable and former ballet student Vilma Espín dressed as a militant on top and ballerina on the bottom. The work encapsulates the general understanding that concert dancers partnered with the Revolution and that ballet had a particularly close connection to state power. Courtesy of Alexis Esquivel.

hope is that future scholars examine these elusive embodied experiences so central to daily life.

Ultimately, choreographic and performative labors helped to make concert dance into a compelling symbol of full body investment in the Revolution. Hopefully it now makes good sense why modern dancers posed for commemorative posters above Paseo in the early 1970s as discussed in the introduction to this book. As the performers improvised to encapsulate revolutionary milestones, they embodied the dramatic physicality of living through politically charged times. Their status as distinguished representatives was not lost on participants in the photo shoot. "It was an honor," modern dancer Isidro Rolando concluded.[11] In the posters inspired by their photographs, abstracted dancers became paradigms of the Cuban everyman and everywoman, or more accurately, the new man and new woman. The path to reach such heights was littered with struggle and disappointment, and dancers had the scars and stories to prove it. Perhaps their hardship made the zenith all the more sweet, or equally possible, profoundly ambivalent.

Above all, their histories attest to the resilience and creativity of dance makers, and Cuban citizens more broadly, who navigated revolutionary politics by using their bodies in motion. In 2013, Cuban modern dancer and choreographer Marianela Boán reflected on the process of cultivating durable originality: "Where ideology is strong, bodies must adapt and resist. I am fascinated by the ways our bodies are pushed by ideology and push back, by the spaces in between the rules and off the grid, where bodies come together, settle, and sometimes dance. Soft, responsive, rebellious, local, our bodies are the first victims of ideology, but are finally unconquerable and unsubmissive."[12] In her rendering, political ideology pushes and pulls, affecting both mind and body. In response, citizens become clever and choreograph to confound absolute control. They kinesthetically engage with structures to live, survive, and sometimes thrive. Coming together to dance also provides precious moments of freedom. Literally and metaphorically dancing with the Revolution meant feeling along the edges of ideology to move alongside and beyond the purview of hegemonic politics. As bodies carved out beats of rhythmic release, they remade the Revolution on repeat, filling it with dance, making history, and corporeally demanding that motion define Cuba's present and future.

Notes

Introduction

1. Luz María Collazo and Isidro Rolando, interview with author, June 6, 2019, Havana, Cuba. Translations, unless otherwise indicated, are my own.

2. "Luz María Collazo: Fui uno de los rostros más fotografiados," September 2006, personal archive of Luz María Collazo.

3. Beneficiaries in M. Cabrera, *El ballet en Cuba*; Pajares Santiesteban, *La danza contemporánea cubana*; Singer, *Fernando Alonso*; Daniel, *Rumba*; victims in Roca, *Cuban Ballet*.

4. Serra, *"New Man" in Cuba*; Quiroga, *Cuban Palimpsests*; L. Guerra, *Visions of Power in Cuba*; Moore, *Music and Revolution*; Bronfman, "'Batista Is Dead.'"

5. Howe, *Transgression and Conformity*; Leal, *Teatro Escambray*; Martin, *Socialist Ensembles*; Mirabal and Velazco, *Hablar de Guillermo Rosales*; Camnitzer, *New Art of Cuba*; de la Fuente, *Grupo Antillano*; Chanan, *Cuban Cinema*; Benson, "Sara Gómez"; Moore, *Music and Revolution*; Serra, *"New Man" in Cuba*.

6. Although other scholars (Pajares Santiesteban, *La danza contemporánea cubana*; John, *Contemporary Dance in Cuba*) have chosen to use the present term "contemporary dance," I stick with the original term "modern dance" to foreground historical trajectories and for the sake of consistency. For a relevant discussion of "modern" versus "contemporary" dance in Argentina, which resonates with Cuba, see Fortuna, *Moving Otherwise*, 10–12.

7. Kraut, *Choreographing the Folk*, 17–24.

8. Resonant with conclusions about a "totalizing, but not total state," Lambe, *Madhouse*, 197.

9. Castro, "Words to the Intellectuals," 220.

10. Bustamante, "Cultural Politics and Political Cultures," 14.

11. Challenges downplayed in M. Cabrera, *El ballet en Cuba*; Pajares Santiesteban, *La danza contemporánea cubana*; Martínez Furé, *Diálogos imaginarios*; Daniel, *Rumba*; Gordon-Nesbitt, *To Defend the Revolution*.

12. Continuities across 1959 also in Lambe, *Madhouse*; Horst, "Sleeping on the Ashes."

13. Benson, *Antiracism in Cuba*; race in earlier eras of Cuban history in de la Fuente, *Nation for All*; Ferrer, *Insurgent Cuba*; Bronfman, *Measures of Equality*; Guridy, *Forging Diaspora*.

14. Recognizing continuities and changes after 1959, as called for by de la Fuente, "La Ventolera," 302.

15. John, *Contemporary Dance in Cuba*; Daniel, *Rumba*; Hagedorn, *Divine Utterances*; Fernandes, *Cuba Represent!*

16. For instance, Grandin, "Off the Beach," 426–29; Joseph and Spenser, *In from the Cold*; Karl, "Reading the Cuban Revolution"; Schlotterbeck, *Beyond the Vanguard*.

17. Bustamante and Lambe, *Revolution from Within*; L. Guerra, *Visions of Power in Cuba*; Ferrer, "History and the Idea," 63–64.

18. Collazo and Rolando, interview, June 6, 2019.

19. Some Latin American histories have discussed dance, including Ramsey, *Spirits and the Law*; Putnam, *Radical Moves*; S. Johnson, *Fear of French Negroes*; Guy, *Sex and Danger in Buenos Aires*; Chasteen, *National Rhythms, African Roots*; or other cultural productions, such as Hertzman, *Making Samba*; Alberto, "El Negro Raúl." Histories of other places and eras may include dance, but concert dance specifically and dance generally remain relatively rare.

20. See, for instance, Garafola, *Diaghilev's Ballets*; Manning, *Modern Dance, Negro Dance*; Ross, *Like a Bomb Going Off*; Foster, *Choreography & Narrative*; Foulkes, *Modern Bodies*; Srinivasan, *Sweating Saris*; Kraut, *Choreographing Copyright*; Croft, *Dancers as Diplomats*; Blanco Borelli, *She Is Cuba*.

21. Resonant with Das, *Katherine Dunham*; Phillips, *Martha Graham's Cold War*; Keilson, "Embodied Conservatism of Rudolf Laban"; in conversation with work on Soviet and Chinese dancers, especially Ezrahi, *Swans of the Kremlin*; Wilcox, *Revolutionary Bodies*; joining

a recent wave of recent scholarship on concert dance in Latin America: Rosa, *Brazilian Bodies*; Fortuna, *Moving Otherwise*; Reynoso, "Choreographing Politics, Dancing Modernity"; Kosstrin, *Honest Bodies*, 85–156; Höfling, *Staging Brazil*, 128–62.

22. Pajares Santiesteban, *Ramiro Guerra*; Pajares Santiesteban, *La danza contemporánea cubana*; Martínez Furé, *Diálogos imaginarios*; M. Cabrera, *El ballet en Cuba*.

23. Different concert dance genres juxtaposed in Brill, "La Escuela Cubana" and Triguero Tamayo, *Placeres del cuerpo*, but there is no discussion of power and privilege differentials. Genre-specific scholarship includes ballet in M. Cabrera, *El ballet en Cuba*; Tomé, "Cuban Ballet"; modern dance in Pajares Santiesteban, *Ramiro Guerra*; Pajares Santiesteban, *La danza contemporánea cubana*; John, *Contemporary Dance in Cuba*; folkloric dance in Martínez Furé, *Diálogos imaginarios*; Hagedorn, *Divine Utterances*; Daniel, *Rumba*.

24. Alicia Alonso, interview with author, March 25, 2015, Havana, Cuba.

25. Following the approach of Benson, *Antiracism in Cuba*, 28.

26. De la Fuente, *Nation for All*, 263–65; L. Guerra, *Visions of Power in Cuba*, 54–55.

27. "El espíritu renovador va a superar," *Revolución*, March 26, 1959, 2.

Chapter One

1. Performance Program, Ballet Alicia Alonso, December 1, 1949, folder 1949 Ballet-Danza, CDAT.

2. Fernando Alonso to Ann Barzel, 1949, folder 144, box 11, ABP.

3. Óscar Abela, "Problemas de nuestra cultura: El Ballet de Cuba en la encrucijada," *Carteles*, September 23, 1956, 37; list of performances 1948–56 for free or low cost also in an untitled document in folder BNC, Historiografía, cajuela 239, CNC.

4. Manuel Villabella, "Yo siempre he creado en función de Cuba," *Adelante*, July 31, 1982; Ángel Rivero, "Lefebre: A través de la danza," *Revolución y Cultura* (September–October 1983), 45–48.

5. Del Toro, *La alta burguesía cubana*; Fariñas Borrego, *Sociabilidad y cultura del ocio*; Thomas, *Cuban Zarzuela*; Stoner, *From the House to the Streets*, 10.

6. M. Cabrera, *El ballet en Cuba*, 214; Ruiz Rodríguez, *Ballet y revolución*, 12.

7. Quote from Palmer, Piqueras, and Sánchez Cobos, "Introduction," 6; my approach also resonates with and builds on work collected in their edited volume. Pacheco Valera, *La Sociedad Pro-Arte Musical*; Guzmán Moré, *De Dirección General a Instituto Nacional de Cultura*; García Yero, "State within the Arts."

8. Foster, *Valuing Dance*.

9. Quoted in Célida Parera Villalón, "Una conversación con el Dr. Guillermo de Zéndegui," *Temas* (April 1998), 13.

10. Estrada Betancourt, *De la semilla al fruto*, 121, 122 (quote); for more on ballet on television, see Rivero, *Broadcasting Modernity*, 72, 75–77, 88, 167, 175.

11. "Dinastía," *Bohemia*, October 25, 1953, 117.

12. Parera Villalón, *Pro-Arte Musical*, 7 (quote), 56–62 (list of foreign performers).

13. Performance Program, La Sociedad Pro-Arte Musical presenta un festival de su Escuela de Baile, May 25, 27, 29, 31, June 1, 1946, folder 19, box 1, Natalia Aróstegui Collection, CHC.

14. Roca, *Cuban Ballet*, 30.

15. Roca, *Cuban Ballet*, 49; Singer, *Fernando Alonso*, 13.

16. Dilettantism in F. Martínez Allende, "La Sociedad Pro-Arte Musical y su Ballet," in Performance Program, La Sociedad Pro-Arte Musical ofrece el Primer Gran Festival de su Escuela de Ballet, May 15, 18, 21, 23, 1943, folder 19, box 1, Natalia Aróstegui Collection, CHC; quote from Renée Méndez Capote, "La Sociedad Pro-Arte Musical y Ballet en Cuba," in Performance Program, La Sociedad Pro-Arte Musical presenta un festival de su Escuela de Baile, May 25, 27, 29, 31, June 1, 1946, folder 19, box 1, Natalia Aróstegui Collection, CHC.

17. Marisabel Sáenz, "El baile como medio de educación física," *Social* (August 1936), 48 (first quote), 54 (second quote).

18. Carmen Rovira, "La danza," in Performance Program, Concierto Infantil, June 1, 1947, folder 4, box 3, Lyceum and Lawn Tennis Club Collection, CHC.

19. *Pro-Arte Musical* 17, no. 1 (October 1, 1940), 1.

20. García-Márquez, *Ballets Russes*, 232, 249, 272–73, 290; M. Cabrera, *El ballet en Cuba*, 76; M. Cabrera, *Alberto Alonso*, 11–12; Parera Villalón, *Pro-Arte Musical*, 92–110.

21. Siegel, *Alicia Alonso*, 40, 44–45; Singer, *Fernando Alonso*, 15–22.

22. John Martin, "'Blue Bird' Ballet Stadium Offering," *New York Times*, August 3, 1940, 13.

23. John Martin, "The Dance: Honor Roll," *New York Times*, June 15, 1941, X8.

24. John Martin, "Alonso in Debut Here as Giselle," *New York Times*, November 3, 1943, 22.

25. John Martin, "Miss Alonso Wins Ovation as Giselle," *New York Times*, October 24, 1945, 27.

26. Siegel, *Alicia Alonso*, 83.

27. Comité Organizador del Homenaje Nacional a Alicia Alonso to Dr. Rafael P. González Muñoz, July 9, 1947, folder Ballet Alicia Alonso, Correspondencias, Notas de Prensa, 1943–1951, cajuela 196, ME-DGC.

28. "Memorandum que el Comité Organizador de la Función en Honor de la Bailarina Cubana Alicia Alonso dirige a la primera dama de la República, Señora Paulina Alsina Viuda de Grau," July 11, 1947, folder Ballet Alicia Alonso Correspondencias, Notas de Prensa, 1943–1951, cajuela 196, ME-DGC.

29. Clippings: [quote in] Francisco Ichaso, "El homenaje a Alicia Alonso," *Diario de la Marina*, August 7, 1947; "Otra junta celebró ayer el comité organizador del homenaje a la gran bailarina cubana Alicia Alonso," *Diario de la Marina*, July 10, 1947; Don Gual, "En esta Habana nuestra: El homenaje a Alicia Alonso," *Información*, July 24, 1947 in folder Ballet Alicia Alonso Correspondencias, Notas de Prensa, 1943–1951, cajuela 196, ME-DGC.

30. Siegel, *Alicia Alonso*, 83.

31. There were instances of pay as low as 175 dollars per performance week (1950–51), and as high as 750 dollars per week in late April and early May 1952. Contracts in folders 1280–81, box 14, ABT.

32. The 1938 contract is in folder 141, box 2, ABT; the 1947 contract is in folder 1284, box 14, ABT.

33. Ballet Theatre Inc. to Alicia Alonso, May 2, 1945, folder 464, box 7, ABT.

34. Folders 1374–76, Sergei Denham Records of the Ballet Russe de Monte Carlo, *ZBD-492, JRDD.

35. M. Cabrera, *El ballet en Cuba*, 51; De Mille, *Portrait Gallery*, 76; Lucille Leimer, "Confidentially," *Los Angeles Times*, January 14, 1947, A5.

36. Célida P. Villalón to Jonathan Mandell, January 12, 1992, in Villalón, Célida Parera, Miscellaneous Manuscripts, (S) *MGZM-Res, Vil C, JRDD.

37. Turnley Walker, trans. Manuel Marsal, "Nuestras glorias en el extranjero: La bailarina que se sobrepuso a la adversidad," *Bohemia*, August 11, 1957, 62–63, 99.

38. De Mille, *Portrait Gallery*, 70.

39. Fernando Alonso to Lucia Chase, August 2, 1948, folder 470, box 7, ABT.

40. John Martin, "'Ballet Alicia Alonso' in Its Bow in Havana," *New York Times*, October 31, 1948, X10.

41. "Alicia Alonso estudió su arte en el extranjero," *Gente*, August 16, 1953, 11–12; Celita [Célida] Parera de Villalón, "Alicia Alonso no estudió su arte en el extranjero," *Gente*, August 30, 1953, 16; Lily Ricard Valdés, "Todo el movimiento de ballet existente en Cuba no es producto exclusivo de Pro-Arte Musical," *Gente*, September 13, 1953, 16–17; Celita [Célida] Parera de Villalón, "Apuntes para la historia del ballet en Cuba," *Gente*, September 27, 1953, 16.

42. Performance Program, Escuela de Ballet Alicia Alonso, June 5, 1955, folder 1955 Ballet-Danza, CDAT.

43. Laura Alonso, interview with author, March 6, 2014, Havana, Cuba.

44. M. Cabrera, *El ballet en Cuba*, 130 (Méndez), 115–16 (Araújo).

45. "El Ballet Nacional y sus propósitos," in Performance Program, Ballet Nacional, folder 1950 Ballet-Danza, CDAT.

46. "Breve historia del ballet en Cuba," in Performance Program, Ballet Nacional, folder 1950 Ballet-Danza, CDAT.

47. "Propósitos que dieron origen y dan vida al Ballet 'Alicia Alonso,'" in Performance Program, Ballet Alicia Alonso, December 22, 1951, folder 1951 Ballet-Danza, CDAT.

48. Fausto Martínez Carbonell, "Aclaraciones en torno al Ballet Alicia Alonso," in Performance Program, Ballet Alicia Alonso, November 13, 1952, SA, BNJM.

49. "Davidacatura," *Bohemia*, June 29, 1958, 138.

50. "Ballerina," *Bohemia*, August 10, 1958, 138.

51. "Telenotas," *Carteles*, January 24, 1954, 23.

52. Miguel Cabrera, "Con Alberto Alonso en sus 50 años con la danza," *Cuba en el Ballet* 2, no. 2 (April–June 1983), 28.

53. Alberto's artistic priorities discussed further in Schwall, "Between *Espíritu* and *Conciencia*"; Schwall, "Sweeping Gestures."

54. "Club Ballerina," expediente 9386, legajo 320, RA, ANC; "Ballet Nacional," expediente 4052, legajo 188, RA, ANC.

55. "Asociación Alicia Alonso Pro-Ballet en Cuba," expediente 2942, legajo 161, RA, ANC; "Institución de Ballet Alicia Alonso," expediente 3503, legajo 175, RA, ANC; "Patronato Ballet de Cuba," expedientes 22775–76, legajo 1085, RA, ANC.

56. Fernando Alonso to Ann Barzel, 1949, folder 144, box 11, ABP.

57. "Dinastía," *Bohemia*, October 25, 1953, 117.

58. Manuel Villabella, "Yo siempre he cre a do en función de Cuba," *Adelante*, July 31, 1982.

59. Parera Villalón, *Pro-Arte Musical*, 21.

60. Performance programs from Grupo de Investigación, Documentación e Información Musical Pablo Hernández Balaguer.

61. Triguero Tamayo, *Placeres del cuerpo*, 143.

62. M. Cabrera, *El ballet en Cuba*, 28.

63. Herminia Grieg de Santos Bush to Nicolai Yavorsky, November 19, 1946, expediente 5, legajo 5, Fondo: Personal de Nicolai Yavorsky, AHPSC.

64. Laura Rayneri de Alonso to A Quien Pueda Interesar [To whom it may concern], October 24, 1944, expediente 9, legajo 1, Fondo: Personal de Nicolai Yavorsky, AHPSC; Parera Villalón, *Pro-Arte Musical*, 95.

65. "Casino de la Playa: Contrato," May 16, 1941, expediente 4, legajo 5, Fondo: Personal de Nicolai Yavorsky, AHPSC; Dr. Luis Varona, Subsecretario de Educación, to Nicolai Yavorsky, April 26, 1944, expediente 2, legajo 4, Fondo: Personal de Nicolai Yavorsky, AHPSC; "Escuela de Ballet Yavorsky," expediente 7, legajo 5, Fondo: Personal de Nicolai Yavorsky, AHPSC.

66. "Contracto," February 5, 1946, expediente 5, legajo 5, Fondo: Personal de Nicolai Yavorsky, AHPSC.

67. Espín Guillois, Ferrer, and Aguilar Ayerra, *El fuego de la libertad*, 603, 676 (image).

68. Triguero Tamayo, *Placeres del cuerpo*, 136; Nilsa, Tobío, and Ramírez in Performance Program, Pro Arte de Oriente presenta su Ballet bajo la dirección del Professor Georges Milenoff, March 10, 1944, Grupo de Investigación, Documentación e Información Musical Pablo Hernández Balaguer.

69. Triguero Tamayo, *Placeres del cuerpo*, 141; Performance Program, Sociedad Pro Arte Oriente presenta su Ballet, June 6, 1949, Grupo de Investigación, Documentación e Información Musical Pablo Hernández Balaguer.

70. Triguero Tamayo, *Placeres del cuerpo*, 139.

71. Isaias Caparrós Otano, "Con los brazos abiertos," *Adelante*, November 20, 1987; quote from Manuel Villabella, "Yo siempre he creado en función de Cuba," *Adelante*, July 31, 1982.

72. Ángel Rivero, "Lefebre: A través de la danza," *Revolución y Cultura* (September–October 1983), 46.

73. "Escuela de Ballet Alicia Alonso, Palma Soriano," expediente 7, legajo 2461, Fondo: Gobierno Provincial de Oriente, AHPSC.

74. Pamphlet, Manuel del Pino, *Panorama histórico del ballet en Camagüey, 1936–1967* (Camagüey: Departamento de Divulgación del Ballet de Camagüey), Biblioteca Provincial Julio Antonio Mella de Camagüey.

75. Ángel Rivero, "Lefebre: A través de la danza," *Revolución y Cultura* (September–October 1983), 46; Manuel Villabella, "Yo siempre he creado en función de Cuba," *Adelante*, July 31, 1982.

76. Studio Sylvia M. Goudie, *Memoria*, 37; Pacheco Valera, "La enseñanza artística."

77. Based on an incomplete series of programs and class offerings, Leontieva taught in 1943–45, 1947, and 1948, and Cuca Martínez, in 1952, 1956, 1958, and 1959. Materials in folders 4, 8–11, box 3, and folder 7, box 5, Lyceum and Lawn Tennis Club Collection, CHC.

78. Pajares Santiesteban, *Ramiro Guerra*, 37.

79. Pajares Santiesteban, *Ramiro Guerra*, 38.

80. Carlos Manuel de Céspedes, "Notas sobre el Departamento de Bellas Artes," *Conservatorio* 7, no. 4 (October–December 1949), 16.

81. "Reglamento" in "Patronato Pro-Ballet Municipal," expediente 3358, legajo 172, RA, ANC.

82. Untitled meeting notes, January 18, 1950, in "Patronato Pro-Ballet Municipal," expediente 3358, legajo 172, RA, ANC.

83. M. Cabrera, *Alberto Alonso*, 19; Elósegui listed in Performance Program, Sociedad Pro Arte Musical, June 27, 1944, folder Ballet Notas de Prensa, box 197, ME-DGC, as well as two more performance programs in the same folder and box; her biography is also in "Personal Actual (Síntesis de los datos)," folder Municipio de la Habana, Academia Municipal de Ballet, Ballet de Cámara, 1960–1961, ME-DGC; Roche mentioned in Reinaldo Cedeño Pineda, "Eduardo Rivero Walker: Ogún eterno," *Del Caribe*, no. 38 (2002), 103.

84. Quote from Reinaldo Cedeño Pineda, "Eduardo Rivero Walker: Ogún eterno," *Del Caribe*, no. 38 (2002), 103; biographical information from Aguirre Molina, "Eduardo Rivero Walker," 10.

85. Parera Villalón, *Pro-Arte Musical*; Pacheco Valera, *La Sociedad Pro-Arte Musical*; for more on patronage and clientelism among Cuban elites, see L. Guerra, *Heroes, Martyrs, and Political Messiahs*, 100–105.

86. Parera Villalón, *Pro-Arte Musical*, 14.

87. Performance Program, La Sociedad Pro-Arte Musical presenta un festival de su Escuela de Baile, May 25, 27, 29, 31, June 1, 1946, folder 19, box 1, Natalia Aróstegui Collection, CHC.

88. Pacheco Valera, *La Sociedad Pro-Arte Musical*, 77–78.

89. M. Cabrera, *El ballet en Cuba*, 115.

90. M. Cabrera, *El ballet en Cuba*, 123–24 (quote on 124); Deyá, *Mirta Plá*, 15–18.

91. Deyá, *Mirta Plá*, 24–25.

92. Miguel Cabrera, "Joaquín Banegas: Maitre del ballet cubano," *Cuba en el Ballet* 10, no. 3 (September–December 1979), 16.

93. Manuel Villabella, "Yo siempre he creado en función de Cuba," *Adelante*, July 31, 1982.

94. Pajares Santiesteban, *Ramiro Guerra*, 36.

95. R. Guerra, "My Experience and Experiments in Caribbean Dance," 51.

96. As illustrated in photos printed in M. Cabrera, *El ballet en Cuba*, 218–19.

97. Nati González Freire, "Con Menia Martínez y Jorge Lefebre," *Bohemia*, July 31, 1970, 24–25.

98. Randall, *Cuban Women Now*, 151.

99. Estrada Betancourt, *De la semilla al fruto*, 72; quote in McElroy and Rodríguez, *Mirror Dance = La danza del espejo*.

100. Studio Sylvia M. Goudie, *Memoria*, 6–7.

101. M. Cabrera, *El ballet en Cuba*, 130.

102. Artículo 47, Título V in Convención Constituyente de la República de Cuba, "Constitución Política de 1940."

103. Ruiz Rodríguez, *Ballet y revolución*, 12.

104. Javier Barahona, "Está en marcha el 'Tren de la Cultura,'" *Carteles*, April 23, 1950, 40–42.

105. Raquel del Valle, "Historia gráfica de las misiones culturales," *Mensuario* (1951), SA, BNJM.

106. M. Millares Vázquez, "Una revolución cultural en Cuba, el campesino cubano y la obra de las misiones culturales," *Carteles*, August 20, 1950, 32–33.

107. Javier Barahona, "Está en marcha el 'Tren de la Cultura,'" *Carteles*, April 23, 1950, 40–42; Singer, *Fernando Alonso*, 11, 72, 85, 87; Raquel del Valle, "Las misiones culturales y el ballet," *Mensuario* (January 1950), 21–22, SA, BNJM; Pajares Santiesteban, *Ramiro Guerra*, 20.

108. Javier Barahona, "Está en marcha el 'Tren de la Cultura,'" *Carteles*, April 23, 1950, 40–42.

109. Raquel del Valle, "Las misiones culturales y el ballet," *Mensuario* (January 1950), SA, BNJM.

110. Angela Grau Imperatori, "Un mes de espera, historia del Ballet Nacional de Cuba," *Cuba en el Ballet* 3, no. 3 (September 1972), 34; Performance Program, Ballet Alicia Alonso, January 7, 1949, SA, BNJM.

111. Performance Program, Ballet Alicia Alonso, December 1, 1949, folder 1949 Ballet-Danza, CDAT.

112. Angela Grau Imperatori, "Un mes de espera, historia del Ballet Nacional de Cuba," *Cuba en el Ballet* 3, no. 3 (September 1972), 33.

113. "Reglamento," 1952, and "Balance General," May 31, 1955, both in "Asociación Alicia Alonso Pro-Ballet en Cuba," expediente 2942, legajo 161, RA, ANC.

114. Angela Grau Imperatori, "Un mes de espera, historia del Ballet Nacional de Cuba," *Cuba en el Ballet* 3, no. 3 (September 1972), 33.

115. Angela Grau Imperatori, "Cuándo, cómo y por qué se fundó la primera compañía de ballet profesional en Cuba," *Cuba en el Ballet* 3, no. 1 (January 1972), 41–45.

116. Angela Grau Imperatori, "La primera gira, historia del Ballet Nacional de Cuba," *Cuba en el Ballet* 4, no. 1 (January 1973), 43.

117. See theorization of dance as a gift in Foster, *Valuing Dance*, 52–87.

118. Angela Grau Imperatori, "Primera gira, hacia el cono sur, historia del Ballet Nacional de Cuba," *Cuba en el Ballet* 4, no. 2 (May 1973), 25–26.

119. Fernando Alonso to Lucia Chase, November 24, 1949, folder 470, box 7, ABT.

120. Fernando Alonso to Ann Barzel, 1949, folder 144, box 11, ABP.

121. Fernando Alonso to Lucia Chase, January 24, 1950, folder 470, box 7, ABT.

122. Arturo Ramírez, "De la farándula," *Carteles*, July 1, 1951, 16.

123. Fernando Alonso to Lucia Chase, March 12, 1952, folder 470, box 7, ABT.

124. L. Guerra, *Heroes, Martyrs, and Political Messiahs*, 75–76, 82.

125. Performance Program, Ballet Alicia Alonso, March 19 and 21, 1952, SA, BNJM.

126. Ballet Alicia Alonso to Señor Presidente, April 7, 1952, cuaderno 1618, FANJ.

127. Fernando Alonso to Carlos González Palacios, May 10, 1952, cuaderno 1618, FANJ.

128. Antonio Núñez Jiménez to Sr. Reinaldo Espinosa, July 19, 1952, cuaderno 1618, FANJ.

129. Undated, but the bound volume of correspondence is organized chronologically, suggesting that the memorandum was written in late 1952. Ballet Alicia Alonso to Sra. Martha Fernández Miranda de Batista, [1952], cuaderno 1618, FANJ.

130. Fausto Martínez Carbonell, "Por que pedimos ayuda al estado," in Performance Program, Ballet Alicia Alonso, August 25 and 29, 1952, SA, BNJM; Fausto Martínez Carbonell, "Los estrenos de ballets y sus costos," in Performance Program, Ballet Alicia Alonso, September 18, 1952, folder 1952 Ballet-Danza, CDAT; Fausto Martínez Carbonell, "Aclaraciones en torno al Ballet Alicia Alonso," in Performance Program, Ballet Alicia Alonso, November 13, 1952, SA, BNJM.

131. Pérez, *Cuba*, 225.

132. Óscar Abela, "Problemas de nuestra cultura: El Ballet de Cuba en la encrucijada," *Carteles*, September 23, 1956, 36–37, 80.

133. Fausto Martínez Carbonell, "Aclaraciones en torno al Ballet Alicia Alonso," in Performance Program, Ballet Alicia Alonso, November 13, 1952, SA, BNJM.

134. Quote in Fausto Martínez Carbonell, "Por que pedimos ayuda al estado," in Performance Program, Ballet Alicia Alonso, August 25 and 29, 1952, SA, BNJM; Fernando Alonso in "Nuestro director habla . . . 'las preocupaciones inmediatas,'" in Performance Program, Ballet Alicia Alonso, August 25 and 29, 1952, SA, BNJM.

135. Iber, "Anti-Communist Entrepreneurs," 175.

136. "Fernando Alonso, y el Congreso Continental de Cultura," in Performance Program, Ballet Alicia Alonso, April 24 and 26, 1953, SA, BNJM; M. Cabrera, *Órbita*, 124–27.

137. Pérez-Stable, *Cuban Revolution*, 14–15, 22–27.

138. First quote from Fausto Martínez Carbonell, "Por que pedimos ayuda al estado," in Performance Program, Ballet Alicia Alonso, August 25 and 29, 1952, SA, BNJM; second quote from "La importancia que tiene el ballet en la cultura de un pueblo," in Performance Program, Ballet Alicia Alonso, November 13, 1952, SA, BNJM.

139. Fausto Martínez Carbonell, "Aclaraciones en torno al Ballet Alicia Alonso," in Performance Program, Ballet Alicia Alonso, November 13, 1952, SA, BNJM; for more on larger educational initiatives of the period, see L. Guerra, *Heroes, Martyrs, and Political Messiahs*, 93–94.

140. Fausto Martínez Carbonell, "Por que pedimos ayuda al estado," in Performance Program, Ballet Alicia Alonso, August 25 and 29, 1952, SA, BNJM.

141. "¡Pero valen más!" *Bohemia*, September 12, 1954, 114.

142. Fernández Guevara, "Constructing Legitimacy"; see also program essay about a pacifist Martí in Performance Program, Comisión Nacional Organizadora de los Festejos del Centenario del Natalicio de José Martí presenta al Ballet Alicia Alonso, January 30, 1953, folder 1953 Ballet-Danza, CDAT.

143. McEwen, *Revolutionary Horizons*, 74–78; Singer, *Fernando Alonso*, 74.

144. Performance Program, Toma de posesión del Presidente Mayor General Fulgencio Batista, función de gala por el Ballet Alicia Alonso programa oficial, February 25, 1955, folder 1955 Ballet-Danza, CDAT.

145. Artículo 29 in Rúber Iglesias F. and Fernando Alonso, "Estatutos," in "Asociación Patronato Ballet de Cuba," expediente 22775, legajo 1085, RA, ANC.

146. *Boletín Informativo, Órgano Oficial del Instituto Nacional de Cultura*, no. 1 (November 1955).

147. Performance Program, Ballet de Cuba, folder 1955 Ballet-Danza, CDAT.

148. Fernando Alonso and Manuel Iribarren, "Asociación Patronato Ballet de Cuba, acta no. 14," December 14, 1955, in "Asociación Patronato Ballet de Cuba," expediente 22775, legajo 1085, RA, ANC.

149. "Polémica y ballet," *Nuestro Tiempo* 3, no. 14 (November 1956).

150. "Para la historia," *Nuestro Tiempo* 3, no. 13 (September 1956), Supplement; "Polémica y ballet," *Nuestro Tiempo* 3, no. 14 (November 1956); more on Nuestro Tiempo in McEwen, *Revolutionary Horizons*, 184–85; L. Guerra, *Heroes, Martyrs, and Political Messiahs*, 209–10.

151. "La carta de Zéndegui," August 5, 1956, in "Para la historia," *Nuestro Tiempo* 3, no. 13 (September 1956), Supplement; "Expone el INC por que niega una subvención," in "Polémica y Ballet," *Nuestro Tiempo* 3, no. 14 (November 1956).

152. Célida Parera Villalón, "Una conversación con el Dr. Guillermo de Zéndegui," *Temas* (April 1998), 13.

153. "Declaración pública de las instituciones culturales de Cuba, con motivo de la agresión económica de la dictadura batistiana al Ballet de Cuba en 1956," repr. in M. Cabrera, *El ballet en Cuba*, 331–32; Óscar Abela, "Problemas de nuestra cultura: El Ballet de Cuba en la encrucijada," *Carteles*, September 23, 1956, 80.

154. Patronato Ballet de Cuba, "Respuesta del Ballet de Cuba a las declaraciones del INC," in "Polémica y ballet," *Nuestro Tiempo* 3, no. 14 (November 1956).

155. "Para la historia," *Nuestro Tiempo* 3, no. 13 (September 1956), Supplement; "Carta dirigida por Alicia Alonso a Guillermo de Zéndegui," August 15, 1956, repr. in M. Cabrera, *El ballet en Cuba*, 329–31.

156. "Expone el INC por que niega una subvención," in "Polémica y Ballet," *Nuestro Tiempo* 3, no. 14 (November 1956).

157. "Un editorial de Nuestro Tiempo," in "Polémica y Ballet," *Nuestro Tiempo* 3, no. 14 (November 1956).

158. "Un atentado a la cultura nacional," *Bohemia*, August 26, 1956, 51; Waldo Medina, "Alicia Alonso, la de Cuba," *El Mundo*, September 8, 1956.

159. For a complete list, see M. Cabrera, *El ballet en Cuba*, 332–33.

160. Ballet Nacional de Cuba and Museo Nacional de la Danza, *El ballet*.

161. Lester Vila Pereira, "Un desagravio para la historia," *Cuba en el Ballet*, no. 112 (September–December 2006), 42.

162. Manuel Corrales, "Presencia estudiantil y popular en XXV años de ballet," *Cuba en el Ballet* 5, no. 1 (January 1974), 24; L. Guerra, *Heroes, Martyrs, and Political Messiahs*, 225.

163. "Homenaje Nacional a Alicia Alonso," *Bohemia*, September 16, 1956, 70.

164. Singer, *Fernando Alonso*, 76.

165. Performance Program, Amigos de la Cultura Cubana presentación del Ballet de Cuba, November 15, 1956, in folder Alonso, Alicia 1950s, [Programs], *MGZB (Alicia Alonso 1950s), JRDD.

166. In the United States: performance programs in folder Alonso, Alicia 1950s, [Programs], *MGZB (Alicia Alonso 1950s), JRDD; in the Soviet Union: "Alicia en la URSS," *Carteles*, March 2, 1958, 33–34; Schwall, "Spectacular Embrace," 279–85; ballet training on the island: Eduardo Muñoz, "Cuba paraíso del ritmo y de la danza: ¿Quiere usted ser artista de ballet?," *Carteles*, May 4, 1958, 72–73, 78; Studio Sylvia M. Goudie, *Memoria*.

167. L. Guerra, *Heroes, Martyrs, and Political Messiahs*, 188–93.

168. Alberto joined the party in 1945 while in New York, according to M. Cabrera, *Alberto Alonso*, 12. Fernando claimed his political views were "made in the U.S.A" in Singer, *Fernando Alonso*, 40.

169. "Acta numero ochenta y seis," February 4, 1956, in "Sociedad Cultural Nuestro Tiempo," expediente 22687, legajo 1080, RA, ANC.

170. Fernando Alonso, "El Ballet de Cuba," *Nuestro Tiempo* 6, no. 27 (January–February 1959).

171. Célida Parera Villalón to Agnes de Mille, August 13, 1990, Agnes de Mille Correspondence and Writings, (S) *MGZMD 100, JRDD.

172. Roca, *Cuban Ballet*, 38.

173. Quoted in Célida Parera Villalón, "Una conversación con el Dr. Guillermo de Zéndegui," *Temas* (April 1998), 13.

174. Performance Program, Amigos de la Cultura Cubana presentación del Ballet de Cuba, November 15, 1956, folder Alonso, Alicia 1950s, [Programs], *MGZB (Alicia Alonso 1950s), JRDD.

175. Fernando Alonso to Carlos González Palacios, May 10, 1952, cuaderno 1618, FANJ.

176. Nati González Freire, "Con Menia Martínez y Jorge Lefebre," *Bohemia*, July 31, 1970, 24–25.

Chapter Two

1. Orlando Quiroga, "Yoruba," *Bohemia*, December 4, 1960, 83.

2. Epigraph corrected for minor spelling mistakes, Irma Obermayer to Katherine Dunham, June 24, 1953, folder 9, box 92, KDP.

3. Blanco Borelli, *She Is Cuba*, 140–43; Cuba's "historical ghosts" in Lambe, "Century of Work," 92; erased dancers in Gottschild, *Digging the Africanist Presence*; Srinivasan, *Sweating Saris*, 43–66.

4. Ramiro Guerra, "Hacia un movimiento de danza nacional," *Lunes de Revolución*, July 13, 1959, 11; also asserted in R. Moore, *Nationalizing Blackness*, 221–28.

5. Resonant with de la Fuente, *Nation for All*, 183–84; R. Moore, *Nationalizing Blackness*; Lane, *Blackface Cuba*; Arnedo-Gómez, *Writing Rumba*; Anderson, *Carnival and National Identity*; Kutzinski, *Sugar's Secrets*.

6. Discussed more in chapter 3, but also alluded to in Ramiro Guerra, "Hacia un movimiento de danza nacional," *Lunes de Revolución*, July 13, 1959, 10–11.

7. Similar to findings on Cuban musicians in Abreu, *Rhythms of Race*, 9.

8. Musicians in Marquetti Torres, "Katherine Dunham y los percusionistas cubanos"; Fernandez, *From Afro-Cuban Rhythms to Latin Jazz*, 64, 67, 90, 119–21; Das, *Katherine Dunham*, 67, 113–14, 129, 130; also building on analysis of transnational connections created by mostly male intellectuals in Guridy, *Forging Diaspora*.

9. Hertzman, *Making Samba*; Chasteen, *National Rhythms, African Roots*; Andrews, "Remembering Africa, Inventing Uruguay"; Lane, *Blackface Cuba*; Alberto, "El Negro Raúl"; R. Moore, *Nationalizing Blackness*; Guridy, *Forging Diaspora*; Das, *Katherine Dunham*.

10. Performance Program, Sociedad Pro-Arte Musical presenta al Ballet Theatre y su Escuela de Baile, May–June 1947, folder 1947 Ballet-Danza, CDAT.

11. M. Cabrera, *El ballet en Cuba*, 33–36; Dino Carrera, "A cuarenta años de *Antes del alba*," *Cuba en el Ballet* 6, no. 2 (April–June 1987), 10–15; Tomé, "Cuban Ballet," 76–80.

12. Chamba mentioned in Dino Carrera, "A cuarenta años de *Antes del alba*," *Cuba en el Ballet* 6, no. 2 (April–June 1987), 13; his real name in Ledón Sánchez, *La música popular en Cuba*, 171.

13. Dino Carrera, "A cuarenta años de *Antes del alba*," *Cuba en el Ballet* 6, no. 2 (April–June 1987), 13.

14. Parera Villalón, *Pro-Arte Musical*, 102.

15. Ledón Sánchez, *La música popular en Cuba*, 171; Fernandez, *From Afro-Cuban Rhythms to Latin Jazz*, 102.

16. Dino Carrera, "A cuarenta años de *Antes del alba*," *Cuba en el Ballet* 6, no. 2 (April–June 1987), 13.

17. Leaf, *Isles of Rhythm*, 41–42.

18. Blanco Borelli, *She Is Cuba*, 25.

19. Dino Carrera, "A cuarenta años de *Antes del alba*," *Cuba en el Ballet* 6, no. 2 (April–June 1987), 14; Performance Program, Sociedad Pro-Arte Musical presenta al Ballet Theatre y su Escuela de Baile, May–June 1947, folder 1947 Ballet-Danza, CDAT.

20. Anderson, *Carnival and National Identity*, 26–27; Schwartz, *Pleasure Island*, 64.

21. Beruff Mendieta, *Las comparsas populares del carnaval habanero*, 7 (first quote), 8 (second quote).

22. Fernando Ortiz, "Informe," repr. in Beruff Mendieta, *Las comparsas populares del carnaval habanero*, 10 (quote), 15–19 (opinions on tourists and racial harmony).

23. De la Fuente, *Nation for All*, 208.

24. Beruff Mendieta, *Las comparsas populares del carnaval habanero*, 6.

25. Bronfman, *Measures of Equality*, 161, 168–71; for more on a whitened version of carnival, see Anderson, *Carnival and National Identity*, 232–52.

26. Martiatu, *Cuba*, 69.

27. Orovio, *El carnaval habanero*, 45.

28. Olga Fernández, "Cara a cara con Nieves Fresneda," *Cuba Internacional* (June 1981), 52–53.

29. Evangelina Chió, "Nieves o el mito de la danza," *Revolución y Cultura* (September 1979), 48.

30. Olga Fernández, "Cara a cara con Nieves Fresneda," *Cuba Internacional* (June 1981), 52–53.

31. Orovio, *El carnaval habanero*, 46 (quote); Olga Fernández, "Cara a cara con Nieves Fresneda," *Cuba Internacional* (June 1981), 52–53.

32. Graziella Garbalosa, "El carnaval en la Habana," *Carteles*, April 2, 1950.

33. "Comparsa habanera," *Carteles*, March 13, 1949, 40–41; "El desfile del carnaval," *Carteles*, March 13, 1949, 47–49.

34. "Santiago de carnaval," *Carteles*, August 5, 1956, 30–31; more on Santiago carnival in Pérez Rodríguez, *El carnaval santiaguero*; Schwall, "Dancing with the Revolution," 110–13.

35. On cross-dressing in Havana, see Orovio, *El carnaval habanero*, 15.

36. Mercer Cook, "Cuba's Dance, the Shuffle, Exhausts Even Spectators," *Afro-American*, August 16, 1941, 1; like Brazilian carnival in Green, *Beyond Carnival*, 199–241; for more about Cook in Cuba, see Guridy, "From Solidarity to Cross-Fertilization," 35.

37. Ramiro Sarteur, "Resurge el carnaval habanero," *Carteles*, March 2, 1947, 30–31.

38. Dino Carrera, "A cuarenta años de *Antes del alba*," *Cuba en el Ballet* 6, no. 2 (April–June 1987), 12.

39. Urban, "'Black Plague' in a Racial Democracy"; Urban, "Plagued by Politics"; Pérez, *To Die in Cuba*, 295.

40. Dino Carrera, "A cuarenta años de *Antes del alba*," *Cuba en el Ballet* 6, no. 2 (April–June 1987), 14–15.

41. Pérez, *To Die in Cuba*, 258.

42. Moore, "Commercial Rumba"; Fernández-Selier, "Making of the Rumba Body"; McMains, "Rumba Encounters"; Jottar, "Acoustic Body."

43. Sublette, *Cuba and Its Music*, 257, 268; Daniel, *Rumba*, 67–70.

44. Leaf, *Isles of Rhythm*, 38.

45. Leaf, *Isles of Rhythm*, 46; for instance, Spanish floor shows noted in Ángel Lázaro, "Las castañuelas de María del Pilar," *Carteles*, February 23, 1947, 15; also Spanish dance classes through Pro-Arte, as discussed in Parera Villalón, *Pro-Arte Musical*, 107; vogue of Spanish dance in Garafola, "Dalí, Ana María, and the Three-Cornered Hat."

46. Moore, *Nationalizing Blackness*, 185.

47. Quoted in Sublette, *Cuba and Its Music*, 269–70.

48. Israel Moliner Castañeda and Gladys Gutierrez Rodríguez, "La rumba," *Del Caribe* 4, no. 9 (1987), 45.

49. Fernández-Selier, "Making of the *Rumba* Body," 95–96.

50. Regina, "Escenario y pantalla: Ballet de Pro Arte," *Diario de la Marina*, May 29, 1947, 8.

51. Arturo Ramírez, "Teatralerías," *Carteles*, April 20, 1947.

52. Parera Villalón, *Pro-Arte Musical*, 102.

53. Regina, "Escenario y pantalla: Ballet de Pro Arte," *Diario de la Marina*, May 29, 1947, 8.

54. Miller, *Voice of the Leopard*, 215; Routon, "Unimaginable Homelands?," 391.

55. Dino Carrera, "A cuarenta años de *Antes del alba*," *Cuba en el Ballet* 6, no. 2 (April–June 1987), 15.

56. Similar to popular music, as discussed in Miller, "Secret Society Goes Public."

57. Abakuá masculinity discussed in Berry, "Now They Are Just about Guapería." I thank the author for sharing this material with me. For more on the warping of Abakuá culture, see Routon, "Unimaginable Homelands?"

58. De la Fuente, *Nation for All*, 382n43; artist-ethnographers of the 1920s in Tomé, "Racial Other's Dancing Body," 185–227; Brandon, *Santeria*, 93–94.

59. Palmié, *Cooking of History*, 56–57.

60. For instance, Ortiz, *Los bailes y el teatro de los negros en el folklore de Cuba*; Miller, *Voice of the Leopard*, 9–10.

61. Hernández Baguer, *Historias para una historia*, 21, 26–27, 289–91.

62. For instance, L. Cabrera, *La sociedad secreta Abakuá*; for more on Cabrera's career, see Maguire, *Racial Experiments*, 104–72.

63. Birkenmaier, *Specter of Races*, 35–37; Lachatañeré, *Manual de Santería*.

64. The group inconsistently referred to as Grupo Nacional de Bailes Folklóricos and Grupo Folklórico Cubano in materials from box 2, Adria Catalá Casey Papers, CHC. The latter name corroborated in "Informe a la Dirección General de Cultura acerca del Grupo Folklórico Cubano," folder CFN Informes 1961, cajuela 300, CNC.

65. Untitled history of the company, box 2, Adria Catalá Casey Papers, CHC; clipping: "Cuban Girls Have Their Own Rhumba," box 2, Adria Catalá Casey Papers, CHC; women appear white, although two dancers could be of mixed European and African descent based on photographs in box 2, Adria Catalá Casey Papers, CHC; for more on the Escuela Normal de Kindergarten, see Stoner, *From the House to the Streets*, 38.

66. Clippings: "Colorful Folk Festival Opens at Auditorium," "Cuban Girls Have Their Own Rhumba," "Cubans Dance to Exhaustion," in box 2, Adria Catalá Casey Papers, CHC.

67. Miller, *Voice of the Leopard*, 199.

68. Garafola, "Travesty Dancer in Nineteenth-Century Ballet."

69. Clipping: "Cubans Dance to Exhaustion," box 2, Adria Catalá Casey Papers, CHC.

70. Untitled history of the company, box 2, Adria Catalá Casey Papers, CHC; clipping: "Cuban Girls Have Their Own Rhumba," box 2, Adria Catalá Casey Papers, CHC.

71. Routon, "Unimaginable Homelands?," 383.

72. Clipping: "The 20th Anniversary National Folk Festival," box 2, Adria Catalá Casey Papers, CHC.

73. Clipping: "Cuban Girls Have Their Own Rhumba," box 2, Adria Catalá Casey Papers, CHC.

74. Routon, "Unimaginable Homelands?," 380, 383.

75. Lam, *Tropicana*, 54–56; Lowinger and Fox, *Tropicana Nights*, 117.

76. Quote from Arturo Ramírez, "Del ambiente teatral," *Carteles*, July 11, 1948, 39; for more on Rodney and the Mulatas de Fuego, see Fernandez, *From Afro-Cuban Rhythms to Latin Jazz*, 147; Blanco Borelli, *She Is Cuba*, 55–56.

77. Alternative title in Orovio, *Cuban Music from A to Z*, 220.

78. Lowinger and Fox, *Tropicana Nights*, 192.

79. Fernandez, *From Afro-Cuban Rhythms to Latin Jazz*, 119–20; "Singing Gods, Cuban Santos," [July 31, 1955], folder 8, box 49, KDP; dates of Dunham's trip to Cuba confirmed by Bench and Elswit, "Everyday Itinerary Dataset, 1950–53."

80. Lowinger and Fox, *Tropicana Nights*, 125–26; Fernandez, *From Afro-Cuban Rhythms to Latin Jazz*, 117–19.

81. Details on *Omelen-ko* in Lowinger and Fox, *Tropicana Nights*, 199–200; *Tambó* in "Apoteósico triunfo de Rodney," *Show* (February 1957), 68.

82. Quotes from "Embrujadora y sensual música africana," *Show* (March 1955), 50–51, image on 50.

83. Lowinger and Fox, *Tropicana Nights*, 239.

84. Raúl Corral, "Cómo se transforma el barro en espíritu," *Carteles*, June 4, 1950, 24–25; Lam, *Tropicana*, 32–33.

85. Performance Program, Sociedad Pro-Arte Musical presenta al Ballet Theatre y su Escuela de Baile, May–June 1947, folder 1947 Ballet-Danza, CDAT.

86. Image of *Prohibido en España* in Arturo Ramírez, "De la farándula," *Carteles*, December 9, 1956, 34; Parés also mentioned in Arturo Ramírez, "De la farándula," *Carteles*, February 10, 1957, 34.

87. Mario Olave Agustí, "Esto es 'Tropicana' un paraíso bajo las estrellas," *Bohemia*, December 20, 1953, 126.

88. As another example, Carmen Curbelo, discussed in Blanco Borelli, *She Is Cuba*, 101.

89. Quote in Irma Obermayer to Katherine Dunham, June 24, 1953, folder 9, box 92, KDP; photograph in folder 54, box 2, Katherine Dunham Photograph Collection, Special Collections Research Center, Southern Illinois University.

90. I have corrected minor spelling errors. Irma Obermayer to Katherine Dunham, June 24, 1953, folder 9, box 92, KDP.

91. Abreu, *Rhythms of Race*.

92. Irma Obermayer to Katherine Dunham, June 24, 1953, folder 9, box 92, KDP.

93. Quote from "El Ballet de Walter Nicks," *Bohemia*, November 22, 1953, 117; pictured in "Sans Souci," *Gente*, January 10, 1953, 23.

94. Irma Obermayer to Katherine Dunham, June 24, 1953, folder 9, box 92, KDP.

95. Marquetti Torres, "Katherine Dunham y los percusionistas cubanos"; Fernandez, *From Afro-Cuban Rhythms to Latin Jazz*, 64, 67, 90, 119–21; Das, *Katherine Dunham*, 67, 113–14, 129, 130.

96. Abreu, *Rhythms of Race*, 3–5; Moreno Vega, "Yoruba Orisha Tradition."

97. Performance Program, Katherine Dunham Stages a Cuban Evening, May 29, 1946, folder 6, box 1, reel 1, ECP.

98. Brunson, "Eusebia Cosme," 392–98.

99. "Guide to the Eusebia Cosme Papers (Sc Micro R-3619)," ECP; López, *Unbecoming Blackness*, 73.

100. Vanguard poetry of the *Afrocubanismo* movement was part of a transnational movement known as *poesía negra, poesía mestiza,* or *poesía afroantillana*. For more, see Arnedo-Gómez, *Writing Rumba*; Anderson, *Carnival and National Identity*.

101. Quoted in "La triunfal tournée de Eusebia Cosme," *Adelante* (October 1938), 14.

102. "Eusebia Cosme," *Adelante* (November 1935), 13; translation by López, *Unbecoming Blackness*, 78–79.

103. Sonic dimensions of Cosme's work in McEnaney, *Acoustic Properties*, 127–32; López, *Unbecoming Blackness*, 94–98; I focus instead on rhythmic movement like Brunson, "Eusebia Cosme," 401.

104. See López, *Unbecoming Blackness*, 65, 73, 87–89; programs in folder 6, box 1, reel 1, ECP.

105. Based on the definition offered in Guridy, *Forging Diaspora*, 4.

106. Katherine Dunham to Nicolás Guillén, June 18, 1946, folder 6, box 8, KDP.

107. Guridy, *Forging Diaspora*, 116, 124–37; Das, *Katherine Dunham*, 107; López, *Unbecoming Blackness*, 89.

108. Performance Program, Katherine Dunham Stages a Cuban Evening, May 29, 1946, folder 6, box 1, reel 1, ECP.

109. Morejón, "Las poéticas," 7.

110. Eusebia Cosme to Katherine Dunham, November 7, 1946, folder 3, box 9, KDP; on Cosme's career limitations, see López, *Unbecoming Blackness*, 61–111.

111. Uldarica Mañas to La directiva de la Sociedad Popular de Conciertos, December 23, 1946, folder 4, box 9, KDP.

112. Uldarica Mañas, "Informe al señor Reinaldo Fernández Rebull," December 23, 1946, folder 4, box 9, KDP.

113. Referred to simply as "Hoy," but assumedly *Noticias de Hoy,* in Uldarica Mañas to Katherine Dunham, August 22, 1947, folder 5, box 10, KDP; Alberto Mola Rodríguez to Katherine Dunham, September 17, 1948, folder 4, box 92, KDP.

114. Uldarica Mañas to Katherine Dunham, May 12, 1947, folder 2, box 10, KDP.

115. Heliodoro García to Katherine Dunham, May 8, 1947, folder 2, box 10, KDP; Katherine Dunham to Heliodoro García, May 29, 1947, folder 2, box 10, KDP.

116. Katherine Dunham to Uldarica Mañas, June 18, 1947, folder 3, box 10, KDP.

117. Katherine Dunham to José Manuel Valdés Rodríguez, June 19, 1947, folder 3, box 10, KDP.

118. Das, *Katherine Dunham*, 103–4.

119. "Katherine Dunham School of Arts and Research [1946–47 Schedule]," folder 1, box 9, KDP.

120. Alberto Mola Rodríguez to Katherine Dunham, September 17, 1948, folder 4, box 92, KDP.

121. García-Márquez, *Ballets Russes*, 290; Pajares Santiesteban, *Ramiro Guerra*, 20.

122. Pajares Santiesteban, *Ramiro Guerra*, 20, 45 (quote), 47.

123. "Katherine Dunham School of Arts and Research [1946–47 Schedule]," folder 1, box 9, KDP; "Dunham School of Dance and Theatre: Class Schedule and Rates, Winter Term, January 5, 1948 to March 27, 1948," 2, folder 2, box 133, KDP.

124. The only mention of Dunham that I found was in Pérez León, *Por los orígenes de la danza moderna en Cuba*, 11. There was no mention of Dunham when Guerra discussed his time in New York in Pajares Santiesteban, *Ramiro Guerra*, 20, 45–48; Pajares Santiesteban, *La danza contemporánea cubana*, 25.

125. See, for instance, "Director y coreógrafo," *Bohemia*, October 16, 1960, 34; R. Guerra, "My Experience and Experiments," 51.

126. Das, *Katherine Dunham*, 106.

127. For more on Dunham's travel in 1946–48, see Das, *Katherine Dunham*, 124–34; also Dunham's limited time in NY in 1947 and 1948 confirmed by Kate Elswit and Harmony Bench, personal communication with the author, September 9, 2019.

128. Pajares Santiesteban, *Ramiro Guerra*, 47.

129. Manning, *Modern Dance, Negro Dance*, xiv.

130. Ramiro Guerra, "La danza moderna," *Lunes de Revolución*, August 10, 1959, 14–15.

131. R. Guerra, "My Experience and Experiments," 49–50.

132. Pajares Santiesteban, *La danza contemporánea cubana*, 25.

133. Katherine Dunham to José Manuel Valdés Rodríguez, June 19, 1947, folder 3, box 10, KDP.

134. Katherine Dunham to Fernando Ortiz, November 11, 1951, folder 9, box 15, KDP.

135. Performance Program, Ballet Alicia Alonso, August 31, 1951, folder 1951 Ballet-Danza, CDAT.

136. Performance Program, Ballet Alicia Alonso, February 9, 1952, folder 1952 Ballet-Danza, CDAT.

137. Renée Méndez Capote, "Toque" in Performance Program, Ballet Alicia Alonso, February 9, 1952, folder 1952 Ballet-Danza, CDAT.

138. Quoted in Das, *Katherine Dunham*, 129.

139. Fernando Ortiz, "¡Buenos augurios del ballet negro! (De una carta a Fernando Alonso)," in Performance Program, Ballet Alicia Alonso, February 9, 1952, folder 1952 Ballet-Danza, CDAT.

140. Ortiz, *Cuban Counterpoint*.

141. Pedro García Suárez, "Ramiro Guerra y la danza moderna," *Bohemia*, May 17, 1963, 18.

142. Das, *Katherine Dunham*, 91.

143. Katherine Dunham to Irma Obermayer, July 23, 1953, folder 9, box 92, KDP.

144. Katherine Dunham to Irma Obermayer, September 9, 1953, folder 10, box 92, KDP.

145. For Obermayer, see Ruth-Ann Hartman to Immigration and Naturalization Service, November 28, 1953, folder 9, box 16, KDP. For documents on other Cuban students, see Rito Ramón Oro in folder 9, box 46, KDP; Oscar Edreia, Jr. in Syvilla Fort to Department Immigration, March 28, 1952, folder 1, box 16, KDP.

146. "Personnel Movements," December 13, 1955, folder 9, box 19, KDP; Irma Obermayer to Martin Leonard, July 17, 1954, folder 3, box 17, KDP.

147. Irma Obermayer to Katherine Dunham, October 19, 1955, folder 14, box 92, KDP.

148. Das, *Katherine Dunham*, 111.

149. Maritza Alonso to Katherine Dunham, May 26, 1955, folder 6, box 18, KDP; Maritza Alonso to Marquen Sutt, January 10, 1956, folder 1, box 20, KDP.

150. Several letters from Jane Kent to Katherine Dunham in April 1955 in folder 4, box 18, KDP; Katherine Dunham to Ernesto Lecuona, May 23, 1955, folder 6, box 18, KDP.

151. Ernesto Lecuona to Katherine Dunham, May 29, 1955, folder 6, box 18, KDP.

152. Katherine Dunham to Giovannella, January 3, 1955 [1956], folder 7, box 17, KDP. Misdated according to Kate Elswit and Harmony Bench, personal communication with the author, August 30, 2019.

153. Copy of letter to Eileen Garrett enclosed in Katherine Dunham to Edith [Bel Geddes], January 6, 1955 [1956], folder 7, box 17, KDP. Misdated according to Kate Elswit and Harmony Bench, personal communication with the author, August 30, 2019.

154. Katherine Dunham to Eileen Garrett, January 6, 1956, folder 1, box 20, KDP; Katherine Dunham to Mario Aguero Medrano, January 7, 1956, folder 1, box 20, KDP.

155. Copy of letter to Eileen Garrett enclosed in Katherine Dunham to Edith [Bel Geddes], January 6, 1955 [1956], folder 7, box 17, KDP. Misdated according to Kate Elswit and Harmony Bench, personal communication with the author, August 30, 2019.

156. See, for instance, letters from Katherine Dunham to Lydia Cabrera from 1970 in folder 15, box 3, Lydia Cabrera Collection, CHC.

157. Das, *Katherine Dunham*, 145.

158. Ángel Rivero, "Lefebre: A través de la danza," *Revolución y Cultura* (September–October 1983), 46–47 (quote on 46); archival evidence of Lefebre dancing with Dunham includes Lee Moselle to Georges Lesebre [*sic*], September 11, 1959, folder 6, box 25, KDP; "Payments Outstanding w/e 9/1/60," January 10, 1960, folder 4, box 26, KDP; several documents in folder 4, box 43, KDP; Lefebre's early years in Cuba are discussed further in chapter 1.

159. Distinct but resonant tensions with Haitians, Das, *Katherine Dunham*, 158–64.

160. Antón Arrufat, "Al hablar con Ramiro Guerra," *Lunes de Revolución*, April 4, 1960, 15.

161. Documents in folder 76, box 136 and folder 135, box 137 in Fulgencio Batista Zaldívar Collection, CHC.

162. Lester Vila Pereira, "Un desagravio para la historia," *Cuba en el Ballet*, no. 112 (September–December 2006), 43; Ballet Nacional de Cuba and Museo Nacional de la Danza de Cuba, *El ballet*; this performance is discussed further in chapter 1.

Chapter Three

1. A. O., "Orfeo antillano," *Mujeres* 4, no. 7 (July 1964), 70; "Orfeo otra vez, siempre Orfeo," *Revolución*, June 29, 1964.

2. Luz María Collazo, interview with author, August 8, 2013, Havana, Cuba.

3. Castro's benevolence in Singer, *Fernando Alonso*, 83–90; Fernando and Alicia's support in Roca, *Cuban Ballet*, 81; the Soviet influence in Guillermoprieto, *Dancing with Cuba*, 75–76.

4. Guevara, "Socialism and Man in Cuba," 219.

5. Quote from O'Connor, *Origins of Socialism in Cuba*, 316; 1960s institutionalization or the lack thereof in Domínguez, *Cuba*, 192; Bengelsdorf, *Problem of Democracy in Cuba*, 77–81, 89–94; Valdés, "Revolution and Institutionalization in Cuba," 18–24.

6. Particularly building on de la Fuente, *Nation for All*; Benson, *Antiracism in Cuba*; L. Guerra, *Visions of Power in Cuba*.

7. Benson, *Antiracism in Cuba*, 5.

8. Carbonell, *Cómo surgió la cultura nacional*, 30.

9. Castro, "Historic Second Declaration of Havana."

10. Reinaldo Cedeño Pineda, "Eduardo Rivero Walker: Ogún eterno," *Del Caribe*, no. 38 (2002), 103.

11. Clipping: "Actuará en Matanzas Conjunto de Danzas," *Girón*, May 11, 1962, folder 1962 Prensa, DCC.

12. "Fiesta de la danza cubana," *Mujeres* 19, no. 11 (November 1979), 52.

13. Mentioned in member lists, "Sociedad Cultural Nuestro Tiempo," expedientes 22684–87, 22690, legajo 1080, RA, ANC.

14. "Inauguran en mayo el Primer Festival de Arte Nacional," *Revolución*, April 20, 1959, 12.

15. Reprinted in Sánchez León, *Esa huella olvidada*, 357–58 (quote on 357).

16. Sánchez León, *Esa huella olvidada*, 48, 231.

17. The fifth department, originally "Departamento de Publicaciones e Intercambio Cultural," became "Departamento de Extensión Teatral" in July 1960, according to Sánchez León, *Esa huella olvidada*, 49. Misidentified as "chorus" in Hagedorn, *Divine Utterances*, 137–38; R. Moore, *Music and Revolution*, 205.

18. Clipping: "Actuará en Matanzas Conjunto de Danzas," *Girón*, May 11, 1962, folder 1962 Prensa, DCC; Pajares Santiesteban, *Ramiro Guerra*, 97.

19. Pérez León, *Por los orígenes de la danza moderna en Cuba*, 21.

20. Pajares Santiesteban, *La danza contemporánea cubana*, 61.

21. Advertisement in *Noticias de Hoy*, September 11, 1959, 6; Lolo de la Torriente, "La danza: Disciplina de la mente y alegría del espíritu," *Bohemia*, October 16, 1960, 75.

22. Sánchez León, *Esa huella olvidada*, 232; for more on Obermayer, see chapter 2.

23. Luz María Collazo and Isidro Rolando, interview with author, June 6, 2019, Havana, Cuba; Fidel Pajares Santiesteban, interview with author, June 8, 2019, Havana, Cuba.

24. Alejandro G. Alonso, "Isidro en tres tiempos," *Juventud Rebelde*, September 19, 1979, 3; Isidro Rolando, interview with author, March 17, 2015, Havana, Cuba.

25. Incorrectly listed as "Rolando Pérez" in Performance Program, Cimarrón, April 21, 1960, SA, BNJM; Rolando, interview, March 17, 2015.

26. Alejandro G. Alonso, "Isidro en tres tiempos," *Juventud Rebelde*, September 19, 1979, 3.

27. Rolando, interview, March 17, 2015.

28. Quote in Tania y Ricardo Villares, "Ensayo general," *Bohemia*, December 6, 1968,

28. Bernabeu was not in an early 1960 budget, repr. in Sánchez León, *Esa huella olvidada*, 366, but she was listed in Performance Program, Danza, September 10, 1960, folder 1959–1961, DCC.

29. A performance program (without cast names) can be found in cajuela 234, CNC.

30. Perla Rodríguez, interview with author, September 23, 2014, Havana, Cuba; Tania Díaz Castro, "Catorce años bailando," *Bohemia*, November 15, 1968, 78.

31. Ángel Rivero, "De la danza al poema," *Revolución y Cultura* (February 1985), 46; Collazo and Rolando, interview, June 6, 2019.

32. Ángel Rivero, "De la danza al poema," *Revolución y Cultura* (February 1985), 46.

33. "Luz María Collazo: Fui uno de los rostros más fotografiados," September 2006, personal archive of Luz María Collazo.

34. Ramiro Guerra, "Hacia un movimiento de danza nacional," *Lunes de Revolución*, July 13, 1959, 11.

35. Performance Program, Marionetas, folder 1965 Ballet-Danza, CDAT.

36. Guillermo Cabrera Infante, "Ballet de Cuba," *Lunes de Revolución*, April 4, 1960, 5; for more on Rodney, see chapter 2.

37. Pajares Santiesteban, *La danza contemporánea cubana*, 62–63.

38. For more, see Schwall, "Spectacular Embrace," 279–86.

39. Laura Alonso, interview with author, March 6, 2014, Havana, Cuba.

40. Adolfo Robal, interview with author, March 21, 2014, Havana, Cuba.

41. Aurora Bosch, interview with author, September 18, 2014, Havana, Cuba.

42. Burdsall, *More than Just a Footnote*, 48, 54.

43. Burdsall, *More than Just a Footnote*, 129; Memorandum, May 18, 1965, folder CDN Asistencia Técnica, '60, cajuela 224, CNC.

44. Lorna Burdsall to Ned and Family, April 3, 1963, folder 1, box 1, BFP.

45. Lorna Burdsall to Mother and Family, April 7, 1973, folder 3, box 1, BFP.

46. Evangelina Chió, "Nieves o el mito de la danza," *Revolución y Cultura* (September 1979), 47; for more on Fresneda and Las Bolleras, see chapter 2.

47. Sánchez León, *Esa huella olvidada*, 120.

48. Performance Program, Yimbula, fiesta de paleros, November 1960, SA, BNJM.

49. Sánchez León, *Esa huella olvidada*, 131–33.

50. Argeliérs León, "La danza folklórica cubana dentro de un proceso de estudio de la misma, informe presentado a Isabel Monal y a Mirta Aguirre," folder CFN Informes 1961, cajuela 300, CNC.

51. For more on León's opinion of folklore in cabaret, see Schwall, "Spectacular Embrace," 288–89.

52. Untitled meeting transcript, 1964, 8, folder CFN Informes 1964, cajuela 300, CNC; Sánchez León, *Esa huella olvidada*, 100.

53. Martínez Furé, *Diálogos imaginarios*, 250–54; for more on Fresneda, Alonso, Torregrosa, and Pérez, see chapter 2.

54. Evangelina Chió, "Nieves o el mito de la danza," *Revolución y Cultura* (September 1979), 47; Marta Blanco, Rogelio Martínez Furé, and Rodolfo Reyes, "Informe del Conjunto Nacional a la Comisión Nacional de Teatro," September 28, 1962, folder CFN Informes 1962, cajuela 300, CNC; Martínez Furé, *Diálogos imaginarios*, 251.

55. Although the document is unsigned, the author mentions working on costumes, which suggests that the founding costume designer María Elena Molinet wrote it. The document has no date, but details the CFN's 1964 international tour, meaning that it was probably written soon after the company returned. [María Elena Molinet], "Antecedentes," folder CFN Informes 1961, cajuela 300, CNC.

56. Tamara Satanowsky to Dirección del Teatro Nacional de Cuba, August 1, 1962, folder CFN Informes 1962, cajuela 300, CNC.

57. Mario Jáuregui Francis, "Autobiografía," May 19, 1975, folder CFN Personal, cajuela 302, CNC.

58. Nati González, "Conjunto Folklórico Nacional, diseño de la danza negra," *Bohemia*, March 17, 1967, 82; Pajares Santiesteban, *La danza contemporánea cubana*, 63.

59. Graciela Chao Carbonero, interview with author, March 25, 2014, Havana, Cuba; Graciela Chao and Caridad Chao to Presidencia del Consejo Nacional de Cultura, December 15, 1964, folder Presidencia—Conjunto Folklorico Nacional, 1960/76, cajuela 300, CNC; Performance Program, Conjunto Folklórico Nacional, July 1965, folder 1965 Ballet-Danza, CDAT.

60. Marilyn Bobes, "Silvina en la danza," *Revolución y Cultura* (March 1986), 2.

61. García Fabras, "Silvina Fabars."

62. Marilyn Bobes, "Silvina en la danza," *Revolución y Cultura* (March 1986), 3–5.

63. "Figuras del Ballet Nacional de Cuba: Amparo Brito y Andrés Williams," *Cuba en el Ballet* 11, no. 1 (January–March 1980), 28–33; Caridad Martínez, personal communication with the author, January 8, 2020.

64. Farrés listed as a modern dancer in Sánchez Léon, *Esa huella olvidada*, 366. She appeared in a student ballet performance in Performance Program, Concierto de Ballet, Escuela de Ballet de la Habana, 1965, folder 1965 Ballet-Danza, CDAT; and in a professional ballet performance in Performance Program, Ballet Nacional de Cuba, June 16–19, 1966, folder 1966 Ballet-Danza, CDAT.

65. Caridad Martínez, interview with author, June 12, 2014, New York, NY.

66. Alicia emphasized unprecedented post-1959 admission of black students in Randall, *Cuban Women Now*, 151–53; Kirk and Padura, *Culture and the Cuban Revolution*, 45–46.

67. Arnold Haskell in Alberto Estron, "Festival para un millón," *Revista Cuba* (July 1967), 60.

68. Tania Díaz Castro, "Alicia del 70," *Bohemia*, June 5, 1970, 5.

69. VC-LL, "Eduardo Rivera [*sic*], un bailarín que llegó," *Revolución*, March 23, 1965, 4.

70. Resonant with the work of scholars discussed in Bustamante, "Cultural Politics and Political Cultures"; see also Schwall, "Footsteps of Nieves Fresneda."

71. Núñez Jiménez, *La Gran Caverna de Santo Tomás*, 84–87.

72. Documents collected and organized in a bound volume labeled "Ballet Alicia Alonso: Sur América y Cuba," FANJ; "Institución Ballet Alicia Alonso," expediente 3503, legajo 175, RA, ANC.

73. Al Burt, "Cuba Ballet Cast in Soviet Mold," *Washington Post*, March 28, 1965, G9; Singer, *Fernando Alonso*, 85.

74. "Objeciones al proyecto de ley de adscripción del Ballet de Cuba a la Dirección General de Cultura, 1960," folder Ballet Nacional Leyes 1960, cajuela 239, CNC.

75. Reprinted in M. Cabrera, *El ballet en Cuba*, 339–42.

76. Raúl Díaz Domínguez, "Aclaración de 'Ballet Nacional,'" *Carteles*, March 22, 1959, 35; for more on Alberto's Ballet Nacional, see chapter 1.

77. Fernando Alonso to Dra. Vicentina Antuña, Edith García Buchaca, and Mirta Aguirre, November 24, 1961, folder Ballet Nacional de Cuba, Historiografía, cajuela 239, CNC.

78. Unión de Escritores y Artistas de Cuba, Sección de Danza y Ballet to Dra. Edith García Buchaca, November 27, 1962, folder Ballet Nacional de Cuba, UNEAC, 1962, cajuela 238, CNC.

79. Guido González del Valle to Helio Armenteros, December 5, 1963, folder D. Contemporánea Informes, 1962–1965, cajuela 225, CNC; "Informe de problemas surgidos con relación al grupo de danza: Danza Contemporánea," February 7, 1964, folder D. Contemporánea Informes, 1962–1965, cajuela 225, CNC.

80. "Proyecto para la formación de un grupo de danza para colaborar con la sección de teatro del Consejo Nacional de Cultura," folder D. Contemporánea Informes, 1962–65, cajuela 225, CNC; "Conjunto de Danza Contemporánea," 1965, folder Conjunto de Danza Contemporánea, cajuela 225, CNC.

81. Guido González del Valle to Dirección de Danza, April 14, 1964, folder D. Contemporánea Informes, 1962–1965, cajuela 225, CNC; "Informe general de las actividades del grupo de Danza Contemporánea," August 1, 1964, folder D. Contemporánea Informes, 1962–1965, cajuela 225, CNC.

82. Undated press release in [*Noticias de*] *Hoy*, folder Conjunto Experimental de Danza de la Habana, cajuela 225, CNC; "Memorandum: Nota de Prensa," folder C. Experimental de Danza, 1964, cajuela 226, CNC; Performance Program, Conjunto Experimental de Danza de la Habana, January 25–26, 1964, cajuela 226, CNC.

83. For example, M. Cabrera, *El ballet en Cuba*; Pajares Santiesteban, *La danza contemporánea cubana*; Daniel, *Rumba*.

84. Guido González del Valle to Amanecer Dotta, November 16, 1964, folder D. Contemporánea Informes, 1962–1965, cajuela 225, CNC.

85. Guido González de Valle to Amanecer Dotta, December 14, 1964, folder D. Contemporánea Informes, 1962–1965, cajuela 225, CNC.

86. "Conjunto Experimental de Danza de la Habana—Informe a la Plenaria Nacional del Consejo Nacional de Cultura," folder C. Experimental de Danza, Informes, 1963, cajuela 230, CNC; Alberto Alonso to Carlos Lechuga, folder C. Experimental de Danza, Informes, 1965–67, cajuela 230, CNC.

87. Guido González del Valle to Eusebio Azcue, November 16, 1964, folder D. Contemporánea Informes, 1962–65, cajuela 225, CNC.

88. "Conjunto de Danza Contemporánea," 1965, folder Conjunto de Danza Contemporánea, cajuela 225, CNC.

89. Orlando Lima to Héctor Quintero, January 14, 1965, folder C. Experimental de Danza, Informes, 1965–67, cajuela 230, CNC; Roberto Álvarez to Antonio Benítez, January 23, 1967, folder C. Experimental de Danza, Informes, 1965–67, cajuela 230, CNC; for more, see Schwall, "Sweeping Gestures," 41–43.

90. Sánchez León, *Esa huella olvidada*, 232.

91. Sánchez León, *Esa huella olvidada*, 365–66, 369–70.

92. Lorna Burdsall to Mother, Dad, Ruth, Ned, etc., February 24, 1959, folder 1, box 1, BFP.

93. Reprinted in Burdsall, *More than Just a Footnote*, 121.

94. Lorna Burdsall to Ned & Family, March 21, 1959, folder 1, box 1, BFP; Burdsall, *More than Just a Footnote*, 116–74.

95. Sánchez León, *Esa huella olvidada*, 30–31.

96. See, for instance, Lorna to Mother, September 26, 1964, folder 2, box 1, BFP.

97. Untitled meeting transcript, 1964, 8, folder CFN Informes 1964, cajuela 300, CNC.

98. [María Elena Molinet], "Antecedentes," folder CFN Informes 1961, cajuela 300, CNC.

99. Rodolfo Reyes to José Llanusa Gobel, February 1967, folder Presidencia—Conjunto Folklórico Nacional, 1960/76, cajuela 300, CNC.

100. María Teresa Linares, "Informe a la Dirección de Teatro y Danza," October 13, 1965, folder CFN Informes 1965, cajuela 300, CNC.

101. Benson, *Antiracism in Cuba*, 33–37.

102. Argeliers León, "La danza folklórica cubana dentro de un proceso de estudio de la misma, informe presentado a Isabel Monal y a Mirta Aguirre," folder CFN Informes 1961, cajuela 300, CNC.

103. Tamara Satanowsky to Dirección del Teatro Nacional de Cuba, August 1, 1962, folder CFN Informes 1962, cajuela 300, CNC.

104. Jesús Pérez, Lázaro Ross, José Oridol, Nancy Rodríguez, Walfredo Isacc, and Jorge Prieto, "Informe," December 14, 1965, folder CFN Informes 1965, cajuela 300, CNC.

105. Tamara Satanowsky to Dirección del Teatro Nacional de Cuba, August 1, 1962, folder CFN Informes 1962, cajuela 300, CNC.

106. "Ballet de Cuba, proyecto de presupuesto, año 1962," folder BNC Economía 60, cajuela 238, CNC.

107. "Bailarines que trabajan en el ballet 'Tierra,'" folder CDN, October–November 1963, cajuela 233, CNC.

108. María E. Molinet and Salvador Fernández to Joaquín Torres, April 16, 1964, folder Presidencia—Conjunto Folklorico Nacional, 1960/76, cajuela 300, CNC.

109. Untitled meeting transcript, 1964, 27, folder CFN Informes 1964, cajuela 300, CNC; meetings happened March 7–13, 1964, as clarified by Jesús Pérez, Lázaro Ross, José Oridol, Nancy Rodríguez, Walfredo Isacc, and Jorge Prieto, "Informe," December 14, 1965, folder CFN Informes 1965, cajuela 300, CNC.

110. Jesús Pérez, Lázaro Ross, José Oridol, Nancy Rodríguez, Walfredo Isacc, and Jorge Prieto, "Informe," December 14, 1965, folder CFN Informes 1965, cajuela 300, CNC.

111. "Relación de directores que ha tenido el Conjunto Folklórico Nacional desde su fundación," folder CFN Historiografía, cajuela 303, CNC; Elena Noriega to Carlos Lechuga, July 1, 1965, folder Presidencia—Conjunto Folklórico Nacional, 1960/76, cajuela 300, CNC.

112. María Teresa Linares, "Informe a la Dirección de Teatro y Danza," October 13, 1965, folder CFN Informes 1965, cajuela 300, CNC.

113. "Cuestionario para el costo previo de obra 'Orfeo' (Ramiro Guerra)," folder Orfeo Antillano, Técnica de un bailarín, La Vida de la Abeja, Teatro García Lorca Junio 1964, cajuela 225, CNC; "Proyecto de presupuesto del Ballet Nacional de Cuba para 1965," folder BNC Economía '60, cajuela 238, CNC.

114. María Teresa Linares, "Informe a la Dirección de Teatro y Danza," October 13, 1965, folder CFN Informes 1965, cajuela 300, CNC.

115. Rodolfo Reyes to José Llanusa Gobel, February 1967, folder Presidencia—Conjunto Folklórico Nacional, 1960/76, cajuela 300, CNC.

116. Rodolfo Reyes to José Llanusa Gobel, February 1967, folder Presidencia—Conjunto Folklórico Nacional, 1960/76, cajuela 300, CNC; a version of these events in Hagedorn, *Divine Utterances*, 159–65.

117. Rodolfo Reyes, interview with author, July 12, 2016, Mexico City, Mexico; Performance Program, Conjunto Folklórico Nacional, July 1965, folder 1965 Ballet-Danza, CDAT.

118. Routon, "Unimaginable Homelands?," 384.

119. Marilyn Bobes, "Silvina en la danza," *Revolución y Cultura* (March 1986), 6, 8.

120. Fernando Oviedo Alfonso to Carlos Lechuga, May 6, 1966, folder CFN Informes 1966, cajuela 300, CNC.

121. Andrés Cortina Rueda, "Autobiografía," folder CFN Personal, cajuela 302, CNC.

122. María Elena Molinet quoted in Sánchez León, *Esa huella olvidada*, 78–79.

123. Sánchez León, *Esa huella olvidada*, 241.

124. Pérez León, *Por los orígenes de la danza moderna en Cuba*, 22.

125. Performance Program, Ballet de Cuba, América del Sur 1959, folder 1959 Ballet-Danza, CDAT; Performance Program, Primer Festival Internacional de Ballet, March 15–April 2, 1960, cajuela 239, CNC.

126. Performance Program, Ballet de Cuba, August 7, 1960, folder 1960 Ballet-Danza, CDAT; Vega, *Alicia en los países maravillosos*.

127. Performance Program, Ballet de Cuba, March 20, 1960, folder 1960 Ballet-Danza, CDAT; quote in Performance Program, Ballet de Cuba, August 7, 1960, folder 1960 Ballet-Danza, CDAT.

128. Guillermo Cabrera Infante, "Ballet de Cuba," *Lunes de Revolución*, April 4, 1960, 4.

129. "Dos protestas de *Lunes*," *Lunes de Revolución*, August 29, 1960, 2.

130. Sánchez León, *Esa huella olvidada*, 233.

131. Antonieta Henríquez, "Danza Moderna en el Teatro," *Noticias de Hoy*, February 24, 1960, 6.

132. Benson, *Antiracism in Cuba*, 221–22.

133. Borges and Maytín, *Arnaldo Patterson*.

134. Ramiro Guerra, "Hacia un movimiento de danza nacional," *Lunes de Revolución*, July 13, 1959, 11.

135. Pérez León, *Por los orígenes de la danza moderna en Cuba*, 16; Collazo and Rolando, interview, June 6, 2019; Borges and Maytín, *Arnaldo Patterson*.

136. Jesús Pérez, Lázaro Ross, José Oridol, Nancy Rodríguez, Walfredo Isacc, and Jorge Prieto, "Informe," December 14, 1965, folder CFN Informes 1965, cajuela 300, CNC.

137. Untitled meeting transcript, 1964, 21, folder CFN Informes 1964, cajuela 300, CNC.

138. José A. Salas to Dirección de Teatro y Danza, March 23, 1966, folder CFN Informes 1966, cajuela 300, CNC.

139. Marilyn Bobes, "Silvina en la danza," *Revolución y Cultura* (March 1986), 9.

140. Alicia the icon also discussed in Schwall, "Between *Espíritu* and *Conciencia*," 157–59; Tomé, "Swans in Sugarcane Fields," 16–20; Brill, "La Escuela Cubana," 176–218.

141. Angela Soto, "Mañana es día de estreno," *Granma*, February 8, 1967, 5.

142. Víctor Gilí, interview with author, June 13, 2015, San Juan, Puerto Rico; Caridad Martínez, interview with author, December 7, 2018, New York, NY.

143. Alonso, *Diálogos con la danza*, 43.

144. Clipping: Waldo Medina, "Honrando a Alicia Alonso," *El Mundo*, March 3, 1967, SA, BNJM.

145. Castro, "Words to the Intellectuals," 229.

146. A. O. "Alicia: Cuba y el ballet," *Mujeres* 7, no. 2 (February 1967), 79.

147. See the image in Jorge Antonio González, "Alicia," *Romances* (May 1967), 3.

148. Alejo Beltrán, "Cuando Giselle se vistió de miliciana," *INRA* 2, no. 8 (August 1961), 97.

149. Guevara, "Socialism and Man in Cuba," 225.

150. For more on this idea, see Schwall, "Between *Espíritu* and *Conciencia*," 160–63.

151. Red Bloy, "El teatro gesticula, baila, canta, ríe, llora," *INRA* 1, no. 3 (March 1960), 14.

152. Lola de la Torriente, "La danza: Disciplina de la mente y alegría del espíritu," *Bohemia*, October 16, 1960, 75.

153. Antón Arrufat, "Al hablar con Ramiro," *Lunes de Revolución*, April 4, 1960, 15.

154. J. M. Valdés Rodríguez, "Tres ballets acertados en la Sala Covarrubias," *El Mundo*, September 18, 1960, B-6.

155. First quote: J. M. Valdés Rodríguez, "Bella noche de arte cubano en la Sala Covarrubias," *El Mundo*, February 21, 1960, B-6; second quote: Guido González del Valle, "¿Por qué danza moderna?," *Revolución*, August 24, 1964, 4.

156. For instance, "Danza vs. Ballet," *Lunes de Revolución*, February 29, 1960, 85; Calvert Casey, "¿Por qué danza moderna?," *Bohemia*, September 20, 1963, 37–38.

157. Muriel Manings, "June 15, 1970," Journal Cuba 1970, folder 18, box 4, Muriel Manings and William Korff Collection, Music Division, Library of Congress.

158. Martínez Furé, *Conjunto Folklórico Nacional*.

159. Palo Monte details from Miller, *Voice of the Leopard*, 218; featured dances detailed in Martínez Furé, *Conjunto Folklórico Nacional*; footage in París, *Nosotros, la música*.

160. Benson, *Antiracism in Cuba*, 114–20; L. Guerra, *Visions of Power in Cuba*, 265–78; de la Fuente, *Nation for All*, 286–96.

161. Martínez Furé, *Conjunto Folklórico Nacional*.

162. José A. Salas to Dirección de Teatro y Danza, March 23, 1966, folder CFN Informes 1966, cajuela 300, CNC.

163. De la Fuente, *Nation for All*, 291–92, 295.

164. Benson, *Antiracism in Cuba*, 112–20; de la Fuente, *Nation for All*, 291–95; L. Guerra, *Visions of Power in Cuba*, 262–63; Moore, *Castro, the Blacks, and Africa*, 308–10.

165. R. Guerra, *De la narratividad al abrastraccionismo en la danza*, 260–70; Performance Program, Conjunto Nacional de Danza Moderna: Suite Yoruba, Huapango, Medea y los Negreros, April 1968, folder 1968 Ballet-Danza, CDAT.

166. Nati González Freire, "Medea y los negreros," *Bohemia*, January 19, 1968, 107.

167. Performance program, Conjunto Nacional de Danza Moderna: Suite Yoruba, Huapango, Medea y los Negreros, April 1968, folder 1968 Ballet-Danza, CDAT.

168. "Cinco años en la danza moderna," *Revista Cuba* (October 1966).

169. Collazo and Rolando, interview, June 6, 2019.

170. Quoted in Pajares Santiesteban, *Ramiro Guerra*, 202–3.

171. Performance Program, Conjunto Nacional de Danza Moderna: Suite Yoruba, Huapango, Medea y los Negreros, April 1968, folder 1968 Ballet-Danza, CDAT.

Chapter Four

1. Kathryn Kenyon, "Cuban Ballet's 'Giselle' Is Success Despite Defections," *Los Angeles Times*, November 17, 1966, D22.

2. L. Guerra, *Visions of Power in Cuba*, 227–31.

3. Albright, *Choreographing Difference*, 57.

4. Castro quoted in Lockwood, *Castro's Cuba, Cuba's Fidel*, 124; Guevara, "Socialism and Man in Cuba," 224.

5. Inspired by "intersectionality" from Crenshaw, "Mapping the Margins."

6. Leiner, *Sexual Politics in Cuba*; Lumsden, *Machos, Maricones, and Gays*; L. Guerra, "Gender Policing"; Sierra Madero, "'El trabajo os hará hombres"; Canaday, *Straight State*; Ben and Insausti, "Dictatorial Rule and Sexual Politics"; Green, "'Who Is the Macho'"; Cowan, *Securing Sex*; Mallon, "*Barbudos*, Warriors, and *Rotos*."

7. For these issues, see Hamilton, *Sexual Revolutions in Cuba*, 172–90, 229–30; L. Guerra, "Gender Policing," 288; Canaday, "LGBT History," 12.

8. Allen, *Venceremos?*, 14.

9. Hartman, *Wayward Lives, Beautiful Experiments*, 217–28, and the rest of the book.

10. Eduardo Conde to Cap. Carlos Chaín, September 3, 1970, folder Presidencia—Conjunto Folklórico Nacional, 1960/76, cajuela 300, CNC; Omar Vázquez, "Tras la gira europea del Conjunto Folklórico Nacional," *Granma*, February 21, 1971, 10.

11. Quoted in Omar Vázquez, "Tras la gira europea del Conjunto Folklórico Nacional," *Granma*, February 21, 1971, 10.

12. Castilla, *Primer Congreso Nacional de Educación y Cultura*, 66; Mesa-Lago, *Cuba in the 1970s*, 105.

13. Clipping: Irina Bielousova, "El Conjunto Folklórico de Cuba en Moscu," *Novedades de Moscu*, December 1, 1970, 1, SA, BNJM.

14. Gabriel Molina, "Sedujo a Argelia el Conjunto Folklórico Cubano," *Bohemia*, July 10, 1964, 76–77.

15. Jesús Pérez, Lázaro Ross, José Oriol, Nancy Rodríguez, Walfredo Isacc, Jorge Prieto, "Informe," December 14, 1965, folder CFN Informes 1965, cajuela 300, CNC.

16. Untitled meeting transcript, 1964, 5, 8, 20, folder CFN Informes 1964, cajuela 300, CNC.

17. Untitled meeting transcript, 1964, 9–10 (quotes on 10), folder CFN Informes 1964, cajuela 300, CNC.

18. Untitled meeting transcript, 1964, 12 (Molinet quote), 20 (Blanco quote), folder CFN Informes 1964, cajuela 300, CNC.

19. Quote from Mariblanca Sabas Aloma, "Total éxito en Europa del Conjunto Folklórico Cubano," *El Mundo*, July 14, 1964; Gabriel Molina, "Sedujo a Argelia el Conjunto Folklórico Cubano," *Bohemia*, July 10, 1964, 76.

20. Mario Martínez to Carlos Lechuga, "Informe no. 4 y conclusiones sobre la jira del Conjunto Folklórico de Cuba," August 29, 1964, folder CFN Relaciones Internacionales Giras 1964, cajuela 302, CNC.

21. Mario Martínez to Carlos Lechuga, "Informe no. 4 y conclusiones sobre la jira del Conjunto Folklórico de Cuba," August 29, 1964, folder CFN Relaciones Internacionales Giras 1964, cajuela 302, CNC.

22. Ferrer, *Insurgent Cuba*, 118; de la Fuente, *Nation for All*, 28.

23. Mario Martínez to Carlos Lechuga, "Informe no. 4 y conclusiones sobre la jira del Conjunto Folklórico de Cuba," August 29, 1964, folder CFN Relaciones Internacionales Giras 1964, cajuela 302, CNC; Rodolfo Reyes to José Llanusa Gobel, February 1967, folder Presidencia—Conjunto Folklórico Nacional 1960/76, cajuela 300, CNC.

24. Mario Martínez to Carlos Lechuga, "Informe no. 4 y conclusiones sobre la jira del Conjunto Folklórico de Cuba," August 29, 1964, folder CFN Relaciones Internacionales Giras 1964, cajuela 302, CNC.

25. Rogelio Martínez Furé to Carlos Lechuga, September 14, 1964, folder CFN Relaciones Internacionales Giras 1964, cajuela 302, CNC.

26. Performance Program, Conjunto Folklórico Nacional: Ciclos Abakuá, Popular y Yoruba-Iyessa, July 1965, folder 1965 Ballet-Danza, CDAT.

27. Ángel Castañeda, "Historia breve del Conjunto Folklórico Nacional y la labor realizada desde su creación," December 1967, folder CFN Historiografía, cajuela 303, CNC; "Relación de directores que ha tenido el Conjunto Folklórico Nacional desde su fundación," December 1967 [?], folder CFN Historiografía, cajuela 303, CNC; Performance Program, Conjunto Folklórico Nacional, September 20, 1968, folder CFN Ciclo Congo, Ciclo Yoruba, Ciclo Yoruba-Iyessa, September 1968, cajuela 307, CNC.

28. The 1970 programs (January, July, and an unspecified month) are in cajuela 305, CNC; Performance Program, Conjunto Folklórico Nacional, El Alafín de Oyó, 1971, SA, BNJM; Performance Program, El Alafín de Oyó, March 1972, SA, BNJM.

29. L. Guerra, *Visions of Power in Cuba*, 265–78.

30. Rogelio Martínez Furé, "Curriculum Vitae de Rogelio Martínez Furé," accessed March 7, 2017, http://www.afrocubaweb.com/fure/Furecv.pdf.

31. For instance, Performance Program, Conjunto Folklórico Nacional de Cuba, Conjunto Campesino, September 1974, SA, BNJM; Performance Program, Conjunto Folklórico Nacional de Cuba, 1975, SA, BNJM.

32. Armando Aguiar Paula to Luis Pavón Tamayo, October 2, 1976, folder Presidencia—Conjunto Folklórico Nacional, 1960/76, cajuela 300, CNC.

33. Rogelio Martínez Furé, "Curriculum Vitae de Rogelio Martínez Furé," accessed March 7, 2017, http://www.afrocubaweb.com/fure/Furecv.pdf.

34. L. Guerra, *Visions of Power in Cuba*, 227–31.

35. Sutherland, *Cuba Now*, 63; Castilla, *Primer Congreso Nacional de Educación y Cultura*, 66; Mesa-Lago, *Cuba in the 1970s*, 103, 105.

36. Quoted in Nancy Morejón, "María Antonia: La muerte de un mito," *Revista Cuba* (January 1968), 48.

37. Conjunto Folklórico Nacional to Departamento de Estadística, "Actividades realizadas por el Conjunto Folklórico Nacional desde noviembre de 1967 a 9 de enero de 1968," February 6, 1968, folder CFN Informes 1968, cajuela 300, CNC; "Una criatura de solo doce años de edad. Conjunto Folklórico Nacional de Cuba," folder CFN Historiografía, cajuela 303, CNC; Nancy Morejón, "María Antonia: La muerte de un mito," *Revista Cuba* (January 1968), 46.

38. Martiatu, "Reflexiones en los cuarenta años de *María Antonia*," 5; Lisandro Otero, "Del otro lado del Atlántico: Una actitud," *El Caimán Barbudo* (June 1968), 7; L. Guerra, *Visions of Power in Cuba*, 273.

39. Georgina Hung Vargas, "De administrador del Conjunto Folklórico Nacional a Departamento de Estadística: Relación de funciones que ha tenido el Conjunto Folklórico Nacional en el trimestre de julio a septiembre 69," November 11, 1969, folder Conjunto Folklórico Nacional Mensuales de Actividades 1969, cajuela 300, CNC; "Grupo 'Conjunto Folklórico Nacional' resumen actividades 1969," March 11, 1970, folder CFN Informes 1969, cajuela 303, CNC.

40. Giral, *María Antonia*.

41. Quoted in Nancy Morejón, "María Antonia: La muerte de un mito," *Revista Cuba* (January 1968), 48.

42. Eduardo Muzio to José Llanusa Gobel, March 29, 1968, folder Ballet Nacional de Cuba Giras Internacionales 1960/1975, cajuela 254, CNC.

43. "Situación operativa de la gira del Ballet Nacional a México," February 28, 1968, folder BNC Relaciones Internacionales 1968, cajuela 261, CNC.

44. Eduardo Muzio to José Llanusa Gobel, March 29, 1968, folder Ballet Nacional de Cuba Giras Internacionales 1960/1975, cajuela 254, CNC.

45. Luis Pavón Tamayo to Belarmino Castilla, July 23, 1971, folder BNC Relaciones Internacionales 1971, cajuela 259, CNC.

46. Marcos, "Asunto: Resumen analítico de las informaciones recibidas por la DGI sobre la jira del Ballet Nacional de Cuba por Checoslovaquia, RDA y Hungría, MUY SECRETO," November 21, 1972, folder BNC Relaciones Internacionales 1972, cajuela 261, CNC.

47. More on gender (especially femininity) and Cuban ballet in Schwall, "Prescribing Ballet."

48. Eduardo Muzio to José Llanusa Gobel, March 29, 1968, folder Ballet Nacional de Cuba Giras Internacionales 1960/1975, cajuela 254, CNC.

49. Marilu Moré to Armando Quesada, August 1, 1972, folder BNC Relaciones Internacionales 1972, cajuela 261, CNC.

50. "Reglamento para delegaciones artísticas por el cual se rigió el Ballet Nacional de Cuba en su gira por Europa Occidental y Yugoslavia," folder R. Internacionales Giras 1974—Restringido, cajuela 260, CNC.

51. M. Cabrera, *Órbita*, 79–81; Performance Program, Conjunto Folklórico Nacional de Cuba, 1982, Archivo de Conjunto Folklórico Nacional de Cuba.

52. Omar Vázquez, "Tras la gira europea del Conjunto Folklórico Nacional," *Granma*, February 21, 1971, 10.

53. R. Guerra, *Coordenadas danzarias*, 123, 125.

54. Guillermoprieto, *Dancing with Cuba*, 271.

55. Orlando Quiroga, "Yoruba," *Bohemia*, December 4, 1960, 83.

56. Clippings: Navarro, "Bejart en Cuba," *Revolución*, June 12, 1964; Bernardo Callejas, "Orfeo se va a Bruselas," *Noticias de Hoy*, September 13, 1964, both in folder 1964 Prensa, DCC; Burdsall, *More than Just a Footnote*, 154; "New Dance Makes Brussels Debut," *New York Times*, October 28, 1964, 50.

57. "Ramiro Guerra," [September 1964], folder Conjunto de Danza Nacional 1962/1975, cajuela 229, CNC.

58. "Eduardo Rivero," [September 1964], folder Conjunto de Danza Nacional 1962/1975, cajuela 229, CNC.

59. "López," [September 1964], folder Conjunto de Danza Nacional 1962/1975, cajuela 229, CNC. For those denounced like López, I included only part of the individuals' names to protect their privacy while helping future researchers locate the report. Unlike the late Guerra and Rivero, who I know have passed, I do not write the full names of those possibly living (i.e., I do not know them personally or did not find them in other records), who were denounced for so-called sexual improprieties.

60. "Menéndez," [September 1964], folder Conjunto de Danza Nacional 1962/1975, cajuela 229, CNC.

61. "Blanco," [September 1964], folder Conjunto de Danza Nacional 1962/1975, cajuela 229, CNC.

62. "Hirme," September 11, 1964, folder Conjunto de Danza Nacional 1962/1975, cajuela 229, CNC.

63. "Francis," September 11, 1964, folder Conjunto de Danza Nacional 1962/1975, cajuela 229, CNC; L. Guerra, *Visions of Power in Cuba*, 198.

64. Burdsall, *More than Just a Footnote*, 155.

65. Lorna Burdsall to E. S. Burdsall, September 26, 1964, folder 2, box 1, BFP.

66. Lorna Burdsall to E. S. Burdsall, October 11, 1964, folder 2, box 1, BFP.

67. Burdsall, *More than Just a Footnote*, 155.

68. "Giras Internacionales" from DCCuba Histórico [Pendrive], DCC.

69. First quote in Jesús [Menéndez] to [Eduardo] Conde, September 30, 1969, folder Danza Nacional Relaciones Internacionales, cajuela 224, CNC; second quote in Jesús Menéndez, December 3, 1969, folder Danza Nacional Relaciones Internacionales, cajuela 224, CNC.

70. "Otra vez Adán y Eva pero con alegre irreverencia," *Cuba Internacional* (April 1970), 52.

71. Based on images published in R. Guerra, *Coordenadas danzarias*, 260–64 (unnumbered).

72. Quotes in "Otra vez Adán y Eva pero con alegre irreverencia," *Cuba Internacional* (April 1970), 56; image in R. Guerra, *Coordenadas danzarias*, 262 (not paginated).

73. R. Guerra, *Eros baila*, 171.

74. Croft, "Introduction," 10.

75. Similar labeling in Wilcox, "Women Dancing Otherwise"; Kosstrin, "Queer Space in Anna Sokolow's *Rooms*."

76. Kosstrin, "Queer Space in Anna Sokolow's *Rooms*," 147; Kennison, "Clothes Make the (Wo)man," 147–56; Hansen, "Pleasure, Ambivalence, Identification," 19.

77. This resonates with dance "for queer activism and community building" in twenty-first-century China, as discussed in Wilcox, "Women Dancing Otherwise," 79.

78. R. Guerra, *Coordenadas danzarias*, 125–26.

79. R. Guerra, *Eros baila*, 168–69; Mousouris, "Dance World of Ramiro Guerra," 67–69.

80. Croft, "Introduction," 16–17.

81. R. Guerra, *Coordenadas danzarias*, 149, 150.

82. R. Guerra, *Coordenadas danzarias*, 157.

83. Image of the human tower published in Mousouris, "Dance World of Ramiro Guerra," 68.

84. Burdsall, *More than Just a Footnote*, 173.

85. Lorna Burdsall, "12 años de danza moderna en Cuba," folder Conjunto de Danza Nacional 1962/1975, cajuela 229, CNC.

86. He alluded to previous U.S. treatments of *Decálogo* that "had caused him trouble." Ramiro Guerra, interview with author, March 12, 2014, Havana, Cuba.

87. Lorna Burdsall to E. S. Burdsall, November 19, 1972, folder 3, box 1, BFP.

88. Mousouris, "Dance World of Ramiro Guerra," 70.

89. Lorna Burdsall to E. S. Burdsall, November 19, 1972, folder 3, box 1, BFP.

90. Lorna [Burdsall] to [Luis] Pavón, January 6, 1973, folder Conjunto de Danza Nacional 1962/1975, cajuela 229, CNC.

91. Lorna Burdsall, "12 años de danza moderna en Cuba," folder Conjunto de Danza Nacional 1962/1975, cajuela 229, CNC.

92. Wambrug Rodríguez and Solés de Dios, "Historia de los seis primeros años de trabajo de la Escuela Nacional de Danza Moderna y Folklórica," 3.

93. Lorna Burdsall, "12 años de danza moderna en Cuba," folder Conjunto de Danza Nacional 1962/1975, cajuela 229, CNC.

94. Armando Quesada to Félix Sautié, March 20, 1973, folder Conjunto de Danza Nacional 1962/1975, cajuela 229, CNC.

95. Lorna Burdsall to E. S. Burdsall, February 11, 1973, folder 3, box 1, BFP.

96. Burdsall, *More than Just a Footnote*, 170; quote from Lorna Burdsall to E. S. Burdsall, March 13, 1973, folder 3, box 1, BFP.

97. Lorna Burdsall to E. S. Burdsall, October 1973, folder 3, box 1, BFP.

98. Lorna Burdsall to E. S. Burdsall, January 28, 1974, folder 3, box 1, BFP.

99. Lorna Burdsall to E. S. Burdsall, April 7, 1974, folder 3, box 1, BFP.

100. For more, see Schwall, "Cuban Modern Dance after Censorship."

101. R. Guerra, *Coordenadas danzarias*, 155.

102. "Luz María Collazo: Fui uno de los rostros más fotografiados," September 2006, personal archive of Luz María Collazo.

103. Performance Program, Ballet Nacional de Cuba, March 5, 1977, folder 1977 Ballet-Danza, CDAT.

104. Armando Hart, "Resolución Ministerial no. 742 de 1961," folder Municipio de la Habana, Academia Municipal de Ballet, Ballet de Cámara, 1960–1961, ME-DGC.

105. Ana Pardo, "Inicia Cuba una nueva escuela de ballet," *INRA* 2, no. 10 (October 1961), 61; Anna Leontieva and Fernando Alonso, "Proyecto para la Escuela de Ballet del Municipio de la Habana," October 8, 1960, folder Municipio de la Habana, Academia Municipal de Ballet, Ballet de Cámara, 1960–1961, ME-DGC.

106. "Proyecto de organización de la enseñanza común en la Escuela de Ballet," folder Municipio de la Habana, Academia Municipal de Ballet, Ballet de Cámara, 1960–1961, ME-DGC.

107. "Escuela Ballet de la Habana Reglamento," folder Municipio de la Habana, Academia Municipal de Ballet, Ballet de Cámara, 1960–1961, ME-DGC.

108. Ana Pardo, "Inicia Cuba una nueva escuela de ballet," *INRA* 2, no. 10 (October 1961), 64.

109. Anna Leontieva and Fernando Alonso, "Proyecto para la Escuela de Ballet del Municipio de la Habana," October 8, 1960, folder Municipio de la Habana, Academia Municipal de Ballet, Ballet de Cámara, 1960–1961, ME-DGC.

110. "Escuela Ballet de la Habana Reglamento," folder Municipio de la Habana, Academia Municipal de Ballet, Ballet de Cámara, 1960–1961, ME-DGC.

111. Ana Pardo, "Inicia Cuba una nueva escuela de ballet," *INRA* 2, no. 10 (October 1961), 64.

112. Dibb, *Classically Cuban*.

113. Coates, *Convicts and Orphans*, 128–29; Morrison, *Bolshoi Confidential*, 24–31.

114. Eduardo Vázquez Pérez, "Esquivel: Un hijo de la Revolución," *El Caimán Barbudo* (August 1979), 16; Miguel Cabrera, "Joaquín Banegas: Maitre del ballet cubano," *Cuba en el Ballet* 10, no. 3 (September–December 1979), 19.

115. Josefina Elósegui to Rolando López del Amo, August 15, 1961, folder Municipio de la Habana, Academia Municipal de Ballet, Ballet de Cámara, 1960–1961, ME-DGC.

116. Miguel Cabrera, "Joaquín Banegas: Maitre del ballet cubano," *Cuba en el Ballet* 10, no. 3 (September–December 1979), 19.

117. Guillermoprieto, *Dancing with Cuba*, 271.

118. For more on medical theories about sexuality, see Lambe, *Madhouse*, 160–65.

119. L. Guerra, *Visions of Power in Cuba*, 292.

120. Ana Pardo, "Inicia Cuba una nueva escuela de ballet," *INRA* 2, no. 10 (October 1961), 66.

121. Nydia Sarabia, "Escuela modelo de ballet en la Habana," *Mujeres* 4, no. 8 (August 1964), 78–79.

122. Almendros and Jiménez-Leal, *Conducta impropia*, 124.

123. Roca, *Cuban Ballet*, 122.

124. Sara Padrón Medina, May 9, 1969, folder Ballet Nacional de Cuba, Bailarines 1968/69, cajuela 242, CNC.

125. Quoted in Sierra Madero, "'El trabajo os hará hombres,'" 327.

126. Noel Navarra, "Un arte exquisito al alcance de todos," *Bohemia*, July 24, 1964, 46–51.

127. Nydia Sarabia, "Escuela modelo de ballet en la Habana," *Mujeres* 4, no. 8 (August 1964), 78.

128. Burt, *Male Dancer*, 10–30; for a recent example in the United States, see Gia Kourlas, "Hey, Lara Spencer, Ballet Is for Boys," *New York Times*, August 23, 2019, https://www.nytimes.com/2019/08/23/arts/dance/lara-spencer-ballet.html.

129. Marian Horosko, "Alicia Alonso, 'The Flower of Cuba,' Diary of a Trip to Havana," *Dance Magazine* (August 1971), 56.

130. Ilse Bulit, "Ballet para hembras y . . . varones," *Bohemia*, February 11, 1977, 7.

131. Castro, "Words to the Intellectuals," 235; Nahmias and Murray, *Unfinished Spaces*.

132. Caridad Martínez, interview with author, December 5, 2018, New York, NY.

133. Guillermoprieto, *Dancing with Cuba*, 23–29, 238–39.

134. Muriel Manings, "June 30, 1970," Journal Cuba 1970, folder 18, box 4, Muriel Manings and William Korff Collection, Music Division, Library of Congress.

135. Rodríguez, *Problemas del arte en la Revolución*, 76–77.

136. M. Cabrera, *El ballet en Cuba*, 259.

137. Marcial Fernández, "Canto vital," January 5, 2017, http://www.balletcuba.cult.cu/canto-vital/.

138. Plisetski, *Canto vital*.

139. Performance Program, Ballet Nacional de Cuba, December 21 and 23, 1973, SA, BNJM.

140. Based on footage available: "Tarde en la siesta (1/2)," accessed May 27, 2020, https://www.youtube.com/watch?v=wsNPZnci6KE; "Tarde en la siesta (2/2)," accessed May 27, 2020, https://www.youtube.com/watch?v=OQUHKAXH_2g.

141. Terry, *Alicia and Her Ballet Nacional de Cuba*, 62.

142. Inspired by the approach in Kosstrin, "Queer Spaces in Anna Sokolow's *Rooms*."

143. Campbell, "Dancing Marines and Pumping Gasoline."

144. Fernando Alonso to Manuel Fernández, May 15, 1973, folder BNC Informes 70, cajuela 243, CNC.

145. Garafola, *Diaghilev's Ballets Russes*, 373–75; Manning, "Looking from a Different Place"; Stoneley, *Queer History of Ballet*, 88, 94–124.

146. Terry, *Alicia and Her Ballet Nacional*, 62.

147. Fernando Alonso to Manuel Fernández, May 15, 1973, folder BNC Informes 70, cajuela 243, CNC.

Chapter Five

1. Nati González Freire, "La Vocacional de Vento: Modelo de la escuela del futuro," *Bohemia*, June 25, 1971, 16, 14 (quotes).

2. Leiner, "Two Decades of Educational Change in Cuba," 209; L. Guerra, *Visions of Power in Cuba*, 323–30.

3. Castilla, *Primer Congreso Nacional de Educación y Cultura*, 85.

4. Castilla, *Primer Congreso Nacional de Educación y Cultura*, 72–73.

5. Building on, but with a different focus than works like Leiner, "Two Decades of Educational Change in Cuba"; Blum, *Cuban Youth and Revolutionary Values*; L. Guerra, "'Feeling Like Fidel'"; Herman, "Army of Educators"; Benson, *Antiracism in Cuba*, 198–230; Schultz, "Liberal Moment of the Revolution." Resonant with scholarship on cultural intermediaries in postrevolutionary Mexico discussed in Joseph and Nugent, *Everyday Forms of State Formation*; Gillingham and Smith, *Dictablanda*; Vaughan, *Cultural Politics in Revolution*.

6. Castilla, *Primer Congreso Nacional de Educación y Cultura*, 72–73.

7. Bustamante, "Cultural Politics and Political Cultures," 4–5; Roth-Ey, *Moscow Prime Time*, 3–4; Caute, *Dancer Defects*; Iber, *Neither Peace nor Freedom*.

8. This means that there was state-artist collaboration, along with the state-artist tensions discussed in chapter 4 and in Coyula, "El trinquenio amargo y la ciudad distópica"; Miller, "Revolutionary Modernity"; Fornet, "El quinquenio gris."

9. Contributing to literature on publics, public sphere, and spectatorship like Warner, *Publics and Counterpublics*; Piccato, *Tyranny of Opinion*; Piccato, "Public Sphere in Latin America"; Fernandes, *Cuba Represent!*; Johnson, *Listening in Paris*; Garafola, *Diaghilev's Ballets Russes*, 273–375; Manning, *Modern Dance, Negro Dance*.

10. Gillingham and Smith, *Dictablanda*, 7–8.

11. "Scenes of School Life," box 37U (Use copy DVD), CRC.

12. Sánchez León, *Esa huella olvidada*, 249, 258–60.

13. For Rivero, Reyes, Patterson, and Obermayer's work, respectively, see Performance Programs, Festival de Teatro Obrero Campesino, [different playbill for each date] March 16, 19, 20, 21, 1961, [all located in] legajo 2, CNC; Veitia Guerra, "Danza moderna y aficionados," 9–10.

14. "Intervención del Dr. Fidel Castro Ruz, Primer Ministro del Gobierno, en la mesa redonda sobre los Instructores de Arte," March 21, 1961, 6–7 (first quote), 29–30 (second quote), folder 11, box 15, Carlos Franqui Collection.

15. Fernando Miguel, "La juventud en todos los frentes: Ejercito del arte," *Bohemia*, September 17, 1961, 80; Dirección de Enseñanza Artística del Ministerio de Cultura, *La enseñanza artística en Cuba*, 147–50; Vicente Cubillas, "Escuelas de Instructores de Arte," *Bohemia*, November 19, 1961, 108–10.

16. Veitia Guerra, "Danza moderna y aficionados," 22–24; Guillermoprieto, *Dancing with Cuba*, 56–63.

17. Fernando Miguel, "La juventud en todos los frentes: Ejercito del arte," *Bohemia*, September 17, 1961, 52.

18. Carlos Nicot Pomar, "Danza, música y teatro de los obreros de Oriente," *Bohemia*, December 3, 1961, 16–20.

19. Veitia Guerra, "Danza moderna y aficionados," Anexo 4.

20. "Los aficionados en escena," *Bohemia*, March 13, 1964.

21. Performance Program, Graduación, Instructores de Arte de Teatro y Danza, December 12–13, 1964, folder 1964 Ballet-Danza, CDAT.

22. Raúl Palazuelos and Luis Coronado, "Ellas en la educación integral del niño," *Bohemia*, April 14, 1972, 24–29, esp. 26.

23. Consejo Nacional de Cultura, "Plan de educación artística CHC-MINED, plan de desarrollo danzario," January 1971, expediente CNC-Aficionados-Cultura Masiva Educación Artística-Danza," legajo 2, anaquel 16, estante 3, CNC.

24. "Plan de danza para el plan de reeducación," expediente CNC Aficionados Programas de Enseñanza de la Danza, legajo 4, anaquel 9, CNC.

25. Sistema Nacional de Capacitación Técnica para Instructores de Arte, *Folclor cubano*.

26. Orovio, *Cuban Music from A to Z*, 203.

27. Fraga, *La nueva escuela*; special thanks to Maya Berry for comparing notes on these dances.

28. "Sobre el movimiento de aficionados," *Revolución y Cultura* (June 1972), 6–7.

29. Mesa-Lago, *Cuba in the 1970s*; Mally, *Culture of the Future*; Giersdorf, *Body of the People*, 26–48.

30. Peters, *Cuban Identity and the Angolan Experience*.

31. Lorna Burdsall to E. S. Burdsall, June 10, 1972, folder 3, box 1, BFP.

32. Performance Program, Graduación, Instructores de Arte de Teatro y Danza, December 12–13, 1964, folder 1964 Ballet-Danza, CDAT.

33. *Danzas revolucionarias* in Performance Program, Graduación, Instructores de Arte de Teatro y Danza, December 12–13, 1964, folder 1964 Ballet-Danza, CDAT; second quote on collective creation in Waldeen de Valencia, "Programas de danza para Círculos de Pioneros e Instructores de Internados de Primaria," expediente CNC Aficionados Programas de Enseñanza de la Danza, legajo 4, anaquel 9, CNC.

34. Veitia Guerra, "Danza moderna y aficionados," 39–40.

35. Chao Carbonero, *Coreografía*, 19 (first quote), 52 (second quote).

36. "Noticias," *Cuba en el Ballet* 3, no. 3 (September 1972), 48.

37. Ismael Santiago Albelo Oti, interview with author, March 19, 2014, Havana, Cuba; Fernando Alonso, "Informe sobre actividades desarrolladas por el Ballet Nacional durante el año 1972," January 10, 1973, folder Ballet Nacional de Cuba Informes 1961/73, cajuela 242, CNC.

38. Fernando Alonso to Lázaro Marcos, 1971[?], folder Ballet Nacional de Cuba Programación, cajuela 258, CNC.

39. "Conjunto Nacional de Danza Moderna," *Ahora*, March 4, 1973, 4.

40. P. Pompeyo, "Danza Nacional de Cuba en festival," *Bohemia*, July 28, 1978, 26.

41. Martínez Furé, *Diálogos imaginarios*, 255–56; Mayra A. Martínez, "Investigación y defensa del folklore nacional: 15 años," *Bohemia*, May 6, 1977, 12–13.

42. Ilse Bulit, "Noches de un festival," *Bohemia*, December 5, 1975, 28 (first quote); Ilse Bulit, "Codo con codo," *Bohemia*, June 4, 1976, 27 (second quote).

43. Veitia Guerra, "Danza moderna y aficionados," Anexo 3; Eddy Veitia, interview with author, March 21, 2014, Havana, Cuba; Ángel Rivero, "Conjunto Folklórico Nacional," *Revolución y Cultura* (April 1976), 50.

44. Milagros Ramírez González, "Proyecto artístico," April 1, 1997, folder Compañía Conjunto Folklórico de Oriente, Centro de Documentación e Investigación de Artes Escénicas de Santiago de Cuba; Millet and Brea, *Grupos folklóricos de Santiago de Cuba*, 98–100, 104–18.

45. "X Aniversario del Conjunto Folklórico de Artes Escénicas Patakín," folder C. Folklórico Patakín 1973–74, cajuela 317, CNC.

46. Bebo Ruiz, "Informe sobre el Conjunto Folklórico de Artes Escénicas Patakín," folder C. Folklórico Patakín, 1973–74, cajuela 317, CNC.

47. Nati González Freire, "Patakín en su décimo aniversario," *Bohemia*, April 14, 1978, 27.

48. "Informe de las actividades realizadas por el grupo Patakín en el mes de abril," May 7, 1973, folder C. Folklórico Patakín 1973–74, cajuela 317, CNC.

49. "Conjunto Folklórico de Artes Escénicas 'Patakín,'" folder C. Folklórico Patakín 1973–74, cajuela 317, CNC; "X Aniversario del Conjunto Folklórico de Artes Escénicas Patakín," folder C. Folklórico Patakín 1973–74, cajuela 317, CNC.

50. Fernandes, "Recasting Ideology, Recreating Hegemony," 312, 324n4; film's gender dynamics discussed in Burton, "Seeing, Being, Being Seen."

51. Vega, *Retrato de Teresa*.

52. Sánchez León, *Esa huella olvidada*, 132.

53. París, *Nosotros, la música*.

54. Muriel Manings, "June 24, 1970," Journal Cuba 1970, folder 18, box 4, Muriel Manings and William Korff Collection, Music Division, Library of Congress.

55. "Actividades realizadas por el Conjunto Folklórico Nacional desde enero al 12 de diciembre de 1967," folder CFN Informes 1967, cajuela 300, CNC.

56. Georgina Hung to Departamento de Estadística, February 6, 1968, folder CFN Informes 1968, cajuela 300, CNC.

57. See chapters 3 and 4.

58. Quoted in Ángel Rivero, "El camino de la danza," *Revolución y Cultura* (January 1984), 36.

59. Antón Arrufat, "Al hablar con Ramiro," *Lunes de Revolución*, April 4, 1960, 15.

60. Massip, *Historia de un ballet*; Schwall, "'Cultures in the Body.'"

61. Omar Vázquez, "Conjunto Nacional de Danza Moderna," *Granma*, November 20, 1968, 5.

62. Clipping: José Manuel Otero, "Danza moderna en el anfiteatro de la Habana," [*Noticias de*] *Hoy*, August 4, 1963, folder 1963 Prensa, DCC.

63. Clipping: "Danza moderna a los centros de trabajo," [*Noticias de*] *Hoy*, September 19, 1965, folder 1965 Prensa, DCC.

64. "Danza moderna en las provincias," *Granma*, March 13, 1966, 15.

65. "I Gran Festival de Ballet Internacional en Cuba," *Bohemia*, March 20, 1960, 67.

66. Clipping: Mariblanca Sabas Aloma, "Festival Internacional de Ballet: 'Un tesoro de arte,'" *El Mundo*, April 7, 1966, SA, BNJM.

67. Quote from clipping: Mariblanca Sabas Aloma, "Gran Festival Internacional de Ballet: Cuatro primeras bailarinas cubanas," *El Mundo,* March 13, 1966, SA, BNJM; more on festivals in M. Cabrera, *Festival Internacional de Ballet de la Habana.*

68. Anecdotes from Arnold Haskell, "Algunas impresiones sobre el Festival Internacional de la Habana Exclusivo para 'O ballet' #7" (1967), 20–21, SA, BNJM; term "four jewels" in "4 páginas de GRANMA: Siete semanas de ballet en Cuba," *Granma,* June 17, 1967, 7–10; also discussed in M. Cabrera, *El ballet en Cuba,* 105–13.

69. Alberto Estron, "Festival para un millón," *Revista Cuba* (July 1967), 59.

70. "4 páginas de GRANMA: Siete semanas de ballet en Cuba," *Granma,* June 17, 1967, 7–10.

71. Annette Solier to Periódico "El Mundo," October 1965, folder Ballet Nac. De Cuba—Maya Plisetskaya (6-C), cajuela 239, CNC.

72. Hilario Molina Vega to Director del Consejo Nacional de Cultura, November 3, 1966, folder Ballet Nacional de Cuba, Relaciones Públicas—Nacionales 1960/1976, cajuela 238, CNC; quote from Hilario Molina Vega to Presidente del Consejo Nacional de Cultura, December 8, 1970, folder Ballet Nacional de Cuba, Relaciones Públicas—Nacionales 1960/1976, cajuela 238, CNC.

73. Marian Horosko, "Alicia Alonso, 'the Flower of Cuba': Diary of a Trip to Havana," *Dance Magazine* (August 1971), 45 (Horosko quotes), 56 (Fernando quote); audio available in Fernando Alonso, interview with Marian Horosko, *MGZTO 5-1114, JRDD.

74. Nati González Freire, "El ballet y su tarea de creación popular," *Bohemia,* July 1, 1977, 10–11.

75. "Informe al Consejo Nacional de Cultura de la jira del Ballet de Cuba del 22 de septiembre al 21 de octubre de 1961," folder BNC Jiras Nacionales 1962, cajuela 254, CNC.

76. Fernando Alonso to Edith García Buchaca, September 24, 1962, folder Ballet Nacional de Cuba, Actividades, Funciones 1960/69, cajuela 242, CNC.

77. Martínez Navarro to Marta Vesa, October 2, 1962, folder BNC Jiras Nacionales 1962, cajuela 254, CNC.

78. Nati González Freire, "El ballet y su tarea de creación popular," *Bohemia,* July 1, 1977, 13.

79. Orlando Quiroga, "De viernes a viernes," *Bohemia,* August 14, 1964, 64.

80. Francisco Pita Rodríguez, "Cursos de apreciación del arte para los trabajadores," *Bohemia,* March 4, 1966, 36.

81. "Brigadas Artísticas Ballet Nacional de Cuba," folder Ballet Nacional de Cuba, Extensión Cultural, cajuela 238, CNC.

82. Sara Pascual, Joaquín Banegas, and Sylvia Marichal to Eduardo Muzio, June 15, 1968, folder BNC Actividades 60, cajuela 242, CNC.

83. Angela Grau to Eduardo Muzio, October 11, 1968, folder BNC Informes 60, cajuela 238, CNC.

84. Silvia Marichal to Eduardo Muzio, October 2, 1968, folder Ballet Nacional de Cuba, Extensión Cultural, cajuela 238, CNC.

85. First quote in Silvia Marichal to Eduardo Muzio, July 10, 1968, folder Ballet Nacional de Cuba, Extensión Cultural, cajuela 238, CNC; second quote in Angela Grau to Eduardo Muzio, October 11, 1968, folder BNC Informes 60, cajuela 238, CNC.

86. Sara Pascual and Sylvia Marichal to Eduardo Muzio, July 24, 1968, folder Ballet Nacional de Cuba, Extensión Cultural, cajuela 238, CNC.

87. Fernando Alonso to Eduardo Conde, September 25, 1969, folder Ballet Nacional de Cuba, Usuarios Servicios Culturales, 1969, cajuela 240, CNC.

88. Cabrera describes a similar incident (potentially the same one) though dated (potentially incorrectly) to 1970 in Estrada Betancourt, *De la semilla al fruto*, 129–30.

89. For more on bourgeois codes, see Johnson, *Listening in Paris*, 231–36.

90. Daly, "To Dance Is 'Female,'" 25.

91. Fernando Alonso to Eduardo Conde, September 25, 1969, folder Ballet Nacional de Cuba, Usuarios Servicios Culturales, 1969, cajuela 240, CNC.

92. Clipping: Bertha Recio, "Curso sobre apreciación de la danza," April 21, 1969, folder 1969 Prensa, DCC.

93. Castilla, *Primer Congreso Nacional de Educación y Cultura*, 73.

94. "Actividades realizadas por grupos artísticos, enero–noviembre 1976, Danza Nacional de Cuba," folder CDN Estadística 1976, cajuela 224, CNC; Jorge Luis Padrón, "Informe estadístico correspondiente al mes de noviembre 1976," December 6, 1976, folder CDN Estadísticas 1976, cajuela 224, CNC.

95. Quoted in Ángel Rivero, "El camino de la danza," *Revolución y Cultura* (January 1984), 36.

96. Administración del Conjunto Folklórico Nacional to Luisa Larriu, December 4, 1974, folder CFN Informes 1974, cajuela 303, CNC.

97. "Anexo no. 1," folder CFN Informes 1975, cajuela 303, CNC; Mayra A. Martínez, "Conferencias en el folclórico," *Bohemia*, February 18, 1977, 29.

98. Mayra A. Martínez, "Investigación y defensa del folklore nacional: 15 años," *Bohemia*, May 6, 1977, 13.

99. Gilberto González to Alexis Vázquez, February 14, 1973, folder CFN Informes 1973, cajuela 303, CNC.

100. Mayra A. Martínez, "Investigación y defensa del folklore nacional: 15 años," *Bohemia*, May 6, 1977, 13.

101. Castilla, *Primer Congreso Nacional de Educación y Cultura*, 72–73.

102. Marcos Portal to Mirtha Atienzar, June 6, 1975, folder CFN Actividades 1972–76, cajuela 303, CNC.

103. Martínez Furé, *Diálogos imaginarios*, 255.

104. Based on observations made during fieldwork in the late 1980s and early 1990s in Hagedorn, *Divine Utterances*, 44–56.

105. "Ciclo de charlas de Alicia Alonso sobre ballet a obreros del transporte," *Granma*, September 21, 1971, 3.

106. "Participarán aficionados de transportes en función con Alicia Alonso, en la Ciudad Deportiva," *Granma*, December 20, 1971, 6.

107. Javier Rodríguez, "El Ballet Nacional en los centros de trabajo de transportes," *Bohemia*, January 7, 1972, 77.

108. Luis Pérez Reyes to Manolo Fernández, June 11, 1973, folder BNC Actividades 70, cajuela 238, CNC.

109. Armando Quesada to Jorge Seguera, June 22, 1971, folder BNC Actividades 70, cajuela 238, CNC.

110. Giselda Domenech, "Reporte de asistencia y recaudación de las funciones de ballet presentadas en el año 1971," December 31, 1971, folder BNC Estadísticas '70, cajuela 241, CNC;

Roberto Pérez, "Informe de la gira del Ballet Nacional por las provincias de Las Villas, Camagüey y Oriente," March 22, 1971, folder BNC Giras Nacionales 1971, cajuela 254, CNC.

111. *Muñecos,* accessed April 17, 2020, https://www.youtube.com/watch?v=jCY7V8c8b4A.

112. Caridad Martínez, interview with author, December 7, 2018, New York, NY.

113. See documents: Eduardo Muzio, "Informe sobre el Festival Internacional de Ballet" and Luis Pavón Tamayo to Belarmino Castilla, May 31, 1972, both in folder IV Festival Internacional de Ballet 1971–72, cajuela 240, CNC.

114. M. Cabrera, *Festival Internacional de Ballet de la Habana,* 21, 75.

115. Fernando Alonso, "Sobre el Festival Internacional de Ballet 1974," folder BNC Festival Internacional de Ballet 1974, cajuela 237, CNC.

116. Un revolucionario amante del ballet to Presidente CNC, December 9, 1974, folder BNC Festival Internacional de Ballet 1974, cajuela 237, CNC.

117. "Noticias," *Cuba en el Ballet* 2, no. 1 (January 1971), 48; Ballet Nacional de Cuba, "Programa radial: Ballet," February 28, 1975, folder BNC Cine, Radio y TV, cajuela 239, CNC.

118. "El mundo de la danza," October 23, 1969, SA, BNJM.

119. "Noticias," *Cuba en el Ballet* 5, no. 1 (January 1974), 46.

120. Castilla, *Primer Congreso Nacional de Educación y Cultura,* 142–44.

121. Angela Grau Imperatori, "Editorial," *Cuba en el Ballet* 1, no. 1 (September 1970), 3; Fernando Alonso, "Informe sobre actividades desarrolladas por el Ballet Nacional de Cuba durante el año 1972," January 10, 1973, folder Ballet Nacional de Cuba, Informes 1961/73, cajuela 242, CNC.

122. Angela Grau to Armando Quesada, January 15, 1972, folder BNC Cine, Radio y TV, cajuela 239, CNC; quote from "Noticias," *Cuba en el Ballet* 3, no. 2 (May 1972), 46; Performance Program, Ballet Nacional de Cuba, April 6, 1973, folder 1973 Ballet-Danza, CDAT.

123. Giselda Demenech Valdés, "Ballet-Visión," January 31, 1975, folder BNC Cine, Radio y TV, cajuela 239, CNC.

124. López-Nussa, "El ballet también es trabajo," *Bohemia,* March 15, 1974, 25.

125. Nati González Freire, "El ballet y su tarea de creación popular," *Bohemia,* July 1, 1977, 11; this incident or a similar one is also mentioned in Tomé, "Swans in Sugarcane Fields," 11.

126. Félix Contreras, "Ballet tierra adentro," *Cuba Internacional* (April 1973), 30–31.

127. Félix Contreras, "Ballet tierra adentro," *Cuba Internacional* (April 1973), 27.

128. "Programación del Ballet de Camagüey durante el año de 1971," May 15, 1971, folder Teatro CNC, Ballet de Camagüey, Camagüey 1971, cajuela 260, CNC.

129. Félix Contreras, "Ballet tierra adentro," *Cuba Internacional* (April 1973), 31 (first quote), 29 (second quote).

130. Tomé, "Swans in Sugarcane Fields," 14.

131. Eduardo Conde to Esteban Torres, December 11, 1969, folder BNC Informes 60, cajuela 238, CNC.

132. Fernando Alonso to Eduardo Conde, December 23, 1969, folder BNC Correspondencia 1969/73, cajuela 242, CNC.

133. [Eduardo] Conde to Fernando Alonso, December 23, 1969, folder BNC Correspondencia 1969/73, cajuela 242, CNC.

134. L. Guerra, *Visions of Power in Cuba,* 305.

135. Ballet dancers had undeniable privileges despite their proletarian image analyzed in Tomé, "Swans in Sugarcane Fields."

136. Fernando Alonso, "Informe sobre actividades desarrolladas por el Ballet Nacional durante el año 1972," January 10, 1973, folder Ballet Nacional de Cuba Informes 1961/73, cajuela 242, CNC; Pablo Moré and Marcos Portal to Armando Quesada, April 4, 1972, folder BNC Informes '70, cajuela 243, CNC.

137. Marian Horosko, "Alicia Alonso, 'the Flower of Cuba': Diary of a Trip to Havana," *Dance Magazine* (August 1971), 58.

138. Alexis Vázquez to Fernando Alonso, November 21, 1973, folder BNC Planes 1974, cajuela 242, CNC.

139. Dibb, *Classically Cuban*.

140. Rodolfo Castellanos and Mirta García, "Situación de la alimentación en el Ballet Nacional de Cuba: Informe 1978," folder BNC Informes 70, cajuela 243, CNC.

141. Fernando Alonso and Luis Pérez Reyes to Félix Sautié, January 7, 1974, folder BNC Informes 70, cajuela 243, CNC.

142. Asunción Sánchez to Juan Lopetegui, December 17, 1974, folder Ballet Nacional de Cuba, Personal, cajuela 242, CNC.

143. Rodolfo Castellanos and Mirta García, "Situación de la alimentación en el Ballet Nacional de Cuba: Informe 1978," folder BNC Informes 70, cajuela 243, CNC.

144. Reckord, *Does Fidel Eat More than Your Father?*, 107.

145. Greer, *Madwoman's Underclothes*, 258.

146. Warner, *Publics and Counterpublics*, 88.

Chapter Six

1. Alejandro G. Alonso, "Qué hay de nuevo," *Juventud Rebelde*, November 8, 1979, 4.

2. Nye, "Public Diplomacy and Soft Power," 94.

3. Feinsilver, *Healing the Masses*, 25 (quote); Kirk and Erisman, *Cuban Medical Internationalism*; Randall, *Exporting Revolution*; Quevedo, "Orquesta Sinfónica Nacional de Cuba"; Keller, "Revolution Will Be Teletyped." My analysis of dance internationalism engages with and builds upon important work on dance diplomacy, including Croft, *Dancers as Diplomats*; Laur, "Dancing for the Nation"; Ezrahi, *Swans of the Kremlin*.

4. Building on work about elite policy calculations like Gleijeses, *Conflicting Missions*; Harmer, "Two, Three, Many Revolutions?"; Kruijt, *Cuba and Revolutionary Latin America*; Domínguez, *To Make a World Safe*; influenced by the approach to Cuban civilians in Angola in Hatzky, *Cubans in Angola*.

5. Randall, *Cuban Women Now*, 158.

6. Rogelio Martínez Furé, "Proyecto para el espectáculo del Conjunto Folklórico Nacional de Cuba," March 16, 1975, folder CFN Mambisa-Palenque 1976, cajuela 304, CNC.

7. Performance Program, Arte del pueblo, folder 1975 Ballet-Danza, CDAT.

8. Castro, *We Stand with the People of Africa*, 8 (quote), 1 (attendance statistics).

9. Peters, *Cuban Identity and the Angolan Experience*, 82.

10. Martínez Furé, *Diálogos imaginarios*, 248–56.

11. Peters, *Cuban Identity and the Angolan Experience*, 6.

12. *Le Peuple* quoted in Gabriela Molina, "Sedujo a Argelia el Conjunto Folklórico Cubano," *Bohemia*, July 10, 1964, 76.

13. Performance Program, Conjunto Folklórico Nacional de Cuba presentan Palenque y Mambisa, 1976, SA, BNJM.

14. Quoted in Performance Program, Conjunto Folklórico Nacional de Cuba presentan Palenque y Mambisa, 1976, SA, BNJM.

15. Rogelio Martínez Furé, "Proyecto para el espectáculo del Conjunto Folklórico Nacional de Cuba," March 16, 1975, folder CFN Mambisa-Palenque 1976, cajuela 304, CNC.

16. Rogelio Martínez Furé, "Proyecto para el espectáculo del Conjunto Folklórico Nacional de Cuba," March 16, 1975, folder CFN Mambisa-Palenque 1976, cajuela 304, CNC; Performance Program, Conjunto Folklórico Nacional de Cuba presentan Palenque y Mambisa, 1976, SA, BNJM.

17. Nati González Freire, "Un coreógrafo de Chango y otros mitos," *Bohemia*, August 9, 1974, 39.

18. Performance Program, Conjunto Folklórico Nacional de Cuba presentan Palenque y Mambisa, 1976, SA, BNJM.

19. Performance Program, Conjunto Folklórico Nacional de Cuba presentan Palenque y Mambisa, 1976, SA, BNJM.

20. Nancy Morejón, "5 preguntas sobre Palenque a Martínez Furé," *Bohemia*, July 16, 1976, 27.

21. Nati González Freire, "Palenque," *Bohemia*, July 9, 1976, 29.

22. Performance Program, Conjunto Folklórico Nacional de Cuba presentan Palenque y Mambisa, 1976, SA, BNJM.

23. Feal, *"Descargas,"* 78.

24. L. Guerra, *Visions of Power in Cuba*, 273.

25. Quotes from Nancy Morejón, "5 preguntas sobre Palenque a Martínez Furé," *Bohemia*, July 16, 1976, 27; for more on multiracial *mambisas*, see Ferrer, *Insurgent Cuba*, 3.

26. Aguirre Molina, "Eduardo Rivero Walker," 29.

27. Performance Program, Conjunto Nacional de Danza Moderna, February 1970, folder 1970 Ballet-Danza Programas, CDAT.

28. Aguirre Molina, "Eduardo Rivero Walker," 30.

29. Casals, *Okantomí*.

30. Quote from Ángel Rivero, "De la danza al poema," *Revolución y Cultura* (February 1985), 51; "Luz María Collazo: Fui uno de los rostros más fotografiados," September 2006, personal archive of Luz María Collazo.

31. Kraut, *Choreographing Copyright*, 49–63.

32. Performance Program, Conjunto Nacional de Danza Moderna, March 1974, [misplaced in] folder 1973 Ballet-Danza, CDAT.

33. Pérez León, *Por los orígenes de la danza moderna en Cuba*, 25.

34. "Luz María Collazo: Fui uno de los rostros más fotografiados," September 2006, personal archive of Luz María Collazo.

35. Casals, *Súlkary*.

36. Apter, "Pan-African Nation," 441.

37. Lorna Burdsall to Mother & All, February 16, 1977, folder 4, box 1, BFP.

38. Alejandro G. Alonso, "Regresó Danza Nacional de Cuba," *Juventud Rebelde*, February 13, 1977, 4.

39. John Darnton, "African Woodstock Overshadows Festival," *New York Times*, January 29, 1977, 6.

40. Reinaldo Cedeño Pineda, "Eduardo Rivero Walker: Ogún eterno," *Del Caribe*, no. 38 (2002), 106.

41. Gilroy, *Black Atlantic*.

42. Lorna Burdsall, "Hacia una escuela cubana de danza moderna," *Bohemia*, January 5, 1979, 13.

43. Puente Sánchez, "Vida y obra de la bailarina Diana Alfonso Valdés," 31.

44. Eddy Veitia, interview with author, March 21, 2014, Havana, Cuba.

45. París and Rodríguez, *Caravana*.

46. Performance Program, Conjunto Folklórico Nacional de Cuba, November 21, 1979, SA, BNJM; Performance Program, Conjunto Folklórico Nacional de Cuba, 1988[?], Archivo de Conjunto Folklórico Nacional de Cuba.

47. Quoted in Lisandro Otero, "Elogio de la artista," *Cuba en el Ballet* 6, no. 4 (October–December 1987), 6; De Mille, *Portrait Gallery*, 70.

48. Discussed further in Schwall, "Spectacular Embrace," 292–96.

49. [Japan] Tadatsugu Sasaki to Alberto Alonso, January 13, 1971, folder BNC Relaciones Internacionales 1971, cajuela 259, CNC; Jorge Lordes Reyes to Celia Labora, February 15, 1973, folder BNC Relaciones Internacionales 1973, cajuela 260, CNC; [Czechoslovakia] Jan Jurista to Celia Labora, January 23, 1973, folder BNC Relaciones Internacionales 1973, cajuela 260, CNC; [Romania] Nistor Ciorogariu to Consejo Nacional de Cultura, April 28, 1973, folder BNC Relaciones Internacionales 1973, cajuela 260, CNC; [Bulgaria] "Noticias," *Cuba en el Ballet* 4, no. 3 (July–September 1985), 39; [Spain] "Noticias," *Cuba en el Ballet* 7, no. 4 (October–December 1988), 39.

50. "Versión cubana de Giselle en la Ópera de París," *Cuba en el Ballet* 3, no. 2 (May 1972), 11; "Noticias," *Cuba en el Ballet* 5, no. 1 (January 1974), 42; "Versión cubana de 'La bella durmiente del bosque' en la Ópera de París," *Cuba en el Ballet* 6, no. 1 (January 1975), 32.

51. Ricardo Rey Mena, "La versión cubana de Giselle en la Ópera de Viena," *Cuba en el Ballet* 11, no. 2 (April–June 1980), 12; Pompeyo Pino Pichs, "La versión cubana de La fille mal gardée en Praga," *Cuba en el Ballet* 12, no. 2 (April–June 1981), 5–6.

52. Chapman, "*Pas de Quatre*."

53. Alejandro G. Alonso, "Alicia coreógrafa," *Juventud Rebelde*, May 12, 1974, 6.

54. Armando Quesada to Luis Pavón, November 5, 1973, folder BNC Relaciones Internacionales 1974, cajuela 259, CNC.

55. Pablo Moré and Marcos Portal to Armando Quesada, April 4, 1972, folder BNC Informes '70, cajuela 243, CNC; "Informe sobre actividades desarrolladas por el Ballet Nacional de Cuba durante el año 1972," folder Ballet Nacional de Cuba Informes 1961/73, cajuela 242, CNC.

56. "Versión cubana de Giselle en la Ópera de París," *Cuba en el Ballet* 3, no. 2 (May 1972), 11.

57. A.G.A. "Giselle, dos bailarinas latinoamericanas y una versión cubana en París," *Juventud Rebelde*, March 27, 1972, 2.

58. Alejo Carpentier, "Josefina Méndez ante el público de París," *Granma*, March 4, 1972, 2.

59. Alejo Carpentier, "Como hubiese querido verla Theophile Gautier," *Cuba en el Ballet* 3, no. 2 (May 1972), 12.

60. Arnold Haskell, "El progreso de los bailarines cubanos," *Cuba en el Ballet* 2, no. 1 (January–April 1971), 29.

61. *Diario Español de Tarragona* quoted in Pompeyo Pino Pichs, "El Ballet Nacional de Cuba: Francia y España 1982," *Cuba en el Ballet* 2, no. 1 (January–March 1983), 35.

62. *La Stampa* quoted in "El BNC ante la crítica extranjera: Gira 1974," *Cuba en el Ballet* 6, no. 1 (1975), 44.

63. Interview in *Solidaridad* quoted in Ballet Nacional de Cuba, *El Ballet Nacional de Cuba en Europa*, 22.

64. Ricardo Rey Mena, "La versión cubana de Giselle en la Ópera de Viena," *Cuba en el Ballet* 11, no. 2 (April–June 1980), 12–13, 14 (quote).

65. Alberto Alonso's work discussed further in Schwall, "Sweeping Gestures"; Schwall, "Between *Espíritu* and *Conciencia*," 160–63.

66. Norma McLain Stoop, "Jorge Lefebre and Oedipus Rex His Afro-Cuban-Ancient Greek Ballet," *Dance Magazine* (August 1971), 38.

67. For Méndez in the modern dance company, see Sánchez León, *Esa huella olvidada*, 366; Leslie Rubinstein, "Red Shoes: In Havana, Jorge Esquivel and Alberto Méndez," *Opera News* 42, no. 22 (June 1978), 19–22.

68. For Danza Contemporánea, see chapter 3; for Tenorio's biography and quote about *Rítmicas*, see Pompeyo Pino Pichs, "Iván Tenorio," *Cuba en el Ballet* 1, no. 3 (July–September 1982), 4.

69. Pompeyo Pino Pichs, "Gustavo Herrera," *Cuba en el Ballet* 3, no. 1 (January–March 1984), 14.

70. García, *Havana USA*, 138; LeoGrande and Kornbluh, *Back Channel to Cuba*, 155–224.

71. Alan Kriegsman, "Dancing across a Political Divide," *Washington Post*, July 30, 1975, E1.

72. Clive Barnes, "A Weekend to See Alicia Alonso," *New York Times*, June 11, 1976, 50; Clive Barnes, "Ballet: An Alonso Triumph," *New York Times*, September 30, 1977, 67; quote from Donald Dierks, "Alonso Earned Ballet Ovation," *San Diego Union Tribune*, November 27, 1977, B-6.

73. Laura Foreman, "Cuban Ballet Will Dance in Two U.S. Cities in 1978," *New York Times*, August 18, 1977, 77.

74. "El Ballet Nacional de Cuba en Estados Unidos y Canadá," *Cuba en el Ballet* 9, no. 3 (September–December 1978), 3.

75. LeoGrande and Kornbluh, *Back Channel to Cuba*, 172 (quote), 130.

76. James Roos, "The Cubans: Ballet Mixed with Politics," [1978?], folder Clippings, box 1, Juan Cueto Roig Collection, CHC.

77. Martin Bernheimer, "Enter Alicia Alonso & Company, Proudly," *Los Angeles Times*, May 30, 1979, G1; image in Simón and Rey Alfonso, *Alicia Alonso*, 73.

78. M. Cabrera, *El ballet en Cuba*, 285; "Ballet Nacional de Cuba: Gira por Estados Unidos, 1979," *Cuba en el Ballet* 10, no. 3 (September–December 1979), 2.

79. Roger Copeland, "Why Cuba Champions the Ballet," *New York Times*, June 11, 1978, 1, 9.

80. Prevots, *Dance for Export*, 71–74.

81. Von Eschen, *Satchmo Blows Up the World*; Iber, *Neither Peace nor Freedom*; Caute, *Dancer Defects*.

82. Olga Maynard, "Alicia Alonso and Ballet Nacional de Cuba," *Dance Magazine* (June 1978), 54.

83. Tomé, "Interracial Choreo-erotics of the Cuban Revolution."

84. Hubert Saal, "The Cubans Are Coming," *Newsweek*, June 26, 1978, 53.

85. Norma McLain Stoop, "Jorge Lefebre and Oedipus Rex His Afro-Cuban-Ancient Greek Ballet," *Dance Magazine* (August 1971), 38.

86. Martin Bernheimer, "A Flourishing Anachronism in Communist Cuba," *Los Angeles Times*, November 26, 1978, Q 90.

87. Brown, "'As Long as They Have Talent.'"

88. Randall, *Cuban Women Now*, 152–53.

89. Caridad Martínez, interview with author, May 10, 2019, New York, NY.

90. Giselda Domenech, "Gira internacional del Ballet Nacional de Cuba, México, Venezuela, Portugal, México de abril 7 a junio 26 de 1975," July 30, 1975, folder Ballet Nacional de Cuba, cajuela 241, CNC.

91. Joaquín G. Santana, "Éxitos del Ballet Nacional de Cuba," *Bohemia*, July 11, 1975, 49.

92. Octavio Roca, "Cuba's Dancing Diplomat: Alonso at Spoleto," *Washington Post*, June 1, 1980, H1.

93. Mesa-Lago, *Cuba in the 1970s*, 17.

94. Caridad Martínez, interview with author, May 22, 2019, New York, NY.

95. For the longer history of Cuban-Soviet exchange, see Schwall, "Spectacular Embrace"; Cuba's increased economic dependence on the Soviet Union in Pérez, *Cuba*, 271.

96. Germán Lahera Almeida to Luis Pavón Tamayo, July 7, 1975, folder BNC Relaciones Internacionales 1975, cajuela 259, CNC.

97. Odessa mentioned in Armando Quesada to Félix Sautié, March 20, 1973, folder Ballet Nacional de Cuba, Personal, cajuela 242, CNC; quote from Félix Sautié Mederos to Miguel Cossio, August 27, 1973, folder Ballet Nacional de Cuba, Personal, cajuela 242, CNC.

98. De Mille, *Portrait Gallery*, 88–89.

99. Caridad Martínez, interview with author, May 24, 2019, New York, NY.

100. Similar understandings of Cuban dancers in South Africa: Lauer, "Dancing for the Nation."

101. Brenner and Castro, "David and Gulliver."

102. Harmer, "Two, Three, Many Revolutions?"

103. Similar to nongovernmental bilateral friendship societies discussed in Pedemonte, "Meeting of Revolutionary Roads," 282–85.

104. Patricio Bunster, "El Dpto. de danza de la Universidad de Chile," *Cuba en el Ballet* 5, no. 2 (May 1974), 23.

105. Quote from Performance Program, Ballet Nacional de Cuba, February 16–18, 1974, cajuela 244, CNC; Giersdorf, *Body of the People*, 160–63.

106. On the early 1960s: Octo Martín Rivera to Vicentina Antuña Tabío, January 22, 1962, folder Ballet Nacional de Cuba, Personal, cajuela 242, CNC; Performance Program, Ballet Nacional de Cuba, May 26, 1962, cajuela 251, CNC; M. Cabrera, *Órbita*, 37; on the 1967 visit: Patricio Bunster to Fernando and Alicia Alonso, folder BNC Festival Internacional de Ballet 1967, cajuela 240, CNC; "4 páginas de GRANMA: Siete semanas de ballet en Cuba," *Granma*, June 17, 1967, 7–10.

107. Pedemonte, "Meeting of Revolutionary Roads."

108. Fernando Alonso to Luis Pavón Tamayo, July 1, 1971, folder BNC Relaciones Internacionales 1971, cajuela 259, CNC; Fernando Alonso to Luis Pavón, July 12, 1971, folder BNC Relaciones Internacionales 1971, cajuela 259, CNC.

109. Patricio Bunster to Fernando Alonso, December 7, 1972, folder BNC Relaciones Internacionales 1972, cajuela 261, CNC.

110. Manolo Fernández to Luis Pavón, May 10, 1973, folder BNC Relaciones Internacionales 1973, cajuela 260, CNC.

111. Miguel Cabrera, "Cuba-México 1975–1980: Un lustro de fructífera colaboración danzaria," *Cuba en el Ballet* 12, no. 2 (April–June 1981), 15; Schwall, "Coordinating Movements," 701–8.

112. "Festival de Ballet en el Peru," *Cuba en el Ballet* 9, no. 1 (January–April 1978), 17–20 (quote on 17).

113. "Segunda Festival Nacional de Ballet: Trujillo y Lima," *Cuba en el Ballet* 11, no. 1 (January–March 1980), 34; Mayda Bustamante, "Latinoamérica 1984: Una gira antológica," *Cuba en el Ballet* 3, no. 4 (October–December 1984), 6; Mayda Bustamante, "Venezuela, Colombia, Perú, Puerto Rico y República Dominicana," *Cuba en el Ballet* 2, no. 2 (April–June 1983), 5; "Noticias," *Cuba en el Ballet* 5, no. 3 (July–September 1986), 39; "Noticias," *Cuba en el Ballet* 5, no. 4 (October–December 1986), 43; Miguel Cabrera, "De nuevo en Perú," *Cuba en el Ballet* 7, no. 3 (July–September 1988), 21.

114. "Noticias," *Cuba en el Ballet* 11, no. 1 (January–March 1980), 38, 39.

115. "Noticias," *Cuba en el Ballet* 3, no. 3 (July–September 1984), 41.

116. Quoted in Javier Rodríguez, "Internacionalismo también en la cultura," *Cuba Internacional* (April 1984), 63.

117. "Noticias," *Cuba en el Ballet* 5, no. 2 (April–June 1986), 51.

118. Harmer, "Two, Three, Many Revolutions?," 82–83; Miguel Cabrera, "Zhandra Rodríguez al reencuentro de un ejemplo," *Cuba en el Ballet* 6, no. 2 (May 1975), 18.

119. "Ballet Nacional de Cuba: Giras en 1975," *Cuba en el Ballet* 6, no. 3 (September 1975), 2–3.

120. María Cristina Anzola, interview with author, January 17, 2019, New York, NY.

121. Anzola, interview, January 17, 2019.

122. For more, see chapter 4 and Schwall, "Cuban Modern Dance after Censorship."

123. Lorna Burdsall to Mother & Family, August 20, 1974, folder 3, box 1, BFP.

124. Lorna Burdsall to Mother, Ned & All, September 1, 1974, folder 3, box 1, BFP.

125. Lorna Burdsall to Mother & All, May 31, 1977, folder 4, box 1, BFP.

126. Performance Program, Conjunto Nacional de Danza Moderna, *Uruguay, hoy*, 1973, folder 1973 Ballet-Danza, CDAT.

127. Burdsall, *More than Just a Footnote*, 177–78.

128. "Relaciones diplomáticas," *Bohemia*, December 29, 1972, 30–31; Bhagirat-Rivera, "Between Pan-Africanism and a Multiracial Nation," 1024.

129. Clipping: "Cultural Centre Praised by Cuban Dancers," *Guyana Chronicle*, July 20, 1976, 10, in folder 1976 Prensa, DCC.

130. Víctor Peñalver Neyra to Armando Aguiar, March 18, 1977, folder CDN Intercambio Cultural '70, cajuela 224, CNC.

131. Polyné, "'To Carry the Dance'"; A.G.A., "Qué hay de nuevo," *Juventud Rebelde*, November 26, 1977; Evangelina Chió, "De Cuba a Guyana," *Revolución y Cultura* (July 1978), 29.

132. Clipping: Raschid Osman, "New Director Stresses Need for National Dance Company," *The Citizen*, August 26, 1977, in folder 1977 Prensa, DCC.

133. Evangelina Chió, "Guyana y la danza moderna," *Bohemia*, January 19, 1979, 31.

134. Clipping: A.G.A., "Qué hay de nuevo," *Juventud Rebelde*, November 26, 1977, in folder 1977 Prensa, DCC.

135. Performance Program, Guyana National School of Dance, Tour of the Republic of Suriname, May 10–17, 1979, SA, BNJM.

136. Evangelina Chió, "De Cuba a Guyana," *Revolución y Cultura* (July 1978), 29.

137. Clipping: Raschid Osman, "New Dance School Director Arrives," *New Nation*, July 27, 1977, in folder 1977 Prensa, DCC.

138. Clipping: Raschid Osman, "No Longer a 'Sissy,' the Male Dancer Must Be Athletic, Virile and Robust," *The Citizen*, October 27, 1977, 5, in folder 1977 Prensa, DCC.

139. Lorna Burdsall to Mother, Ned & All, September 23, 1977, folder 4, box 1, BFP.

140. Gabriel, "Qué hay de nuevo," *Juventud Rebelde*, September 8, 1974, 4.

141. Alejandro G. Alonso, "Por una forma caribeña para la danza moderna," *Juventud Rebelde*, February 12, 1980, 4.

142. Reinaldo Cedeño Pineda, "Eduardo Rivero Walker: Ogún eterno," *Del Caribe*, no. 38 (2002), 107.

143. Nettleford, *Dance Jamaica*, 194.

144. Nati González Freire, "Solo," *Bohemia*, February 29, 1980, 30–31.

145. Javier Rodríguez, "Internacionalismo también en la cultura," *Cuba Internacional* (April 1984), 63.

146. Lorna Burdsall to Mother, Ned & All, September 23, 1977, folder 4, box 1, BFP.

147. "Acutará en Nicaragua Danza Nacional de Cuba," *Juventud Rebelde*, March 9, 1981, 1; Borland, "Marimba," 89–90.

148. Clipping: "La escuela cubana de danza: Las ventajas del bloqueo," *Revista del Departamento de Filosofía* 8 (April–June 1978), folder 1978 Prensa, DCC.

149. Miguel Cabrera, "La danza: Encuentro latinoamericano en Brasil," *Cuba en el Ballet* 2, no. 4 (October–December 1983), 22–23.

150. Mayda Bustamante, "Latinoamérica 1984: Una gira antológica," *Cuba en el Ballet* 3, no. 4 (October–December 1984), 4.

151. Quotes from Pompeyo Pino, "Lázaro Carreño: Triunfo en Rio de Janeiro," *Cuba en el Ballet* 5, no. 3 (July–September 1986), 22; "Noticias," *Cuba en el Ballet* 4, no. 3 (July–September 1985), 40.

152. Quote from "Noticias," *Cuba en el Ballet* 5, no. 2 (April–June 1986), 52; "Noticias," *Cuba en el Ballet* 4, no. 3 (July–September 1985), 42; "Noticias," *Cuba en el Ballet* 6, no. 2 (October–December 1987), 37.

153. Mayda Bustamante and Pompeyo Pino, "Ballet Nacional de Cuba: Gira latinoamericana 1987," *Cuba en el Ballet* 6, no. 3 (July–September 1987), 3; "Noticias," *Cuba en el Ballet* 6, no. 2 (April–June 1987), 35; "Noticias," *Cuba en el Ballet* 8, no. 1 (January–March 1989), 42.

154. Miguel Ángel Sirgado, "Una escuela para América Latina," *Bohemia*, February 6, 1987, 7–8.

155. Pompeyo Pino, "II Congreso Latinoamericano y Caribeño de Danza," *Cuba en el Ballet* 8, no. 1 (January–March 1989), 36–38.

156. More on Fernando's 1953 proposal in chapter 1; the new organization's goals in "Fundación Latinoamericana y Caribeña de la Danza," folder Fundaciones 1989, box AD Manu, Carlota Carrera, Archivo de la Danza, Universidad de Puerto Rico, Río Piedras.

157. Leonardo Padura, "Entrevista: ¿Un bueno momento para los jóvenes?," *El Caimán Barbudo* (November 1982), 10–11.

158. Martínez, interview, May 24, 2019; quote from Caridad Martínez, interview with author, May 29, 2019, New York, NY.

159. Randall, *Cuban Women Now*, 158.

160. Clipping: Nadia Karandashov Robinson, "Al talento hay que darle oportunidades," *Trabajadores*, September 3, 1987, folder 1987 Prensa, DCC.

161. Javier Rodríguez, "Internacionalismo también en la cultura," *Cuba Internacional* (April 1984), 60–63.

162. Assumedly U.S. dollars, but unspecified in Eckstein, "Cuban Internationalism," 379.

Chapter Seven

1. Performance Program, Grupo Danza Abierta, December 15–18, 1988, folder 1988 Ballet-Danza, CDAT.

2. Fornet, "El quinquenio gris."

3. "Centralized decentralization" from Bengelsdorf, *Problem of Democracy in Cuba*, 99; Mesa-Lago, "Cuba's Economic Counter-reform (*Rectificación*)," 102.

4. Hernández-Reguant, *Cuba in the Special Period*; Fernandes, *Cuba Represent!*; John, *Contemporary Dance in Cuba*.

5. Guzmán Moré, *Creación artística y crisis económica en Cuba*, 28; I also build on Fusco, *Dangerous Moves*. However, the performers that Fusco examines differ from the establishment artists in Guzmán Moré's work and in my study, since they often operated outside of nationalized institutions.

6. Alejandro G. Alonso, "Rosario Cárdenas: Gioconda tropical," *Juventud Rebelde*, September 5, 1979, 4.

7. Bustamante, "Anniversary Overload?," 226.

8. Bustamante, "Confronting (and Forgetting) Return." I thank the author for sharing this paper with me.

9. Pérez-Stable, *Cuban Revolution*, 150.

10. Caridad Martínez, interview with author, May 22, 2019, New York, NY; requisite happiness also analyzed by Lillian Guerra in her manuscript, as cited by Bustamante, "Anniversary Overload?," 243n87.

11. "Noticias," *Cuba en el Ballet* 3, no. 4 (October–December 1984), 43.

12. "Ponencia sobre la fundamentación y desarrollo de la Joven Guardia del Ballet Nacional de Cuba," folder Cuballet, 1991, Archivo de Centro de ProDanza.

13. José Rafael Vilar, "Adolescencia de un sueño: La Joven Guardia del BNC (1984–1989)," *Cuba en el Ballet* 8, no. 4 (October–December 1989), 18–20; "Noticias," *Cuba en el Ballet* 5, no. 1 (January–March 1986), 44; "Noticias," *Cuba en el Ballet* 4, no. 4 (October–December 1985), 34.

14. "Noticias," *Cuba en el Ballet* 7, no. 1 (January–March 1988), 44; "Noticias," *Cuba en el Ballet* 7, no. 2 (April–June 1988), 44.

15. "Figuras del Ballet Nacional de Cuba," *Cuba en el Ballet* 12, no. 3 (July–September 1981), 22–23.

16. Caridad Martínez, interview with author, June 12, 2014, New York, NY.

17. Caridad Martínez, interview with author, January 18, 2019, New York, NY.

18. Caridad Martínez, interview with author, May 24, 2019, New York, NY; Martínez, interview, January 18, 2019.

19. Martínez, interview, June 12, 2014.

20. Martínez, interview, January 18, 2019.

21. Martínez, interview, June 12, 2014.

22. Martínez, interview, January 18, 2019.

23. Performance Program, Ballet Teatro de la Habana, folder 1988 Ballet-Danza, CDAT.

24. Martínez, interview, June 12, 2014.

25. Armando López, "No hice 'Giselle' por ser negra," *Cubaencuentro*, July 2, 2009, http://www.cubaencuentro.com/entrevistas/articulos/no-hice-giselle-por-ser-negra -190821/(galleryslide)/8/(gallerynode)/190837; Caridad Martínez, interview with author, May 29, 2019, New York, NY.

26. Performance Program, Ciclo de experimentación en la imagen escénica, folder 1987 Ballet-Danza, CDAT; Performance Program, Ballet Teatro de la Habana, folder 1988 Ballet-Danza, CDAT.

27. Martínez, interview, May 22, 2019.

28. Quoted in Martin, *Socialist Ensembles*, 164; changes also detailed in Guzmán Moré, *Creación artística y crisis económica en Cuba*.

29. Martínez, interview, May 24, 2019.

30. Performance Program, Ciclo de experimentación en la imagen escénica, folder 1987 Ballet-Danza, CDAT.

31. "Esquivel, un hijo de la revolución," *El Caimán Barbudo* (August 1979), 16–18.

32. Isaías Caparrós Otano, "Jorge Esquivel habla de . . . ," *Bohemia*, January 2, 1987, 14.

33. Performance Program, Ciclo de experimentación en la imagen escénica, folder 1987 Ballet-Danza, CDAT.

34. Performance Program, Ciclo de experimentación en la imagen escénica, folder 1987 Ballet-Danza, CDAT; Martínez, interview, May 22, 2019.

35. Performance Program, Ballet Teatro de la Habana, Test, folder 1989 Ballet-Danza, CDAT; Martínez, interview, May 22, 2019.

36. Pedro Ángel, "Test: Laberinto de significados," *Juventud Rebelde*, August 18, 1989, 5.

37. Performance Program, Ballet Teatro de la Habana, Test, folder 1989 Ballet-Danza, CDAT.

38. Martínez, interview, May 24, 2019.

39. Martínez, interview, May 22, 2019.

40. Martínez, interview, May 22, 2019.

41. Martínez, interview, May 22, 2019.

42. Pedro Ángel, "Test: Laberinto de significados," *Juventud Rebelde*, August 18, 1989, 5.

43. Martínez, interview, May 22, 2019.

44. Manning, *Modern Dance, Negro Dance*, xix.

45. Pedro de la Hoz, "Eppure si muove: De la gesticulación al gesto," *Tablas* 2 (1989), 44–45.

46. Martínez, interview, May 22, 2019.

47. Mesa Martell, "Vida institucional," 42–43.

48. Navarro, "In Medias Res Publicas," 198.

49. Performance Program, VII Festival Internacional de Ballet de la Habana, November 14, 1980, folder 1980 Ballet-Danza, CDAT; Marilyn Bobes, "Silvina en la danza," *Revolución y Cultura* (March 1986), 7.

50. Roca, *Cuban Ballet*, 95.

51. Martínez, interview, June 12, 2014; Martínez, interview, January 18, 2019.

52. Ruiz Rodríguez, *Fernando Alonso*, 12, 124.

53. Fernando Alonso in Yolanda Ferrera Sosa, "Maestros de maestros," *Bohemia*, November 17, 1978, 25.

54. Ruiz Rodríguez, *Fernando Alonso*, 125.

55. Unpublished manuscript shared by its author: Lourdes María Cepero Estrada, "Ballet de Camagüey, 1967–2007: Raigambre y vuelo," 7.

56. Jaime Sarusky, "Fernando Alonso habla de el Ballet de Camagüey," *Bohemia*, March 12, 1976, 4–5.

57. Manuel Rodríguez Viamontes to Luis Pavón Tamayo, September 17, 1973, folder Ballet de Camagüey, cajuela 259, CNC.

58. Joaquín Banegas to Manolo Fernández, April 13, 1973, folder Teatro CNC Ballet de Camagüey, Camagüey 1973, cajuela 260, CNC.

59. Armando Quesada to Luis Pavón, November 28, 1973, folder Ballet de Camagüey 68/74, cajuela 260, CNC.

60. Luis Pavón Tamayo to Armando Quesada, December 13, 1973, folder Teatro CNC Ballet de Camagüey, Camagüey 1973, cajuela 260, CNC.

61. Manuel González to Armando Quesada, June 14, 1974, folder Teatro CNC Ballet de Camagüey, Camagüey 1974, cajuela 260, CNC.

62. Magda Martínez, "Sobre la punta de los pies," *Bohemia*, August 30, 1974, 23; "Ballet de Camagüey," folder Año 77, ABC.

63. Roberto Méndez, "Ballet de Camagüey: Un sueño de dos décadas," *Revolución y Cultura* (June 1989), 9.

64. Fernando Alonso to Félix Sautié, May 20, 1975, folder Ballet Nacional de Cuba, Personal, cajuela 242, CNC; Alicia Alonso to Luis Pavón, August 30, 1975, folder Ballet Nacional de Cuba, Personal, cajuela 242, CNC; Fernando Alonso to José Ramón Artilles Díaz, June 8, 1976, folder BNC Personal 70, cajuela 241, CNC; Alicia Alonso to Armando Aguiar, July 7, 1976, folder BNC Personal 70, cajuela 241, CNC.

65. Folder Ana Lidice del Río González, ABC.

66. Alicia Alonso to Ibarbia, September 13, 1976, folder BNC Personal 70, cajuela 241, CNC.

67. "Entrevista Fernando Alonso realizada en la sede del ballet de Camagüey," May 6, 1983, folder Fernando Alonso, ABC.

68. "Entrevista Fernando Alonso realizada en la sede del ballet de Camagüey," May 6, 1983, folder Fernando Alonso, ABC.

69. Roberto Méndez, "Ballet de Camagüey: Un sueño de dos décadas," *Revolución y Cultura* (June 1989), 9–10.

70. Senel Paz, "Fernando Alonso y el Ballet de Camagüey," *Bohemia*, April 21, 1978, 31.

71. Rosa Elvira Peláez, "Para una función infinita," *Bohemia*, November 29, 1985, 21.

72. Roberto Méndez, "Ballet de Camagüey: Un sueño de dos décadas," *Revolución y Cultura* (June 1989), 7.

73. Rosa Elvira Peláez, "Para una función infinita," *Bohemia*, November 29, 1985, 21.

74. Ángel Tomás, "Aquí hemos pasado los años más difíciles," *El Caimán Barbudo* (May 1976), 12.

75. Interview transcript with Fernando Alonso for *Adelante*, ABC.

76. Guillermo Leyva, interview with author, October 13, 2017, Wheaton, IL.

77. Cepero Estrada, *Memorias del Ballet de Camagüey*, 21, 33; Roberto Méndez, "Ballet de Camagüey: Un sueño de dos décadas," *Revolución y Cultura* (June 1989), 10; Pompeyo Pino Pichs, "Ballet en Lorca," *Bohemia*, September 1, 1978, 26.

78. Departamento de Divulgación Ballet de Camagüey, "Fernando Alonso Rayneri," 1984, folder Sobre Fernando Alonso y Metodología del Profesor, ABC; clipping: Angelina Camargo, "México tiene condiciones para contar con una magnifica compañía de ballet," *Excelsior*, May 13, 1984, 4, ABC; "La vocación de enseñar: Fernando Alonso," 4, folder Sobre Fernando Alonso y Metodología del Profesor, ABC.

79. Sergio Vitier García Marruz and Fernando Alonso Rayneri, "Convenio: Complejo cultural 'Julio Antonio Mella'," November 27, 1983, folder Fernando Alonso, ABC; Roberto Méndez, "Ballet de Camagüey: Un sueño de dos décadas," *Revolución y Cultura* (June 1989), 11.

80. For details, see Cepero Estrada, *Memorias del Ballet de Camagüey*, 33–62.

81. Ferrales Racet and Vidal Savigne, "Historia de los festivales de la danza en Camagüey," 82.

82. Rosa Elvira Peláez, "Para una función infinita," *Bohemia*, November 29, 1985, 20.

83. Fernando Alonso to Fidel Castro, November 11, 1985, folder Miscelánea de Fernando Alonso, ABC.

84. Emilio Suri Quesada, "Entrevista con Fernando Alonso, por donde andan las señales," *Juventud Rebelde*, February 19, 1989, 12.

85. Elías Rodríguez Rodríguez to Ana Marlene Fonseca, December 22, 1979, folder Ana Marlene Fonseca, ABC; Guillermo Leyva, "Cuestionario," May 10, 1982, folder Leyva Barley, Guillermo, ABC.

86. For instance, Juan Carlos González Almora came from Pinar del Río, Esperanza Torres García from Havana, Rafael Villalón Barreras from Santiago de Cuba, and Isbert Ramos Mediaceja from Guantánamo. Ondina María Arteaga came from Venezuela, María Teresa García Schlegel from Colombia, Fidel Orrillo Puga from Peru, Christine Marie Ferrando from France, Fausto Renato Arroyo Quezada from Ecuador, and Gysele Ascarrunz Novo from Brazil. See folders named for and containing documents about these individuals in ABC.

87. Dpto. Divulgación e Historia to Christine Ferrando, October 8, 1986, folder Ferrando, Mª Christine, ABC.

88. See, for instance, several "Valoración Sistemática de los resultados del trabajo" from 1987, 1988, 1989 in folder Mercedes Delgado Prado, ABC.

89. Jorge Luis Valdés Roque, "Cuestionario," February 27, 1980, folder Biografía [unintelligible], ABC; *escoria* discussed in Quiroga, "Unpacking My Files," 149, 158.

90. Burdsall, *More than Just a Footnote*, 175–76.

91. Performance Program, Danz-Escultura, Lorna Burdsall y su grupo, September 24–27, 1990, folder 1990–1991 Ballet-Danza, CDAT.

92. Her name appears in Performance Program, Así Somos, folder 1989 Ballet-Danza, CDAT.

93. Camnitzer, *New Art of Cuba*, 5.

94. Camnitzer, *New Art of Cuba*, 3–4, 175, 177.

95. Performance Program, Danz-Escultura, Lorna Burdsall y su grupo, September 24–27, 1990, folder 1990–1991 Ballet-Danza, CDAT.

96. "Cubanness" from Performance Program, Moda '86, Espectáculo 'Multi-medias' por el Grupo de Danza Contemporánea Así Somos, folder 1986 Ballet-Danza, CDAT; Burdsall, *More than Just a Footnote*, 192 (second quote).

97. Performance Program, Moda '86, Espectáculo 'Multi-medias' por el Grupo de Danza Contemporánea Así Somos, folder 1986 Ballet-Danza, CDAT.

98. Pamphlet, "Un salto al nuevo milenio, Así Somos . . . teatro de imágenes," personal archive of Gabriela Burdsall.

99. Burdsall, *More than Just a Footnote*, 184–85.

100. Burdsall, *More than Just a Footnote*, 192.

101. Quoted in Performance Program, Así Somos, personal archive of Gabriela Burdsall.

102. Triguero Tamayo, *Placeres del cuerpo*, 195–99.

103. Rivero quoted in Triguero Tamayo, *Placeres del cuerpo*, 200; Luz María Collazo and Isidro Rolando, interview with author, June 6, 2019, Havana, Cuba.

104. Performance Program, Compañía Teatro de la Danza del Caribe, February 16–19, 1989, folder 1989 Ballet-Danza, CDAT.

105. Reinaldo Cedeño Pineda, "Eduardo Rivero Walker: Ogún eterno," *Del Caribe*, no. 38 (2002), 107.

106. Viddal, "Vodú Chic," 20.

107. De la Fuente, *Grupo Antillano*, 71 (quote), 72–73.

108. Photograph in de la Fuente, *Grupo Antillano*, 219.

109. Nati González Freire, "Ómnira," *Bohemia*, April 20, 1979, 29; Pompeyo Pino Pichs and Roberto Méndez, "Danza Nacional en el año de su XX aniversario: Un salto adelante," *El Caimán Barbudo* (June 1979), 17; Eduardo Rivero, "Guión de Dúo a Lam," folder Dúo a Lam 1979, DCC.

110. "Luz María Collazo: Fui uno de los rostros más fotografiados," September 2006, personal archive of Luz María Collazo.

111. Collazo and Rolando, interview, June 6, 2019.

112. Triguero Tamayo, *Placeres del cuerpo*, 201.

113. Performance Program, Teatro de la Danza del Caribe, October 27–29, 1989, folder 1989 Ballet-Danza, CDAT.

114. Triguero Tamayo, *Placeres del cuerpo*, 202.

115. Muriel Manings, "March 9, 1984," Journal Cuba 1984, folder 20, box 4, Muriel Manings and William Korff Collection, Music Division, Library of Congress; Muriel Manings, interview with author, November 1, 2012, New York, NY; Roberto Lavastida, interview with author, March 7, 2014, Havana, Cuba.

116. Ángel Rivero, "El juego de la danza," *Revolución y Cultura* (June 1985), 48, 49.

117. Performance Program, Danza Nacional de Cuba, Sexto Festival Internacional de Ballet, November 18 and 19, 1978, folder 1978 Ballet-Danza, CDAT.

118. Ángel Rivero, "El juego de la danza," *Revolución y Cultura* (June 1985), 49–50.

119. Performance Program, Grupo Danza Abierta, December 15–18, 1988, folder 1988 Ballet-Danza, CDAT.

120. Tomás Guilarte, interview with author, March 29, 2014, Havana, Cuba; Raquel Mayedo, "Danza Abierta: Reto a la vanguardia," *Tablas* 2 (April–June 1989), 48.

121. Gabri Christa, interview with author, September 25, 2016, Staten Island, NY.

122. Christa quoted in John, *Contemporary Dance in Cuba*, 106.

123. Caridad Martínez, interview with author, May 10, 2019, New York, NY.

124. Clipping: Raquel Mayedo, "Abierta, abrir, abriendo," *Cartelera* 354 (December 8–14, 1988), folder 1988 Prensa Nacional, DCC.

125. Raquel Mayedo, "Danza Abierta: Reto a la vanguardia," *Tablas* 2 (April–June 1989), 51.

126. Guilarte, interview, March 29, 2014.

127. Printed in Pedro Ángel, "Danza abierta código cerrado," *Juventud Rebelde*, December 26, 1988, 5.

128. Marianela Boán, interview with Shanna Lorenz, July 2001, Monterrey, Mexico, http://hidvl.nyu.edu/video/001010723.html.

129. Guilarte, interview, March 29, 2014.

130. Pedro Ángel, "Danza abierta código cerrado," *Juventud Rebelde*, December 26, 1988, 5.

131. Clipping: Lina de Feria, "Danza Abierta," *La Gaceta de Cuba* (March 1989), 18, folder 1989 Prensa Nacional, DCC.

132. Discussion of open-minded young collaborators in Boán, interview, July 2001; quote from clipping: Raquel Mayedo, "Abierta, abrir, abriendo," *Cartelera* 354 (December 8–14, 1988), folder 1988 Prensa Nacional, DCC.

133. Pajares Santiesteban, *La danza contemporánea cubana*, 97–98.

134. Clipping: Lina de Feria, "Danza Abierta," *La Gaceta de Cuba* (March 1989), 18, folder 1989 Prensa Nacional, DCC.

135. Rosa Elvira Peláez, "Marianela no quiere sentarse en el sillón," *Granma*, October 12, 1988, 7.

136. Quote in "Noticias," *Cuba en el Ballet* 7, no. 1 (January–March 1988), 43; "Noticias," *Cuba en el Ballet* 7, no. 3 (July–September 1988), 43.

137. "Rosario Cárdenas," *EcuRed*, accessed November 3, 2015, http://www.ecured.cu/index.php/Rosario_Cárdenas; Helson Hernández, "Choreographer & Director Rosario Cárdenas," *Havana Times*, April 10, 2011, http://www.havanatimes.org/?p=41337.

138. Performance Program, Recital Marianela Boán, Danza Nacional de Cuba, folder 1981 Ballet-Danza, CDAT.

139. Raquel Mayedo, "Danza Abierta: Reto a la vanguardia," *Tablas* 2 (1989), 48.

140. Mireya Castañeda, "Sensibilidad, riesgo y provocación de Rosario Cárdenas," *Granma*, October 1, 1989, 7.

141. Clipping: Raimundo Díaz Rosell, "Sueño en la memoria de Ramiro Guerra," *Bastion*, August 3, 1989, folder 1989 Prensa Nacional, DCC.

142. Rosa Elvira Peláez, "Ramiro Guerra, el maestro: Danza de sueños y trabajo," *Granma*, August 16, 1988, 5.

143. R. Guerra, *De la narratividad al abstraccionismo en la danza*, 258.

144. "De la memoria fragmentada: Guión de Ramiro Guerra," folder De la Memoria Fragmentada 1989, DCC.

145. Guerra quoted in Mireya Castañeda, "Sentir el pulso del momento," *Granma*, September 3, 1989, 7; critic quotes from clipping: Milsania, "Donde convencionalismo no tuvo lugar," *Tribuna de la Habana*, September 5, 1989, folder 1989 Prensa Nacional, DCC.

146. Luis Roblejo, interview with author, August 12, 2013, Havana, Cuba; "De la memoria fragmentada: Guión de Ramiro Guerra," folder De la Memoria Fragmentada 1989, DCC.

147. Lavastida, interview, March 7, 2014; Guilarte, interview, March 29, 2014.

148. Guilarte, "Análisis acerca del surgimiento y desarrollo de la Compañía Danza Libre," 16–17; Víctor H., "Nacimiento del Conjunto de Danzas de Guantánamo," *Venceremos*, January 28, 1990.

149. Guilarte, "Análisis acerca del surgimiento y desarrollo de la Compañía Danza Libre," 9.

150. Guilarte, interview, March 29, 2014; Manings, interview, November 1, 2012.

Epilogue

1. Rubén Gallo, "Is This the End of Cuba's Astonishing Artistic Freedom?," *New York Times*, February 19, 2019, https://www.nytimes.com/2019/02/18/opinion/cuba-censorship-arrufat.html.

2. Peter Kornbluh, "Covid-19: Cuba Deserves Relief from U.S. Sanctions," *The Nation*, March 31, 2020, https://www.thenation.com/article/world/coronavirus-cuba-sanctions-aid.

3. John, *Contemporary Dance in Cuba*.

4. Rogelio Martínez Furé, telephone interview with author, September 23, 2014, Havana, Cuba; Hearn, *Cuba*, 47.

5. Caridad Martínez, interview with author, June 12, 2014, New York, NY.

6. Luz María Collazo and Isidro Rolando, interview with author, June 6, 2019, Havana, Cuba.

7. Caridad Martínez, interview with author, May 24, 2019, New York, NY.

8. Alicia Alonso, interview with author, March 25, 2015, Havana, Cuba.

9. Amelia Durarte de la Rosa, "Obama Meets Alicia Alonso," *Granma*, March 23, 2016, http://en.granma.cu/cuba/2016-03-23/obama-meets-alicia-alonso.

10. According to the archivists helping me, I saw all the boxes that were available. It is possible that there were other boxes that were not yet organized or that I was not allowed to see.

11. Collazo and Rolando, interview, June 6, 2019.

12. Marianela Boán, "Artist Statement," accessed April 26, 2020, https://en.marianelaboan.site/artist-statement.

Bibliography

Primary Sources

ARCHIVES

Cuba

Archivo de Ballet de Camagüey, Camagüey, Cuba

Archivo de Centro de ProDanza, Havana, Cuba

Archivo de Conjunto Folklórico Nacional de Cuba, Havana, Cuba

Archivo de Danza Contemporánea de Cuba, Teatro Nacional de Cuba, Havana, Cuba

Archivo de Sala de Arte, Biblioteca Nacional José Martí, Havana, Cuba

Archivo General del Ministerio de Cultura, Biblioteca Juan Marinello

    Fondo: Consejo Nacional de Cultura

    Fondo: Ministerio de Educación (1940–61), Dirección General de Cultura

Archivo Histórico Provincial de Santiago de Cuba

    Fondo: Gobierno Provincial de Oriente

    Fondo: Personal de Nicolai Yavorsky

Archivo Nacional de Cuba

    Fondo: Registro de Asociaciones

Biblioteca Provincial Julio Antonio Mella de Camagüey, Camagüey, Cuba

Centro de Documentación e Investigación de Artes Escénicas de Santiago de Cuba, Santiago de Cuba, Cuba

Centro de Documentación y Archivo Teatral, Teatro Nacional de Cuba, Havana, Cuba

Fundación Antonio Núñez Jiménez, Havana, Cuba

Grupo de Investigación, Documentación e Información Musical Pablo Hernández Balaguer, Santiago de Cuba, Cuba

Museo Nacional de la Danza, Havana, Cuba

Personal Archive of Gabriela Burdsall, Havana, Cuba

Personal Archive of Isidro Rolando, Havana, Cuba

Personal Archive of Luz María Collazo, Havana, Cuba

Puerto Rico

Archivo de la Danza, Universidad de Puerto Rico, Río Piedras, San Juan, Puerto Rico

United States

Ann Barzel Papers, The Newberry Library, Chicago, IL

Carlos Franqui Collection, Manuscripts Division, Department of Rare Books and Special Collections, Princeton University Library, Princeton, NJ

Cuban Heritage Collection, University of Miami Libraries, Coral Gables, FL

    Adria Catalá Casey Papers

    Alberto Alonso and Sonia Calero Papers

Burdsall Family Papers
Fulgencio Batista Zaldívar Collection
Juan Cueto Roig Collection
Lyceum and Lawn Tennis Club Collection
Lydia Cabrera Collection
Natalia Aróstegui Collection
Cuban Revolutionary Collection, Yale University, New Haven, CT
Jerome Robbins Dance Division, New York Public Library for the Performing Arts,
  New York, NY
  Agnes de Mille Correspondence and Writings
  American Ballet Theatre Records
  Marian Horosko Writing and Research Files
  Sergei Denham Records of the Ballet Russe de Monte Carlo
  Villalón, Célida Parera, Miscellaneous Manuscripts
Music Division, Library of Congress, Washington, DC
  Muriel Manings and William Korff Collection
Personal Archive of Caridad Martínez, New York, NY
Schomburg Center for Research in Black Culture, New York Public Library, New York, NY
  Eusebia Cosme Papers
Special Collections Research Center, Southern Illinois University, Carbondale, IL
  Katherine Dunham Papers
  Katherine Dunham Photograph Collection

NEWSPAPERS AND MAGAZINES

Adelante
Afro-American
Ahora
Bohemia
*Boletín Informativo, Órgano Oficial del
  Instituto Nacional de Cultura*
El Caimán Barbudo
Carteles
Conservatorio
Cuba en el Ballet
Cuba Internacional
Dance Magazine
Del Caribe
Diario de la Marina
Gente
Granma
Havana Times
INRA
Juventud Rebelde
Los Angeles Times
Lunes de Revolución

Mensuario
Mujeres
El Mundo
Nation
New York Times
Newsweek
Noticias de Hoy
Nuestro Tiempo
Opera News
Pro-Arte Musical
Revista Cuba
Revolución
Revolución y Cultura
Romances
San Diego Union Tribune
Show
Social
Tablas
Temas
Venceremos
Washington Post

BOOKS AND FILMS

Ballet Nacional de Cuba, ed. *El Ballet Nacional de Cuba en Europa, 1969 críticas.* Havana, 1969.

Beruff Mendieta, Antonio. *Las comparsas populares del carnaval habanero, cuestión resuelta.* Havana: Molina y Cia, 1937.

Cabrera, Lydia. *La sociedad secreta Abakuá: Narrada por viejos adeptos.* Havana: Collección del Chicherekú, 1958.

Carbonell, Walterio. *Cómo surgió la cultura nacional.* Havana: Ediciones Bachiller, Biblioteca Nacional José Martí, 2005.

Casals, Melchor, dir. *Okantomí: Todo mi corazón.* Havana: Instituto Cubano del Arte e Industria Cinematográficos, 1974.

———. *Súlkary.* Havana: Institutio Cubano del Arte e Industria Cinematográficos, 1974. https://www.youtube.com/watch?v=le1jJDdiU1U.

Castilla, Belarmino, ed. *Primer Congreso Nacional de Educación y Cultura.* Havana: Instituto Cubano del Libro, 1971.

Castro, Fidel. "The Historic Second Declaration of Havana," February 4, 1962. http://media.smithsonianfolkways.org/liner_notes/paredon/PAR01013.pdf.

———. *We Stand with the People of Africa.* New York: Venceremos Brigade, 1976.

———. "Words to the Intellectuals." In *Fidel Castro Reader,* edited by David Deutschmann and Deborah Shnookal, 213–40. Melbourne: Ocean, 2007.

Chao Carbonero, Graciela, ed. *Coreografía: Guía de estudio.* Havana: Editorial Pueblo y Educación, 1980.

Convención Constituyente de la República de Cuba. "Constitución Política de 1940," 1940. http://pdba.georgetown.edu/Constitutions/Cuba/cuba1940.html.

Dibb, Michael, dir. *Classically Cuban: Alicia Alonso and the Cuban National Ballet.* London: British Broadcasting Corporation, 1982.

Fraga, Jorge, dir. *La nueva escuela.* Havana: Instituto Cubano de Arte e Industria Cinematográficos, 1973. https://www.youtube.com/watch?v=5IuYmZbp_YQ.

Giral, Sergio, dir. *María Antonia.* Havana: Instituto Cubano de Arte e Industria Cinematográficos, 1990.

Guevara, Ernesto. "Socialism and Man in Cuba." In *Che Guevara Reader: Writings on Politics and Revolution,* edited by David Deutschmann, 212–28. Melbourne: Ocean, 2007.

Lachatañeré, Rómulo. *Manual de Santería.* Havana: Editorial Caribe, 1942.

Leaf, Earl. *Isles of Rhythm.* New York: A. S. Barnes, 1948.

Lockwood, Lee. *Castro's Cuba, Cuba's Fidel.* New York: Vintage Books, 1969.

Martínez Furé, Rogelio. *Conjunto Folklórico Nacional.* Havana: Consejo Nacional de Cultura, 1963.

Massip, José, dir. *Historia de un ballet.* Havana: Instituto Cubano del Arte e Industria Cinematográficos, 1962. https://www.youtube.com/watch?v=SeJD4X6x3QI.

Ortiz, Fernando. *Cuban Counterpoint: Los bailes y el teatro de los negros en el folklore de Cuba.* Havana: Publicaciones de Ministerio de Educación, 1951.

———. *Tobacco and Sugar.* New York: Knopf, 2013.

París, Rogelio, dir. *Nosotros, la música.* Havana: Instituto Cubano del Arte e Industria Cinematográficos, 1964. https://www.youtube.com/watch?v=NlauZTe7OW4&t=430s.

París, Rogelio, and Julio César Rodríguez, dirs. *Caravana*. Havana: Instituto Cubano del Arte e Industria Cinematográficos, 1990. https://www.youtube.com/watch?v =RsuMLeRtVII&t=2537s.

Pérez León, Roberto. *Por los orígenes de la danza moderna en Cuba*. Havana: Departamento de Actividades Culturales, Universidad de la Habana, 1986.

Plisetski, Azari, choreographer. *Canto vital*. Puerto Rico, 1979. https://www.youtube.com /watch?v=CnULIqdsaeo.

Randall, Margaret. *Cuban Women Now: Interviews with Cuban Women*. Toronto: Women's Press, 1974.

Reckord, Barry. *Does Fidel Eat More than Your Father? Conversations in Cuba*. New York: New American Library, 1972.

Rodríguez, Carlos Rafael. *Problemas del arte en la Revolución*. Havana: Editorial Letras Cubanas, 1979.

Sistema Nacional de Capacitación Técnica para Instructores de Arte. *Folclor Cubano*. Havana: Ministerio de Cultura, 1977.

Studio Sylvia M. Goudie. *Memoria: 1949–1959*. Havana, 1959.

Sutherland, Elizabeth. *Cuba Now*. New York: Dial, 1968.

Vega, Pastor, dir. *Alicia en los países maravillosos*. Havana: Instituto Cubano del Arte e Industria Cinematográficos, 1962.

———. *Retrato de Teresa*. Havana: Instituto Cubano del Arte e Industria Cinematográficos, 1979.

Secondary Sources

Abreu, Christina D. *Rhythms of Race: Cuban Musicians and the Making of Latino New York City and Miami, 1940–1960*. Chapel Hill: University of North Carolina Press, 2016.

Aguirre Molina, Anna Arelis. "Eduardo Rivero Walker, danza y tradición." Undergraduate thesis, Instituto Superior de Arte Filial Camagüey, 2007.

Alberto, Paulina L. "El Negro Raúl: Lives and Afterlives of an Afro-Argentine Celebrity, 1886 to the Present." *Hispanic American Historical Review* 96, no. 4 (November 2016): 669–710. https://doi.org/10.1215/00182168-3677639.

Albright, Ann Cooper. *Choreographing Difference: The Body and Identity in Contemporary Dance*. Middletown, CT: Wesleyan University Press, 2010.

Allen, Jafari S. *Venceremos?: The Erotics of Black Self-Making in Cuba*. Durham, NC: Duke University Press, 2011.

Almendros, Nestor, and Orlando Jiménez-Leal. *Conducta impropia*. Madrid: Editorial Playor, 1984.

Alonso, Alicia. *Diálogos con la danza*. Edited by Pedro Simón. Havana: Editora Política, 2000.

Anderson, Thomas F. *Carnival and National Identity in the Poetry of Afrocubanismo*. Gainesville: University Press of Florida, 2017.

Andrews, George Reid. "Remembering Africa, Inventing Uruguay: Sociedades de Negros in the Montevideo Carnival, 1865–1930." *Hispanic American Historical Review* 87, no. 4 (November 2007): 693–726. https://doi.org/10.1215/00182168-2007-040.

Apter, Andrew. "The Pan-African Nation: Oil-Money and the Spectacle of Culture in Nigeria." *Public Culture* 8, no. 3 (1996): 441–66.

Arnedo-Gómez, Miguel. *Writing Rumba: The Afrocubanista Movement in Poetry.* Charlottesville: University of Virginia Press, 2006.

Ballet Nacional de Cuba and Museo Nacional de la Danza. *El ballet: Un sueño en manos del pueblo.* Havana: Museo Nacional de la Danza, 2016. https://www.youtube.com/watch?v =PIoKc26aGLg.

Ben, Pablo, and Santiago Joaquín Insausti. "Dictatorial Rule and Sexual Politics in Argentina: The Case of the Frente de Liberación Homosexual, 1967–1976." *Hispanic American Historical Review* 97, no. 2 (May 2017): 297–326.

Bench, Harmony, and Elswit, Kate. "Everyday Itinerary Dataset, 1950–53." *Dunham's Data: Katherine Dunham and Digital Methods for Dance Historical Inquiry, 26 Countries, 1950–1953.* Inter-university Consortium for Political and Social Research [distributor], July 30, 2020. https://doi.org/10.3886/ICPSR37698.v1.

Bengelsdorf, Carollee. *The Problem of Democracy in Cuba: Between Vision and Reality.* New York: Oxford University Press, 1994.

Benson, Devyn Spence. *Antiracism in Cuba: The Unfinished Revolution.* Chapel Hill: University of North Carolina Press, 2016.

———. "Sara Gómez: Afrocubana (Afro-Cuban Women's) Activism after 1961." *Cuban Studies* 46 (2018): 134–58. https://doi.org/10.1353/cub.2018.0008.

Berry, Maya. "Now They Are Just about Guapería: Sacred Swagger for a 'New Man' 2.0." Paper presented at the Dance Studies Association Conference, Northwestern University, Evanston, IL, 2019.

Bhagirat-Rivera, Ramaesh Joseph. "Between Pan-Africanism and a Multiracial Nation: Race, Regionalism, and Guyanese Nation-Building through the Caribbean Festival of Creative Arts (CARIFESTA), 1972." *Interventions* 20, no. 7 (October 3, 2018): 1022–36. https://doi.org/10.1080/1369801X.2018.1487798.

Birkenmaier, Anke. *The Specter of Races: Latin American Anthropology and Literature between the Wars.* Charlottesville: University of Virginia Press, 2016.

Blanco Borelli, Melissa. *She Is Cuba: A Genealogy of the Mulata Body.* New York: Oxford University Press, 2016.

Blum, Denise F. *Cuban Youth and Revolutionary Values: Educating the New Socialist Citizen.* Austin: University of Texas Press, 2011.

Borges, Mercedes, and Pedro Maytín, dirs. *Arnaldo Patterson, el maestro.* Havana: Consejo Nacional de las Artes Escénicas, 2017. https://vimeo.com/317148191.

Borland, Katherine. "Marimba: Dance of the Revolutionaries, Dance of the Folk." *Radical History Review* 84, no. 1 (Fall 2002): 77–107.

Brandon, George. *Santería from Africa to the New World: The Dead Sell Memories.* Bloomington: Indiana University Press, 2000.

Brenner, Philip, and Soraya Castro. "David and Gulliver: Fifty Years of Competing Metaphors in the Cuban–United States Relationship." *Diplomacy & Statecraft* 20, no. 2 (2009): 236–57.

Brill, Deirdre. "La Escuela Cubana: Dance Education and Performance in Revolutionary Cuba." Ph.D. diss., University of Pennsylvania, 2007.

Bronfman, Alejandra. "'Batista Is Dead': Media, Violence and Politics in 1950s Cuba." *Caribbean Studies* 40, no. 1 (2012): 37–58.

———. *Measures of Equality: Social Science, Citizenship, and Race in Cuba, 1902–1940.* Chapel Hill: University of North Carolina Press, 2004.

Brown, Lauren Erin. "'As Long as They Have Talent': Organizational Barriers to Black Ballet." *Dance Chronicle* 41, no. 3 (November 2018): 359–92.

Brunson, Takkara. "Eusebia Cosme and Black Womanhood on the Transatlantic Stage." *Meridians* 15, no. 2 (March 1, 2017): 389–411. https://doi.org/10.2979/meridians.15.2.06.

Burdsall, Lorna. *More than Just a Footnote: Dancing from Connecticut to Revolutionary Cuba.* Quebec: AGMV Marquis, 2001.

Burt, Ramsay. *The Male Dancer: Bodies, Spectacle, Sexualities.* London: Routledge, 2007.

Burton, Julianne. "Seeing, Being, Being Seen: Portrait of Teresa, or Contradictions of Sexual Politics in Contemporary Cuba." *Social Text*, no. 4 (1981): 79–95. https://doi.org/10.2307/466277.

Bustamante, Michael J. "Anniversary Overload? Memory Fatigue at Cuba's Socialist Apex." In *The Revolution from Within: Cuba, 1959–1980*, edited by Michael J. Bustamante and Jennifer L. Lambe, 218–43. Durham, NC: Duke University Press, 2019.

———. "Confronting (and Forgetting) Return: The *Visitas de la Comunidad* of 1979." Paper presented at the American Studies Association Meeting, Chicago, IL, 2017.

———. "Cultural Politics and Political Cultures of the Cuban Revolution: New Directions in Scholarship." *Cuban Studies* 47 (2019): 3–18.

Bustamante, Michael J., and Jennifer L. Lambe, eds. *The Revolution from Within: Cuba, 1959–1980.* Durham, NC: Duke University Press, 2019.

Cabrera, Miguel. *Alberto Alonso: Una vida para la danza.* Havana: Ediciones ENPES, 1990.

———. *El ballet en Cuba: Apuntes históricos.* Havana: Cúpulas, 2011.

———. *Festival Internacional de Ballet de la Habana, (1960–2004): Una cita de arte y amistad.* Havana: Letras Cubanas, 2006.

———. *Órbita del Ballet Nacional de Cuba, 1948–1978.* Havana: Editorial ORBE, 1978.

Camnitzer, Luis. *New Art of Cuba.* Austin: University of Texas Press, 2003.

Campbell, Jennifer L. "Dancing Marines and Pumping Gasoline: Coded Queerness in Depression-Era American Ballet." In *Queer Dance: Meanings and Makings*, edited by Clare Croft, 125–43. New York: Oxford University Press, 2017.

Canaday, Margot. "LGBT History." *Frontiers: A Journal of Women Studies* 35, no. 1 (2014): 11–19.

———. *The Straight State: Sexuality and Citizenship in Twentieth-Century America.* Princeton, NJ: Princeton University Press, 2009.

Caute, David. *The Dancer Defects: The Struggle for Cultural Supremacy during the Cold War.* New York: Oxford University Press, 2008.

Cepero Estrada, Lourdes María. *Memorias del Ballet de Camagüey.* Camagüey: Editorial Ácana, 2014.

Chanan, Michael. *Cuban Cinema.* Minneapolis: University of Minnesota Press, 2010.

Chapman, John. "*Pas de Quatre.*" In *International Encyclopedia of Dance*, edited by Selma Jeanne Cohen. New York: Oxford University Press, 2009.

Chasteen, John Charles. *National Rhythms, African Roots: Latin American Popular Dance before the Twentieth Century.* Albuquerque: University of New Mexico Press, 2004.

Coates, Timothy J. *Convicts and Orphans: Forced and State-Sponsored Colonizers in the Portuguese Empire, 1550–1755.* Stanford, CA: Stanford University Press, 2001.

Cowan, Benjamin A. *Securing Sex: Morality and Repression in the Making of Cold War Brazil.* Chapel Hill: University of North Carolina Press, 2016.

Coyula, Mario. "El trinquenio amargo y la ciudad distópica: Autopsia de una utopía." *Archipélago: Revista cultural de nuestra América* 14, no. 56 (2007): 52–55.

Crenshaw, Kimberlé. "Mapping the Margins: Intersectionality, Identity Politics, and Violence against Women of Color." *Stanford Law Review* 43, no. 6 (1991): 1241–1300.

Croft, Clare. *Dancers as Diplomats: American Choreography in Cultural Exchange*. New York: Oxford University Press, 2015.

———. "Introduction." In *Queer Dance: Meanings and Makings*, edited by Clare Croft, 1–33. New York: Oxford University Press, 2017.

Daly, Ann. "To Dance Is 'Female.'" *TDR: The Drama Review* 33, no. 4 (1989): 23–27.

Daniel, Yvonne. *Rumba: Dance and Social Change in Contemporary Cuba*. Bloomington: Indiana University Press, 1995.

Das, Joanna Dee. *Katherine Dunham: Dance and the African Diaspora*. New York: Oxford University Press, 2017.

de la Fuente, Alejandro. *Grupo Antillano: The Art of Afro-Cuba*. Pittsburgh: Pittsburgh University Press, 2013.

———, ed. *A Nation for All: Race, Inequality, and Politics in Twentieth-Century Cuba*. Chapel Hill: University of North Carolina Press, 2001.

———. "La Ventolera: Ruptures, Persistence, and the Historiography of the Cuban Revolution." In *The Revolution from Within: Cuba, 1959–1980*, edited by Jennifer L. Lambe and Michael J. Bustamante, 290–305. Durham, NC: Duke University Press, 2019.

De Mille, Agnes. *Portrait Gallery*. Boston: Houghton Mifflin, 1990.

del Toro González, Carlos. *La alta burguesía cubana, 1920–1958*. 2nd ed. Havana: Editorial Ciencias Sociales, 2011.

Deyá, Giselle. *Mirta Plá: Una joya de la cultura cubana*. Havana: Letras Cubanas, 2011.

Dirección de Enseñanza Artística del Ministerio de Cultura. *La enseñanza artística en Cuba*. Havana: Editorial Letras Cubanas, 1986.

Domínguez, Jorge I. *Cuba: Order and Revolution*. Cambridge, MA: Harvard University Press, 2009.

———. *To Make a World Safe for Revolution: Cuba's Foreign Policy*. Cambridge, MA: Harvard University Press, 1989.

Eckstein, Susan. "Cuban Internationalism." In *Cuba: Twenty-Five Years of Revolution, 1959–1984*, edited by Sandor Halebsky and John M. Kirk, 372–90. New York: Praeger, 1985.

Espín Guillois, Vilma, Yolanda Ferrer, and Carolina Aguilar Ayerra. *El fuego de la libertad*. Havana: Editorial de la Mujer, 2015.

Estrada Betancourt, José Luis. *De la semilla al fruto: La compañía*. Havana: Casa Editora Abril, 2008.

Ezrahi, Christina. *Swans of the Kremlin: Ballet and Power in Soviet Russia*. Pittsburgh: University of Pittsburgh Press, 2012.

Fariñas Borrego, Maikel. *Sociabilidad y cultura del ocio: Las élites habaneras y sus clubes de recreo (1902–1930)*. Havana: Fundación Fernando Ortiz, 2009.

Feal, Rosemary Geisdorfer. "*Descargas*: Exploring Identity in Rogelio Martínez Furé's Afro-Cuban Poetic Forms." *Afro-Hispanic Review* 37, no. 2 (Fall 2018): 76–94.

Feinsilver, Julie Margot. *Healing the Masses: Cuban Health Politics at Home and Abroad*. Berkeley: University of California Press, 2001.

Fernandes, Sujatha. *Cuba Represent!: Cuban Arts, State Power, and the Making of New Revolutionary Cultures.* Durham, NC: Duke University Press, 2008.

———. "Recasting Ideology, Recreating Hegemony." *Ethnography* 7, no. 3 (2006): 303–27.

Fernandez, Raul A. *From Afro-Cuban Rhythms to Latin Jazz.* Berkeley: University of California Press, 2006.

Fernández Guevara, Daniel J. "Constructing Legitimacy in 'Stone' and 'Words' during Cuba's Second Republic: Building and Contesting Fulgencio Batista's José Martí." *History and Memory* 31, no. 2 (2019): 117–54.

Fernández-Selier, Yesenia. "The Making of the Rumba Body: René Rivero and the Rumba Craze." *Sargasso*, no. 1 & 2 (2012–13): 85–100.

Ferrales Racet, Mirna, and Yulia Vidal Savigne. "Historia de los festivales de la danza en Camagüey, 1982–1997." Undergraduate thesis, Instituto Superior de Arte Filial Camagüey, 2000.

Ferrer, Ada. "History and the Idea of Hispanic Caribbean Studies." *Small Axe: A Caribbean Journal of Criticism* 20, no. 3 (51) (November 1, 2016): 49–64. https://doi.org/10.1215/07990537-3726854.

———. *Insurgent Cuba: Race, Nation, and Revolution, 1868–1898.* Chapel Hill: University of North Carolina Press, 1999.

Fornet, Ambrosio. "El quinquenio gris, revisando el término." Paper presented at the Casa de las Américas, Havana, Cuba, 2007. http://www.rebelion.org/noticia.php?id=45857.

Fortuna, Victoria. *Moving Otherwise: Dance, Violence, and Memory in Buenos Aires.* New York: Oxford University Press, 2019.

Foster, Susan Leigh. *Choreography & Narrative: Ballet's Staging of Story and Desire.* Bloomington: Indiana University Press, 1998.

———. *Valuing Dance: Commodities and Gifts in Motion.* New York: Oxford University Press, 2019.

Foulkes, Julia L. *Modern Bodies: Dance and American Modernism from Martha Graham to Alvin Ailey.* Chapel Hill: University of North Carolina Press, 2006.

Fusco, Coco. *Dangerous Moves: Performance and Politics in Cuba.* London: Tate, 2015.

Garafola, Lynn. "Dalí, Ana María, and the Three-Cornered Hat." In *Dalí and the Ballet: Set and Costumes for the Three-Cornered Hat*, edited by Curtis Carter. Milwaukee, WI: Haggerty Museum of Art, Marquette University, 2000.

———. *Diaghilev's Ballets Russes.* New York: Oxford University Press, 1989.

———. "The Travesty Dancer in Nineteenth-Century Ballet." *Dance Research Journal* 17, no. 2 and 18, no. 1 (Autumn 1985–Spring 1986): 35–40. https://doi.org/10.2307/1478078.

García, María Cristina. *Havana USA: Cuban Exiles and Cuban Americans in South Florida, 1959–1994.* Berkeley: University of California Press, 1996.

García Fabras, Oddebí. "Silvina Fabars, intérprete excepcional de la danza folclórica cubana." *La Jiribilla: Revista de cultura cubana*, June 19, 2017. http://www.lajiribilla.cu/articulo/silvina-fabars-interprete-excepcional-de-la-danza-folclorica-cubana.

García Yero, Cary Aileen. "The State within the Arts: A Study of Cuba's Cultural Policy, 1940–1958." *Cuban Studies* 47 (2019): 83–110.

García-Márquez, Vicente. *The Ballets Russes: Colonel de Basil's Ballets Russes de Monte Carlo, 1932–1952.* New York: Knopf, 1990.

Giersdorf, Jens Richard. *The Body of the People: East German Dance since 1945.* Madison: University of Wisconsin Press, 2013.

Gillingham, Paul, and Benjamin T. Smith, eds. *Dictablanda: Politics, Work, and Culture in Mexico, 1938–1968.* Durham, NC: Duke University Press, 2014.

Gilroy, Paul. *The Black Atlantic: Modernity and Double Consciousness.* London: Verso, 2007.

Gleijeses, Piero. *Conflicting Missions: Havana, Washington, and Africa, 1959–1976.* Chapel Hill: University of North Carolina Press, 2003.

Gordon-Nesbitt, Rebecca. *To Defend the Revolution Is to Defend Culture: The Cultural Policy of the Cuban Revolution.* Oakland, CA: PM Press, 2015.

Gottschild, Brenda Dixon. *Digging the Africanist Presence in American Performance: Dance and Other Contexts.* Westport, CT: Greenwood, 1996.

Grandin, Greg. "Off the Beach: The United States, Latin America, and the Cold War." In *A Companion to Post-1945 America*, edited by Jean-Christophe Agnew and Roy Rosensweig, 426–45. Malden: Blackwell, 2002.

Green, James Naylor. *Beyond Carnival: Male Homosexuality in Twentieth-Century Brazil.* Chicago: University of Chicago Press, 2002.

———. "'Who Is the Macho Who Wants to Kill Me?' Male Homosexuality, Revolutionary Masculinity, and the Brazilian Armed Struggle of the 1960s and 1970s." *Hispanic American Historical Review* 92, no. 3 (August 2012): 437–70.

Greer, Germaine. *The Madwoman's Underclothes: Essays and Occasional Writings.* New York: Atlantic Monthly Press, 1990.

Guerra, Lillian. "'Feeling Like Fidel': Scholarly Meditations on History, Memory, and the Legacies of Fidel Castro." *Cuban Studies* 47 (2019): 111–42.

———. "Gender Policing, Homosexuality and the New Patriarchy of the Cuban Revolution, 1965–70." *Social History* 35, no. 3 (2010): 268–89.

———. *Heroes, Martyrs, and Political Messiahs in Revolutionary Cuba, 1946–1958.* New Haven, CT: Yale University Press, 2018.

———. *Visions of Power in Cuba: Revolution, Redemption, and Resistance, 1959–1971.* Chapel Hill: University of North Carolina Press, 2012.

Guerra, Ramiro. *Coordenadas danzarias.* Havana: Ediciones Unión, 1999.

———. *De la narratividad al abstraccionismo en la danza.* Havana: Centro de Investigación y Desarrollo de la Cultura Cubana Juan Marinello, 2003.

———. *Eros baila: Danza y sexualidad.* Havana: Editorial Letras Cubanas, 2001.

———. "My Experience and Experiments in Caribbean Dance." In *Making Caribbean Dance: Continuity and Creativity in Island Cultures*, edited by Susanna Sloat, translated by Melinda Mousouris, 49–61. Gainesville: University Press of Florida, 2010.

Guilarte, Tomás. "Análisis acerca del surgimiento y desarrollo de la Compañía Danza Libre." Undergraduate thesis, Instituto Superior de Arte, 1994.

Guillermoprieto, Alma. *Dancing with Cuba: A Memoir of the Revolution.* Translated by Esther Allen. New York: Vintage Books, 2006.

Guridy, Frank A. *Forging Diaspora: Afro-Cubans and African Americans in a World of Empire and Jim Crow.* Chapel Hill: University of North Carolina Press, 2010.

———. "From Solidarity to Cross-Fertilization: Afro-Cuban/African American Interaction during the 1930s and 1940s." *Radical History Review* 87, no. 1 (Fall 2003): 19–48.

Guy, Donna. *Sex and Danger in Buenos Aires: Prostitution, Family, and Nation in Argentina.* Lincoln: University of Nebraska Press, 1995.

Guzmán Moré, Jorgelina. *Creación artística y crisis económica en Cuba (1988–1992).* Havana: Editorial de Ciencias Sociales, 2010.

———. *De Dirección General a Instituto Nacional de Cultura.* Havana: Editora Historia, 2014.

Hagedorn, Katherine J. *Divine Utterances: The Performance of Afro-Cuban Santería.* Washington, DC: Smithsonian Institution Press, 2001.

Hamilton, Carrie. *Sexual Revolutions in Cuba: Passion, Politics, and Memory.* Chapel Hill: University of North Carolina Press, 2014.

Hansen, Miriam. "Pleasure, Ambivalence, Identification: Valentino and Female Spectatorship." *Cinema Journal* 25, no. 4 (1986): 6–32.

Harmer, Tanya. "Two, Three, Many Revolutions?: Cuba and the Prospects for Revolutionary Change in Latin America, 1967–1975." *Journal of Latin American Studies* 45, no. 1 (2013): 61–89.

Hartman, Saidiya V. *Wayward Lives, Beautiful Experiments: Intimate Histories of Social Upheaval.* New York: W. W. Norton, 2019.

Hatzky, Christine. *Cubans in Angola: South-South Cooperation and Transfer of Knowledge, 1976–1991.* Translated by Mair Edmunds-Harrington. Madison: University of Wisconsin Press, 2015.

Hearn, Adrian H. *Cuba: Religion, Social Capital, and Development.* Durham, NC: Duke University Press, 2008.

Herman, Rebecca. "An Army of Educators: Gender, Revolution and the Cuban Literacy Campaign of 1961." *Gender & History* 24, no. 1 (April 2012): 93–111.

Hernández Baguer, Grizel. *Historias para una historia.* Havana: Ediciones Museo de la Música, 2012.

Hernández-Reguant, Ariana, ed. *Cuba in the Special Period: Culture and Ideology in the 1990s.* Basingstoke: Palgrave Macmillan, 2010.

Hertzman, Marc A. *Making Samba: A New History of Race and Music in Brazil.* Durham, NC: Duke University Press, 2013.

Höfling, Ana Paula. *Staging Brazil: Choreographies of Capoeira.* Middletown, CT: Wesleyan University Press, 2019.

Horst, Jesse. "Sleeping on the Ashes: Slum Clearance in Havana in an Age of Revolution, 1930–1965." Ph.D. diss., University of Pittsburgh, 2016.

Howe, Linda S. *Transgression and Conformity: Cuban Writers and Artists after the Revolution.* Madison: University of Wisconsin Press, 2004.

Iber, Patrick. "Anti-Communist Entrepreneurs and the Origins of the Cultural Cold War in Latin America." In *De-Centering Cold War History: Local and Global Change,* edited by Jadwiga E. Pieper Mooney, 167–86. New York: Routledge, 2013.

———. *Neither Peace nor Freedom: The Cultural Cold War in Latin America.* Cambridge, MA: Harvard University Press, 2015.

John, Suki. *Contemporary Dance in Cuba: Técnica Cubana as Revolutionary Movement.* Jefferson, NC: McFarland, 2012.

Johnson, James H. *Listening in Paris: A Cultural History.* Berkeley: University of California Press, 2008.

Johnson, Sara E. *The Fear of French Negroes: Transcolonial Collaboration in the Revolutionary Americas*. Berkeley: University of California Press, 2012.

Joseph, Gilbert M., and Daniel Nugent, eds. *Everyday Forms of State Formation: Revolution and the Negotiation of Rule in Modern Mexico*. Durham, NC: Duke University Press, 2012.

Joseph, Gilbert M., and Daniela Spenser, eds. *In from the Cold: Latin America's New Encounter with the Cold War*. Durham, NC: Duke University Press, 2008.

Jottar, Berta. "The Acoustic Body: Rumba Guarapachanguera and Abakuá Sociality in Central Park." *Latin American Music Review* 30, no. 1 (June 1, 2009): 1–24. https://doi.org/10.5555/lamr.2009.30.1.1.

Karl, Robert A. "Reading the Cuban Revolution from Bogotá, 1957–62." *Cold War History* 16, no. 4 (October 2016): 337–58. https://doi.org/10.1080/14682745.2016.1218848.

Keilson, Ana Isabel. "The Embodied Conservatism of Rudolf Laban, 1919–1926." *Dance Research Journal* 51, no. 2 (August 2019): 18–34. https://doi.org/10.1017/S0149767719000160.

Keller, Renata. "The Revolution Will Be Teletyped: Cuba's Prensa Latina News Agency and the Cold War Contest over Information." *Journal of Cold War Studies* 21, no. 3 (2019): 88–113.

Kennison, Rebecca. "Clothes Make the (Wo)man: Marlene Dietrich and 'Double Drag.'" *Journal of Lesbian Studies* 6, no. 2 (2002), 147–56.

Kirk, John M., and H. Michael Erisman. *Cuban Medical Internationalism: Origins, Evolution, and Goals*. New York: Palgrave Macmillan, 2009.

Kirk, John M., and Leonardo Padura, eds. *Culture and the Cuban Revolution: Conversations in Havana*. Gainesville: University Press of Florida, 2001.

Kosstrin, Hannah. *Honest Bodies: Revolutionary Modernism in the Dances of Anna Sokolow*. New York: Oxford University Press, 2017.

———. "Queer Space in Anna Sokolow's *Rooms*." In *Queer Dance: Meanings and Makings*, edited by Clare Croft, 145–65. New York: Oxford University Press, 2017.

Kraut, Anthea. *Choreographing Copyright: Race, Gender, and Intellectual Property Rights in American Dance*. New York: Oxford University Press, 2016.

———. *Choreographing the Folk: The Dance Stagings of Zora Neale Hurston*. Minneapolis: University of Minnesota Press, 2008.

Kruijt, Dirk. *Cuba and Revolutionary Latin America: An Oral History*. London: Zed, 2017.

Kutzinski, Vera M. *Sugar's Secrets: Race and the Erotics of Cuban Nationalism*. Charlottesville: University Press of Virginia, 1994.

Lam, Rafael. *Tropicana: Un paraíso bajo las estrellas*. Havana: Editorial José Martí, 1997.

Lambe, Jennifer L. "A Century of Work: Reconstructing Mazorra, 1857–1959." *Cuban Studies* 43 (2015): 90–117.

———. *Madhouse: Psychiatry and Politics in Cuban History*. Chapel Hill: University of North Carolina Press, 2017.

Lane, Jill. *Blackface Cuba: 1840–1895*. Philadelphia: University of Pennsylvania Press, 2005.

Lauer, Meryl. "Dancing for the Nation: Ballet Diplomacy and Transnational Politics in Post-Apartheid South Africa." *Dance Research Journal* 50, no. 3 (December 2018): 85–98.

Leal, Rine, ed. *Teatro Escambray*. Havana: Editorial Letras Cubanas, 1978.

Ledón Sánchez, Armando. *La música popular en Cuba*. Oakland, CA: El Gato Tuerto, 2003.

Leiner, Marvin. *Sexual Politics in Cuba: Machismo, Homosexuality, and AIDS*. Boulder, CO: Westview, 1994.

———. "Two Decades of Educational Change in Cuba." *Journal of Reading* 25, no. 3 (1981): 202–14.

LeoGrande, William M., and Peter Kornbluh. *Back Channel to Cuba: The Hidden History of Negotiations between Washington and Havana*. Chapel Hill: University of North Carolina Press, 2016.

López, Antonio M. *Unbecoming Blackness: The Diaspora Cultures of Afro-Cuban America*. New York: New York University Press, 2016.

Lowinger, Rosa, and Ofelia Fox. *Tropicana Nights: The Life and Times of the Legendary Nightclub*. Orlando: Harcourt, 2005.

Lumsden, Ian. *Machos, Maricones, and Gays: Cuba and Homosexuality*. Philadelphia: Temple University Press, 2010.

Maguire, Emily A. *Racial Experiments in Cuban Literature and Ethnography*. Gainesville: University Press of Florida, 2011.

Mallon, Florencia E. "*Barbudos*, Warriors, and *Rotos*: The MIR, Masculinity, and Power in the Chilean Agrarian Reform, 1965–74." In *Changing Men and Masculinities in Latin America*, edited by Matthew Gutmann, 179–215. Durham, NC: Duke University Press, 2003.

Mally, Lynn. *Culture of the Future: The Proletkult Movement in Revolutionary Russia*. Berkeley: University of California Press, 1990.

Manning, Susan. "Looking from a Different Place: Gay Spectatorship of American Modern Dance." In *Dancing Desires: Choreographing Sexualities On and Off the Stage*, edited by Jane C. Desmond, 403–13. Madison: University of Wisconsin Press, 2001.

———. *Modern Dance, Negro Dance: Race in Motion*. Minneapolis: University of Minnesota Press, 2008.

Marquetti Torres, Rosa. "Katherine Dunham y los percusionistas cubanos." *Desmemoriados: Historias de la música cubana*. http://www.desmemoriados.com /katherine-dunham-percusionistas-cubanos/. Accessed August 31, 2019.

Martiatu, Inés María. *Cuba: Costumbres y tradiciones*. Havana: Prensa Latina, 2006.

———. "Reflexiones en los cuarenta años de María Antonia." In *Una pasión compartida: María Antonia*, edited by Inés María Martiatu. Havana: Letras Cubanas, 2004.

Martin, Randy. *Socialist Ensembles: Theater and State in Cuba and Nicaragua*. Minneapolis: University of Minnesota Press, 1994.

Martínez Furé, Rogelio A. *Diálogos imaginarios*. Havana: Editorial Letras Cubanas, 1997.

McElroy, Frances, and María Teresa Rodríguez. *Mirror dance = La danza del espejo*. Philadelphia: Shirley Road Productions & Pata de Perro Productions, 2005.

McEnaney, Tom. *Acoustic Properties: Radio, Narrative, and the New Neighborhood of the Americas*. Evanston, IL: Northwestern University Press, 2017.

McEwen, Abigail. *Revolutionary Horizons: Art and Polemics in 1950s Cuba*. New Haven, CT: Yale University Press, 2016.

McMains, Juliet. "Rumba Encounters: Transculturation of Cuban Rumba in American and European Ballrooms." In *Making Caribbean Dance: Continuity and Creativity in Island Cultures*, edited by Susanna Sloat, 37–48. Gainesville: University Press of Florida, 2010.

Mesa Martell, Iliana. "Vida institucional del Conjunto Folklórico Nacional de Cuba." Undergraduate thesis, Instituto Superior de Arte, 1991.

Mesa-Lago, Carmelo. *Cuba in the 1970s: Pragmatism and Institutionalization.* Albuquerque: University of New Mexico Press, 1978.

———. "Cuba's Economic Counter-reform (Rectificatión): Causes, Policies and Effects." *Journal of Communist Studies* 5, no. 4 (December 1, 1989): 98–139. https://doi.org/10.1080/13523278908414994.

Miller, Ivor. "A Secret Society Goes Public: The Relationship between Abakuá and Cuban Popular Culture." *African Studies Review* 43, no. 1 (April 2000): 161–88. https://doi.org/10.2307/524726.

———. *Voice of the Leopard: African Secret Societies and Cuba.* Jackson: University Press of Mississippi, 2011.

Miller, Nicola. "A Revolutionary Modernity: The Cultural Policy of the Cuban Revolution." *Journal of Latin American Studies* 40, no. 4 (November 2008): 675–96. https://doi.org/10.1017/S0022216X08004719.

Millet, José, and Rafael Brea. *Grupos folklóricos de Santiago de Cuba.* Santiago de Cuba: Editorial Oriente, 1989.

Mirabal, Elizabeth, and Carlos Velazco. *Hablar de Guillermo Rosales.* Miami, FL: Editorial Silueta, 2013.

Moore, Carlos. *Castro, the Blacks, and Africa.* Los Angeles: University of California, Center for Afro-American Studies, 1991.

Moore, Robin D. "The Commercial Rumba: Afrocuban Arts as International Popular Culture." *Latin American Music Review / Revista de Música Latinoamericana* 16, no. 2 (1995): 165–98. https://doi.org/10.2307/780372.

———. *Music and Revolution: Cultural Change in Socialist Cuba.* Berkeley: University of California Press, 2006.

———. *Nationalizing Blackness: Afrocubanismo and Artistic Revolution in Havana, 1920–1940.* Pittsburgh: University of Pittsburgh Press, 1997.

Morejón, Nancy. "Las poéticas de Nancy Morejón." *Afro-Hispanic Review* 15, no. 1 (Spring 1996): 6–9.

Moreno Vega, Marta. "The Yoruba Orisha Tradition Comes to New York City." *African American Review* 29, no. 2 (1995): 201–6. https://doi.org/10.2307/3042291.

Morrison, Simon Alexander. *Bolshoi Confidential: Secrets of the Russian Ballet from the Rule of the Tsars to Today.* New York: Liveright, 2016.

Mousouris, Melinda. "The Dance World of Ramiro Guerra: Solemnity, Voluptuousness, Humor, and Chance." In *Caribbean Dance from Abakuá to Zouk: How Movement Shapes Identity*, edited by Susanna Sloat, 56–72. Gainesville: University Press of Florida, 2002.

Nahmias, Alysa, and Benjamin Murray, dirs. *Unfinished Spaces.* Oley: Bullfrog Films, 2011.

Navarro, Desiderio. "In Medias Res Publicas: On Intellectuals and Social Criticism in the Cuban Public Sphere." Translated by Alessandro Fornazzari and Desiderio Navarro. *Boundary 2* 29, no. 3 (2002): 187–203.

Nettleford, Rex. *Dance Jamaica: Cultural Definition and Artistic Discovery; The National Dance Theatre Company of Jamaica, 1962–1983.* New York: Grove, 1985.

Núñez Jiménez, Antonio. *La Gran Caverna de Santo Tomás: Monumento nacional.* Havana: Ediciones Plaza Vieja, 1990.

Nye, Joseph S., Jr. "Public Diplomacy and Soft Power." *The Annals of the American Academy of Political and Social Science* 616 (March 2008): 94–109.

O'Connor, James R. *The Origins of Socialism in Cuba*. Ithaca, NY: Cornell University Press, 1970.

Orovio, Helio. *El carnaval habanero: Su música y sus comparsas*. Havana: Ediciones Extramuros, 2005.

———. *Cuban Music from A to Z*. Durham, NC: Duke University Press, 2009.

Pacheco Valera, Irina. "La enseñanza artística en la memoria de dos asociaciones de la república." *Libínsula: La isla de los libros*, May 31, 2013. http://librinsula.bnjm.cu /secciones/317/nombrar/317_nombrar_2.html.

———. *La Sociedad Pro-Arte Musical: Testimonio de su tiempo*. Havana: Ediciones La Memoria, Centro Cultural Pablo de la Torriente Brau, 2011.

Pajares Santiesteban, Fidel. *La danza contemporánea cubana y su estética*. Havana: Unión, 2005.

———. *Ramiro Guerra y la danza en Cuba*. Quito: Casa de la Cultura Ecuatoriana, 1993.

Palmer, Steven, José Antonio Piqueras, and Amparo Sánchez Cobos. "Introduction: Revisiting Cuba's First Republic." In *State of Ambiguity: Civic Life and Culture in Cuba's First Republic*, edited by Steven Palmer, José Antonio Piqueras, and Amparo Sánchez Cobos, 1–21. Durham, NC: Duke University Press, 2014.

Palmié, Stephan. *The Cooking of History: How Not to Study Afro-Cuban Religion*. Chicago: University of Chicago Press, 2013.

Parera Villalón, Célida. *Pro-Arte Musical y su divulgación de cultura en Cuba, 1918–1967*. Montclair, NJ: Senda Nueva de Ediciones, 1990.

Pedemonte, Rafael. "The Meeting of Revolutionary Roads: Chilean-Cuban Interactions, 1959–1970." *Hispanic American Historical Review* 99, no. 2 (May 2019): 275–302.

Pérez, Louis A., Jr. *Cuba: Between Reform and Revolution*. 3rd ed. New York: Oxford University Press, 2006.

———. *To Die in Cuba: Suicide and Society*. Chapel Hill: University of North Carolina Press, 2007.

Pérez Rodríguez, Nancy. *El carnaval santiaguero*. Vol. 2. Santiago de Cuba: Editorial Oriente, 1988.

Pérez-Stable, Marifeli. *The Cuban Revolution: Origins, Course, and Legacy*. New York: Oxford University Press, 1999.

Peters, Christabelle. *Cuban Identity and the Angolan Experience*. New York: Palgrave Macmillan, 2012.

Phillips, Victoria. *Martha Graham's Cold War: The Dance of American Diplomacy*. New York: Oxford University Press, 2020.

Piccato, Pablo. "Public Sphere in Latin America: A Map of the Historiography." *Social History* 35, no. 2 (May 1, 2010): 165–92. https://doi.org/10.1080/03071021003795055.

———. *The Tyranny of Opinion: Honor in the Construction of the Mexican Public Sphere*. Durham, NC: Duke University Press, 2010.

Polyné, Millery. "'To Carry the Dance of the People Beyond': Jean León Destiné, Lavinia Williams and 'Danse Folklorique Haïtienne.'" *Journal of Haitian Studies* 10, no. 2 (Fall 2004): 33–51.

Prevots, Naima. *Dance for Export: Cultural Diplomacy and the Cold War*. Middletown, CT: Wesleyan University Press, 1998.

Puente Sánchez, Marta Emilia. "Vida y obra de la bailarina Diana Alfonso Valdés." Undergraduate thesis, Instituto Superior de Arte, 2006.

Putnam, Lara. *Radical Moves: Caribbean Migrants and the Politics of Race in the Jazz Age.* Chapel Hill: University of North Carolina Press, 2013.

Quevedo, Marysol. "The Orquesta Sinfónica Nacional de Cuba and Its Role in the Cuban Revolution's Cultural Project." *Cuban Studies* 47 (2019): 19–34.

Quiroga, José. *Cuban Palimpsests.* Minneapolis: University of Minnesota Press, 2005.

———. "Unpacking My Files: My Life as a Queer Brigadista." *Social Text* 32, no. 4 (121) (2014): 149–59.

Ramsey, Kate. *The Spirits and the Law: Vodou and Power in Haiti.* Chicago: University of Chicago Press, 2011.

Randall, Margaret. *Exporting Revolution: Cuba's Global Solidarity.* Durham, NC: Duke University Press, 2017.

Reynoso, Jose Luis. "Choreographing Politics, Dancing Modernity: Ballet and Modern Dance in the Construction of Modern México (1919–1940)." Ph.D. diss., University of California, Los Angeles, 2012.

Rivero, Yeidy M. *Broadcasting Modernity: Cuban Commercial Television, 1950–1960.* Durham, NC: Duke University Press, 2015.

Roca, Octavio. *Cuban Ballet.* Layton, UT: Gibbs Smith, 2010.

Rosa, Cristina F. *Brazilian Bodies and Their Choreographies of Identification: Swing Nation.* Basingstoke: Palgrave Macmillan, 2015.

Ross, Janice. *Like a Bomb Going Off: Leonid Yakobson and Ballet as Resistance in Soviet Russia.* New Haven, CT: Yale University Press, 2015.

Roth-Ey, Kristin. *Moscow Prime Time: How the Soviet Union Built the Media Empire That Lost the Cultural Cold War.* Ithaca, NY: Cornell University Press, 2014.

Routon, Kenneth. "Unimaginable Homelands?: 'Africa' and the Abakuá Historical Imagination." *Journal of Latin American Anthropology* 10, no. 2 (2005): 370–400. https://doi.org/10.1525/jlca.2005.10.2.370.

Ruiz Rodríguez, Raúl Rubén. *Ballet y revolución.* Havana: Comité Central del Partido Comunista de Cuba, 1973.

———. *Fernando Alonso: Danza con la vida.* Havana: Ediciones Letras Cubanas, 2000.

Sánchez León, Miguel. *Esa huella olvidada: El Teatro Nacional de Cuba (1959–1961).* Havana: Editorial Letras Cubanas, 2001.

Schlotterbeck, Marian. *Beyond the Vanguard: Everyday Revolutionaries in Allende's Chile.* Berkeley: University of California Press, 2018.

Schultz, Rainer. "The Liberal Moment of the Revolution: Cuba's Early Educational Reforms, 1959–1961." *Cuban Studies* 49 (2020): 215–35.

Schwall, Elizabeth. "Between *Espíritu* and *Conciencia*: Cabaret and Ballet Developments in 1960s Cuba." In *The Revolution from Within: Cuba, 1959–1980,* edited by Michael J. Bustamante and Jennifer L. Lambe, 146–69. Durham, NC: Duke University Press, 2019.

———. "Coordinating Movements: The Politics of Cuban-Mexican Dance Exchanges, 1959–1983." *Hispanic American Historical Review* 97, no. 4 (November 2017): 681–716.

———. "Cuban Modern Dance after Censorship: A Colorful Gray, 1971–1974." In *The Futures of Dance Studies,* edited by Susan Manning, Janice Ross, and Rebecca Schneider, 303–20. Madison: University of Wisconsin Press, 2020.

———. "'Cultures in the Body': Dance and Anthropology in Revolutionary Cuba." *History of Anthropology Review* 41 (December 14, 2017): http://histanthro.org/notes /cultures-in-the-body/.

———. "Dancing with the Revolution: Cuban Dance, State, and Nation, 1930–1990." Ph.D. diss., Columbia University, 2016.

———. "The Footsteps of Nieves Fresneda: Cuban Folkloric Dance and Cultural Policy, 1959–1979." *Cuban Studies* 47 (2019): 35–56.

———. "Prescribing Ballet: A History of Gender and Disability in Cuban Psicoballet." *Gender & History* 32, no. 2 (July 2020): 373–92.

———. "A Spectacular Embrace: Dance Dialogues between Cuba and the Soviet Union, 1959–1973." *Dance Chronicle* 41, no. 3 (November 2018): 275–302.

———. "Sweeping Gestures: Alberto Alonso and the Revolutionary Musical in Cuba." *Studies in Musical Theatre* 13, no. 1 (2019): 37–51.

Schwartz, Rosalie. *Pleasure Island: Tourism and Temptation in Cuba.* Lincoln: University of Nebraska Press, 1999.

Serra, Ana. *The "New Man" in Cuba: Culture and Identity in the Revolution.* Gainesville: University Press of Florida, 2007.

Siegel, Beatrice. *Alicia Alonso, the Story of a Ballerina.* New York: F. Warne, 1979.

Sierra Madero, Abel. "'El trabajo os hará hombres': Masculinización nacional, trabajo forzado y control social en Cuba durante los años sesenta." *Cuban Studies* 44 (2016): 309–49.

Simón, Pedro, and Francisco Rey Alfonso. *Alicia Alonso, órbita de una leyenda.* Madrid: Sociedad General de Autores y Editores, 1996.

Singer, Toba. *Fernando Alonso: The Father of Cuban Ballet.* Gainesville: University Press of Florida, 2014.

Srinivasan, Priya. *Sweating Saris: Indian Dance as Transnational Labor.* Philadelphia: Temple University Press, 2012.

Stoneley, Peter. *A Queer History of the Ballet.* London: Routledge, 2010.

Stoner, K. Lynn. *From the House to the Streets: The Cuban Woman's Movement for Legal Reform, 1898–1940.* Durham, NC: Duke University Press, 1991.

Sublette, Ned. *Cuba and Its Music: From the First Drums to the Mambo.* Chicago: Chicago Review Press, 2007.

Terry, Walter. *Alicia and Her Ballet Nacional de Cuba: An Illustrated Biography of Alicia Alonso.* Garden City, NY: Anchor Press/Doubleday, 1981.

Thomas, Susan. *Cuban Zarzuela: Performing Race and Gender on Havana's Lyric Stage.* Urbana: University of Illinois Press, 2009.

Tomé, Lester. "The Cuban Ballet: Its Rationale, Aesthetics and Artistic Identity as Formulated by Alicia Alonso." Ph.D. diss., Temple University, 2011.

———. "Interracial Choreo-erotics of the Cuban Revolution: Ballet, Social Taboo and the Postracial Hyperreality." Paper presented at the Dance Studies Colloquium, Temple University, Philadelphia, PA, 2018. https://www.youtube.com/watch?v =Q1DloB3ix1Q.

———. "The Racial Other's Dancing Body in *El Milagro de Anaquillé* (1927): Avant-Garde Ballet and Ethnography of Afro-Cuban Performance." *Cuban Studies* 46 (2018): 185–227. https://doi.org/10.1353/cub.2018.0010.

————. "Swans in Sugarcane Fields: Proletarian Ballet Dancers and the Cuban Revolution's Industrious New Man." *Dance Research Journal* 49, no. 2 (August 2017): 4–25. https://doi.org/10.1017/S0149767717000171.

Triguero Tamayo, Ernesto. *Placeres del cuerpo: La danza en Santiago de Cuba*. Santiago de Cuba: Fundación Caguayo y Editorial Oriente, 2015.

Urban, Kelly. "The 'Black Plague' in a Racial Democracy: Tuberculosis, Race, and Citizenship in Republican Cuba, 1925–1945." *Cuban Studies* 45 (2017): 319–39.

————. "Plagued by Politics: Cuba's National Sanatorium Project, 1936–59." *Bulletin of the History of Medicine* 91, no. 4 (December 2017): 772–801. https://doi.org/10.1353/bhm .2017.0081.

Valdés, Nelson. "Revolution and Institutionalization in Cuba." *Cuban Studies* 6, no. 1 (1976): 1–37.

Vaughan, Mary Kay. *Cultural Politics in Revolution: Teachers, Peasants, and Schools in Mexico, 1930–1940*. Tucson: University of Arizona Press, 1997.

Veitia Guerra, Ángel Eduardo. "Danza moderna y aficionados." Undergraduate thesis, Instituto Superior de Arte, 1992.

Viddal, Grete. "Vodú Chic: Cuba's Haitian Heritage, the Folkloric Imaginary, and the State." Ph.D. Diss., Harvard University, 2013.

Von Eschen, Penny M. *Satchmo Blows Up the World: Jazz Ambassadors Play the Cold War*. Cambridge, MA: Harvard University Press, 2009.

Wambrug Rodríguez, Idania, and María de los Ángeles Solés de Dios. "Historia de los seis primeros años de trabajo de la Escuela Nacional de Danza Moderna y Folklórica." Undergraduate thesis, Instituto Superior de Arte, 1990.

Warner, Michael. *Publics and Counterpublics*. New York: Zone Books, 2014.

Wilcox, Emily. *Revolutionary Bodies: Chinese Dance and the Socialist Legacy*. Berkeley: University of California Press, 2019.

————. "Women Dancing Otherwise: The Queer Feminism of Gu Jiani's Right & Left." In *Queer Dance: Meanings and Makings*, edited by Clare Croft, 67–82. New York: Oxford University Press, 2017.

Index

Note: Illustrations are indicated by page numbers in *italics*.

Envisioning Cuba

Elizabeth B. Schwall, *Dancing with the Revolution: Power, Politics, and Privilege in Cuba* (2021).

Daniel A. Rodríguez, *The Right to Live In Health: Medical Politics in Postindependence Havana* (2020).

Tiffany A. Sippial, *Celia Sánchez Manduley: The Life and Legacy of a Cuban Revolutionary* (2020).

Ariel Mae Lambe. *No Barrier Can Contain It: Cuban Antifascism and the Spanish Civil War* (2019).

Henry B. Lovejoy. *Prieto: Yorùbá Kingship in Colonial Cuba during the Age of Revolutions* (2018).

A. Javier Treviño, *C. Wright Mills and the Cuban Revolution: An Exercise in the Art of Sociological Imagination* (2017).

Antonia Dalia Muller, *Cuban Émigrés and Independence in the Nineteenth-Century Gulf World* (2017).

Jennifer L. Lambe, *Madhouse: Psychiatry and Politics in Cuban History* (2017).

Devyn Spence Benson, *Antiracism in Cuba: The Unfinished Revolution* (2016).

Michelle Chase, *Revolution within the Revolution: Women and Gender Politics in Cuba, 1952–1962* (2015).

Aisha K. Finch, *Rethinking Slave Rebellion in Cuba: La Escalera and the Insurgencies of 1841–1844* (2015).

Christina D. Abreu, *Rhythms of Race: Cuban Musicians and the Making of Latino New York City and Miami, 1940–1960* (2015).

Anita Casavantes Bradford, *The Revolution Is for the Children: The Politics of Childhood in Havana and Miami, 1959–1962* (2014).

Tiffany A. Sippial, *Prostitution, Modernity, and the Making of the Cuban Republic, 1840–1920* (2013).

Kathleen López, *Chinese Cubans: A Transnational History* (2013).

Lillian Guerra, *Visions of Power in Cuba: Revolution, Redemption, and Resistance, 1959–1971* (2012).

Carrie Hamilton, *Sexual Revolutions in Cuba: Passion, Politics, and Memory* (2012).

Sherry Johnson, *Climate and Catastrophe in Cuba and the Atlantic World during the Age of Revolution* (2011).

Melina Pappademos, *Black Political Activism and the Cuban Republic* (2011).

Frank Andre Guridy, *Forging Diaspora: Afro-Cubans and African Americans in a World of Empire and Jim Crow* (2010).

Ann Marie Stock, *On Location in Cuba: Street Filmmaking during Times of Transition* (2009).

Alejandro de la Fuente, *Havana and the Atlantic in the Sixteenth Century* (2008).

Reinaldo Funes Monzote, *From Rainforest to Cane Field in Cuba: An Environmental History since 1492* (2008).

Matt D. Childs, *The 1812 Aponte Rebellion in Cuba and the Struggle against Atlantic Slavery* (2006).

Eduardo González, *Cuba and the Tempest: Literature and Cinema in the Time of Diaspora* (2006).

John Lawrence Tone, *War and Genocide in Cuba, 1895–1898* (2006).

Samuel Farber, *The Origins of the Cuban Revolution Reconsidered* (2006).

Lillian Guerra, *The Myth of José Martí: Conflicting Nationalisms in Early Twentieth-Century Cuba* (2005).

Rodrigo Lazo, *Writing to Cuba: Filibustering and Cuban Exiles in the United States* (2005).

Alejandra Bronfman, *Measures of Equality: Social Science, Citizenship, and Race in Cuba, 1902–1940* (2004).

Edna M. Rodríguez-Mangual, *Lydia Cabrera and the Construction of an Afro-Cuban Cultural Identity* (2004).

Gabino La Rosa Corzo, *Runaway Slave Settlements in Cuba: Resistance and Repression* (2003).

Piero Gleijeses, *Conflicting Missions: Havana, Washington, and Africa, 1959–1976* (2002).

Robert Whitney, *State and Revolution in Cuba: Mass Mobilization and Political Change, 1920–1940* (2001).

Alejandro de la Fuente, *A Nation for All: Race, Inequality, and Politics in Twentieth-Century Cuba* (2001).